NEWSGATHERING
SECOND EDITION

Ken Metzler
University of Oregon

Prentice-Hall, Inc., Englewood Cliffs New Jersey 07632

Library of Congress Cataloging in Publication Data

Metzler, Ken.
  Newsgathering.

  Bibliography: p.
  1. Reporters and reporting. I. Title.
PN4781.M45 1986   070.4'3   85-9538
ISBN 0-13-617002-1

For Barbara, Scott, and Douglas

Editorial/production supervision and
    interior design: Debbie Ford
Cover design: Joseph Curio
Manufacturing buyer: Harry P. Baisley

© 1986, 1979 by Prentice-Hall, Inc., Englewood Cliffs, New Jersey 07632

Printed in the United States of America

10 9 8 7 6 5 4 3 2 1

ISBN   0-13-617002-1   01

Prentice-Hall International (UK) Limited, *London*
Prentice-Hall of Australia Pty. Limited, *Sydney*
Prentice-Hall Canada Inc., *Toronto*
Prentice-Hall Hispanoamericana, S.A., *Mexico*
Prentice-Hall of India Private Limited, *New Delhi*
Prentice-Hall of Japan, Inc., *Tokyo*
Prentice-Hall of Southeast Asia Pte. Ltd., *Singapore*
Editora Prentice-Hall do Brasil, Ltda., *Rio de Janeiro*
Whitehall Books Limited, *Wellington, New Zealand*

Contents

Preface

In the first edition of this book, I said its impetus had come from a year in the newsroom of the *Honolulu Advertiser* where I learned that what I was teaching in the classroom was not quite what I was doing in the newsroom. I had been covering a variety of news and feature assignments for Honolulu's morning newspaper ranging from interviewing runaway girls to interviewing visiting Army generals. I learned from both those encounters.

From the child I learned how it feels when your mother dies when you're only ten years old. You go to live with your father; you assume responsibility for all household chores, and your reward is to get beat up every few weeks by your drunken father, and that's why you've run away from home. The encounter changed my opinions about runaways: Sometimes running away is the most mature thing a youngster can do. From the visiting Army general, a woman who headed the U.S. Women's Army Corps, I learned an interviewing method I can only describe as the staccato–machine gun technique: rapid-fire questions to match the general's rapid-fire answers.

That year I became, I think, a better journalist and perhaps also a more understanding, tolerant human being.

Through the year I also learned that what the journalism textbooks and I had been teaching was not quite on target. We were not covering the essentials of *getting* news. We said almost nothing about chatting informally with news sources to ferret information out of reluctant bureaucrats. Or about talking with bereaved families to get a more adequate report on a person's life than what you'd get from a funeral home. Or about the kind of interviewing that elicits quotes and anecdotes that will make your story come alive with real people instead of the fuzzy facades of bureaucratic jargon.

The years that have elapsed since publication of the first edition of *Newsgathering* have not changed my views. They've only strengthened my resolve to try to improve in this second edition what I started in the first.

In those years I've talked with many editors and reporters. I've participated in editorial retreats where the news staff lets down its collective hair and talks about the *real* problems of day-to-day reporting. One woman, a writer for a major news magazine, remarked that journalism education (and by implication, textbooks) tends to emphasize writing at the expense of interviewing, documentary research, and "synthesis," the thought process whereby a reporter arrives at the essence of the topic being written about.

That's not to denigrate the importance of writing. I attended a newspaper retreat at Flathead Lake in Montana where editors and reporters at *The Missoulian* spent some considerable time berating the staff's problems in grammar, spelling, and story organization. But they spent more time talking about making the paper more interesting and more palatable to people through more features, more humor, more fun. And that, they concluded, means good writing, yes, but it also means more aggressive reporting, more creative ideas, more contact with people, more sensitive interviewing, better listening with ears and eyes and, indeed, *heart* more keenly attuned to the human beings about whom we journalists profess concern.

Like the previous edition, this new work is based in part on extensive interviews with practicing journalists whose experiences run the gamut from tiny weeklies to major metro dailies.

As in the first edition, I have relied heavily on case histories as a means of describing the excitement of reporting. I hope students will read them for what they tell you by indirection. Some find that a case history yields several levels of information. A case history about an interviewing success—or even a failure—becomes different, somehow deeper, after you've done several interviews yourself. You often find yourself saying, "Yes, now I understand why the reporter asked the question that way. I didn't see that the first time I read it."

Teachers who have used the first edition will find the emphasis is just about the same in this new edition. However, some new ideas have been included.

1. A new chapter on documentary research, including exotic new methods of computerized data base acquisition. The changes also include a section on the use of numbers and statistics, which I find a serious weakness among students. (Chapter 10)
2. A new chapter on the ethics of journalism. (Chapter 19)
3. Updated examples throughout the book, with references to new research materials.
4. Greater attention to the "literary" aspects of journalism, shown largely through examples such as a prize-winning account of the explosion of Mount St. Helens in

Washington and a dramatic case-history account of a fatal traffic accident. (Chapters 14 and 16)

Some of the major points of the previous edition have, of course, been retained.

1. Continued emphasis on case histories combined with step-by-step instructions on how to gather information, organize it, and write it. The case histories will, I hope, demonstrate some of the excitement of reporting.
2. Continued emphasis on interviewing and observation, along with the new emphasis on documentary research.
3. Lots of attention to newsfeatures and people reporting. Current practices suggest that it's hard sometimes to distinguish the features from the straight news.
4. Continued discussion of "service journalism."
5. Ongoing emphasis on the notion that, compared to most occupations, reporting is fun.
6. Continued prodding of students to deal with their language skills deficiencies.
7. Continued encouragement of students to put their classroom and laboratory learning to work by getting onto the journalistic firing line through internships or work on community or campus papers.

The latter point is important because ultimately the student comes to understand that professional reporters get news mostly by talking to people. Sometimes these people are hostile, anxious, angry, despondent, or scared. Much news coverage, after all, involves reporting a crisis or a tragedy. Talking to sources under such conditions is not easy, but it can be learned, and a good reporter is always better as a human being for having learned it.

Learning and growing make reporting worthwhile. If there were ever a profession suited to people who want to be "students" all their lives—students of the human condition and the world around us—this is it.

ACKNOWLEDGMENTS

I don't know where the idea got started that authors are lonely souls, forever working alone at their typewriters. You get information for books like this largely the same way you get information for news—by getting out and talking to people. And reading. The more experience I gain as a writer of books, the more I realize that nothing need be lost on an author. Every experience counts, every conversation, every idea picked up from, say, a colleague or a former teacher or a former editor.

Among the most pervasive influences on the writing of this book is my first editor, the late Charles V. Stanton of the *Roseburg* (Oregon) *News-Review*. It was he who told a cantankerous county official to go to hell when the official angrily remonstrated against something I had written. "Don't worry about it," Charles Stanton told me later. "I expect my reporters to get me into trouble once in awhile. If they don't they're not doing their job."

I cannot name them all—the people who have influenced this work—for the list would fill half the pages in the book. Some, however, must be singled out.

My most recent reporting class at the University of Oregon Journalism School, for instance. I told them they were guinea pigs in a noble project: the development of a second edition of *Newsgathering*. They helped to show me what worked and what didn't in the first edition, and thereby immensely improved the second edition. Thanks to Jo An Conway, Shira Fadeley, Kate Fogleman, Willene Long, Deb Monnier, Steve Mozena, Dale Sinner, Theron Thompson, Valerie Morgan, and Cynthia Whitfield.

Also members of the editorial staffs of these newspapers: *The Oregonian, Seattle Times, Register-Guard, Daily Camera, Honolulu Advertiser, Star-Bulletin, Missoulian, Chronicle of Higher Education, Education Week, Walla Walla Union-Bulletin, Grants Pass Courier.*

Especially helpful in developing the two editions were Barrie Hartman, Mike Thoele, Jeremy Cohen, Bob Bone, Janice Wolf, Jane Evinger, Gordon Sabine, Tom Jaques, Lee Wilkins, Dean Rea, Jack Hart, Roy Halverson, Martha Matzke, Ron Wolk, Corbin Gwaltney, John Crowl, Phil Semas, Buck Buchwach, George Chaplin, Gerry Keir, Mike Middlesworth, Helen Altonn, Patricia Smith, Steve Arthur, Neale Copple, Al Hester, Jay Black, Chuck Whitney, Eric Jones, Sharon Brock, Wil Sims, Bill Oliver, Steve Dalphin, Debbie Ford, Hilda Tauber, Ev Dennis, Carolyn Kortge, Kit Smith, Tom Kaser, Marijoy Rubiloff, Jerry Burris, Ann Portal, Jim Dooley, Barbara and Ed Clendaniel, Matt McVay, Dan Dillon, Randy Rasmussen, Duncan McDonald, Mike Fancher, Terry and Heidi Brennan, Galen Rarick, Lyle Nelson, Vickie Ong, and—most important—my wife, Betty Jane, who understands the wayward methods of authors better than anyone I know. Many others who helped are mentioned in the body of the text.

I especially appreciate the helpful suggestions of the manuscript readers for this second edition: Rob Phillips, Oregon State University; Jim Willis, Northeastern University; and T. J. Scanlon, Carleton University.

To all the above, and many more, I remain deeply grateful.

Ken Metzler

Eugene, Oregon

1

Your Career in Journalism

This book has a single-minded mission. It's designed to help you, the prospective journalist, learn about news: how to recognize it, how to get it, how to write it. It is not intended to tell you "everything you ever wanted to know about newspapers"—or about mass media or communications research. It may dip in to research findings occasionally, of course, to relate the information you must know to be an effective journalist. But the topics meander too much for a text intended to teach you how to write news and features for newspapers. News reporting is not simple. You'll have to employ your full attention just to catch up with today's news practices.

The title, *Newsgathering,* reflects emphasis on the process of getting information from news sources. The best journalists will tell you that writers are never any better than the information they convey. They will also suggest that the real pleasure of journalism lies not in the writing of news but in the gathering of it. Reporting is fun, even exciting. Perhaps this is what attracts young people to consider it as a career.

Few other fields offer the opportunity to meet such a wide variety of personalities and situations. As Mark Twain wryly observed in 1872, a typical reporter might spend one day interviewing the governor or the military commandant and the next interviewing prisoners in the lockup, forming lasting friendships with some of the "worst people in the world." Reporters do rub shoulders with the rich and famous—and also with the outcasts. One young newspaper woman undertook to interview five convicted rapists in the penitentiary. This showed great

(Photo by Randy L. Rasmussen.)

courage. But the story she wrote was worth the effort, a feature article about rape that seemed truly helpful to women seeking to protect themselves against violence. The insights she gained by interviewing the five convicts were genuinely useful to her readers. Hers was, indeed, a noble purpose.

"Noble purpose," then, is a second reason journalism has attracted increasing numbers of young people in recent years. It's a good feeling to know that you have helped people—often in a personal way—by bringing them news and ideas about the world around them. And this is precisely what the readers want. A research study titled *Changing Needs of Changing Readers* (Ruth Clark, 1979) suggests that readers want the important news but they also want the kind of information that will help them cope. "Most especially," says the report, "they want more attention paid to their personal needs, help in understanding and dealing with their own problems in an increasingly complex world, news about their neighborhood . . . and advice on what to buy, where to play, how to cope." By paying attention to such needs, a journalist can have positive impact on people's lives. This is true even when conveying bad news or writing about people most of us do not admire.

A third reason for entering journalism may be the most basic of all: You've always wanted to write. That's a cliche in most newsrooms. You would be wise not to emphasize it in job interviews. But it's true—a cliche only because people repeat it so often. Writing has become such a compulsion that out of the newsroom of the *Wilmington* (Delaware) *News Journal* there mysteriously appeared a spoof checklist to determine whether one is in fact addicted to writing. It was patterned after a similar document for potential alcoholics:

Do you write to escape from worries or trouble?
Do you write alone?
Has a physician ever treated you for writing?

Call it an addiction or a compulsion, but in truth many journalists find writing hard, grubby work—much more fun to interview your favorite ax murderer.

A fourth reason for entering journalism may seem strange at first: an interest in some highly specialized field such as medicine, education, technology, politics, government, nutrition, or any one of a hundred other fields. Hundreds of highly specialized newspapers and magazines have emerged in recent decades to become respected journals: The *Wall Street Journal,* for example, or the *Chronicle of Higher Education.* Journalists find increasingly that writing about such fields as business, education, or medicine can be more interesting than practicing them.

Finally, you like people. That is a special reason for pursuing journalism. You'll get to know more people through a reporting career, and a wider variety of individuals, than you would in just about any other field. You are a gregarious sort, and meeting new people comes naturally to you—and so reporting is the place to be. Or you are shy, and meeting new people comes hard. Reporting is still the place to be. It will *force* you to get out and meet people. It can change your life for the better. Your liking for people involves more than meeting them and interviewing them as sources of information, however. As a writer you must like and appreciate people as your readers. You will, if you're a good, sensitive writer, work hard to make your articles interesting, easy to read, even *fun* to read.

No doubt you can find other reasons for entering journalism as a career. You are curious about the world around you; reporting is a good way to discover more. You are interested in everybody and everything; journalism is a way to keep in touch with the world. Or you enjoy being a student, believe it or not. Journalism is a way to continue to learn, to grow intellectually and socially. Perhaps you like the good feeling that comes from seeing in print the words that have popped out of your mind. You like the recognition from others, parents, teachers, peers, when you have produced a piece of writing that strikes a responsive chord within them.

THE REALITIES OF THE NEWSROOM

The foregoing thoughts are, of course, from the perspective of the beginning journalist. Perhaps, therefore, they represent a naive and idealistic view. What are some of the realities of the newsroom?

Recently a retirement party was held for a newspaper writer-editor, Dan Sellard. He had completed more than 37 years at the *Eugene* (Oregon) *Register-Guard* in jobs ranging from covering city hall to running the newsroom as city editor. A scrapbook stood at the center of a table surrounded by certificates depicting the various writing awards he had won. Photos showed him with various celebrities he had met. One photo showed him with his arm around the 1960s sex goddess, Jayne Mansfield, whom he had just interviewed.

He'd interviewed lots of important people. He found John F. Kennedy "charismatic." Nelson Rockefeller was "stuffy," Hubert Humphrey "folksy, fun," Richard Nixon "very impressive," and Harold Stassen "dull." He reminisced about the awesome spectacles—and the tragedies. He remembered a highway accident: "holding a bleeding woman's head in my lap and lying to her about her husband who had just died." He recalled writing so many stories about fathers backing cars over their children that he could never back his own car without making doubly sure no one was behind. He remembered watching an ambulance crew remove the bodies of two children from a burning house while police combed taverns searching for the mother—the kids had been locked in the bedroom.

He'd covered city council meetings where discussion ranged from curb cuts to dogs at large. He'd taken an early morning walk with Harry S Truman. He'd witnessed a pioneer episode of open heart surgery. He'd covered the building of the Alaska oil pipeline. One time he even held Judy Garland's hand, a moment, he said, "that I wished would last forever."

"It all sounds exciting, doesn't it?" he remarked as he summed up these and other highlights. "But for every fun and exciting story there were all those thousands that weren't. Most stories are hard work, hard digging for facts. It's hard to explain them when you do have the facts. It's not a glamorous job, but it's satisfying most of the time. It's never easy."

True, not every moment of a reporter's life brims with ecstatic excitement. Covering the meetings of governmental agencies plodding through jargon-filled agendas can tax the staying power of any reporter. Certainly today's reporting will seldom match the glamour of the *Front Page* era of hell-for-leather journalism. But it's a worthy and interesting field that offers plenty of opportunity to make noteworthy contributions to the betterment of humankind.

And, unlike the earlier days when Dan Sellard started his career, the pay isn't bad. Not fabulous, exactly, but better than the 60 cents an hour at which he started. And the sky is the financial limit when you consider that reporters do occasionally write best-selling books, such as the Woodward-Bernstein epic, *All the President's Men*.

HOW YOU FIT IN

The earlier comments about why a young person might consider journalism as a career represent the first step toward a self-analysis. You need more qualifications than having "always wanted to write" if you are to enjoy success in this field. Here are some of those qualifications:

1. Skills in handling the language. This is the most important of all. To put it bluntly, no one wants you when you can't spell, can't use words

properly, or can't construct grammatically correct sentences. The self-test at the end of this chapter can either reassure you if you pass with a high score—or set you on a track toward improvement if you don't.

2. Tolerance. You'll meet all kinds of people in this business. Consider yourself a professional when you truly feel you can interview outcasts—such as the five rapists mentioned earlier—and listen to their comments without showing your scorn.

3. Listening skills. Reporting is, or should be, a listening profession, not a talking one. You must develop the ability not only to listen tolerantly to outcasts but also to those who would try to intimidate you, evade your questions, bamboozle you, throw their weight around, or otherwise prevent you from learning about the public's business.

4. Perception. This means the ability to receive information, analyze it, and figure out what it really means to your community, your readers. It takes a broad education and some experience to develop this skill; it never comes easily.

5. Curiosity. Here's a quality some say is closely linked to intelligence. It's essential to the journalist.

6. Perseverance. This is essential to any field, of course, but journalism particularly requires the quietly persistent (but not arrogant) pursuit of elusive details.

7. Self-confidence, tempered with an ability to accept criticism and learn from it. Persons entering journalism, suggests Professor Jim Willis of Northeastern University, should know that it will be a lonely job at times. Sources, even readers, will sometimes turn on you for publishing the facts when the facts are unpopular. At times the only source of strength may be within the reporters themselves. But the ability to accept criticism gracefully is equally necessary. Without it, a reporter could become dogmatic, even retreating into a cynical kind of fortress mentality and defensiveness.

Some traits suggest your *not* going into journalism. Among the poorest risks in journalism are zealots, power brokers, politicians, and other assorted ax-grinders: the kinds of people who hold strong points of view and want to change the world to conform to their perceptions of it. As noted, another poor risk is the person with poor language skills. Poor listeners—those who talk too much and never give others a chance—have troubles, too. Failure to listen carefully results in factual errors, misinterpretations, and misquotations.

THE BREADTH OF JOURNALISM

Learning to gather and write news can be useful in a hundred different ways, not all of which mean working for a newspaper. Material in this book will be sufficiently basic to apply more or less to the news function of all media: newspapers, magazines, broadcast, newsletters, organizational publications, public relations writing, and even to some extent to advertising copywriting.

The basic thrust of the chapters to follow will, however, run toward writing for newspapers. That's where the examples and case histories come from. To attempt to apply the principles to any and all media would render the book unnecessarily complicated.

Keep in mind, though, that what you learn here can lead to careers in other fields. Reporting itself is a general and a liberal education when you consider what you learn from the wide range of experiences. The person successful in reporting is generally alert, open-minded, intelligent, perceptive, and communicative. These are precisely the qualities demanded by most any position that needs a communicative generalist. Reporters do frequently enter other positions, including management.

The news media offer many opportunities. At this writing 1,710 dailies and about 7,600 weeklies operate in the United States with another 116 dailies in Canada. About 8,150 radio and 960 television stations also operate here, along with perhaps 18,000 to 20,000 magazines. Untold numbers of books, pamphlets, flyers, brochures, and technical manuals are being produced by public agencies and industrial concerns. Most of them employ journalistically trained persons to write and edit their materials. They find it easier to teach technical concepts to an intelligent journalist than to try to make a writer out of a technician.

We have a much broader definition of journalism today. It's more than just newspapers and broadcast news. Some contemporary definitions suggest that it means the communication of *all* factual information, ideas, and opinions. It includes essays, commentary, and even the work of "literary" writers who often turn to the reporting of factual materials. In 1966, for instance, the late novelist Truman Capote published a nonfiction classic entitled *In Cold Blood* about a Kansas murder. He emerged from the experience to proclaim "reportage" as the "great, unexplored literary art form of the future." Tom Wolfe's 1979 book, *The Right Stuff*, about the seven pioneer astronauts, is another example. Newspapers have also encouraged writers to employ literary trappings—such as scenes, dialogue, description, suspense, irony—in their reporting.

Journalism also allows a person to explore the world in its broadest sense. You can pursue most any interest—politics, travel, science, education, social problems—from the journalistic perspective. Instead of being an accountant, you write about business. You can retool for another interest (sports, perhaps, or politics?) much more quickly and less expensively than an accountant can. And you can move from the general reporting in a newspaper into the more specialized work of a magazine writer for, say, *Business Week* or *Medical Economics*.

To be sure, the doors that permit such interchanges are more open to the skilled and perceptive journalist than to the mediocre one. But the doors are there, slightly ajar. Such opportunities can make journalism an exciting career.

Not only are journalists permitted to grow and change through their careers, but circumstances may *require* them to do so. Dramatic changes in both social mores and in the technological means of communicating information will require future journalists to be tolerant, perceptive, and flexible. This is good. Journalism demands young men and women who are intellectually alive, curious, interested in the world about them. It especially needs the ones who enjoy meeting all kinds of people from kings to outcasts.

POINTS TO REMEMBER

1. This text has a singular purpose: to teach you how to write news and features for newspapers.
2. Journalism is a gateway to varied experiences. It is a means of helping people by keeping them informed, of fulfilling a long-standing desire to write, or pursuing specialized interests. It's especially nice for those who enjoy people.
3. The work of a reporter is wide-ranging and even exciting at times, though it can be routine and tedious as well.
4. Traits of successful journalists include highly developed language and listening skills, perception, tolerance, curiosity, perseverance, and self-confidence. It is not a field for zealots and power brokers.
5. Journalism today tends to be broadly defined to include most all nonfiction work. Career opportunities go beyond newspapers and broadcast stations; one can work in specialized periodicals, even books. Some aspects of nonfiction writing can even be considered "literary."

A QUIZ

Can we assume you have mastered the fundamentals of spelling, punctuation, grammar, and word usage? Let's hope so. Planning to be a professional reporter with a serious language deficiency is like planning a career in engineering when you can't master fifth-grade arithmetic. Just as the engineering student must bear down on trigonometry, algebra, and calculus, so must the journalism student master the tools of writing.

The professionals for whom you will one day work certainly consider them important. A survey of newspaper editors, published in 1980, ranked language skills at the top of the list of deficiencies noted among recent journalism school graduates.

One managing editor remarked that if carpenters were as poorly trained as some journalism graduates, they wouldn't even know how to use a hammer and nails. "I feel journalism students better learn the ABCs of the profession," he said.

This self-administered quiz will help you to determine your strengths and weaknesses. Take it privately—only you will know the result. In this quiz are the most common mistakes in spelling, grammar, and punctuation, assembled from the mistakes most often seen on student papers and reporters' stories. They are, in short, everyday problems, the kind all journalism students should recognize.

Number a sheet of paper from 1 to 100. Write down the correct answers for each choice.

SPELLING

Select the correct word from the choices below. Use the *preferred* (dictionary's first choice) spelling where applicable.

1. accidently, accidentally, acidentaly
2. accomodate, accommodate, acommodate
3. all right, alright
4. anceint, ancient
5. baloon, balloon
6. batallion, battallion, battalion
7. beleive, believe
8. cieling, ceiling
9. collabborate, collaborate, colabborate
10. commitment, committment
11. conceive, concieve
12. debateable, debatable
13. defendent, defendant
14. dependant, dependent
15. desireable, desirable
16. development, developement
17. diesel, deisel
18. embarrassment, embarassment
19. firey, fiery
20. flourescent, fluorescent, flouresent
21. guage, gauge
22. holliday, holiday
23. hygiene, hygeine
24. incidently, incidentally
25. interchangeable, interchangable
26. irrelevant, irrelevent, irelevant
27. liesure, leisure
28. maintainance, maintainence, maintenance, maintanance
29. mispell, misspell, mispel
30. newsstand, newstand
31. occassional, occasional, ocassional
32. oppulence, opulence, oppulance
33. paralell, parralell, parallel
34. peir, pier
35. professor, proffessor, proffesor
36. recommend, reccomend, reccommend
37. resistant, resistent
38. rythm, rhythum, rhythm
39. satellite, sattelite, sattellite

40. sieze, seize
41. seperate, separate
42. sargent, sargeant, sergeant
43. temperment, temperament
44. truly, truely, truley
45. vinager, vinegar, vineger

GRAMMAR AND WORD USAGE

Select the correct word from each of the choices below.

46. He said he felt [bad, badly] about the accident.
47. The committee announced [its, their] agenda.
48. Jones, [who, whom] they said was sick, came anyway.
49. [Who, Whom] does Jones prefer for governor?
50. "[Its, It's] about time you got here," she said.
51. She spun around and [lay, laid] the book on the table.
52. She gave the book to [I and her, me and she, me and her].
53. The president, together with his wife, [is, are] under indictment.
54. Even as we speak, the victim [lays, lies] in the street.
55. Debbie is a better runner than [I, me].
56. If [your, you're] grammar and spelling are good, you can work for the school paper.
57. Neither Smith nor Jones [was, were] present.
58. Neither Smith nor his daughters [was, were] present.
59. [Like, As] you said, the answer is nowhere to be found.
60. Give the prize to [whoever, whomever] wants it most.
61. Jim went to visit his dad [who, whom] he had never seen.
62. She doesn't mind [him, his] coming home late.
63. The number of qualified applicants [is, are] small.
64. Rusting in the rain [is, are] the remnants of my old car.
65. It sounds [like, as if] she's the person for the job.
66. She's the woman [who, whom] police want for questioning.
67. In the bag [was, were] a doughnut and seven apples.
68. The troops moved [further, farther] inland yesterday.
69. She pledged [further, farther] support for his proposal.
70. The doctor told her patient to [lay, lie] down.
71. She [laid, lay] there for an hour.
72. He wishes he [was, were] a millionaire.
73. The dog dug up [it's, its] bone.
74. She was hurt [bad, badly] by her defeat at the polls.
75. Johnson is a man [who, whom] we have long admired.
76. Sally and her friend, Billie, [is, are] in Canada.
77. Present at the meeting [was, were] Jane, Sally, and Jo.
78. The president gave Smith and [I, me] a stern lecture.

79. He drives [careless, carelessly].
80. They [hung, hanged] the prisoner at dawn today.

PUNCTUATION

On your answer sheet, write any corrections for punctuation errors you find in the following sentences. Some are okay as they stand.

81. James, and his mother went to Cincinnati.
82. The witness testified as follows: "The gunman came to my counter and said, "Stick 'em up, lady, or I'll shoot.' So I gave him all the money."
83. What became of the childrens toys?
84. They're in Charles garage.
85. "Its a girl!" exclaimed the doctor.
86. Captain McDonald, commander of the brigade fell from his horse.
87. Captain Smith honored his two "heroes": Smith and Marx.
88. The slim-tanned actor visited the island of Molokai.
89. My favorite celebrity Mary Tyler Moore visited my home town last week.
90. The inflation rate dipped sharply the unemployment rate remained high. [Punctuate, only, do not change wording.]
91. Killed in the collison were John Doe, 37, Chillicothe; Jane Roe, 33, Boston; and Henry Fisk, 44, Los Angeles.
92. The captain said; "We have the fire under control."
93. Sally, my oldest sister, left for Kansas yesterday.
94. "Where," he asked, "is the stadium"?
95. "It's near the Civic Center", she replied.

SENTENCE FRAGMENTS

Some of the following are complete sentences and others are fragments. On your answer sheet identify each one as *complete* or *fragment*.

96. Although she knows it's hopeless.
97. Stop!
98. Kids love snow.
99. After a hard night's snowfall.
100. Jennifer, although she is one of the most prosperous, perspicacious, and talented actresses we have seen, and despite her rather uneven temperament and mean disposition, and with high regard for her station in life.

When you have finished, score your paper by using the key in Appendix C.

2

Reporters at Work

Journalism, it has been said, is a window open to the world. The world seen from the window can be an exciting adventure, a hopeless bore, or somewhere in between. It all depends on you.

It never bored I.F. Stone, who edited an iconoclastic weekly newspaper that specialized in politics and government. He loved what he was doing. He once remarked that he was having so much fun that he "ought to be arrested." Perhaps it's your own attitude that determines the fun quotient. For most people it's the adventure of meeting new people and of seeing the sometimes rusty, usually awkward machinations of public affairs and government from an intimate vantage point. It's a learning experience and some of what you learn may surprise you. Examine, if you will, a case in point.

BONNIE: A CASE HISTORY

Surprises? Young reporters entering journalism often do encounter situations they hardly expected. The surprises often come in relationships with news sources—people chemistry. Some young people think that no one will talk with them. Not true. Others think reporters have some kind of inalienable right to barge right into a tense situation and start asking questions without even bothering to explain who they are or why they've come. That's not true either. And some seen quite astonished to discover that when you're a news reporter, some people may fear you. Others may hate you; a few may "love" you. Some will try to exploit

(Photo by John C. Froschaver.)

you. But quite a few will come to respect you, particularly if you do your job with accuracy, fairness, and common sense.

These are among the lessons one young reporter, Bonnie Henderson, learned while working for a weekly newspaper on the Oregon coast and later for a small daily in southern Oregon, her first two jobs out of college.

She covered the police beat for the daily, where she learned a lot about crime and tragedy. She also learned that cops are terrible flirts, especially on those occasions when she wore a dress, which was about once a week.

Not that she minded. She flirted back a little, not a bad way for a woman reporter to ease into more serious conversations for getting information for news stories, she decided. Maybe that's not true in every city, but it certainly worked in the isolated western community where she worked. She was the first woman ever to cover the police beat in that town, a little lumbering and tourist town called Grants Pass.

It took awhile for them to get used to one another. The cops teased her quite a bit, but she eventually gained their respect, largely, she believes, by careful reporting. She took great pains to be accurate and complete, and she was careful to avoid misrepresentation or sensationalizing.

Her open and amiable style of talking to people served her well when interviewing common people hit by tragedy. She interviewed a man whose son had been shot, and her sympathetic, sensitive style of conversation made the session easy for the man, possibly even therapeutic. On the other hand, she tried to interview a relative of a murder victim outside the courthouse during a trial. The woman burst into tears and fled from the encounter while the rest of the family glowered disdainfully at Bonnie. At that point Bonnie felt herself intrusive—"doing a dirty job of questionable importance."

It was on the police beat, in any event, that she learned about the dark side of society, covering stories of murder, tragedy, violence. One story touched her deeply.

A young woman had killed her six-day-old baby. The woman, unmarried, impoverished, of less-than-average intelligence, had hoped that the baby would improve her relationship with the child's father. She was disappointed. He refused to marry her. Bonnie was touched by her plight—"It was the kind of thing that could happen to anyone, one of those 'there but for the grace of God go I' kinds of situations." Bonnie kept an eye on the woman at a courtroom hearing: "She had this frightened look in her eye, like a scared jackrabbit." Bonnie wanted to reach out to her, say something. She did wish her "good luck" while passing by during a courtroom recess, but the woman ignored her.

Bonnie was seldom emotionally touched by the plight of people involved in crime and tragedy. Almost never, in fact. It would be almost impossible to do the job if you got excessively emotional each time.

A more severe problem was the tension—the constant adversarial style of newsgathering that somehow seemed necessary to get the job done. The worst problems were never the big stories, but the trivial ones. A homosexual psychiatrist was attacked one day, and the cops didn't want to provide any details. Bonnie had to piece the story together from multiple sources such as other police agencies and hospital reports.

And she found that cops can be temperamental sometimes. The chief of detectives wouldn't speak to her for a month because she happened onto a story about a detective being replaced. He'd made a mistake in dealing with several narcotics arrests, all of which had to be dropped for insufficient evidence.

Even a mellow attitude toward flirtatious cops couldn't compensate for the harsh reality of having to write a story that displeases a bureaucrat. This was not the first time, nor would it be the last. But it is at least a mild surprise to find that cops all too eager to tease you one day would refuse even to speak to you in a fit of pique the next. Bonnie eventually formed a certain professional insensitivity to those kinds of problems and went on about her job.

But it's a job full of surprises, pleasant and unpleasant. One of the first occurred early in her career. She worked as a reporter for the weekly newspaper at Seaside, a coastal resort community that holds a beauty pageant each summer to select Oregon's contestant in the Miss America pageant. Bonnie drew the assignment to cover the various areas of competition, talent, evening gown, and swimsuit.

Bonnie, whose feminist proclivities are fairly mellow, found the "girls," as they called each other, extraordinarily talented and attractive. But they were "women" in her eyes, not girls. What *really* got her "grossed out," to use her term, was the swimsuit competition. The contestants paraded around in bathing suits and high heels, and they wore ribbons on their hips.

"Just like U.S.D.A.prime beef," Bonnie declared indignantly a time or two around the office. Another point hit her: The age limit for the beauty competition was 26. Bonnie was 26.

Later, on vacation at her family's cabin near Mount Hood, Bonnie had a strange dream. She was in the audience watching the final event in the beauty pageant, and the judges were about to announce the winner. But the judges couldn't agree on the official candidates, and so they turned to Bonnie. The contest officials called her from the audience and asked her to accept the Miss Oregon crown and to compete in Atlantic City for the title of Miss America.

Bonnie felt a little uncomfortable about the ensuing dilemma. In the simple logic of a dream, not even her feminist principles prevailed as a consideration. It was strictly a matter of getting on with her journalistic career versus the instant fame her selection would bring. Perhaps she could justify her acceptance on the basis of regional chauvinism—"It's *my* state," she reasoned, "so maybe I should be willing to represent it. . . ."

The world will never know her decision for, according to Bonnie, she awakened before making up her mind.

And what symbolic meaning does she attach to the dream?

"Well, at least it shows that I have a sense of humor," she says. She could hardly wait to tell people at the office about the dream and its ironic twist in the light of her earlier indelicate remarks about pageant traditions. She also thinks that her subconscious had undertaken to prod her with an important messsage: She was now an awesome 26 years of age, just about over the hill, at least for beauty competition.

Bonnie returned to college for a graduate degree in journalism after three years of reporting; she planned to return to work after graduation, preferably in a field that permitted more demanding and comprehensive writing than covering police and courts for a small daily newspaper. On one occasion one of the professors, a woman, was casting about for someone to play a role for a hypothetical news incident the students were to report in a lab exercise. The part required a young woman to play a "beauty queen" who refuses to pose in a bikini for publicity pictures and thereby touches off a community controversy.

The professor—who knew nothing of Bonnie's dream or her feminist principles—selected Bonnie for the part. Bonnie played to rave reviews. She even referred to her fellow beauty contestants as "the girls," a touch of realism in which she takes a certain perverse pride.

HOW YOU LEARN FROM EXPERIENCE

When young people get out of college and enter professional journalism, they tend to have common experiences. Bonnie's activities were by no means exceptional. Interviews with more than 100 young journalism graduates over the past ten years suggest the following:

1. The comments confirm the notion that reporting is fun. "It's a blast!" says one. "I still get a rush out of seeing my byline," says another; "anybody who doesn't admit that is a liar or should be in some other field." What makes reporting fun? Among the suggestions are (1) the thrill of seeing something you've researched and written in print, (2) the excitement of meeting and interviewing important people others have only heard about, and (3) the novelty of discovering interesting human qualities in just about everybody from celebrities to convicted criminals. One young man interviewed a convicted murderer and was astonished to find him "not a monster"—not much different, in fact, from people you meet every day on the street.

2. Learning to conduct interviews—indeed, to talk to people in all stations of life—is a skill that does not always come easily to some beginners. Young people seldom know how to deal with a bereaved family or with the emotions brought on by sudden crises, but they can learn. And they often do. They even learn that arrogant or contentious behavior is far less effective in getting people to talk than sympathetic, nonjudgmental listening.

3. Mistakes are all too easily made, and many of them are not even the reporter's fault (or perhaps the reporter's fault only for not having doublechecked more carefully). Sources will relate "facts" they believe to be true but which, on further investigation, prove to be twisted, colored, or otherwise misstated. The problem is often the result of the sources' faulty memory rather than deliberate distortion.

4. It's shocking to beginners to discover the many "human" ways in which people respond to mistakes or, indeed, even to factually correct statements that somehow rub a raw nerve. One reporter wrote an article quoting a government agency that "pilot error" had caused a fatal airplane crash. The father of the dead pilot stormed into the newsroom and threatened to smash the reporter into pulpwood. The father had to be physically restrained and removed from the newsroom. And yet the reporter's story had accurately quoted a government agency. The father's quarrel was with the agency, not the reporter. Even the most outrageous comments by journalism professors on students' papers could never match that experience.

5. New reporters quickly discover that news stories tend to run in sequences, many of them never-ending, rather than in singles. Reality seems to be just one gigantic soap opera. Reporters see the human drama every day, especially on such newsbeats as police, fire, courts, politics, and many others where fate often determines the winners, the losers, and even the casualties among innocent bystanders.

6. In contacting news sources, young women are often unnerved by vulgar sexual innuendoes, particularly when they enter male bastions not often frequented by women in the past. One young woman, upon hearing a crude suggestion made to her by a police chief, was so mortified that she could never bring herself to go back. She had to be reassigned to another newsbeat. Police officers often are dreadful

teases. A group of them prepared an elaborate hoax on another woman, giving her gruesome and sexually crude details about a phony murder case. Only when she was about to report the details to her editor did they confess their ruse. They said they'd done it only because they liked her a lot. After all, hadn't they prevented her from making a fool of herself with her boss?

7. Frustration comes frequently to young reporters, usually in these forms: (1) difficult or evasive news sources, (2) problems in establishing ongoing relationships with the news sources you must contact regularly, (3) overcoming shyness, (4) unwanted editing of stories—including nagging remarks about grammar and spelling problems, (5) lack of knowledge about the way government works and who's who within the local power structure, and (6) deadlines, too much work, too many routine assignments, too many meetings to cover, not enough time to do the stories you'd like.

8. Beginners find ethical concerns much more prevalent than they ever imagined. Learning ethics in the classroom is vastly different from encountering a tearful mother concerned about whether her daughter's name will be published in a drunk driving arrest. One reporter called the school superintendent in her community to ascertain the superintendent's reaction to being named in open court as a party to an illicit sexual liaison. To her astonishment, the superintendent had not heard about the court testimony. "My God," he exclaimed, "you can't put that in the *paper*!" Not knowing how to respond, the reporter passed the phone to the city editor—who said the paper would, indeed, report what was said in open court about a public official. The editor's decision has been mildly controversial in that community ever since. The superintendent eventually resigned.

9. In smaller communities where many beginners get their first jobs, a reporter is often still viewed with respect, deference, even a little awe. "What a great feeling," says one. "In some cases, people see you as having tremendous power over their lives. What you write can make their day—or ruin it. That's where a sense of ethics comes in because it would be easy to abuse that power." The power may be illusory, however.

10. Moving from a college paper to a professional one can cause unique traumas. One young woman—a star on the campus daily—was surprised to find her new editors fussing over such things as objectivity, grammatical errors, and "holes" in her stories: things she didn't think to ask her sources about. When she wrote a story about a $45,000-a-year school official shoplifting $750 worth of merchandise, the editors asked her to change the story so that the two figures did not appear in the same sentence. A close juxtaposition would bring out the irony, they said, thereby suggesting a writer's bias.

11. Most young people find that after a trial period lasting from six months to a year, an interesting change occurs, something like a runner's "second wind." Where before they were never quite sure of their

talents or their skills, *now* they're sure. Reasonably sure. Or at least comfortable with their talents. One young man, who describes himself as shy, found that he could be surprisingly at ease with important people during interviews. He learned that the day he showed up in jeans and T-shirt to interview the new owner of a furniture store in the community. The owner, a woman, was flanked by colleagues and lawyers, all dressed in tuxedos and gowns. It was one of those absurd situations that happen occasionally. He'd planned to spend the day on a Florida sound with a fisherman but the weather turned bad. So he was hustled instead to a hurry-up interview with the elegant business folks—no time to change clothes.

"And here I was dressed like a bum," the reporter recalls. The situation was so splendidly ludicrous that he forgot to be shy. The interview went well, one of his best. It still astonishes him when he thinks about it. Out of the experience he learned that "instead of worrying, you just go out and do what you have to do." His new self-confidence extended into other areas of his work. He discovered that he had more talent than he had realized and that his shyness was no longer getting in the way. He even concluded that his sensitivity, curiosity, and love of the written word were assets indeed.

And so it goes for most young reporters newly out of journalism school. The profession loses a few, of course, out of frustration, disappointment, or inability to cope with the problems. But most do fine. It's often at this stage that they find themselves wondering what the next step will be.

The young Florida reporter—the one who showed up at the black tie occasion wearing blue jeans—is a case in point. His name is Scott Martell, and at this writing he works for the *Islander,* a weekly on Sanibel Island, a classy resort and residential area off the west coast of Florida. There he covers the environment, the schools, business, sports, and some elements of city and county government. He also writes features, his greatest love. If he learned anything from the black tie–blue jeans interview it is that most journalism students "will be surprised by how well they can handle situations when the pressure is actually put upon them."

Much of Scott's work for the paper is routine, to be sure: the usual news coverage of agency meetings, new business openings, construction projects, and bureaucratic waffling. But in a year's time he had managed to have himself quite a few adventures, many of them related to western Florida's unique island geography. He had fished Pine Island Sound, explored the remote and mysterious Upper Captiva Island (accessible only by boat), patrolled the Caloosahatchee River in search of the endangered manatee (sea cow), sailed the Gulf of Mexico with commercial crab fishermen, and run a canoe down the Sanibel River with a wildlife expert to greet such denizens as playful baby alligators, Cuban tree frogs, green herons, and even the big, clumsy anhinga or water turkey. Later Scott would describe the route as a "mystical utopian fantasy."

After a year Scott says he is frustrated some by time pressures. He feels his work is spread too thin. But on the whole he likes his job. He hopes to expand on the

Scott Martell on the job in Florida.

aspects he enjoys the most such as environmental issues, travel, and features about interesting people, such as a 65-year-old man who swam for his health in the swift currents of Pine Island Sound. This man once saved an injured pelican stranded on a sandbar. Scott wrote a story about the rescue and then found it particularly heart-warming to write a follow-up story about the pelican's release back to the wild after a two-month stay at a wildlife rehabilitation center.

Eventually Scott will move on to explore other horizons, but for now he says his job is satisfying.

Diversity of career paths is a nice aspect of journalism, he says. He hopes eventually to write fiction, perhaps returning to the forest fire lookout where he first decided to go into journalism or perhaps returning to the farm he owns in Oregon. Or he may work on a magazine. Or stay with newspapers.

"Maybe what I like best about this profession is that there are so many alternatives," he says. "It's exciting having so many possibilities. But it is also scary in a way. You have to make choices. But at least the choices exist. You're not confined to a closed existence."

POINTS TO REMEMBER

1. Reporting may not be for everyone, but those who try it usually find it interesting, enjoyable, even exciting at times.

2. The experiences of a beginning reporter can run the gamut from writing about beauty pageants to people's personal tragedies.

4. A sensitive, caring, conversational style of interviewing can ease you through difficult reporting situations, as can care and caution in accurately representing what sources tell you.

4. Professional mistakes can be traumatic when compared to classroom mistakes.

5. The work can be frustrating at times, particularly when coping with human problems or having your time spread too thin.

6. Ethical concerns are paramount in the professional world, as are the demands and concerns of editors, particularly when compared to one's work on a college paper.

7. Most people earn their wings as professional reporters after six to twelve months on the job. It's a good feeling that will even see you through such calamities as having to interview an elegantly dressed group while wearing jeans.

PROJECT

Interview a professional journalist such as a reporter for one of the local papers or broadcast stations and write an account similar to the material on Bonnie Henderson and Scott Martell in this chapter.

Topic of the interview. "The real world of professional reporting and writing: What's it like?"

Depending on the quality of the material gathered, the class may want to duplicate excerpts of the best interviews for use in this class and possibly in other classes. Thus the material gained through the interviews will have a practical value, and you can tell the respondents that this is *not* a "wastebasket" academic assignment.

Suggestions. Please understand that the purpose of the interviews is narrowly defined: descriptions of experiences and insights into the world of the professional journalist for the edification of students who have not yet entered the profession. Some points that might be covered within this context include having the journalists discuss some of their early experiences in the profession. What kinds of experiences surprised them? What professional tasks do they find easiest? Hardest? What do they wish they'd learned in college—particularly in journalism school if they attended one? What suggestions can they offer to journalism students? Please make the answers as specific as you can.

It would also be useful to include a brief biographical sketch of the journalist you interview.

Your interview report should contain: (1) a summary of the main points you covered in the interview, (2) outstanding quotes or insights, (3) personal anecdotes that illustrate points made in the interview, and (4) brief descriptions of appearance, mannerisms, gestures, and so forth. *Avoid inserting your own opinions* with phrases such as, "She seemed to feel sad when she told the story about. . . ." Avoid first person altogether in your report. Do not let your interview slide into generalities. Get specifics. Probe. Find out *why* your respondent is saying certain things: What life experiences has she or he had to produce a certain point of view?

Tips on interviewing. Pick a reporter by identifying bylines. Familiarize yourself with the written work of that reporter so that you can talk comfortably about it. Make an interview appointment explaining that this is part of a class project designed to provide material for class discussion and learning. (This will make the reporter a "teacher" of sorts; a little bit of teacher dwells in just about everybody.) Seek a quiet place for the conversation, and try to make it an informal chat rather than a rigid question-and-answer session. Let the reporter do most of the talking. Consider using material in this chapter as a guide to the kind of information you might seek through your interview. Try to get details of specific incidents to illustrate principles. Sometimes you can "prime the pump" by reciting stories like those in this chapter. Telling about Scott Martell's blue jeans–black tie interview, for example, might prompt your reporter to recall a similar story that you can use in your report. Or you can ask about a concept drawn from your reading. Is asking questions of a victim's relative in a court case actually a "dirty job of questionable importance," as Bonnie Henderson suggests? In asking questions, be specific but brief. Be sure to ask follow-up questions to affirm your understanding and to secure greater detail.

3

How to Recognize News

What is "news"? Both practitioners and scholars have struggled with that question, and their answers can only be described as bewildering. Historically the question seemed far less difficult than it does now.

"When a dog bites a man, that's not news. But when a man bites a dog, that *is* news." It was John B. Bogart, city editor of the *New York Sun,* who uttered that famous dictum more than a century ago. To some extent it still stands today, because news often is the account of something rare or out of the ordinary.

"News is what will make people talk." Charles Dana, editor of the *New York Sun,* made that point, which certainly is true today. If you walked past ten houses on the street and found house seven engulfed in a roaring fire, which one would *you* talk about when you got home? To a large extent, news is guided by human nature. It is not human nature to talk about house three or five where all is calm, when house seven is on fire. And it is human nature to wonder about the occupants. Did they get out safely? Will their house be saved? How much loss will they suffer? Do they have insurance? It's the kind of curiosity that produces good reporters. The much-vaunted "nose for news" is little more than a professionally disciplined curiosity, the kind that evolves from human nature.

"News is anything that makes the reader say, 'Gee, whiz.' " That statement, made by Arthur McEwan, editor of the *San Francisco Examiner,* holds true even today, though today's news is often highly complex. Events that might have caused you to say "Gee, whiz" at one time hardly rate a second notice today. Take space travel, for instance. We remember many of the pioneering efforts—John Glenn's

(Photo by Dan Dillon)

first ride, Neil Armstrong's walk on the moon, Sally Ride's pioneering venture as the first American woman in space—but we tend to take only passing note of the routine ventures in between.

"One big trouble with news is that nobody knows what it is. The other trouble is that nobody knows what it means." That remark came not from an editor but from a political scientist, Leon V. Sigal. He took an insightful excursion into the world of the working journalist and reached that conclusion in his book *Reporters and Officials,* published in 1973.

Today's definitions of news are no less bewildering. In 1982 the American Society of Newspaper Editors published a pamphlet entitled "What is news? Who decides? And how?" The definitions of news from some 500 journalists who responded to a survey ranged from "News is what raises eyebrows" to "News is what I want to write about."

The variety of definitions, the uncertainty, may sound ominous to the aspiring journalist, though it need not be. News is a recounting of the events, situations, and ideas that human nature prompts us—as reasonably intelligent, alert, and interested people—to take note of. Or we *would* take note of them if we knew about them. The journalist's job is to second-guess human nature and to anticipate the elements that audiences will find interesting, important, and useful.

THE BOTTOM LINE—DEFINING NEWS

Contrary to Leon Sigal's view, most people tend to know what news is, at least on an elemental level. We use news every day in normal conversation. The way we tell others about our own personal news bears an uncanny resemblance to the way the news media relate events and situations of major public importance.

You might call it a "bottom line" style of conversation. If you suddenly encounter an old friend you haven't seen for years, one of the first questions likely to come up is, "What's new in your life?" So you tend to hit the highlights. You finished school and you just got your first job. Or you bought a new car. You took a trip to Bermuda. Next year, finances permitting, it will be Hawaii. You met someone new and you're thinking of getting married. You're studying yoga.

Usually you present the bottom line first—you got a new job—with elaborating details later: You'll be working at the computer information center, earning $19,000 a year, and you're really enthusiastic about the opportunities, and so on.

You probably haven't given much thought to a definition that guides your choice of subjects to talk about when someone asks you what's new. Most of us don't; we just seem to know. We say what comes to mind naturally. Given a chance to consider, we might even accept one or more of the academic definitions common in the profession. Here's one:

> *News is a prompt, "bottom line" recounting of factual information about events, situations, and ideas (including opinions and interpretations) calculated to interest an audience and help people cope with themselves and their environment.*

To that definition you can add ten elements useful in the gathering and writing of news as practiced on most newspapers.

Timeliness.   Something that happened last night is more newsworthy than something that happened a month or a year ago. News must be "new." When you read it or hear about it, it should be for the first time. *Discovery* of old events can be news, however, such as finding the wreckage of an eighteenth-century sailing ship in 90 fathoms of water off the coast of Florida. It is that discovery that is news, not the sinking 200 years ago.

Consequence.   The more people affected by an event, the greater its news value. A tax reform bill in Congress affects all taxpayers and has more news value than, say, a federal project in Texas affecting only residents of that state. Sometimes a reporter must ferret out the consequences. Let's say 50 false fire alarms have been reported in a week. The story may have greater consequence value if the reporter, quoting the fire chief, touches on the problem of a real fire occurring when equipment is involved in a false run.

Prominence.   More news value is placed on better-known persons or institutions. If the President breaks a leg, the whole world is interested. If you break your leg, chances are only your family and friends will care.

Rarity.   Like precious metal, the less frequently something exists or happens, the greater the news value. If you fell 1,000 feet off a cliff and broke *only* your leg, it would be news. Why? Because most people do not survive such falls. Yours is a rare occurrence. This is why America's first woman in space is news; when women routinely fly space missions, the news value will diminish.

Proximity.   Human nature dictates that we are more concerned about things near us than far away. Foul weather in Maine contains scant interest to someone living in California and vice versa. The size of a community is a factor: The larger the city the more distance we feel. A brutal but routine murder is page-one news in a tiny rural community but hardly worth a paragraph in Chicago or Los Angeles.

Conflict.   Human nature also dictates that we pay more attention to clash than to routine. A fight in Congress. A fire crew battling an inferno. A lively political debate. A violent labor strike. A personal struggle to surmount an obstacle such as defeating cancer or climbing a mountain in a raging storm. We take particular note of such things because they are human drama, the kind of stuff from which novels emerge. Clashes of opinion also suggest the unsettled nature of certain situations.

Change.   Unsettled situations do contain the prospect of change, of course. You have a bigger story when it suggests either an uncertain future or the likelihood of a different course. It is human nature either to resist change or to welcome it. Either way you know that people are interested.

Action.   The concept of people *doing* things is more dramatic and thus more newsworthy than people merely thinking or talking about them. People marching on city hall to protest higher taxes makes a bigger story than random, disorganized dissatisfaction. That Mr. A is angry at Mr. B is hardly news, unless A shoots B or burns his house down or files a lawsuit.

Concreteness.   The tangible always takes precedence over the abstract on the scale of news values. A single body on the street is more noteworthy than abstract discussion about the dangers of violent crime. We have a sliding scale of values: A $100,000 bank robbery obviously supersedes a $1,000 robbery.

Personality.   The human dimension—journalists call it "human interest"—clearly enters the scale of news values. People like to read about people, from celebrities to ordinary folks involved in extraordinary matters.

FURTHER DEFINITIONS

These elements tend to overlap, of course, such as when a "prominent personality" takes a "concrete action" calculated to produce "change" of massive "consequence." Clearly, the more elements involved in the story, the bigger the story.

Some other elements, not part of the basic list, deserve mention. They are not on the original list because they tend to be a little artificial, even though they represent modern journalistic practices. Some of them lean toward techniques of story presentation.

Celebration. Anniversaries, civic events and awards, parades, milestones— these are routinely newsworthy. They often present a reason to write a story, a "newspeg" it's called: "Today marks the 50th anniversary of the Japanese attack on Pearl Harbor" and similar milestones.

Adventure. Readers vicariously identify with physical or intellectual exploits of daring men and women. Reader interest in sports falls largely into this category. The choice of news events can range from space flight to a swimmer's dramatic rescue of a drowning child. Articles presented in narrative form—almost like a short fiction story—can heighten the suspense and the vicarious enjoyment.

Mystery. Enigmas intrigue people. A murder victim is discovered, and the game is afoot, to paraphrase Sherlock Holmes, the intriguing game of learning what happened and who did it.

Drama. If art imitates life, then it follows that many real events contain the elements of good art. The classic plot line of fiction deserves study by journalists. A character confronts a conflict, struggles with problems and crises, and then encounters a grim "darkest moment." The character wins (happy ending) or loses (tragic ending). Three types of conflict are traditional: hero versus human, hero versus nature, hero versus self. Reality is full of examples. A pilot brings a crippled airliner to a dramatic but safe landing after a midair collision. A young couple, camped near Mount St. Helens, tell a harrowing story of escape after the mountain explodes with a force of 500 atomic bombs. An average man plunges into an icy river to rescue a survivor of an air crash. Because of the drama involved, these stories are sometimes bigger than if the worst had happened.

Ethics. The history of the human race is a constant search for what's right and just. You'll find news value here, too, in such things as persons convicted of crimes they didn't commit, people winning Pulitzer prizes for stories that were fakes, or investigations of malfeasance in political office.

Self-improvement. This is a latecomer to the traditional list of news elements, for newspapers at least. It remains a little controversial among editors. Readership studies have demonstrated high interest in "service" journalism—the kind of journalism magazines have traditionally practiced all along. It includes stories on home maintenance, food, finances, human relationships, entertainment, travel, health, beauty, and fashions.

A final set of definitions deserves brief mention because they are terms of the trade.

Hard news.   News of important public events such as actions of government, social or economic trends, education, international relations.

Soft news.   Information that is less important than hard news but often more interesting, even tantalizing sometimes: gossipy items about celebrities, offbeat incidents, sensational crime cases, items noted for reader interest.

Straight news.   Presentation of unvarnished facts without attempt to analyze, interpret, or capture human interest.

Spot news.   A sudden happening, such as a fire, a jury verdict, or a Congressional decision, as opposed to trend stories.

LIFE CYCLE OF A NEWS ISSUE

Journalists must also distinguish between a "news issue" and a "news event." The *news issue* is largely an ongoing situation or problem, such as a long-standing dispute between labor and management at Company X. *News events* arise when, as a result of the dispute, labor goes on strike, or when the strike erupts into violence, or when it's settled.

News issues fall into two categories. Let's label them the *sudden explosion* type and the *running fever* type.

The "sudden explosion" begins with a dramatic, unexpected, and sometimes violent incident. Two airplanes collide over a busy airport with awesome loss of life, and the issue is joined. Why did it happen? Who's to blame? An investigation ensues, debate continues, and ultimately, perhaps, some action results.

The "running fever" category is the kind of issue you hardly notice at first. If it's violent at all, the violence comes toward the end, not at the beginning. Consider an example:

The scene is Ponderosa College, a tiny, mythical college set, let us say, amid the pine trees on a hill in northern California. For years students have lived with an administrative dictum that bars political speakers from the campus. A mild fever of discontent edges in. At first the public dialogue is mellow.

"Why can't we have political speakers?"

"Because Ponderosa must remain a bulwark against crass political manipulation."

The fever has begun, even if not entirely noticed yet by the news media. The question will be asked again, more sharply. Perhaps the fever will go away, perhaps not. It may continue with the dictum fought against, petitioned against, even picketed against. Appeals are made to higher authority, the Board of Trustees or maybe the courts. Ever more strident letters appear in newspapers, graffiti appears suddenly on the walls. Perhaps a "test case" is tried—students bring in a controversial political speaker in direct challenge to the administration. The lid blows off. A climax approaches. What will happen next?

The whole fever bears the markings of a well-plotted work of fiction, except that it's totally factual. It's reportable most any time something specific happens or is about to happen: a protest petition, a picket line, the arrival of the controversial politician, the reaction (or even the lack of reaction) of the college president.

The more perceptive a reporter you are, the earlier you'll notice subtle signs of change. It is not necessary or even desirable to await a sudden, explosive confrontation before perceiving that newsworthy change is in the wind. By contrast, inability to perceive subtle but significant fevers with the potential for change can lead to the "sudden explosion" type of issue. Recent history has shown us many, such as urban race riots, political discontent, or labor strife. If you see a wall of snow tumbling down the mountainside, you do not have to await its arrival at your location to start sounding an avalanche warning.

IDENTIFYING WITH YOUR READERS

A perceptive reporter must do more than memorize the traditional elements of news. The best reporters and writers are "audience oriented" in two ways. First, they like people. They enjoy being with them, asking questions of them, writing about them. Second, because they like people, they strive to play to the needs and interests of their audiences, just as a good speaker works an audience with a mixture of factual information, thematic message, humor, and inspiration. The more you know about your audience—which is to say the more you know about human nature—the better you can match your message to its interests.

A lot of this has, over the four centuries of newspaper tradition, been intuitive. Depending on the newsperson's skill in reading an audience, it is better than guesswork, but far short of scientific. It's largely flying by the seat of your pants. It is, in the words of magazine journalist John Fischer, a "cross between playing the horses and practicing psychiatry without a license."

It probably will always remain so. But in recent decades newspapers have turned to research, particularly study of audience characteristics and interests, to remove some of the guesswork. Marketing studies have become commonplace. Some big newspapers, the *Chicago Tribune,* for example, employ full-time research departments.

Most of their work centers around advertising and circulation concerns. The idea of using scientific research methods to determine what kinds of information should go into the newspaper is a new concept, and one not always supported by reporters and their editors. News, these journalists say, is something more precious, more ephemeral, than corn flakes or computer hardware. If you were selling a new brand of breakfast cereal, you'd conduct marketing studies in selected areas, and you'd guide your decisions on the results.

Can the marketing of news be handled in a similar manner?

The answer assumes more importance to newspaper publishers than ever before because of competition with other media. While broadcast news has attracted ever-increasing audiences, newspaper circulation has not kept pace with

U.S. population growth. Circulation actually declined in the early 1970s, prompting publishers and editors to ask, "What do our readers want from us?" And they turned increasingly to audience research for the answers.

The answers continue to come. Full discussion of them is beyond the scope of this book, but some are of particular interest to those striving to acquire skill as writers of news and features. Research certainly has impact on newswriting practices, enough impact that student journalists should pay heed, if not homage.

Research—and common sense among the more perceptive journalists— suggests that reader interests start with "self" and expand out from there to the more remote interests of community, national, and international affairs. Research combined with theory suggests that anyone who reads a newspaper expects a payoff, a specific reward for the time and effort involved. One research giant, Wilbur Schramm, divides these rewards into "immediate" and "delayed."

Immediate rewards stem from news of crime, corruption, sports, disasters, recreation, human interest, and social events. Delayed rewards come from news of public affairs, economic conditions, problems of society, science, education, community health.

"News of the first kind pays its reward at once," Schramm wrote in 1947. "A reader can enjoy a vicarious experience without any of the dangers or stresses involved. He can shiver luxuriously at an axe-murder, shake his head sympathetically and safely at a tornado. . . . News of the second kind, however, requires the reader to endure unpleasantness or annoyance—as, for example, when he reads of the ominous foreign situation, the mounting national debt, rising taxes, falling market, scarce housing, cancer, epidemics, farm blights. It has a kind of 'threat value.' It is read so that the reader may be informed and prepared."

The trouble with audience research, many journalists insist, is that audiences tend toward the immediate rewards. Most people will select the light, frothy material that one editor condemns as "bubble gum journalism." Editors argue that their job is to maintain a balance, like a nagging parent determined that the child shall consume everything on the dinner plate.

While the argument continues, it is safe to say that newspapers have changed over recent years, partly as a result of some of the research findings. The notion of the "self-centered" reader of the 1970s has produced many new sections devoted to "service journalism," a term borrowed from magazines. New sections on Entertainment, Lifestyles, and Fashions appeared. The term "use-paper" emerged. Editors redefined news as something either inherently interesting or "useful within 24 hours" to most readers. A research finding that large numbers of young people were indifferent to newspapers has produced material—entertainment sections, for example—calculated to serve their interests.

Then in the 1980s the idea emerged that readers really expected "hard news" from the newspaper after all, though they didn't want to lose anything else. A young professional woman, responding to a research project, declared, "I think of a newspaper as a big information supermarket where I can pick and choose what I want."

Even younger people showed concern about the economy, especially in such areas as finding jobs or buying cars and homes amid high interest rates. Foreign affairs gained sometimes-chilling personal implications: the threat and occasional reality of armed conflict, the rising cost of imported oil and other commodities, for instance. Serious news was "in," but self-help information was not necessarily "out." One survey showed that almost half the respondents were seriously concerned about the prospect of nuclear war, and 48 percent were worried about losing their jobs. Editors began to think "balance": avoiding excesses on either side.

The study, "Changing Needs of Changing Readers" (Ruth Clark, 1979), was part of a six-year study sponsored by the newspaper industry and run through the Newspaper Advertising Bureau in New York. The studies ranged from readership patterns of persons with eyesight problems to analysis of children's reading patterns. Table 3–1 shows one pattern of reader results, an analysis of what respondents say they "usually read" in the newspaper.

Both the working reporter and the student journalist may find some research useful as a means of getting closer to the reader. That's the most important aspect: Never lose sight of the person you're trying to inform or help. Here are some of the most useful research findings for doing so.

1. Readers spend 30 to 50 minutes with the daily paper (the bigger the paper, the more they read). About two-thirds of the readers thumb through the entire paper page by page; the rest go directly to specific sections such as sports or the comics. (For reference, see *Newspaper Readership Project,* 1984, in the bibliography.)

2. Most people get their national and international news from television, their local and regional news from newspapers. (Grotta, Larkin, & DePlois, 1975.)

3. People who subscribe to newspapers tend to have higher incomes, better education, and longer residencies in their communities than non-subscribers. (Rarick, 1973.)

4. News with high reader interest tends to have an unpleasant aspect. (Clyde, 1968.) Given dual choices, the participants in a study preferred to read the unpleasant over the pleasant, the important over the unimportant, the interesting over the boring, and the unpleasant over the important.

5. Readers and professional journalists tend to agree on the elements of high readership: (1) impact or consequence—something that affects lots of readers, and (2) conflict. (Atwood, 1970.)

6. Readers want more *local* news and features. (Grotta et al., 1975.)

7. Newspaper readers find advantages to newspapers not present in other media, notably an ease in quickly obtaining desired information; you don't have to listen to an hourlong newscast to get the one or two items you want, such as a sports score or election result. (Newspaper Readership Project, 1984.)

Table 3-1 Kinds of Newspaper Items "Usually Read" by Education within Sex

	MEN		WOMEN	
Editorial	*Some Coll+*	*HS Grad or Less*	*Some Coll+*	*HS Grad or Less*
News about local community	87%	86%	92%	89%
Economic news: jobs, inflation, etc.	91	87	87	81
International or world news	92	84	90	75
News about President, Congress	85	79	82	70
News briefs, summary of news	84	75	84	71
News about local politics, gov't.	81	73	78	68
News about celebrities	69	61	82	73
TV program listings	63	66	66	71
Advice columns	46	45	83	80
Calendar of local events	57	56	71	61
Letters to the editor	63	52	69	59
Food pages	27	39	81	81
Editorials, editor's opinions	61	56	66	53
Comic strips, funnies	59	61	56	54
Obituaries	38	51	51	63
Sports news: local schools, etc.	59	66	41	40
Business and financial news	67	54	47	37
Sports news: professional teams	71	70	32	28
Political opinion columns	55	50	53	38
Book reviews	33	16	28	26
Crossword puzzle	20	19	28	26
Advertising				
Supermarket advertisements	36%	52%	77%	82%
Store ads for clothing	44	48	75	77
Classified or want ads	59	67	53	60
Movie ads	63	51	56	55

Source: "Meeting Readers' Multiple Needs," Newspaper Advertising Bureau, 1984.

Precisely how much of this research can be applied to the day-to-day work of the reporter depends on competence and imagination. To one informed observer, Leo Bogart, a lot of research findings merely suggest that newspapers try to do better what they've been doing all along: a balance of news and features. Bogart, vice president and general manager of the Newspaper Advertising Bureau, once gave a talk on how newspapers can attract more young people. Encourage good writing, he said. Leave space for routine news. Try to articulate the concerns of the readers: "Does your paper reflect what they talk about at home?"

BASIC QUESTIONS

Much of the foregoing material can be summarized in a set of basic questions dealing with an event or topic under discussion. The more affirmative answers you can give to these questions, the higher the news value.

Is it really *new*? Does it represent change, progress, regression, a new trend? Has an old situation occurred in a new context (hijacking of a passenger ferry, perhaps, instead of an airliner)?

Is it specific and concrete rather than vague or abstract?

Is action involved? Has money been spent, blood spilled, court papers filed, invasions begun rather than merely threatened?

Does it threaten the future of important people or institutions? Will heads roll, giants fall, or VIPs tumble from their thrones?

Does it involve unusual circumstances?

Is a significant philosophical issue or principle involved?

Who cares? Will it affect lots of people? How many?

Does it affect the future?

Are people likely to hate it or oppose it?

Can people do anything about it on an individual basis?

Does it reward the reader (teach something, reassure, warn, alert, offer a reason to laugh or cry)?

Does it contain such seductive elements as mystery, adventure, romance, drama, sex, violence, wealth, celebrity status, suspense, irony, or humor?

Is it urgent? Is it important *now*? Can mileposts or news pegs offer a reason to write about it now?

Is it practical or useful? Can the reader build it, ride it, eat it, feel it, kick it, or at least go see it?

IS NEWS WHAT YOU MAKE IT?

Questions like those in the above list may help the beginner sort out news on a primary level. Even so, identifying news remains a difficult question for the person thrown into the jungle of human activities and charged with the responsibility of sorting news from nonnews. If only the distinction were as simple as separating edible mushrooms from the poisonous ones.

Experience does suggest to reporters that to an extent news is what you make it. That sounds arrogant, so let's examine the issue. Walter Lippmann, the late, great pundit of journalism, remarked in 1922 that if you see a building leaning at a dangerous angle, you need not wait for it to fall to decide that it's worthy of note, therefore news. That remains true today. But the question is complicated by subtle nuances, not to mention bureaucratic complexities. At what degree of list does the building become dangerous? One degree? Five, ten? Who decides? What agency is in charge? City, county, state, federal? Will an engineering consultant be hired?

How will it be funded? Has an environmental impact statement been filed? Is it a matter for the courts? How simple the Lippmann dictum seems today in this era of legal and bureaucratic mazes.

In fact, a perceptive reporter can tap into the building problem at just about any step along the way, at just about any degree of building list or at any level of governmental concern.

News can, indeed, be what a journalist says it is as long as it can be presented as a matter of public interest and concern. It depends to a great extent on the skill and perception of the journalist. Clearly the journalists who have the public's interests more closely in mind—with fairness, accuracy, and completeness their major guidelines—will produce more newsworthy material. A "people-oriented" journalist seems to do this best. Within the breast of every living person, a famous editor once said, lies buried at least one significant story. (Ellery Sedgwick, *The Happy Profession,* 1946.) The task of the journalist is to find it and to recognize its significance. It begins with reportorial enthusiasm: being interested in just everything and everybody you meet.

Meanwhile, you shouldn't despair if you're still uncertain and frustrated by the elusive nature of news. Half a century ago a Baltimore newspaperman, Gerald W. Johnson, wrote a small book entitled *What Is News?* One of his answers remains valid today: "In the last analysis 'What is News?' may be restated in the words of the Roman governor who asked, 'What is truth?' and whose question remains unanswered although the man who asked it has been twenty centuries dead."

POINTS TO REMEMBER

1. News is not easily defined, though it tends to be the factual recounting of events and situations that interest people.
2. Most people know what news is when they recount it daily in their conversations.
3. Traditional news elements include timeliness, consequence, prominence, rarity, proximity, conflict, change, action, concreteness, personality.
4. Much news consists of specific events that fall from a basic and ongoing news "issue."
5. Studies of readers suggest that they are increasingly interested in "hard" or important news, but they don't want to forego recent developments in reader-service news.
6. Readers expect a reward for their efforts, which can be either immediate or delayed.
7. News sometimes actually is what you make it, depending on the skill and perception of the reporter.

PROJECT

Clip three page-one articles from a daily newspaper. Write a paper analyzing the ways in which the ten elements of news, as discussed in this chapter, are involved in each story. *Purpose:* Learn to recognize the elements of news as they appear in actual news stories. *Suggestions:* Try to find three stories that are distinctly different from one another so that you have a range of news elements to deal with. By referring to the news elements, explain why you think the article was given a position of importance on page one instead of an inside page. Do you believe the article is on page one because of a high level of consequence or prominence or what? Which news elements are the most important in each story? The least important? Which are missing altogether? Which, if any, of the minor criteria for news (celebration, adventure, mystery, drama, ethics, self-improvement) are present? Are any news elements misplaced in your view? That is, did the reporter fail to give sufficient attention to one or more elements?

4

Organization of a News Story

In its simplest form, the news story bears a striking resemblance to our own "bottom line" style of presenting personal news. We usually just blurt it out: "Guess what? I'm engaged!" The most important element comes first, the elaborating details later. ("Yes, Tom finally popped the question. . . . The wedding's in June. . . . We're spending three weeks in Hawaii. . . .")

Or let's say a friend of yours is in the hospital with a broken leg. Consider how you might tell someone about it, compared to how a newspaper might approach it. They bear a remarkable similarity.

First, the personal approach: "Did you hear—Judy Long's in the hospital. Broke her leg yesterday. She was learning hang gliding, of all things. It was her first big flight and she hit a log trying to land that contraption down at Sandy Beach. I told her flying was dangerous, but you know how adventurous these young folks are nowadays. . . ."

A newspaper report would leave out the opinion. But the facts themselves would be arranged in a pattern similar to our bottom line method.

The opening paragraph, called the "lead" (leed) in news jargon, would capture the essence of the situation: A young woman named Judy Long hurt herself in a hang gliding accident and is in the hospital with a broken leg.

The second paragraph would tell what happened: She had flown the craft off a local landmark called Bald Mountain and was trying to land it at Sandy Beach, another landmark stretched along the Chickahominy River below the mountain. (It's important to identify specific locales.) The news story would usually quote

(Photo by Randy L. Rasmussen.)

some authority or a witness, such as, "A sheriff's deputy said an unexpected gust of wind sent the glider crashing into a log on the beach."

Further details would follow, either in chronological order or more or less in order of descending importance. The details might include such items as an eyewitness account and background information (such as the area's popularity with hang gliding enthusiasts or the number of times similar accidents have occurred in the past). The story might even include speculation about the future—not the writer's speculation but that of some official such as the sheriff. As a writer you would not say hang gliding is dangerous, but you might quote the sheriff as saying so, even if you didn't personally agree.

In reporting such an event personally or as a newspaper item, you have observed an ancient journalistic custom: answering the six questions known as the five W's and the H. They are Who, What, Where, When, Why, and How. They are classics. Rudyard Kipling lyrically called them "six honest serving men who taught me all I knew." And as we communicate news events and situations—from personal gossip to international crises—we tend to reach for them even when we are not always conscious of doing so.

Who? Our friend, Judy Long, of course.

What? Broke her leg in a glider accident.

Where? On Sandy Beach, alongside the Chickahominy River, below Bald Mountain.

When? Yesterday.

How? The glider, caught by a sudden gust of wind, crashed into a log on the beach.

Why? This question runs deeper than the others, as you might imagine. The answer could be deeply embedded into Ms. Long's psychological profile (she's always exhibited a spirit of adventure) or it could be quite simple: She unwittingly lost control of the craft. More about this later.

How do such stories get into the paper? It is possible that someone on the paper knows Judy Long personally or that someone witnessed the crash and called to tell the paper about it. More likely it came off a police report. To paraphrase a pioneer journalist named John L. Given (*Making a Newspaper*, 1907), newspapers do not keep a watch on all humankind, but they do station watchers at a few places where it becomes known whenever events worth talking about occur or when people's lives stray from routine pathways.

These include places like city hall, the courthouse, police headquarters. And it is at the latter, specifically the Sheriff's Office, that it becomes known that Judy Long's life has strayed from ordinary pathways.

A CASE HISTORY

To understand how to organize a news story, you may find it helpful to view it in context. It is more than rhetorical, for it involves the entire process of story selection, research (documents and interviews), and writing. Let us therefore present a case history involving the hypothetical story about Judith Long. The story is based on a real incident. No doubt hundreds of routine glider flights have been made off Bald Mountain onto Sandy Beach. How come this one gets attention? Probably because the newspaper's definition of news is not unlike most people's: It's what people talk about. People talk about unusual events, celebrities they've met, and people or situations that deviate from routine pathways. Journalists write about the same nonroutine events when they learn of them.

To understand the process of organizing a simple news story, you must first understand three principles of newsgathering.

1. First you must recognize the event as "news." Often this is not as easy in the field as it might have been in the classroom or a textbook. But failure to do so is akin to a farmer failing to distinguish between the potato plants and the weeds.

2. Having ascertained the news value, you must decide which details to seek, whom to talk to, what questions to ask. You know that out of your search for detail must come a "bottom line" or *essence* of the news. This

you will present as your opening or "lead" paragraph. You know that the story organization will proceed with elaborating details that answer the five-W's-and-H questions.

3. Having gathered the appropriate information, you must "package" the information in a coherent news article: the "bottom line" first, the elaborating details to follow.

So in this case history we'll say that you are employed by a small daily newspaper published in a town called River City. The paper is delivered to doorsteps within the community each afternoon around 4:30. You work in a large, open-spaced office called a newsroom with about 20 other reporters under the direction of an executive called the "city editor."

As the paper's police reporter you come to work around 6:30 each morning and are usually making the rounds of police and fire agencies by seven o'clock. Today, on your Monday morning rounds, you stop at the office of the county sheriff and happen across a minor but potentially newsworthy item involving the young woman named Judy (or Judith) Long.

Your first word that the life of Judith Long has strayed from ordinary paths comes when you skim what used to be called the "police blotter," a listing of police activities during the past day or so. It's called the blotter because in the early days of newspapering reporters sometimes learned of police activities by reading the blotter used to dry the ink on the police records. They read it backwards. Today they're more likely to read a computer printout. It records each action taken during the previous day's shifts of the deputies in the Sheriff's Office. It includes notations of crimes and accidents reported, persons arrested, miscellaneous public services performed, and stacks of other routine minutiae typical of police work. It is raw material for the reporter. It does not tell what is news, nor does it tell you what questions to ask should you decide a particular item is news. It's merely a starting point for the reporter. It's up to you to separate the nuggets from the raw ore. Here is a portion of a printout:

DAILY POLICE BULLETIN

C-05627	MINOR ACCIDENT LAINE, M. RPDT MVA, MINOR INJ/NO TOW	P/LOT 94-144 PARK HWY OF 777 HILL ST	1230/05.07.85
C-05628	HARASSMENT-NO PHYSICAL CONTACT WILKINS, L. RPTD UNK THREW BEER BOTTLE INTO SWIMMING POOL	95 ARGYLE RD OF SAME	0345/05.08.85
C-05629	LARCENY, THEFT HALVERSON, R. RPTD THEFT OF RIFLE FROM VEH/VAL $200	RT 1 WEST ACRES OF SAME	1835/05.07.85
C-05630	MISC PUBLIC LANDERS, R. RPTD HANG GLIDER ACC/ONE INJ	SANDY BEACH OF 555 WESTWAY #4	1450/05.07.85

```
C-05631   DEL CHILD-RUNAWAY        1777 BEACON DR #235      0800/05.07.85
          JOHNSON, J.              OF 1777 BEACON #235
          ABOVE LEFT HOME & FAILED TO RETURN

C-05632   BURGLARY                 KAISER RD               1600/05.07.85
          CREST ELEM SCHOOL        OF 98-375 KAISER RD
          RPTD ENTRY INTO CAFETERIA VIA WINDOW, NOTHING TAKEN

C-05633   ALL OTHER OFFENSES       ACE TAVERN              0322/05.08.85
          FOSDICK, F.              OF S.O.
          ARRESTED ONE FOR RESISTING ARREST
```

You may skim a hundred or more such items and find only a handful of newsworthy incidents. Chances are your newspaper has some guidelines on what is important enough to be reportable. Armed robberies are reportable, for example; minor thefts are not. Tavern brawls are not unless serious injuries result or unusual circumstances prevail. Minor arrests such as disturbing the peace or driving while intoxicated are reportable only if the accused is convicted by a court. Burglary and theft are reportable only if the loss is above $5,000 or if circumstances are unusual. Accidents are reported only if serious injuries or fatalities resulted or if circumstances are unusual. Rapes are reportable but the victim is not to be identified. Juveniles (under eighteen) are not to be identified by name.

And so on. As a reporter you also monitor the police bulletin for trends. A rash of burglaries, an upward climb of violence in a certain district, an increase in intoxicated drivers—all these are news even if any single example is not.

From this morning's log you check out two items, RESISTING ARREST and HANG GLIDER ACCIDENT. The former is a routine tavern brawl in which four persons were arrested; you skip it in accordance with your paper's policy. (Some papers, of course, might have a policy that would include such an item.)

That leaves the hang glider accident. You ask to see report C-05630. (You're lucky to have a cooperative Sheriff's Office; many police agencies will not allow newswriters to read reports. They fear a reckless reporter might prematurely release information that hinders an investigation, such as naming a suspect who is under surveillance. You're especially careful to avoid that kind of problem, and you have thereby gained the confidence of the department. Even so, police-reporter relations are often uneasy.)

Here is the police report.

INCIDENT REPORT

```
Case No. C-05630
Time:1450      Date 5-7-85
Officer: Fosdick
Location: Sandy Beach
INJURED:     LONG, JUDITH ANN, d.o.b. 3-22-57
             555 Westway Avenue, Apt. #4
             River City

CONTACTED:   LANDERS, ROSALEE JANICE, d.o.b. 7-24-62
             555 Westway #4
             River City
```

DETAILS: Writer was advised of an injured woman at Sandy Beach. Upon arrival writer determined that LONG has possible broken leg and numerous scratches. LANDERS said Long had taken off from Bald Mountain in a hang glider and was airborne for a period of approximately five minutes. Upon landing the glider, a sudden gust of wind apparently caused it to fall a height of five to ten feet. Long struck a log on the beach, causing a possible fracture to left leg. Ambulance removed subject to Mercy Hospital at 1507 hrs.

F. Fosdick, Badge 0976

Basic Questions

The police report, though sketchy, gives you sufficient details to allow you to make some preliminary decisions about the incident.

Is it a news story? Yes, probably, for two reasons. It is an unusual accident, therefore more noteworthy than, say, the same person's breaking her leg falling in the bathtub. Second, it may, justifiably or not, imply an inherent danger in a relatively new leisure activity that so far has undergone little public scrutiny. In short, the accident could represent the start of a "news issue" dealing with the safety of hang gliding.

How big a story? Probably not more than two or three paragraphs for the accident itself. However, if the accident has touched off a full-scale investigation by the sheriff or another agency on the safety of hang gliding, you'll have a longer story. It also depends on time. Your deadline for the first of the two editions your paper publishes daily is (we'll say) 10:30 A.M. It's 7:30 now. If an important story turns up as you make the rounds of other police agencies, you may have to settle for a brief report of the accident. If nothing else turns up, then you may devote more attention to this one. Such are the vagaries of daily news reporting.

What belongs in the story? As you gain experience, you develop a kind of mental checklist. The reporting of a news event starts with six basic questions: Who? What? Where? When? Why? How? Let's examine how they fit this story and what additional questions need to be asked.

Who? You already have the names and ages (d.o.b. means "date of birth") but you may need further identification. Newspapers generally identify persons by one or more of the following: address, age, occupation, family connection, noteworthy accomplishments ("first woman in space," etc.), or their connection with the incident being reported (a witness, for example). Who is Judith Long? Is she well known in town? How about Rosalee Landers? You make a mental note to check the *City Directory*, a fat reference book that lists the names, addresses, and occupations of residents of the community.

What? You have a fair picture of what happened, assuming the police report is correct. Experienced reporters, however, learn not to trust a single source, preferring corroboration and additional details from other sources. So you plan to call Rosalee Landers, who appears to have been a witness. You will also call Mercy Hospital for a report on the extent of injuries and her current condition.

Where?   No problem here. You consult a map and find that Bald Mountain (elevation 1,120 feet) overlooks Sandy Beach (elevation 505 feet), a large and popular recreation spot about twenty miles east of River City.

When?   "Sunday afternoon" is close enough for your report.

How?   The police report seems clear enough—a gust of wind caught the glider, causing it to fall. Your sense of professional curiosity causes you to wonder about some aspects of the accident, however. Was Long an experienced glider pilot? Are wind gusts common at Sandy Beach? Did the glider collapse, or fall nose-first, or flip to one side, or what? Exactly how did the woman strike the log? How big was the log? How fast was she going? How hard was the wind blowing? Did many people witness the accident? Where was Landers at the time? You may not fit *all* of these details into your report, but you need them to enhance your understanding of the incident. This will enable you to write a more accurate and precise report. Your writing must not be vague.

Why?   This should not be confused with "how?" Why the accident happened can be explained superficially by the how: A wind gust caught the glider and caused it to fall. "Why?" is a deeper, more intriguing question. Why did Judy Long take up hang gliding in the first place? What inherent quest for adventure is she attempting to fulfill by such a sport? How about gliding itself? If it is inherently dangerous, why is it not regulated? Do glider pilots receive instruction and follow rules of safety? Who teaches them? What are their credentials for teaching? Answers to these and similar questions can contribute to the understanding of "why?" These questions may not be asked immediately, certainly not in a routine report about a single accident. But in the long run, "why" is the most important question a journalist can ask.

Two other questions belong on the reporter's basic list.

Background.   Is this the first such accident? Does it represent any kind of trend? How long has hang gliding been popular at Sandy Beach? Have any complaints been received about it from the public? What attempts, if any, have been made to regulate or limit the activities of hang gliding enthusiasts at Sandy Beach? Inquiries along these lines help to put the event in perspective. It may be that hang gliding has been a festering issue that could erupt into public controversy. It may not be, of course. These are merely lines of questioning to be pursued when you really don't know much about the subject. One way to find out about the subject is to read what's been written before. So you make a mental note to check the clip files in the newspaper library when you get back to the office.

So what?   This final question explores the deeper implications of an event or situation. Most events are not just isolated happenings; they are connected with trends and issues that people care about. So your investigation and your story should, if possible, answer the question: What does this mean to people? Is safety indeed an issue? Is annoyance to other people on the beach an issue? Is regulation an issue? If a problem exists, what are some solutions? What boards, commissions, or other public agencies might be involved? In short, what are the implications for the future? And what about the personal future of Judith Long? Will she fly hang gliders again?

True, not every minor incident warrants the full treatment. Maybe it's the fifth or the eleventh hang glider incident at Sandy Beach that gets the full investigation. Yet a good reporter, which is to say a curious reporter, always considers the implications that might make the story more than routine. A reporter with curiosity and imagination can do this better than one who cannot see beyond the immediate facts.

Developing the Story

It is now 8:30, and you have completed your check of the police and fire agencies. It is a quiet day. Had an important story turned up, you would have phoned the city editor. The editor then would have decided whether to let you proceed with the important story or whether to assign it a to a G.A. (general assignment) reporter. It depends on circumstances and the availability of reporters.

This time the news is routine. "A quiet weekend," you tell the city editor on your return to the office. "A few drunk drivers, a couple of minor burglaries, a tavern brawl, and, oh, yes, this thing about a woman in Mercy Hospital—broke her leg trying to land a hang glider at Sandy Beach."

"Hang glider? Is she badly hurt?"

"Broken leg and scratches so far as I know now. I'll check the hospital."

"How did it happen?"

The questions are calculated to help the city editor determine how big and what kind of story to run. To make this determination, the editor balances the reporter's enthusiasm for the story against other demands on news space, including stories that the reporter doesn't even know about.

"It's an unusual kind of accident," the city editor says. "I don't think we've had one like it around here. Be sure to check the clip files to verify that. I'd say the story is worth six or eight inches on the front page of the second section. As for the safety angle, let's talk about a follow-up story later."

Six to eight column inches in the paper equal about 150 to 200 words. Not a long story, but sufficient for detailing a minor but novel kind of accident. You make a few notes on what information you still need.

1. Check hospital for condition of injured person.
2. Verify spelling of names in telephone directory and/or *City Directory*. Also check addresses. It's important that your story be totally accurate down to the last detail.

3. Check clip files in newspaper library for background on hang gliding, safety, and so forth.
4. Check Sheriff's Office again to verify that this is the first glider accident at Sandy Beach. Ask whether there have been safety or public nuisance complaints about gliders.
5. Find out who Rosalee Landers is; call for verification of details of accident and possible eyewitness report.

From your desk at the office you pick up the phone and start making the first of several calls. Most of your routine interviewing, in fact, is done by phone.

Mercy Hospital's director of community relations—the person you always call for hospital information—tells you that Judith Long is in "good" condition. This is hospital terminology meaning that the patient is conscious, vital signs (pulse, respiration, blood pressure) are stable, and the prognosis is good. The director confirms that Judith Long has a compound fracture of the left leg.

You check the *City Directory* for two listings.

LONG, JUDITH ANN, emp US Natl Bank, 555 Westway #4, 123-0001
LANDERS, ROSALEE JANICE, emp City Health Dept, 555 Westway #4, 123-0001

You guess that they share an apartment and that therefore Landers should be able to tell you quite a bit about the accident and about Judy Long. You decide to call Landers, but first you check the newspaper library for stories published previously in the paper about hang gliding.

The librarian finds only a few clippings of previous stories on the subject. One is a feature done by a reporter for the paper's Sunday magazine. The story, titled "Soar Subject," describes the writer's experience in learning hang gliding at Bald Mountain (he took a nose dive at the end of a one-minute flight but wasn't hurt). Another story reports a fatal accident in another part of the state, 300 miles away. A third reports the state Department of Parks and Recreation's closure of certain state parks to hang gliding activities. Sandy Beach, a county park, was not among the closures. A fourth story, with a Chicago dateline, quotes a surgeon predicting a rash of hang gliding injuries in the years ahead as more people take up the sport. And that's all the clippings on the subject. Perhaps (you think to yourself) you'll check into the subject again later and write a longer story about hang gliding.

But first things first. You call the City Health Department and ask for Rosalee Landers. To your good fortune, she's at her desk. You have done many telephone interviews under similar circumstances—checking the details of a police report with a witness—and you've gradually learned the best way to approach people. Not all people are enthusiastic about answering such inquiries, so you've learned to start such interviews innocuously. You don't hit her too soon with the "What happened?" approach. If you come on too strong, she'll feel threatened and clam up. But if you come on informally, demonstrating interest in her and her feelings, then you'll be told a lot. You always start your interview by identifying yourself and explaining your purpose. Thus:

A. Hello?

Q. Rosalee Landers?

A. Yes.

Q. Good morning. My name is Cindy Johnson. I'm a reporter for the *Daily Express*. I'm writing a report for today's paper based on some information the Sheriff's Office has provided me about Judith Long. Am I correct that Judith Long is your apartment mate?

A. Yes, that's right.

Q. Okay. Well, I just wondered if you could tell me how she's getting along in the hospital. [Yes, it's true that you already have the hospital report, but the need here is to establish conversational rapport by asking a "human" question: one that suggests you care about people. Asking about the state of someone's health is demonstrating that kind of concern. It is the kind of question *anyone* would ask who cares about Judith Long. Landers has probably answered the very same question a dozen times already this morning.]

A. Oh, she's all right, but she's going to be in the hospital for awhile.

Q. Oh, I'm sorry to hear that.

A. Well, I think she must have whacked that log a lot harder than we thought at first.

Q. I guess so. Did you see the accident? [This is a "filter question" to determine her qualifications for answering the question that comes later: "What happened?"]

A. From a distance, yeah. I was on the top of the hill—

Q. Bald Mountain, you mean?

A. Right. I was watching her through binoculars.

Q. As I understand it from the Sheriff's Office, she got off from the mountain okay and made about a five-minute flight and—

A. I doubt if it was five minutes. More like two minutes or less.

Q. I see. Can you tell me what you saw as you watched her?

A. Well, Judy just had tough luck. It was a freak accident. The wind currents around Sandy Beach are usually quite dependable, and that's why we like to go there. Well, I was watching Judy through the glasses, and she was doing fine for her first flight, making a fine landing approach right into the wind. From what I could see, just as she was coming down, a sudden gust of wind came and she kind of flipped to one side and hit this big log. Then some people at the beach started running toward her, and I got pretty scared.

Q. I see. You say this was her first flight?

A. Yes, first extended flight off the mountain clear on down to the beach.

Q. She'd done shorter flights before?

A. Yeah, like, you know, just down the slopes. Maybe three or four feet off the ground to get the feel of the glider. Like the saying goes, when you're learning to fly, don't go any higher than you're willing to fall.

Q. Sounds like good advice. These were short kinds of practice training flights, I gather. [Such questions are necessary for clarification. The reporter, don't forget, must have sufficient detail to write an accurate report.]

A. Right.

Q. So this longer flight onto the beach was the first time she got higher than she'd want to fall.

A. Right. Quite a bit higher.

Q. How high?

A. Well, the actual distance from the ground would have been as much as a couple hundred feet at one point, I'd say. But of course she didn't fall from that height.

Q. I understand she fell from somewhere between five to ten feet.

A. I couldn't tell from where I was, but that's what some people said. Judy said the wind caught her unawares. You know? Like she didn't expect this sudden crosswind, and it kind of slammed her into that log. Frankly, she wasn't too clear on just what happened. The first thing she said to me when I finally got to her and we were waiting for the ambulance, she says, "Oh, Rosie—would you like to see that on instant replay?"

Q. (Chuckles.) It takes a woman with strong moral fiber to make a joke at a time like that.

A. Oh, Judy's got spirit. I talked to her for a minute this morning at the hospital, and she's planning to fly again when she gets out of the hospital.

Q. That *is* spirit, all right. Can you tell me how long she's been flying?

A. Just a week. She spent about three afternoons taking lessons from Larry Jones—he runs informal classes for hang gliding afternoons and weekends and so Judy and I decided to go out there.

Q. So you fly, too?

A. Oh, sure. I've made three long flights off Bald Mountain already.

Q. Sounds scary.

A. Oh, it's really neat—I mean you really feel like an eagle feels, all alone, you know? You ought to try it.

Your interview continues in this vein, an easygoing kind of conversation but clearly directed by the reporter. You listen carefully and react to her comments to *show* that you are listening. You encourage further comments by inquiring further about points she raised, such as her "first flight" remark. That this was Long's first extended flight off Bald Mountain deserves a brief mention in the story. If you were in a hurry you might make your questions more pointed and brisk, but no need to this time. You glance at the clock. It is 9:25—65 minutes to deadline.

You ask a few final questions. You learn that Judy Long is a teller at the Eastside branch of the U.S. National Bank, that Landers is a nutritionist at the City Health Department, that Larry Jones is a mathematics teacher at South High School who learned hang gliding in Hawaii while with the Air Force. Landers believes there must be 40 or 50 gliding enthusiasts around River City, and Bald Mountain is a favorite spot because the mountain has gradual slopes and (usually) dependable wind currents. Hang gliding, Rosie Landers tells you, is quite safe, and she hopes your story will emphasize that and not sensationalize the whole thing out of perspective. In fact, there hasn't been a hang gliding accident at Sandy Beach in the two years or so that people have been flying there. At least that's what Larry Jones told her last night when she talked to him by phone.

You thank her for her help. Next you call Sheriff Ira Carter. Yes, he tells you, this is the first injury from hang gliding at Sandy Beach that the Sheriff's Office has had any word on.

> A. I'd say our biggest problem at Sandy Beach is cars, not sailplanes. It's against the state law to drive motor vehicles on that beach but people do it anyway. Each summer we get a hundred complaints about cars driving on the beach endangering kids.
>
> Q. Have you had accidents there with cars?
>
> A. Two that I can remember, and probably more. One was a motorcycle accident and the other was a kid who drowned when his car fell into the river.

You make a mental note to check further about the car problem at Sandy Beach. For now, you must get on with your story, and so you thank the sheriff, and you get to work organizing your story.

Writing the Article

Throughout your interviews you have made mental notes on the major elements of the story, points you might call "noteworthy facts." By the time you are ready to write, you have them organized in your head or perhaps on paper. Here they are in random order.

1. young woman in hospital
2. good condition with broken leg
3. hang glider accident
4. victim's first extended flight off Bald Mountain
5. hit log landing at Sandy Beach
6. apparently caused by unexpected wind gust
7. "freak accident"; bad luck (witness quote)
8. wants to fly again
9. identify: J. Long, bank teller
10. "instant replay" remark
11. first serious glider accident at Sandy Beach
12. sheriff more concerned about cars on beach

Your next step is to arrange the elements in a logical order. Your story will start with the most important or the most "newsworthy" element. How would you tell a friend if you wanted the friend to get the essential information right away? Probably something like, "Judy's in the hospital with a broken leg . . . hurt herself flying a hang glider yesterday . . . hit a log as she was landing. . . ."

Once you have stated the essence of the situation, you then elaborate with details that support the opening. These details explain it, they provide additional particulars, and they answer questions that logically arise (the question of safety, for example).

Journalists call this structure the *inverted pyramid*. It simply suggests that the most important facts go at the top of the story, with the elaborating details arranged more or less in order of descending importance.

So what *is* the most important element? That a young woman is in the hospital? That's certainly important to anyone who knows her. But lots of people go to the hospital every day without newspaper attention. Why single out this one?

What's different about this one is the manner of injury. It's more dramatic and unusual. It also has public implications. A bathtub injury, unlike a glider injury, does not raise questions of whether some public agency should regulate bathtubs. Not that your story would editorialize about safety. It will merely let the incident speak for itself. But you know that safety implications are inherent in such an accident, justifiably or not.

So you arrange your elements in order of descending importance, as a kind of outline for your story:

1. hang glider accident
2. woman in hospital
3. identification of woman
4. "good condition"
5. caused by freak wind gust
6. first serious glider accident at Sandy Beach
7. victim's first extended flight
8. witness account with details
9. miscellaneous details, space permitting (such as victim wants to fly again, and so forth)

It is 9:45. You have 45 minutes to complete your story. You could do it in 20 if you had to, but 45 will give you a comfortable margin and allow you to rewrite the story for greater clarity. You turn to your video display terminal and begin your story.

> Judith Long, 28, a bank teller at the Eastside branch of the U.S. National Bank, was injured Sunday—

No. No good. You're using too many words to get to the point. Judith Long is not a celebrity. That she's a bank teller is not important. Save those kinds of details until later. *Get that woman in the hospital with injuries from a glider accident.* Those are the newsworthy elements. So you try again.

> A River City woman is in good condition today in Mercy Hospital following a hang glider accident Sunday afternoon at Sandy Beach.
> A hospital spokeswoman said the woman, Judith Ann Long, 555 Westway Ave., suffered a fractured leg when she hit a log while landing her glider on the beach.
> Witnesses said a "sudden wind gust" caught the glider and. . . .

It's not bad. If you had the 20 minute deadline, you might settle for that version. But you decide to give it one more try. You've allowed yourself to lapse into a kind of newspaper cliche in this version—"accident victim in hospital today"—which gives the story a routine aspect. Let's get that "hang glider accident" into the first line of type, if possible; that's the most noteworthy aspect of it. Here is your final version (the paragraphs are numbered as reference points for the comments that follow the story):

1. A hang glider accident at Sandy Beach sent a River City woman to Mercy Hospital Sunday afternoon with a broken leg.
2. The hospital said the woman, Judith Ann Long, 28, of 555 Westway Ave., was in good condition today.
3. A sheriff's deputy said an unexpected gust of wind apparently caused the glider to fall from a height of five to ten feet during a landing on the beach. Long was hurt when she hit a log in the fall.
4. Sheriff Ira Carter said today that this was the first serious glider accident reported to his office in the two years that gliding enthusiasts have been flying off 1,120-foot Bald Mountain, which rises 615 feet above Sandy Beach.
5. "Our biggest problem at Sandy Beach is cars, not sailplanes," he said. "Every summer we get a hundred complaints about cars driving on the beach."
6. Long, a bank teller, had taken up gliding about a week ago. A friend, Rosalee Landers, who witnessed the accident, said the flight lasted about two minutes. It went well until the glider neared the beach and "kind of flipped to one side," said Landers. It was Long's first extended flight off Bald Mountain. Landers called it a "freak accident."
7. "Judy just had tough luck," she said. "The wind currents around Sandy Beach are normally quite dependable, but this time a freak gust came up."

Commentary

The story totals about 200 words, or about eight column inches. However, it can be cut at several points: after paragraph 3 or 4 or 6. Cutting the story at those points would not interfere with the reader's understanding of the essentials. It is not necessary to know the safety information in paragraphs 4 and 5, for example, and paragraphs 6 and 7 merely add details that establish the circumstances of the accident.

Some other points should be noted:

Attribution. Note how information is attributed to sources: the sheriff, a witness, the hospital. Reporters do not generate news; they merely report events, and the information should be attributed to the sources from which it came.

Quotes. Used sparingly, direct quotations add color and realism to a story, as for example the eyewitness commentary in paragraphs 6 and 7. For maximum effectiveness they should be used as separate paragraphs rather than buried within a paragraph, unless the quote is fragmentary as in paragraph 6.

Identification. Persons prominent in a story should be identified precisely. In this example, three elements of identification are present: age, address, and occupation. (Note that the age is based on date of birth and therefore will change in the hypothetical example as time goes on.)

Sentences. They should be short for easy reading.

Paragraphs. They also should be short, seldom more than six typewritten lines (which approximate twelve lines of type).

Inconsistent information. Often a reporter's sources will give conflicting details. This is common enough that a reporter should take it in stride. Did the flight last five minutes as in the officer's report or two minutes as described by an eyewitness? You must use common sense, or you can hedge: "The flight lasted between two and five minutes, according to various accounts." In this instance, an eyewitness account by someone who has flown herself seems more credible than a second-hand version by a nonwitness. To solve such problems, keep pressing for specific details and try to interview more than one source.

STRUCTURE OF A NEWS STORY

What goes into a news story can be separated into these five parts:

1. An opening designed to capture the essence of a situation clearly and (if possible) dramatically. The opening or lead need not be confined to one paragraph. The first sentence of your story, however, should draw the reader into the second sentence and so on through the story.

2. A catchall paragraph that elaborates on the lead and provides any necessary details. In the hang glider story the name and the condition of the injured person are reserved for the catchall in order to streamline the lead. The lead and the catchall, working together, should answer the who, what, when, and where, leaving perhaps the why and the how for subsequent paragraphs.

3. A "sales message" if appropriate. This could be an appealing quote or a statement of what an event or situation means to the reader (such as the cost of living has gone up or the streets are more dangerous because of violence, etc.). In the glider story, short as it is, no sales message is necessary.

4. A transition to the details, such as "police said the accident occurred when . . ." or "the council broke into open debate when Mayor Smith announced . . ." or (in the hang glider story) "Sheriff Ira Carter said today that this was the first. . . ."

5. Details as needed to complete the story. Generally, the details should be organized into blocks with each block representing a unified set of details. In the hang glider story you find two blocks of details once you get past paragraph 3. One block

deals with the sheriff's comments about beach safety; the other gives an eyewitness account of the accident. The more complex the story, the harder you have to work to confine material into blocks, like chapters in a book. Again, these blocks are usually organized in order of descending importance.

Newspapers have several reasons for structuring stories with the most important aspects first and the remaining details more or less in order of descending importance. One is that the high speed of newspaper production often requires that stories be cut in length after having been set in type. The cuts are easier if the editors merely have to remove the last paragraphs, thereby eliminating the least important details.

Another reason is that a newspaper is designed for quick reading. Most readers do not complete a story. One study (Schramm, 1947) showed that of every 100 persons who started a story, an average of only 30.7 remained by the end of paragraph 15.

POINTS TO REMEMBER

1. Newspapers write news much the way people speak—"bottom line first."
2. News elements are: who, what, where, when, why, and how.
3. Much news comes from reporters covering "beats," places where news happens or becomes known, such as police headquarters.
4. Once tips and leads are picked up, reporters pursue details through documents and interviews.
5. Typical news story structure includes the essence in the lead, followed by catchall and transitional paragraphs, elaborating details next, usually in order of descending importance.

EXERCISES

Below are details for two brief single-incident newspaper articles. Write stories for today's afternoon newspaper based on the information provided. *Purpose:* Practice handling inverted pyramid organization of simple news stories as discussed in this chapter. *Suggestions:* Keep your stories to no more than four or five paragraphs or about six to eight column inches. Make a clear outline of what's important, and don't get bogged down in unnecessary detail. The material here is purposely rambling and cluttered to give you practice in ferreting out the essentials.

STORY 1

0402 hours (4:02 A.M.) this date: James O. Small calls the Sheriff's Office. He's 33, lives at 234 Apple Street, River City. He's a member of REACT, a local citizen's band radio club. He says he's picked up a radio call moments ago from a truck driver who said he'd seen a serious vehicle accident involving injury or possible fatality five miles east of River City on U.S. Highway 123. Sheriff dispatches a patrol car and ambulance.

0412. Deputy Sheriff Charles Curtis arrives at scene, milepost 244.3, five miles east of River City. This is a hilly and curvy portion of the highway. Mr. Gooding, the truck driver, is present. Weather: rainy. Highway condition: wet.

0413. Curtis inspects vehicle, a 1982 VW Rabbit. It lies upside down partially submerged in the Chickahominy River, which flows beside the highway at this point. Site is 37 feet from edge of highway. Driver inside. Doors jammed. Driver appears to be alone. Back of vehicle rests in river, front on shore.

0414. Curtis wrenches door open with crowbar. Driver unconscious. Blood oozing from mouth. Breathing irregular. Appears to have broken arm and leg.

0421. Ambulance arrives, removes patient from scene.

0422. Dept. Curtis checks ID of driver: Harold Alan Kennedy, age 33, of San Jose, California.

0433. Dep. Curtis takes statement from truck driver, Peter Gooding, 456 Cherry Street, River City. "A little before four I was driving my rig eastward with a load of veneer. The highway was slippery. Raining hard. I saw these car lights shining kind of eerie through the rain from down below. That's when I stopped to check and found this car kind of halfway in the river. Got my flashlight and got out to take a look. I could see this guy inside. Wasn't moving or nothing. I couldn't get the damned door open. So I got on the radio and called for help."

0445. Dep. Curtis takes measurements. Vehicle rests 37 feet from edge of highway. Skid marks on highway extend 57 feet along the westbound lane of highway, then veer off highway toward river. Vehicle traveled a total distance of 94 feet from start of skid marks to resting place.

0455. Ambulance arrives at Mercy Hospital with patient.

0533. Harold Alan Kennedy expires as he's being prepared for operating table. Cause of death not yet known. Victim had multiple injuries, including concussion, punctured lung, internal bleeding, fractures of right leg and left arm.

0601. Next of kin notified: wife, Helen Kennedy of San Jose. Arrangement made with River City Mortuary to ship remains to San Jose.

STORY 2

Last night an annual "First Citizen Banquet" was held at the Riverview Hotel. About 300 persons attended. Sponsored by East River City Kiwanis Club. Purpose: name the community's "First Citizen of the Year."

Mayor (and Kiwanian) Henry W. Wadsworth got up to introduce the honored first citizen, whose identity is kept secret until after dinner. Here are notes on what he said:

> I'm not gonna give a long speech [laughter, applause]. Our selection committee consisted of four women and three men, including myself as chair. We considered 43 outstanding citizens, both men and women. It was not an easy decision. After three weeks and seven meetings a decision was reached and unanimously agreed on. So

now we come to that long-awaited moment. We are proud to announce that our committee most enthusiastically chose for the First Citizen of River City Judge Sarah Jane Benchly of the Holcomb County Court of Domestic Relations. We proudly recognize Judge Benchly for her unstinting efforts on behalf of underprivileged children over a period of ten years. . . .

A two-minute standing ovation ensues. Judge Benchly comes forward to be recognized and to receive a plaque from Mayor Wadsworth. Here are notes on what she said:

I'm deeply honored—so much so that for perhaps the first time in my life, words fail me. Thank you, thank you. I want to also thank my husband, John, and our two sons, Charles and Dana, for their unselfish encouragement and support for my activities. And their patience. Because they, um, because . . . [wipes away a tear], because they so unselfishly gave of their own time in things like household chores—my goodness, Charles and Dana even do their own laundry—well, they are the ones who made it possible for me to give my attention to Bixby House and the work with the children of Holcomb County. I must say, also, that this honor has come as a complete surprise to me. When John suggested we attend this banquet he said it was our anniversary celebration—our 21st anniversary is tomorrow—and I was naively unsuspicious. I somehow thought it was John's way of providing a romantic interlude to our busy lives. How wrong I was! [Laughter, applause.] Thank you.

Background on Judge Benchly. Age 44. Lived in River City 15 years. Was in private practice of law until appointment as judge of Court of Domestic Relations four years ago. First appointed judge by governor to fill unexpired term of the late Judge Allen W. Bixby who died in office. Benchly ran unopposed for reelection a year later. She has a BA degree from Stanford University and law degree from the University of Southern California. She is on the board of trustees for Ponderosa College and the Bank of River City. She is married to Dr. John E. Benchly, a pediatrician. They have two sons, Charles 17, and Dana, 14. She taught high school English for four years before going to law school. She is the first woman to be chosen First Citizen in the five-year history of the award. Mayor Wadsworth was the first winner five years ago. Judge Benchly has spent the past ten years organizing camping, skiing, and river-rafting excursions for underprivileged children. She was the founder and first president of Bixby House, a shelter home for girls (runaways, abused children, etc.), named in honor of the late Judge Bixby. She was born in Sacramento, California.

Write a short *news* story (assume that a personality interview will be done later). When you've finished both stories, turn to Appendix C and compare your work with the model stories. Please resist the temptation to look first. This is the first of several programmed newswriting exercises that will help you learn on your own. This kind of practice will aid you with your laboratory newswriting exercises and also with writing for actual publication.

5

Writing a News Lead

From the reader's view, nothing is more important than the opening or "lead," as it's called in newspaper jargon. A young engineer once impatiently flung down the day's newspaper after trying to read a complex story about land-use planning.

"I read two paragraphs and still couldn't figure out what the hell they were talking about," he explained. "So I decided to bag it."

The moral of that incident is, *Get to the point quickly.* And that is the role of the lead. A good news lead is more than a beginning, however. It serves four vital functions.

1. It summarizes succinctly the content of the news article, thereby making clear the point of the story.
2. It quickly gets the reader interested in the story.
3. It facilitates headline writing by the copy desk.
4. It makes overall reading of the paper more efficient. The point of each story is clear from its lead, so readers waste less time with material in which they have little interest.

To accomplish these goals, reporters use many kinds of leads such as the summary lead or the quotation lead. No category of leads is quite so useful, though, as knowing the news values cited in Chapter 3. It also helps to understand human nature enough to have an instinctive feeling about what will attract a reader's attention. An effective lead sentence can sometimes entice readers to

Dennis McCarthy, in Oregonian library doing clip research. *(Photo by Randy L. Rasmussen.)*

pursue a topic they might otherwise avoid. Probably not many would be interested in this:

> The School Board moved to prioritize the implementation of interfacing utilization factors in its regularly scheduled meeting last night.

Reporters must get away from the jargon of government agencies and into the cares and concerns of their readers. Most people are interested in themselves, their families, their community, usually in that order. So newspaper leads that extract out of school board meetings such news as ways to educate their kids better or to cope with problems such as discipline or drug addiction will get more attention.

Writing a good lead is not easy. Feature stories and complex stories are particularly difficult. By contrast, some stories—the big, simple, important ones such as the death of an important figure, a major crime or tragedy, the election of a President—almost dictate their own openings.

> The King is dead.
> Jesse Jackson will visit River City next week.
> Five teenagers died in a car accident last night.

A complicated story, on the other hand, makes lead writing difficult. It's almost impossible when reporters themselves don't understand the event. The writing of a good lead is more than a rhetorical exercise. It is a lesson—sometimes traumatic—in thinking. It forces you to sift through masses of material you have compiled from various sources. It forces you to give a succinct answer to the question, "Just what *is* my story?"

Consider a hypothetical example. You have spent three hours covering a meeting of the Board of Trustees of Ponderosa College, a small liberal arts institution in River City. For three hours they wrangled over the problems of the college. Costs are up. Alumni contributions are down. Foundation and government grants are down. The faculty is restless about promised raises. Tuition might have to be raised. Buildings are deteriorating. Construction of new buildings has been delayed by financial problems. The institution is not bankrupt, exactly, but the talk meanders along grim financial pathways. And this is the first time these problems have been discussed in public.

You might conclude that those three miserable hours have produced no news. Nothing really happened. The board passed no motions, took no vote, hired no president, fired no coach. The trustees merely talked. Is that news?

Yes. And it may be more important in this unsettled state than if the board had fired the president. The news is that Ponderosa may be in financial difficulty. The talk is largely in that direction. It leads to that conclusion.

Once you understand *that* as the essence of the news—you're no longer looking for an *event* that has obtruded itself—then you'll find it easier to write the lead. It's your *understanding of the situation,* not the problem of stringing words together, that produces your lead. Here is one possibility:

1. Ponderosa College, faced with rising costs and dwindling income, may be in financial trouble.
2. Talk of money problems dominated a rambling three-hour discussion of the college's Board of Trustees last night. The board took no formal action, but Chairman Ebenezer Johnson summarized the college's plight with this remark:
3. "The board has four choices. We can cut student enrollment by 30 per cent. We can raise tuition. We can beat the bushes for more money. Or we can all resign and turn the problem over to a new board better equipped to deal with financial crisis."
4. Not all board members agreed with Johnson's proposed solutions, but. . . .

SOME NEW TRENDS IN LEADS

Analysis of the sample lead on Ponderosa College's troubles suggests one way in which leads have changed over the years. Some leads contain several stages spanning three or four paragraphs. Essentially, the lead must answer the five W's and the H, but it need not do so in a single paragraph.

Paragraph 1 succinctly states the essence, covering the *who* (Ponderosa College), *what* (financial trouble), and *why* (dwindling resources, rising costs).

Paragraph 2 supplies the *where* and *when.* It also documents the opening: The reporter didn't fabricate the information but got it from an official source, the meeting of the board, which was open to the public.

Paragraph 3 provides further documentation through the words used by a college official to summarize the problem. It also provides a little of the *how* (how the college might handle the situation).

Paragraph 4 is a transition to the elaborating details that follow the lead.

The three-paragraph lead is common today. In the past writers tried to cram everything into a single paragraph with tedious results:

> James G. Bridlington, 57, of 345 Gooseneck Lane, and George C. Jones, 33, of 322 Partridge Ave., both of River City, sustained minor injuries yesterday when their pickup truck, traveling east on Highway 123 with a load of strawberries, swerved out of control on wet pavement and plummeted over a 15-foot embankment and into the Chickahominy River, the Holcomb County Sheriff's Office reported this morning.

The modern, streamlined style of lead writing would break that lump into more easily digested bits in short paragraphs.

> A pickup truck swerved on wet Highway 123 and plunged down an embankment into the Chickahominy River yesterday, sending two River City men to Mercy Hospital with minor injuries.
> The Sheriff's Office identified them as. . . .

This new freedom of style allows writers to add touches of drama to complex stories. Sometimes the stories are so subtle and complicated that it helps to focus on a microcosm—that is, a small example—rather than trying to grasp the entirety. Note this opening of a story about a major national problem—missing children.

> Rita and Layton Frost's nightmare began April 2.
> "I remember going to Eric's room that morning," says Mrs. Frost. "And he wasn't there."
> Eric, 12, was missing from his Winston, Ore., home for five weeks—apparently abducted by a man who promised to make him a movie star.
> In a panic, the Frosts searched, called the police, then called Child Find, one of some 60 groups begun in the last three years to help find missing children. On May 3, the FBI found Eric—confused, unmolested and safe—400 miles away in Sacramento.
> "It's a very happy ending," Mrs. Frost says softly. "It couldn't be happier."
> The system worked for the Frosts. And the June 13 opening of the National Center for Missing and Exploited Children in Washington, D.C., may bring more happy endings. . . .
>
> *—David Fink, USA Today*

By focusing on the small picture, the Frosts, the writer helps the reader grasp the big picture: Lots of similar abduction traumas add up to a major national problem.

The new freedom for imaginative leads also causes frustration among writers. Perhaps it helps to know that even experienced writers have troubles with the opening paragraphs. Consider a typical example—we'll call it the Jimmy Rawlins saga—which is based on an actual event. First the details:

Jimmy, age nine, is the son of Sandy and Fred Rawlins. Yesterday about 5 P.M. Jimmy's father took him to the emergency room of Mercy Hospital where a doctor treated him for minor burns on the right side of his face. Not much of a story in it at first glance. But some stories run deeper if you'll just inquire.

"I asked Jimmy to check the gas in a five-gallon can I had lashed to the back of my Jeep," explained Fred Rawlins. "It seemed to be taking him a long time. I went outside and I found Jimmy trying to strike a match to see if there's any gas in the can. I yelled, 'Jimmy, watch out!' That's when the gas exploded. Blew the top right off the can. There's a flash of flame shooting fifteen feet in the air. I was plenty scared. Jimmy's hair was smoldering a little, but he seemed okay otherwise. I took him to the hospital just to make sure. Whew, that was a close call. "Jimmy's a mighty lucky boy."

Jimmy says, "Wow. I just didn't think. I was lucky, I guess. Wow."

How do you fashion a lead out of that? First you must decide—just what *is* the news? No one killed, no major property damage, no public issue is at stake.

But perhaps your reporter's instincts tell you that the story is an important one—something that people will talk about and from which both parents and kids can learn. Those are important kinds of stories, too. You can, of course, reach for the traditional lead.

> A nine-year-old River City boy was treated yesterday at Mercy Hospital for burns suffered when a gas can exploded. . . .

That's too passive. It doesn't do justice to the "nugget of learning" kind of story you have. Try again.

> A fiery explosion of a gas can sent a nine-year-old River City boy to Mercy Hospital with minor burns yesterday. . . .

That's still not right. You must try to emphasize the lesson to be learned from Jimmy's experience. The traditional news lead doesn't seem to accomplish that. How about:

> Jimmy Rawlins is lucky to be alive today. . . .

That's editorializing. You're making a judgment. But you're not a judge; you're a reporter, and as such you must learn to *get out of the way of your own material.* That is, do not insert personal opinions, no matter how obvious the conclusion might be. Your job is to gather the facts, assemble them in a coherent manner, and let them speak for themselves.

> "Jimmy's a mighty lucky boy," his father said today after the boy suffered minor burns. . . .

Not much better, it seems. Traditional news leads just won't do the job here. Perhaps this calls for a nontraditional—that is, a more creative—solution. Perhaps, too, you can introduce some of the suspense the father must have felt seeing Jimmy hold a lighted match at the mouth of a gas can.

> When Jimmy Rawlins's father asked him to check the gas in a five-gallon can, Jimmy picked up a match and. . . .

Now you're on the right track. But as Ernest Hemingway used to say, "Simplify!" When writing a narrative lead, get into the story at *the last possible moment*—just before some climactic action. Eliminate the long preamble.

> Nine-year-old Jimmy Rawlins lit a match yesterday to see if there was any gas in a five-gallon can.
> There was.
> The explosion ripped off the top of the can and sent a fountain of flame 15 feet into the air, but Jimmy escaped with only minor burns on the right side of his face. He was treated and released from the emergency room of Mercy Hospital.
> "Wow!" said Jimmy later. "I just didn't think. I'm just lucky, I guess."
> Jimmy, the son of. . . .

TYPES OF NEWS LEADS

Narrative Lead

The Jimmy Rawlins story uses a narrative lead, as does the missing-child story cited earlier. The narrative—also called an "anecdotal lead"—is particularly useful for complicated stories. Sometimes a small but revealing conversational exchange will produce a good lead. Here's an example from a story depicting a rancher versus wildlife conflict.

> The rancher from Steamboat Springs was wearing a leather vest adorned with ornamental buttons made of elk's teeth.
> He had appeared before the Colorado Wildlife Commission in Denver to complain about too many elk and deer living on his property and eating his hay. One commissioner, eyeing the elks-tooth vest, said, "It looks like you've been killing your share of elk."
> The rancher smirked. "Yeah, and each one of those teeth represents a missing haystack."
> It was a typically hyperbolic exchange in what may as well be called The Great Elk Hassle. . . .
>
> —Bob Saile, *Denver Post*

Summary Lead

The summary lead is by far the most prevalent in newspaper writing. It gives a succinct summary of the event or situation. It is most useful in straight news, especially news that is important and uncomplicated. It can be adapted to trends and situations as well as incidents, as these examples suggest.

> WICHITA—The Kansas Wheat crop this summer most likely will fall far short of last year's 448-million bushel crop, a team of experts determined after a tour of the state this week.
>
> —*Jim Suber, Topeka Capital Journal*

> The careers of two award-winning San Francisco vice squad officers ended today when the Police Commission fired them for hiring a prostitute to perform at a police academy graduation party.
>
> —*Leslie Guevarra, San Francisco Examiner*

> Judy Canova, the self-described cowgirl-entertainer who came to be known for hillbilly humor and an ear-bursting yodel, died of cancer Friday at a Hollywood hospital. She was 66.
>
> —*Mark Gill, Los Angeles Times*

> Women don't give up smoking as easily—or willingly—as men, a new study shows.
>
> —*Sally Ann Stewart, USA Today*

Summary leads can be worded to draw attention to a particular aspect of a news story. If timing is important, for instance, the lead might start, "Tuesday is the last day for. . . ." If the "why" is important, the lead should emphasize it: "Arson is the suspected cause of yesterday's $2 million fire at Amalgamated Widget. . . ."

Question Lead

Sometimes a news story defies an easy summary because it may raise questions rather than answering them. The question lead is useful in such cases or when the answers themselves are unclear or debatable.

> What are teens watching, saying, wearing, listening to or otherwise tuned in to? Youth News reporters asked a selection of teens for their opinions on what's in and what's out this month.
>
> —*Youth News Service*

> Which are the best, the scariest, the dippiest, the most stomach-crunching, scream wrenching, heart-stopping roller coasters of them all?
>
> —*Knight-Ridder News Service*

HOLLYWOOD—It's the topic that won't go away: What has happened to situation comedy on television?

Ten years ago, eight of the top 10 shows were sitcoms. This season none made the top 10.

—*Tom Green, USA Today*

The Quotation Lead

Most news stories quote sources, official and unofficial. A common means of opening a news story is to use a quote that either succinctly summarizes the situation or provides a sufficiently colorful insight to interest the reader.

Watch out for pitfalls in the quotation lead, however. Of all the lead types discussed here, the quote lead is the most often abused. That's because the quote doesn't always give the reader a clear idea of what the story is about. For example, note this lead (from an actual story except for the fictitious name):

"There are a lot of us around," said Jane Doe. "We're sort of a new class of people."

Is the story talking about vegetarians, joggers, or what? Without the headline and the subsequent paragraphs, the quoted material neither delivers a succinct summary nor entices the reader—two major things a lead must do.

In truth, Jane Doe, age 41, is dying of cancer. The quote is from a speech she gave to the Ninth Euthanasia Conference of the Right to Die lobby. Had the context of the quotation been clear, it might have contained greater meaning. Thus:

Jane Doe, dying of cancer at 41, insists on her right to die with dignity.
"There are a lot of us around," she said yesterday. "We're sort of a new class of people."

Even that lead fails to capture the poignancy of the situation. Subsequent comments attributed to Mrs. Doe seem much more compelling, and they might have been used more effectively in the lead. She said, for example, that she had obtained a prescription for a lethal quantity of sleeping pills, but she doubted that she would ever use them. Then she added a remark that could have been a more powerful quotation lead:

"I have no doubt my death will involve pain, and it may involve incontinence. But I can get permission from my friends to commit suicide but not from my sons."

The quote has a better chance of attracting the reader because suicide is something most people can understand and because the concept of "asking permission" to commit suicide is rare. Under what circumstances, the reader wonders, would a person ask permission to commit suicide?

This discussion is not meant to discourage use of quotation leads, only to suggest that reporters apply a two-pronged test to any contemplated quote lead: (1) Does it (without help of headline) summarize what the story is about? (2) Does it prick the curiosity of casual readers and make them want to read on? One negative answer should make you wary; two should make you discard the lead.

Here are two examples that seem to stand the test:

> "The most significant aspect of political reportage so far this year is how wrong it has been," says Paul Duke, moderator of PBS's Washington Week in Review.
>
> —*Arthur Unger, Christian Science Monitor*

> "I've burglarized a lot of homes," Charles B. Lankford told a meeting of the Capitol East Community Crime Council last week, "and I can tell you that 99 per cent of all burglars will get out fast if they hear some noise or see a light."
>
> —*Anne H. Oman, Washington Post*

The Flashby Lead

Complex news stories involving many diverse elements present a special problem to the reporter. If a big storm hits your community, which of the following belongs in the lead? Air and ground transportation halted? Twenty thousand people without electricity? Three deaths? Some 50,000 livestock animals in danger of starving? Seventeen persons in the hospital? Forecast for still more snow? Schools closed? Forty-two skiers trapped in a mountain lodge? Three million dollars in property damage? Most severe storm in ten years?

Most of them are important. The "flashby" lead allows a brief glimpse of each of them (or as many as you want to fit into the opening). Subsequent paragraphs, of course, give further details. Here are two possible ways to open such a story:

> River City can expect more snow tomorrow in the wake of last night's storm that killed three persons, hospitalized 17, caused $3 million property damage, halted transportation, and threatened to starve some 50,000 cattle.

> River City's worst storm in 10 years will bring more snow tomorrow. Authorities, meanwhile, began to tally the devastation of last night's 15-inch snowfall:
> Three lives lost.
> Seventeen persons hospitalized.
> Some $3 million property damage.
> About 20,000 residents without electricity.
> [And so on, with as many elements as necessary.]

The key to the flashby is parallel structure, using the same rhetorical pattern to introduce each new item. The first of the two examples uses verbs followed by nouns (with an occasional intervening adjective): *killed* three persons, *hospitalized* three others, and so on. The second example starts each item with a number (with qualifying adjective as necessary). Below are some variations of the flashby technique.

> SAN DIEGO—High school students tapped into a school computer, electronically wiping out some files, deleting grades and altering fellow students' homework, San Diego school officials have reported.
>
> —*Lanie Jones, Los Angeles Times*

> DENMAN ISLAND—The craftsmen are afraid of losing their big sales season, the tofu factory is worried about propane supplies and the fire truck is nearly out of gasoline.
>   Those are just a few of the problems facing this small island now that the government workers' strike has wiped out its ferry connection to Vancouver Island.
>
> —*Moira Farrow, Vancouver Sun*

> Two Houston football fans, upset over a referee's call in a championship game which their team lost, sue the referee and the National Football League for "consumer fraud."
>   A happily married woman in Boston, after falling and breaking her pelvis, sues her husband for $35,000 for failing to keep the sidewalk clear of ice and snow.
>   A 24-year-old Boulder, Colo., man sues his parents for $350,000 because he doesn't like the way they brought him up.
>   These are all examples of what many critics of the American legal system might regard as frivolous lawsuits that are increasingly clogging court calendars. . . .
>
> —*Edwin Chen, Los Angeles Times*

The Direct Address Lead

The key to the direct address lead is the word "you," meaning the reader. Your story simply addresses itself to the reader in the second person. This lead is especially useful for the service sections of the newspaper—those dealing with travel, food, entertainment, medicine, crafts, housing, and similar areas. It is also useful for stories that are intimate or personal by nature: *Your* shyness, *your* quest for a fuller life, etc.

> If you want to own companies with fast-growing earnings, high technology still is a good place to be.
>
> —*Tom Petruno, USA Today*

> Yes, folks, just another 160 or so shopping days left until Christmas. And if your kids expect to find a Cabbage Patch doll under the tree next year, you'd better line up to buy one now.
>
> —*Knight-Ridder News Service*

Descriptive Lead

Newspaper stories rarely start out with novel-like descriptions, but sometimes descriptive openings can set an appropriate mood for what's to follow. Here's an example in a lengthy story about the fate of seven fraternities and two sororities ordered disbanded by the trustees of a small college in Maine. The description of dreary weather conditions casts a somber light on what, to the organizations involved, is an unhappy situation.

> A week of unseasonably mild weather in mid-February wrapped Colby College's campus on Mayflower Hill in restless, rainy fog and began melting the winter's snow. Shallow lakes formed on the terraced lawns in front of the library, and water ran in desultory streams over the sidewalks on fraternity row, stopping here and there in dark puddles and then dripping in thin sheets down the stairs toward the student union.
> The fog and the chilly rain lent the several houses that line fraternity row a melancholy aspect that seemed appropriate to their situation, which is all but hopeless. . . .
>
> —*Lawrence Biemiller, Chronicle of Higher Education*

Teasers

The teaser can be in any form; the distinction is that it is cold-bloodedly calculated to seduce the reader. Examples:

> The hottest new thing in air conditioning is ice.
> The idea is that you make ice overnight, when rates are cheaper, and then melt it slowly during the day to absorb heat and cool the building.
>
> —*Brad Kuhn, Wall Street Journal*

> SACRAMENTO—Not that the Legislature is boring, but it apparently takes an Elizabeth Taylor or a Burt Lancaster to generate *real* excitement around here.
> Just about everybody in the Capitol found an excuse to wander up to room 4202 yesterday afternoon as Taylor, Lancaster and fellow actor Ed Asner appeared at a meeting of the Assembly Judiciary Committee.
>
> —*Steven A. Capps, San Francisco Examiner*

> "Oh, Harry," the college girl said, softly, tears in her eyes, "I'm sorry, Harry, to be doing this to you."
> "That's all right," Harry, a rather intense young man of about 19, said unconvincingly, his eyes focused on his feet.
> "But it wouldn't have worked, Harry, it had to stop," she said.
>
> —*Gay Talese, New York Times*

The last lead is a vintage classic, written by a man who later gained fame as a writer of articles and nonfiction books in a style then known as "New Journalism." Does it arouse your curiosity? What is the college girl doing to poor old Harry? What is such a story doing on the front page of the *Times?* (For answers, see Appendix C.)

PITFALLS TO AVOID

The major problems to be avoided in the writing of leads are so common that they can be anticipated in student writing. You'll do your writing teacher (and, ultimately, yourself and your future readers) an immense favor by thinking twice the next time you produce leads like the bad examples cited in this section.

Vagueness

Vagueness is often the result of lack of understanding of the news value and/or the nature of the event. Example:

> River City Police Chief Darrell McManus spoke yesterday at the weekly luncheon of the Downtowners Club.

The important question is not whether the police chief spoke but whether he said anything. Below are two better examples:

> Police Chief Darrell McManus yesterday predicted that in 10 years some 20 to 25 per cent of River City's police force will be women.
> Speaking to the weekly luncheon meeting of the Downtowners Club, McManus explained. . . .

> In 10 years, some 20 to 25 per cent of River City's police force will be women, Police Chief Darrell McManus told the Downtowners Club yesterday. . . .

Clutter

Clutter is the result of a reporter's trying to get too much into the first sentence. The underbrush often obscures the sense of the story.

> According to an eyewitness account, a hitchhiker from River City, Roger S. Smith, 24, of 1010 Paradise St., was killed at 5:10 A.M. today when he stepped into the path of an oncoming car on U.S. Highway 123, just east of the Goodpasture overpass, about 11 miles east of the outskirts of River City.

Avoid starting a lead with a dependent clause ("According to an eyewitness account . . ."). Another good rule: Never let your lead run more than about 30 words. Twenty would be even better. Keep paragraphs short, especially at the beginning of the story—preferably not more than three or four typewritten lines. Here's a better version of the hitchhiker fatality:

> A River City man died instantly early today when he walked into the path of a car on Highway 123 about 11 miles east of River City.
> Police identified him as. . . .

Gilding the Lily

Sometimes reporters try too hard for a clever turn of phrase or a dazzling play on words. A good rule is: Use one hand to pat yourself on the back for your cleverness, and use the other to cross out your rhetorical jewel. It probably says nothing. It merely gets in the reader's way, blocking access to the facts.

> SEATTLE—This city's famous drizzle is a fizzle.

What, precisely does that say? Nothing. Later in the story the readers learn what they should have been told in the first place: November 1976 was an extremely dry month in Seattle. A better lead would have stated that news clearly and simply.

> SEATTLE—November set an all-time record for drought in this city—a mere half-inch of rain compared to a normal November of six or seven inches.

Buried Lead

Often a potentially exciting story is made dull and routine by an unthinking reporter. Every story should be examined for elements of drama, novelty, mystery, intrigue, and adventure, as well as for significance, prominence, and other traditional elements. Here's a case of misplaced emphasis, making a potentially exciting story just a ho-hum account:

> Two River City children were in good condition today in Mercy Hospital after an automobile accident on Highway 123 east of River City, police said.
> Police identified the children as. . . .
> Officers said the auto, driven by the children's mother, ran off the highway and into the Chickahominy River. The mother was thrown clear as the vehicle rolled down an embankment, but the two children were trapped inside the vehicle, half submerged and upside down, about 25 feet from shore. A girl ran into the water, turbulent and swollen from winter rains, and swam to the car, rescuing the two children. Police identified the rescuer as Linda McCormack, 17, a competitive swimmer at South High School.

The imaginative reporter tries to capture the drama of the rescue in the lead, rather than settling for the routine. Thus:

A high school swimming champion plunged into the swollen, turbulent waters of the Chickahominy River early today to rescue two River City children trapped in a partly submerged car.

Linda McCormack, 17, state champion in the women's high school 100-meter freestyle, swam the 25 feet. . . .

Prominence is a news element that can change the nature of the lead. Suppose Linda is the daughter of the governor of the state, Edward W. McCormack. Then the lead would likely read:

Gov. Edward W. McCormack's 17-year-old daughter, Linda, plunged into the swollen, turbulent waters of. . . .

Passiveness

The ways in which passiveness can weaken your leads can be seen in these examples:

Weak: River City was covered by an inch of snow last night.

Better: An inch of snow covered River City last night.

Weak: It is believed by police that John Doe, wanted for questioning in a River City murder case, has fled to Nebraska.

Better: Police believe John Doe, wanted for questioning in a River City murder case, has fled to Nebraska.

Better: John Doe, wanted for questioning in a River City murder case, has fled to Nebraska, police believe.

Weak: There were a lot of people at the annual River City rock concert last night, with all 300 seats taken and people standing in the hallway.

Better: The audience overflowed the 300-seat auditorium at River City rock concert last night, forcing some to stand in the hallway.

In each case, the weak versions are passive—sleepy—rather than active. The problems of passiveness usually arise from a tendency, rampant in academic circles, to be impersonal: *It is believed* rather than *police believe.* This produces a dreadful stuffiness that makes difficult reading. The most noxious usages are *there is, it is, there are,* and similar variations. When you see them in your article, pull them out, just as you'd remove noxious weeds from your garden. Always try to express your material specifically and concretely. Don't say *John was there.* Say *John stood in the audience* or *John sat on a rock near the ocean.*

You will, however, find occasions when the passive voice is proper. Suppose you want to focus attention on the person or thing *being acted upon* rather than on whatever or whoever is doing the acting. Thus:

The girl was kidnapped. (Not: Unknown person or persons kidnapped the girl.)

John Smith was killed yesterday in a car accident. (Not: A car accident killed John Smith yesterday.)

Failed Promises

A common mistake is promising something in the lead that the story fails to deliver. A lead should be considered a promissory note. If you say the mayor delivered a "humorous speech," you'd better deliver humor sooner or later. Here's one that does.

> Laughter, metaphors, whoops and hollers punctuated the graduation Tuesday of 285 students at Hudson's Bay High School. It was the school's 28th commencement ceremony.
>
> —*Sally James, Vancouver Columbian*

The story delivered on its promise, quoting one student speaker expressing trepidation at opening the cafeteria doors only to be struck down by "the flying milk cartons of life," and another drawing laughter with his account of life's major trials just ahead: moving 1,000 miles to face a tough new environment in a larger city, trying to make new friends, and—worst of all—having to do his own laundry.

POINTS TO REMEMBER

1. A lead should get to the point quickly.
2. It also speeds reading comprehension and the writing of heads.
3. Don't expect leads to come easy; even professionals have trouble, probably because leads require writers to find the point or essence of the story.
4. Complex events must be summarized by all-encompassing leads.
5. Leads today are often more succinct than those of earlier years. They also vary more in style.
6. Summary leads are the most prevalent in newspapers today, but the array of leads includes narrative, question, quotation, flashby, direct address, descriptive, and teaser leads.
7. Avoid vagueness in your leads, also clutter, too-clever plays on words (gilding the lily), passiveness, and jargon. Stories must live up to the "promise" of the lead.

EXERCISES

Below are rudimentary facts for six news stories. For each situation, write an appropriate lead for a news story. Assume that you are writing for an afternoon daily and that it is now 10:30 in the morning, about an hour before your deadline. *Purpose:* Practice writing leads. *Suggestions:* Be brief and succinct. You need not write the entire story (unless you want to; it's good practice). Just write the first two or three paragraphs, whatever constitutes your lead. Use only the information given here; do not make up facts. Don't get bogged down in unnecessary detail. Try writing a variety of leads for each situation, and rewrite your first efforts until you are satisfied. After completing the exercises, turn to Appendix C for sample stories.

The following facts are basic to all exercises:

Last night at 0030 hours (30 minutes past midnight) River City police responded to a report of an accident that had just occurred.

Time of accident: Approximately 0023 hours this date.

Place of accident: Intersection of Main Street and River Avenue, River City.

Vehicles involved: Car A, 1977 Chevrolet Vega, operated by Charles A. Rush, 3005 Ponderosa Avenue, River City. Sex M, age 33, occupation computer programmer.

Car B, 1976 Volkswagen Rabbit, operated by Harry A. Allen, 1176 Chicago Avenue, Evanston, Illinois. Sex M. age 72, occupation writer and retired professor of history, Northwestern University.

Circumstances: Car A traveling south on Main Street. Car B traveling east on River Avenue. Car B was struck broadside by Car A. Skid marks left by Car A indicated that Car A skidded 40 feet on pavement; apparently unable to stop because of slick pavement.

Traffic lights: Car B had green light. Car A had red light.

Weather: Light rain and high winds gusting to about 45 miles an hour. Pavement slick.

Passengers: Both men traveling alone.

Witness: John H. Roe, pedestrian, age 35, of 45 Deadwood Lane, River City, saw the accident from the southeast corner of the intersection.

Source of information: River City Police Department unless otherwise specified.

Situation 1: Both cars sustained about $200 damage. No injuries. No arrests or citations. Both cars drove away under their own power.

Situation 2: Same as number 1 except the driver of B is the governor of your state.

Situation 3: Same as 1, except that impact caused Car B to swerve onto the sidewalk at the southeast corner of intersection, striking pedestrian Roe. Roe taken by ambulance to Mercy Hospital emergency room where he was treated for scalp lacerations and released. No other injuries.

Situation 4: Cars heavily damaged. Driver of B removed to Mercy Hospital by ambulance. He is listed in satisfactory condition in hospital, with two broken ribs, broken left arm, and numerous lacerations. Driver of Car A unhurt. Cars towed away. No arrests. No citations issued.

Situation 5: Cars heavily damaged. Driver of B was removed by ambulance to Mercy Hospital. At 9:45 this morning driver of B died. Cause of death not yet known. Autopsy scheduled for this afternoon after which the body is to be shipped to Evanston. Driver of A was not hurt but was arrested at the scene on a charge of driving while under the influence of intoxicating liquor. Lodged in city jail in lieu of $500 bail. Police Chief Darrell McManus tells you: "We're still investigating that accident this morning. . . . I can't really tell you anything more at this time."

Situation 6: Same basic information as situation 1 (minor damage, no injuries). But when Car B was hit, some 1,000 pages of a book manuscript spilled out of Car B through the right-hand door that had sprung open as a result of impact. The pages scattered to the wind over an eleven-block area. Police Chief Darrell McManus tells you at 10:30 A.M.: "We have a crew of about twenty people out there searching for those pages, mostly residents of the neighborhood and about eight or ten kids from South High School, which is in that general vicinity. I think we got about 700 pages so far, and they're all in Mr. Allen's motel room laid out to dry. Some of the kids climbed trees to get pages, and a couple of times they had to go on rooftops. I guess you could call this a freak accident all right." You call Mr. Allen at his motel and get the following background information.

A. It's my life's work. The pages are a book manuscript about my work with the French underground during the Nazi occupation of World War II. I've been working on this book for thirty years.

Q. What brought you to River City?

A. There are some original documents in the library of Ponderosa College about the French underground. I came here to examine them. As it turned out, they contained nothing I didn't already have.

Q. What's the name of your book?

A. It's called *An Underground View.* It's under contract with a publisher in New York, and it should be published in about a year. I'm just finishing the last portion this week.

Q. Is it fiction or nonfiction?

A. Nonfiction. It's a personal account of some of my adventures and narrow escapes during the Nazi occupation. I was a U.S. Army officer with the OSS—Office of Strategic Services—and I parachuted into France in 1942 and remained there until 1944.

Q. Do you have a duplicate copy of the manuscript?

A. No. But I just counted all the soggy pages located by the search party, and I find I have exactly 814 pages so far. I'm sure we'll find most of the others, and what we don't find I can redo. So it's not the disaster I had rather imagined it to be last night. Just a little inconvenient, that's all. The people of River City have been wonderful to me—I can't thank them enough.

6

Developing Your Newswriting Skills

Newswriting is like playing the violin or shooting pool. Once you learn the fundamentals, the rest is practice. To develop your technique in violin playing, you start with a simple composition, practice it, perfect it, and then you move on to something else. So it is with newswriting. You assemble information for a simple news story, write it, rewrite it, perfect it, and then you go on to another story.

This chapter gives you an opportunity to practice and perfect your techniques. Six writing exercises demonstrate the techniques of assembling information for and writing six common types of news articles: spot news, advances, speeches, obituaries, follow-ups, and meetings. To get in the mood for this chapter, imagine yourself a newly hired young reporter for a small daily newspaper. We'll call it the *River City Express*, circulation 87,443. River City is a community of 120,000 located in your state. You work in the newsroom with about twenty other reporters, all under the direction of the city editor.

These exercises focus on short and relatively uncomplicated news articles. They average six or seven column inches in length, which is about 150 to 175 words (less than a manuscript page, double spaced). Each depicts a single incident or situation. The information in each comes largely from a single source, although another source or two may be consulted for additional information. The exercises show how the information is obtained: the angles explored, the questions asked, the problems encountered.

All you have to do is write the story. You may have trouble assembling many bits of random information into a coherent news story. You are not alone. Experi-

(Photo by Randy L. Rasmussen.)

enced professionals have the same problem, and they must work hard to achieve the simple, lean prose that makes reading easy and pleasant.

Each exercise gives you sufficient information for your news article. Indeed, it gives you far too much information. That's to help you cope with one of the alluring traps for the inexperienced writer: trying to cram *everything* into your story. Don't. You must learn to distinguish the newsworthy kernels from the routine chaff. In other words you must *think*. What are the essentials of the event or situation? What is important? What is newsworthy? Sometimes important and newsworthy are not the same. A dramatic human interest story about, say, the rescue of two children trapped in a submerged car is eminently newsworthy but of limited importance.

Having too much information is a problem typical of the good reporter. It is, in fact, an asset. The best reporters invariably gather more information than they can possibly use in a story. By so doing, they will know the event or situation better and be able to describe it more precisely. If they have gathered enough for a 2,000-word story and can write only 200 words, they'll know which 200 words most succinctly tell the story.

Each news story in this chapter is based on a real news item published in a newspaper. Names and some circumstances, however, are fictitious. The first exercise below is a dry run. That is, the process by which the reporter researched, organized, and wrote her story will be depicted step by step right on through the finished article. By this means some further fundamentals of news story organization can be demonstrated.

Exercises 2 through 6 are yours to write. After you have read through the material for an exercise, give yourself one hour to write the story. This method will simulate the newsroom practice of writing stories against deadlines. If you finish early, rewrite as much of the story as you can. It is in the rewriting that your skills will come through. After finishing a story, turn to Appendix C in the back of the book for a sample story.

EXERCISE 1: SPOT NEWS

Assume that a house fire occurred last night in River City. The city editor asks you to handle the story by calling the fire chief, Charles Pickering. Before placing the call you think about the kinds of information you'll need. The most important qualities of a fire story, by most news standards, are loss of life, injuries, and property damage. You'll look for other details such as the cause of the fire, personnel and equipment used to fight it, insurance coverage, plans for rebuilding. You'll also look for unusual circumstances: daring rescues, narrow escapes, twists of irony.

Your interview with Fire Chief Pickering, depicted below, may strike you as rambling. But it's typical. Don't expect information to be handed to you in a 5-W-inverted-pyramid package. Often you must dig, asking lots of questions, even when the source is cooperative, as here. The fire chief doesn't know how to write a news story; you do.

Q. Mr. Pickering, my name is Cindy Johnson, a reporter for the *Express*. I understand you had a house fire last night.

A. I suppose you could say that. We had two fire trucks and eleven men out to an apartment fire last night.

Q. I see. Well, I'm planning to write a story about that fire for today's paper—can you tell me what happened?

A. I'll be glad to tell you what details I have. We got this call at the fire department around 12:30 and—

Q. Excuse me—do you mean last night? Thirty minutes past midnight?

A. That's right. The trucks arrived at this location at 456 Partridge Avenue, that's a brick building that houses Charlie Brinkman's sporting goods store. It also has a second story with an apartment and some storage areas, and the fire was in the apartment. We had to take this lady off a ledge with her two little kids. Then we got up in there with a couple of inch-and-a-halfs, and we had it under control in maybe twenty minutes. I guess that's about all there was to it, unless you have some questions.

Q. Yes, could I have the lady's name, please?

A. Okay, that's Mrs. Mary Westerman, and the address of the apartment is 456½ Partridge Avenue here in River City. I don't know the names of the little kids—they're just babies, really, two little girls.

Q. Do you know what caused the fire?

A. No, not completely. We're still poking around this morning, trying to figure out what happened. It was a funny kind of fire.

Q. Funny?

A. Well, don't put this in the paper but for a few moments it looked like it was going to get away from us—the whole inside of that apartment seemed to be going like kindling. There must have been some highly combustible material in there, but we're going to have to look at it more carefully. Lucky the fire station was only three blocks from the apartment. I think if we'd been 30 seconds later we would have lost the whole building.

Q. What was the amount of damage?

A. About 40 thousand dollars. Most of that damage was in the apartment, except there was quite a bit of water damage in the store underneath.

Q. I see. The fire itself was pretty much confined to the apartment, then?

A. That's right. Destroyed the apartment—a total loss.

Q. Was anyone hurt?

A. Well, Mrs. Westerman had a bad gash in her arm, bleeding pretty bad. Bill Taylor, one of the firemen, ran her down to Mercy Hospital where they sewed her up.

Q. Do you know how she got hurt?

A. Well, that's quite a story. She told Bill Taylor that she woke up and smelled smoke and then there was some kind of muffled explosion in the living room. She started to open the door from the bedroom to the living room, but she could see the whole thing was in flames. She went back to the bedroom, got the little kids, and broke out a window of the bathroom, one that leads out to a ledge about 15 feet off the ground. That's where she was when we got there.

Q. She got hurt getting out?

A. Yeah, she got that nasty gash getting the kids through the bathroom window. Her nightgown was all covered with blood.

Q. She went out in a nightgown?

A. Oh, she was smart—when she saw those flames she didn't wait for nothing. She just grabbed the kids and out she went. By doing that she probably saved all their lives. It's smart not to wait around inside where the smoke might get you.

Q. How wide is this ledge?

A. Oh, I'd say about six feet.

Q. So she wasn't in danger of falling.

A. No. We took her down with a ladder. Wrapped her in a blanket and took her down to the hospital.

Q. Was she the only one hurt?

A. Yes.

Q. Was anyone else in the apartment at the time?

A. No, just the two little kids.

Q. Where was *Mister* Westerman all this time?

A. A good question. Don't quote me, but I'm told he left her about six months ago and hasn't been seen since.

Q. Is the fire loss covered by insurance?

A. I don't know. You better call Charlie Brinkman about that—it's his building.

Q. Okay. Do you have Mary Westerman's age?

A. Nineteen.

Q. Did you have any problems fighting this fire, or was it largely routine?

A. I'd say routine. We're still looking at the cause so I can't comment on that.

You call Charles Brinkman, owner of the building and partner in the sporting goods store known as Brinkman and Sons Sporting Goods. He tells you the loss is indeed covered by insurance and that he'll be repairing the damage as soon as the insurance settlement comes. You ask how you can get in touch with Mary Westerman, and he replies: "At my house. My wife and I took them in last night and they'll stay with us until they get resettled."

You call Westerman, telling her you're sorry to hear about the fire but glad she and the children got out safely. She confirms the story of her escape and adds a few comments: "I just couldn't *believe* it when I opened the door to the living room—it was just a ball of flame. I thought to myself I'm sure glad I didn't pay cash for that new coffee table I bought last week because I didn't see how we were *ever* gonna get out because you had to go through the living room to get to the door. That's when I thought of the bathroom window. . . . The children's names are Patricia, age twenty-one months, and Priscilla, age five months. . . . Mister Westerman? That *rat!* . . . It took six stitches to sew up my arm. . . . It's the left arm and I'm left-handed, darn it. . . . Some day why don't you write about left-handed people? We're the most oppressed minority group in America today. . . . I honestly don't know how the fire started; everything happened so fast. . . .

Discussion. After you've gathered your information, your next step is to evaluate it. What is the essence of the situation? What is the most important element? What are some of the secondary points? Just as important, what can be eliminated? Some elements are too trivial or private to be included. Certainly Westerman's troubles with her husband can be discarded as being unrelated to the essence of the story. Her remarks about left-handedness are equally unimportant. Her professed relief at not having paid cash for the coffee table is a nice touch for a feature story but probably not for straight news.

Some elements, on the other hand, clearly are part of the story. The fact that a fire had occurred, that people in an apartment had a close call but escaped largely unharmed, that the fire department put out the blaze in twenty minutes, and that $40,000 damage occurred—all these seem to describe the incident and should be part of your news account.

In addition, some of the remarks by Westerman give an intimate account of what it's like to see your residence enveloped in flames. Comments like "ball of flame" and "I didn't see how we were ever gonna get out" add color to your story.

But quotes can also get in the way of a good story. Some student writers tend to put *everything* in quotes, thereby destroying their effectiveness. You, being a professional writer, surely can relate the incident more effectively than a witness can describe it off the top of the head. The quotes are more effective when used sparingly to provide a touch of human reaction to the incident. So use your own words to describe the incident; save the quote for the person's "Gee whiz" reaction.

An experienced reporter selects and rejects these elements almost automatically. The beginner, however, often finds it convenient to list the elements as was done for the hang glider story (Chapter 4). Eventually you, too, will do them in your head. But for practice, let's identify the main elements of this story. This list is not necessarily in order of importance.

> $40,000 damage
> plans for rebuilding
> mother and children safe
> gash on arm
> cause of fire under investigation
> how fire started
> quick action by mother probably saved lives
> quick spread of flames
> how firemen brought it under control
> narrow escape through window
> rescue of trio from ledge

The next step is organization: arranging the elements into a logical order. Under the principle of important things first, details in order of descending importance, you can rate each element for its news value.

If you rated the elements solely on the basis of importance, however, you might miss the best story. It depends on what you consider important. You might select the $40,000 damage or the quick action of the fire department because, after all, no one was hurt. And that would be a mistake.

Therefore the concept of importance might well be tempered with another: What is the most *interesting* or *fascinating* aspect? Which aspect are people most likely to respond to? Take a guess on which of the following aspects people would most like to hear about. Better yet, try them out on some friends.

1. A fire occurred last night.
2. Some $40,000 occurred in fire damage.
3. Mr. Brinkman plans to rebuild his fire-damaged sporting goods building.
4. A young woman in nightclothes, carrying two babies, narrowly escaped a fire.

Common sense, or the empirical evidence from quizzing your friends, surely will convince you that number 4 is far and away the most interesting. It is the kind of stuff from which literature is fashioned—an appealing heroine outwits tragedy—and it therefore tickles our curiosity. So perceptive reporters judge news partly on their knowledge of people. If you see something that profoundly affects people—makes them laugh or say "for gosh sakes"—write it down in your notebook. Put it in your story and your readers will also say "for gosh sakes."

So your organization of the story might stack up something like this:

1. Narrow escape through window.
2. Rescue from ledge.
3. Minor injury to woman; children safe. (Had there been deaths or serious injury, this element would have been at the top of the story.)
4. Some $40,000 damage. (Had it been greater, this, too, would have been higher in the story.)
5. How the fire was controlled.
6. How the fire started. (This is not really known, thus is low in story priority.)
7. Plans to rebuild.

Once you have made these decisions, you are ready to write your story. The hardest part, reporters almost universally agree, is the lead. It is here that you must present in a few words the essence of the situation—indeed it is here that you must *think*. A reporter, struggling to capture the fire story, might start out with several tries before capturing the essence.

> Fire engulfed a River City apartment last night, causing $40,000 damage and forcing the occupants, a young woman and her two small daughters, to crawl through a bathroom window to a ledge from which they were rescued by firemen. . . . [No, it won't do. Too cluttered and rambling.]
>
> Fire destroyed a River City apartment last night, forcing a young woman to flee. . . . [Too routine. And how about the babies?]
>
> A young mother and her two tiny daughters were rescued from a second-story ledge last night after fleeing from a fire that. . . . [Too passive.]
>
> A young woman carried her two babies to safety last night when fire engulfed her apartment. . . . [You're getting closer.]

Once the lead is completed, you must make a transition to the main body of the article. You then follow your outline to record the remaining points of the story. In general, each point should be treated in a separate paragraph. Keep your paragraphs short, averaging three or four typewritten lines.

You do not always strictly and literally follow the principle of descending importance, however. The so-called inverted pyramid principle can get you into trouble if followed too literally. For the sake of coherence and logical order, you sometimes have to finish a series of related thoughts in a story before you go on to the next series. This is true even though the first thoughts of the second series may be more important than the last of the first series. (More about this problem in Chapter 7.)

Nor can you always follow your outline rigidly. Sometimes it is more important merely to let one thought merge naturally into another than to force a concept to fit the particular location called for in the outline.

Some writers claim that they don't really know what they will write in paragraph two until they've finished paragraph one. They may have a general organization in mind, but they leave the details to improvisation at the typewriter. They find that this approach results in a smoother flow of ideas and makes transitions easier.

Transitions are essential to a smooth and coherent article. A transition is a rhetorical device that links one thought to another or one paragraph to another. To understand it, think of the phrase, "Meanwhile, back at the ranch. . . ." It means that where you have an abrupt change of thought, you must insert a phrase or a word that alerts the reader to the change. It may not be so clumsy as "meanwhile, back at the ranch," but it's essential nonetheless. The usual transitions fall into three categories.

1. The use of a word or phrase to indicate the direction of the next thought. Included are such terms as *however, moreover, meanwhile, in any event, but, so, then, on the other hand,* and many others. They're little signposts that tell the reader what's coming.

2. Repeating a word or phrase. Note the link between the two paragraphs immediately preceding point number 1 above. The first of those two ends with the phrase, ". . . makes transitions easier." The next paragraph starts out, "Transitions are essential. . . ." The repeated word, *transitions,* is the link between the two paragraphs, a slight but essential redundancy.

3. A logical progression of thought that really needs no literal transition. One thought follows logically from the earlier one. If you say in the first paragraph, "Marsha fell down," you could say in the next, "She skinned her knee." A skinned knee is a logical result of falling down. It is only when the second thought is unexpected that a transition may be necessary. Suppose "she found a diamond ring" is the second thought. A transition may be necessary to introduce it: "*As she lay there,* she found a diamond ring."

Note the use of transitions in the following story about the fire. Note, too, the way the story organization follows the original outline—not precisely, but close.

A young woman carried her two small daughters to safety by breaking a bathroom window to escape the flames that rapidly engulfed their apartment in River City last night.

Firemen used a ladder to rescue the woman, Mary Westerman, 19, and her two tiny children from the second-story ledge to which they had escaped when the fire blocked the apartment door.

She was treated at Mercy Hospital for a severe cut on the arm. The children, ages 5 months and 21 months, were not hurt.

The fire destroyed the apartment, located in the Brinkman and Sons Sporting Goods building, 456 Partridge Ave. Water also damaged the store below, said Fire Chief Charles Pickering, who estimated the loss at $40,000.

Westerman said she first noticed the fire when she awakened shortly after midnight and smelled smoke.

She found the living room "a ball of flame."

"I didn't see how we were ever going to get out because you had to go through the living room to get to the door," she said. "That's when I thought of the bathroom window."

The quick exit probably saved their lives, the fire chief said. "It's smart not to wait around inside where the smoke might get you."

The chief said 11 fire fighters controlled the blaze in about 20 minutes. Cause of the fire was under investigation this morning.

Charles Brinkman, the building's owner, plans repair work soon.

Lead focuses on most dramatic element. Woman's name is not used here to streamline the lead and focus attention on the drama. Writer refrained from using phrases like "fled in a nightgown"; it didn't seem to fit the context of carrying babies to safety.

Note transitional device: repeat of the word "woman." A second, more subtle transition comes in the use of the phrase "firemen used a ladder to rescue," which follows logically from the escape.

The transition is a logical follow-up to previous paragraph. It answers the implied question, "What happened next?"

Finally the damage report. Terms such as "the fire" and "the apartment" are sufficient for transition, even though this is a distinct change in thought. Some readers might quit the story here as the essential questions are answered by this point.

Notice how the phrase "first noticed the fire" introduces a new thought, which is the woman's personal account.

Short paragraphs here speed the reading and connote "action."

Direct quote follows logically and adds the "I was there" flavor of an involved witness.

The term "quick exit" follows logically from the preceding quote. The comment from the chief is a logical conclusion presented by a person of authority, suggesting a lesson to be heeded by others.

Continued reference to "the chief" makes this transition to minor details.

A final note tacked on at the end has a logical where-do-we-go-from-here aspect.

EXERCISE 2: AN ADVANCE STORY

The word "advance" as a newspaper term has several meanings (see Glossary); here it simply means a story announcing an upcoming event such as a lecture or a meeting. The city editor asks you to call John Small, a River City attorney and president of the Downtowners Club, for a story about a meeting coming up in a couple of days. "I understand they're having the governor speak," says the city editor. The Downtowners Club is a civic betterment group composed of business and professional people in River City. You telephone John Small, introduce yourself, and proceed to assemble the information you need.

Q. Mr. Small, I'm writing a story for today's paper on your next meeting of the Downtowners Wednesday—is it true that the governor is speaking?

A. Yes, we just completed the arrangements for his speech this morning. How did you get the news so fast?

Q. I think our city editor has built-in radar—can you give me the time and place of the speech?

A. It's at noon this Wednesday at the Riverview Hotel. The speech itself will begin promptly at 12:45. And I'd like you to make a note, if you will, that it's open to the general public without charge. We'll be setting up chairs for those who don't plan to eat lunch.

Q. Okay. Is this an unusual procedure—inviting the public?

A. We're always delighted to have the public attend as guests, but this time we're issuing special invitations to city and county officials who are *not* members to come and hear the speech.

Q. You're actually sending them written invitations?

A. No, there's no time for that. We just want to let them know through the media that Governor [Edward W.] McCormack is speaking.

Q. What's the topic of the speech?

A. As you know, the biennial session of the state legislature begins in Valley City next month. So the governor plans to outline some ideas that he'll be taking to the legislature.

Q. What kind of ideas?

A. His press secretary wasn't specific about that.

Q. How about a title to the speech?

A. We don't have that, either.

Your curiosity prompts you to call the governor in Valley City, the state capital, 100 miles away. Ken Farmer, the governor's press secretary, tells you:

> The governor is not entirely sure at this point what the speech will be about, but he will, as always, be forthright and candid on matters of importance as related to the forthcoming sessions of the legislature. I rather imagine these will include a selection of the major issues, such as taxation, school finances, mass transportation, land-use planning, and law enforcement. I think it's safe to say that law enforcement will be the primary topic, with school finances not far behind.

Suggestions. Though some of the information is vague, it's sufficient for a small story. Emphasize what you know of the content of the speech rather than the mere fact that the governor is speaking. Assume that today is Monday and the speech is this coming Wednesday. Information about the speech's content should be attributed to the press secretary or to Mr. Small.

EXERCISE 3: A SPEECH

You have been assigned by the paper to cover Governor McCormack's speech to the River City Downtowners Club (Exercise 2). As the governor's party enters, you spot Ken Farmer, the press secretary, and obtain from him a copy of the speech. The governor is introduced by Judge Sarah Benchly, judge of the Holcomb County Court of Domestic Relations and winner of this year's "Citizen of the Year" award. About 200 persons are present, the largest audience in the 23-year history of the club, says John Small, club president. Following is a segment of the speech. Write a story for tomorrow's (Thursday's) paper based on this segment.

I'd like to talk for a few moments about one of the primary issues of my administration. This is the issue of corrections. With the growth of crime in this state— property crime is up 30 percent over last year and violent crime is up an astounding 47 percent!—the cry is inevitably raised:
"Put these people in prison"
"Lock them up!"
"Put them away!"
"Take them off the streets!"
"Make our streets safe once more!"
Unfortunately it is not that simple. In the first place, our prisons are full. Right now we have more than a thousand prisoners in facilities built to house 675.
But the cry comes again—"Build a new prison!"
Hardly a week goes by that I do not get some such communication. I have not spoken publicly on this subject before, but I do so now in answer to all those whose cries for more repressive corrections methods have become ever more shrill. I simply must make my position clear. It's simply this:
I am opposed to building another concrete fortress, a fortress that has all the earmarks of a medieval castle, a fortress that represents the dark ages with its 20 foot walls built at a cost of 50 million dollars.
No, there has to be a better way. I favor a policy that makes better use of our available resources. I favor a policy that insures that those who can be helped—*are* helped. I prefer that this help come in the form of rehabilitation centers at the regional level, not at a central penal facility.
Now, some people wish to go beyond the mere locking up of felons. They favor a return to capital punishment.
You will recall that we once had capital punishment in this state—the gas chamber. Before that we had the gallows. In the state's history, we hanged 17 men, and we dispatched by the gas chamber another 14 men and one woman. Then ten years ago the legislature referred the matter of capital punishment to a vote of the people. And the people in their wisdom voted it out.
Today, however, you'll find those who favor a return to capital punishment. I am told that at least two bills to this end are being prepared for the state legislature. Though I have not addressed myself publicly to this question in the five years I have been your governor, I do so now in the hope that there will be no mistake on where I stand.
I stand unalterably opposed to capital punishment.
I do not believe society has the right to deliberately take a human life.
I do not make a habit of threatening a veto. But if the legislature should pass a bill restoring capital punishment in this state, I shall veto that bill. And if the legislature

refers the question of capital punishment to a vote of the people, I shall lead the fight to defeat it. We have come too far in this state to fall back to the Dark Ages. Next month, when the legislature convenes, I shall address to the session some specific proposals for penal reform. Rest assured that a new prison and capital punishment will not be among them.

Suggestions. Avoid the "Governor McCormack spoke yesterday" type of lead. The opening paragraph should summarize the most newsworthy part of his message. The structure of the typical speech story is this:

Section 1: A lead that summarizes the most newsworthy comments. Avoid dependence on the quotation lead—you probably can summarize more succinctly in your own words.

Section 2: One or more "catchall" paragraphs that cite the circumstances of the speech: time, place, type of audience, etc. This section often contains an additional snippet of comment: "He explained that . . ." or "He added that. . . ."

Section 3: A strong, succinct quote that supports the lead: It reinforces it, elaborates on it, explains it, or adds a colorful insight.

Section 4: A continuing summary of the speech's major points. This may extend to several paragraphs. It usually consists of restating the main points in your own words, but with direct quotations used judiciously to support each point. The material usually comes in order of descending importance. Avoid using synonyms for "said" (averred, declared, stated, etc.). "Said" is a comfortable verb, not officious, and can be used unless a specific meaning is sought (shouted, whispered, etc.).

The hypothetical example below illustrates the structure of a typical speech story. Note that the name of the speaker need not be in the opening paragraph when the message seems more noteworthy than the name.

> The world is coming to an end within 18 months, a Ponderosa College professor told members of the Downtowners Club in River City yesterday.
>
> John J. Farad, professor of phrenology, told the 65 members attending the weekly luncheon meeting that little hope exists for a reprieve.
>
> "I have consulted the charts and the stars," he said, "and I am convinced that the ultimate catastrophe will overtake us in fewer than 18 months."
>
> Professor Farad said he had reached that conclusion after 40 years of study. . . .

EXERCISE 4: AN OBITUARY

In a newspaper office, death is a daily occurrence. That's because a newspaper like the mythical *River City Express* can expect to carry anywhere from two to ten articles a day on the deaths of citizens of the community. On most newspapers the task of writing the routine obituary falls to the youngest reporters. They soon learn that writing an obit is neither traumatic nor difficult; it is merely routine.

Not always, of course. The death of a celebrity, a major public official, a notorious criminal—all these may call for long stories recapping an extraordinary life. Wire services and many newspapers maintain biographical files on prominent citizens who are in their mature years so that obituaries can be prepared quickly. Indeed, obits of the most important people are already written; should one of them suddenly die, the editors need only add the circumstances of death to the beginning of the story.

Most obits, however, are routine, based on information provided by the mortuary in charge of the funeral arrangements. The information comes to the newspaper in the form of a questionnaire filled out by the family or as an obit already prepared by the mortuary. Often the mortuary will call by phone if a deadline is close. The mortuary's information usually includes circumstances of death, highlights of the person's life, names of survivors, and details of funeral services. A reporter may supplement this information by checking clips in the newspaper library or by interviewing the family. (The task of interviewing a bereaved family is seldom as difficult as most young reporters imagine.)

The routine obit follows a fairly standard story organization:

1. The lead sentence includes the name, age, identification, and circumstances of death. The identification usually summarizes a career or cites a highlight of the person's life. Thus: "John L. Doe, 77, who coached five football teams to state championships during an 18-year career at South High School, died yesterday."

2. A follow-up or "catchall" paragraph follows the lead. It includes any noteworthy information not cited in the opening. "Doe died at Mercy Hospital three days after collapsing of an apparent heart attack." If circumstances are unusual, this catchall section may run to several paragraphs.

3. Next come details of funeral services. "Services will be held at the First Congregational Church, 976 Partridge Avenue, River City, Thursday at 10 A.M. A private burial will follow at the Pine Tree Cemetery." (Some newspapers prefer to have this information at the end of the story.)

4. Next comes a recap of the person's life, brief or extended depending on the prominence of the individual. This includes details of employment, civic honors, awards, public service, professional and social affiliations. Doe, for example, probably will be described by his coaching accomplishments: "Doe retired from coaching after compiling a South High career of 93 victories, 70 losses, and 11 ties. . . . Doe twice served as president of the State Coaches Association, and was honored as 'Coach of the Year' in 1959 after his South team amassed 17 consecutive victories. . . ."

5. Survivors come next. Most newspapers confine the list of survivors to grandparents, parents, brothers, sisters, spouse, children. Sometimes the number of grandchildren is included.

6. Minor details come to the end: "The family requests no flowers," or "Contributions may be made in Doe's memory to. . . ."

Pitfalls to avoid.   Steer clear of euphemisms for death: *expired, passed away, laid to rest, gone to a final reward.* Avoid platitudinous eulogies in your own writing, and use them sparingly in quotations. Try to make your article a recap of the highlights of a person's life, not a grim report of death. It might even be a cheerful obit as, for example, the recapping of the life of a humorist.

"A good obit is like a good personality feature," explains one editor-teacher, Professor Lillian (Lee) Wilkins of the University of Colorado. "The only difference is that the subject doesn't show up for the final interview."

Write a succinct obit based on the following information provided to you by the Hickman-Edwards Chapel of the Gardens, 747 River Avenue, River City.

Memorial services for Walter Samuel Stewart will be held in the Hickman-Edwards Chapel of the Gardens tomorrow afternoon at 1 o'clock. Officiating will be Dr. Cyrus Churchman, pastor of the United Methodist Church of River City, of which the late Mr. Stewart was a member. Concluding rites and interment will take place at the Valley View Memorial Park, located three miles south of River City. Contributions may be made in Mr. Stewart's memory in lieu of flowers to the Stewart Scholarship Fund for American Indians, care of Ponderosa College. Walter S. Stewart was born the son of Charles L. Stewart and the former Minnie Miller on November 14, 1907 at Bismarck, North Dakota. He moved with his parents as a child to Sioux City, Iowa, where he lived for more than 30 years. He graduated from high school in Sioux City, and attended the University of Minnesota. He first went to work for Western Union as a messenger boy and later learned bookkeeping while working for the Moon Insurance Company at Sioux City. On June 3, 1934, he was joined in holy wedlock with the former Mary Jane Witherspoon, of Sioux City, his lifetime companion, who survives. Of this union were born three children, all girls, Elaine May, born in 1935 (now Mrs. Alexander Wyman, of Prairie View, Texas), Heather Louise, born in 1938 (now Mrs. Joseph Simmons of Sandy, Oregon), and Cynthia Ann, born in 1943 (now Mrs. Charles Gonzales, of Spearfish, South Dakota). In 1939 the Stewart family moved from Sioux City to River City, where Mr. Stewart was an auto salesman and bookkeeper for several years. In 1946 he founded the Stewart Chevrolet Sales and Service in River City, which he ran until his retirement in 1971. His interests were varied and his concern for people was genuine as shown by his being a sponsor of a boys' summer baseball team for teenagers and his interest in antique cars. In June of each of the last ten or twelve years of his auto dealership he devoted one full floor of his auto dealership to a display of antique cars. As a young man he became interested in American Indians, their culture and their plight on the reservations. He assembled a lifetime collection of writings by and about Indians, totaling about 1,600 volumes, including many unpublished manuscripts, monographs, and photographic collections, all of which he donated to the library of Ponderosa College in a ceremony two years ago. Throughout his life he was interested in community affairs, and he served on the River City School Board from 1952 to 1960. He was also a founder of the River City Antique Cars Club and served as its first president in 1956–60. In addition to his wife, the late Mr. Stewart is survived by the aforementioned children, and five grandchildren. Mr. Stewart will be sorely missed by members of the River City community.

After reading the above material, you call the mortuary for additional details. You learn that Mr. Stewart collapsed yesterday about noon while working on one of his antique cars, a 1934 Dodge coupe. He was taken by ambulance to Mercy Hospital, and he expired yesterday afternoon around four. Cause of death was a postmyocardial infarction (heart attack). You also check library clips on Mr. Stewart. In 1958 he established the Stewart Scholarship for young men and women of American Indian origin to attend a college of their choice at a stipend of $2,000 a year. A feature interview about Mr. Stewart and his antique cars appeared about a year ago. It notes that Mr. Stewart has four old cars, including the 1934 Dodge, a 1924 Model-T, a 1929 Chevrolet, and a 1937 Ford V-8. All are in running order, restored personally by Mr. Stewart in some 20 years of painstaking work. "Old cars are an addiction with me," he was quoted as saying. "Some guys take to alcohol or drugs. Me, I never did drink or smoke. These old cars suit me just fine. I drive the old Dodge to church every Sunday, and Mary Jane and I have a fine time driving the '37 Ford to picnics in the country."

EXERCISE 5: A FOLLOW-UP STORY

A reporter, when interviewing for one story, keeps alert for other stories. Some of them will be new stories that happen to drop in the conversation. Others will be "follow-up" stories that report new developments in an ongoing news issue. The other day, for example, you called Fire Chief Pickering for a story on an apartment fire (Exercise 1). Today you call him again to see if his investigation of that mysterious fire has produced any new details. Has he determined the cause of the fire yet? Has he cleared up the puzzle of the fire's rapid spread through the apartment? You place your call, and this is what Pickering tells you:

> Yes, we've checked it thoroughly now; we even had a man over from the State Fire Marshal's Office. We're pretty sure the cause was a lighted cigarette––better make that read "probable cause" because sometimes you can't be one hundred percent sure. But the big problem, we discovered after some tests on the unburned portion in the bedroom, was the paint. They had some cheap paint in there that must have been put on 25 or 30 years ago, long before Charlie Brinkman bought that building, and it was in the apartment, cracking and peeling and flaking, and when it got hot enough it caught fire and just flashed through the living room. It had the living room in flames within seconds. Well, we're checking around town to see if there's any more of that old paint in buildings. Starting next week we're going to go out and inspect a few old buildings around town to see if the paint is a fire hazard. And if anybody has some old paint in their houses or business buildings they're suspicious about, why, give us a call and we'll send someone out to check. . . . No, there's no charge; we normally have an annual fire inspection program where we send firemen out to inspect houses for fire hazards. The more time we spend doing that, the less time we spend fighting fires. . . .

Suggestions.   Assume that the fire occurred about 12:30 A.M. on a Wednesday and that it is now Friday morning, two days later. You are writing for today's paper. Don't assume that your readers know about Wednesday's fire. They may have missed your original story or they may have forgotten the details. You have to include a paragraph to remind them. Go back to the notes for Exercise 1. Your story structure for this follow-up story will be something like this:

Lead
Background
Elaborating details

EXERCISE 6: A MEETING STORY

We live in a meeting-oriented society. Sometimes reporters attend public meetings to get stories—the city council or the school board, for example. But reporters can't be everywhere at once, so a lot of meetings are covered merely by interviewing one or more of the participants. Such is the case in this exercise. The city editor brings to your desk an athletic-looking man named Paul Nelson, who is president of a statewide organization called the Mountain Rescue and Safety Council. He lives at 333 High Pass Avenue, River City.

"Mr. Nelson has a story about a meeting that several outdoor groups held yesterday at the Riverview Hotel," says the city editor. "They passed a resolution recommending the use of citizen's band radios by mountain climbers. Let's have a story on that for today's paper." With that he leaves you alone with Mr. Nelson, who takes a seat beside your desk.

This is a typical newspaper situation. You don't know much about mountain climbing or CB radios, but you're going to have to learn enough in the next fifteen minutes to write a story. You have two things in your favor, however. First, Nelson is as eager as you to have a successful interview. Second, you're a professional; you know how to ask questions and probe for detail. So. . . .

Q. Mr. Nelson, just what is this resolution you passed about CB radios?
A. I can read it to you: "Resolved: that for safety and to facilitate the work of rescue parties, the following agencies request that all mountain climbers carry citizen's band radios and that prior to beginning an ascent they register with an appropriate agency information about their planned routes, departure times, expected return times, radio equipment, and frequencies (channels) in use."
Q. What does the resolution mean by the term "the following agencies"?
A. The agencies represented at the meeting were the Mountaineers (a River City mountaineering club), the U.S. Forest Service, REACT (a citizen's band radio emergency monitoring club), the Civil Air Patrol, and the State Mountain Rescue and Safety Council.
Q. How does it happen that this group got together?
A. The meeting was called by MRSC—Mountain Rescue and Safety Council. We're a volunteer agency that coordinates rescue teams whenever there's a lost or overdue climbing party. We've had a lot of problems, particularly in winter, with lost or overdue climbers. Sometimes a search

mission has to be conducted under extremely hazardous conditions. So we called this meeting.

Q. And out of this meeting, then, came this resolution?

A. Yes, we passed the resolution unanimously last night about ten o'clock.

Q. And the problem you are trying to solve is the hazard of searching for lost climbing parties, particularly in winter?

A. Yes. We think portable two-way radios have become small and efficient enough that it's reasonable to ask a climbing party to carry one. They weigh only a couple of pounds.

Q. Does the signal carry far?

A. It depends, but you can usually get at least three or four miles with a decent radio. Our procedure will be that if a climbing party is twelve hours overdue, we'll establish a radio monitoring network on the frequencies they're using.

Q. Would three or four miles be enough range for a rescue party?

A. Definitely so if the rescuers know roughly where the climbers should be.

Q. Do you anticipate that mountain climbers will readily accept your proposal?

A. It may take an educational campaign on our part. Climbers are an independent bunch. Quite a few will resent the intrusion of "civilization" into their pristine mountain environment. We had some pretty wild discussions about that yesterday.

Q. But I gather that you finally reached agreement.

A. Yes. Our contention is that climbers don't have to use the radio unless they're in trouble. Our *major* argument, however, is that when a climber gets lost, a lot of people risk their lives searching for them. A couple of pounds of radio gear in a climber's backpack is a small price to pay to make it easier and safer for rescue parties.

Q. Have your rescue parties had casualties in the past?

A. Yes, in the five years I've been engaged in these rescue missions, MRSC has gone on nineteen missions for lost climbers. We've also had other kinds of missions, but I'm talking now only about mountain-climbing parties. In that time we've had no one killed, but we had four hurt. Nothing serious, fortunately. About two years ago a rescue spotter plane had a crash landing on Mount Multnomah. Suddenly we were searching for two lost parties. But the plane turned out to be no problem because it had a radio "beeper" in the tail that led the searchers right to it within minutes. The climbers weren't so lucky. One out of the three died of hypothermia—that's a lowered body temperature caused by the cold. That incident is what started us thinking about using CB radios.

Your interview continues in this vein. You learn the following additional details: The radios are the small walkie talkie type, costing between $50 and $200. They operate on batteries. Seventeen persons attended yesterday's meeting. Nelson presided over the meeting. The seventeen persons come from all over the state and represent one or another of the five agencies involved in the resolution. Three persons are from River City. They are Nelson and two representatives of the Mountaineers, John Polanski, 2114 Canal Street, and Carol Gibson, 893 Mountain Highway. The meeting started yesterday noon and ran continuously until about 10:30 last night with only a break for dinner. Within the next 30 days, Nelson says, the five agencies will develop an educational campaign to inform mountain climbers of the resolution and the reasons behind it.

Suggestions. Keep your story simple and uncluttered. Don't rely heavily on quotes. Tell the story in your own words, starting with the action taken, identifying the agencies involved, and moving quickly to the reasons for the action. Save direct quotes for succinct summaries of explanation or touches of color. Be sure to attribute the information in your story to Mr. Nelson. (If your state has no mountains, then assume your locale is northern California and that references to "this state" actually mean northern California, not the entire state.) A meeting story is not unlike other stories—the important aspect is not that a meeting was held but that a certain action took place at the meeting.

Discussion question. Is the story worth further attention? What kinds of approaches might be taken to a follow-up story?

POINTS TO REMEMBER

1. Practice makes perfect, as they say.
2. Having too much information, though it complicates the writer's job, helps to secure a better understanding of the topic, thus produces a better article.
3. Information comes mostly through interviews and arrives in raw, rambling form. It requires careful thought to determine what can be included and what eliminated from your story. You must organize the material into a coherent whole.
4. The drama inherent in some situations, such as narrowly escaping tragedy, can be an important consideration in judging news values.
5. Careful use of transitions can smooth the flow of your story.
6. Organization of a typical speech story starts with a summary lead and catchall paragraph followed by a strong quote to back up the lead, and then the elaborating details.
7. An obituary should be a celebration of an interesting life, not a funeral dirge.
8. Organization of a typical obit starts with name and identification followed by a recounting of highlights of the person's life. Usually included are time and place of funeral services and a list of survivors.
9. Many stories don't end with a single installment; some, like soap operas, continue with new developments. So reporters seek "follow-ups."

7

Writing the Complex Story

Until now we've concentrated on single-incident, single-source stories. You interviewed one fire chief for the fire story. You did talk to others for additional facts, but only after you had the nature of the story firmly in mind. And for your meeting story on radios for mountain climbers, you again interviewed only one person. He filtered out a lot of useless information from the hours of discussion. Had you been there you might have been hopelessly confused by the rambling, sometimes-rancorous discussion.

That's typical of meetings. You'll hear many viewpoints, expressed through wayward and redundant discussion. Often you'll find little agreement. The arguments in public meetings—such as a school board or Congress—proceed with the efficiency of rusty machinery. That's democracy. Chances are you wouldn't want to change it, but it does make the reporter's job difficult. And meetings are simple compared to other kinds of complex stories. Let's say the county sheriff suddenly and unexpectedly resigns with nothing more than this puzzling remark: "I could give you a thousand reasons, but let's just say I'm darned tired and fed up." Those were the words actually used by a sheriff in a small Oregon community to announce his resignation.

If the sheriff won't tell you the reasons, perhaps others will. By checking a wide variety of sources, you can compare, contrast, verify, cross-check, corroborate, and eventually fill in the missing details. From all this work can emerge a mosaic of understanding that no one person could ever provide—not even the sheriff. Your investigation of the situation has literally made *you* the expert. Your overall

(Photo by Randy L. Rasmussen.)

understanding of a situation thereby becomes greater than any one of the sources you consult. Your work takes on new meaning. No longer are you a "recording secretary." You're a *thinking* reporter, the best kind. No longer are you at the mercy of manipulative or uncooperative bureaucrats. What one doesn't tell you another will.

Once you think you understand a complex situation, your next task is to sort through the fragments of information and form them into conceptual building blocks for your story. Like the simple story, the complex one starts with an essence or point that you will describe in the lead. The rest of your story consists of the major supporting points or concepts. You will present them to your readers in a controlled, logical fashion, one at a time like chapters in a book.

TYPICAL KINDS OF COMPLEX STORIES

If the level of understanding required here seems intimidating, keep in mind that some stories are less complex than others. You can start with the merely frustratingly complex stories and, as you gain experience, gradually work toward the hopelessly complex ones. Here are some typical ways complex situations emerge in news reports.

A Roundup Story

The term "roundup" (also called "wrapup" or "wrap") is newspaper jargon for stories that wrap several similar events into a single story. You call the Highway Patrol on a Monday morning, and the sergeant gives you details of three accidents. Accident number one killed two persons and injured five. Accident number two killed one and injured three. Accident number three put three persons in the hospital, one of whom died three hours later. Instead of writing separate stories, you put them together: "Four persons died in three separate highways accidents in Holcomb County over the weekened, the Highway Patrol reported. . . ."

A Multisource Story

Many stories are based on interviews with more than one source. But in the simple kinds of stories, one of the sources is dominant, the others secondary. In complex stories, such as a major winter storm, no one source is dominant. You must fit many diverse elements into a coherent mosaic. You get material on snarled transportation from the police, on casualties from the hospitals, on weather data from the Weather Service, and on colorful sidelights from observation and eyewitness reports. By fitting the pieces together, you present the big picture, as in this example:

> Bands of thunderstorms dumped as much as seven inches of rain Sunday across parts of the sodden Upper Midwest, causing new flooding in South Dakota and Wisconsin, and threatening more floods in waterlogged Nebraska.
>
> —*Associated Press*

A Multiple-Viewpoint Story

The reporting of public meetings often involves multiple viewpoints. Let's say Ponderosa College's Board of Trustees takes a divergent set of views on whether to fire a football coach who has lost too many games. Three trustees argue vehemently for dismissing the coach, four are vigorously opposed, and several others are noncommittal. It's all discussion, no action. How do you handle such a story? You might try a question lead—"Should Ponderosa football coach Roy Wolfe be dismissed for losing too many games?"—and then go on to cite the highlights of discussion on either side of the issue. Or you might characterize the discussion in a summary lead such as this:

> The future of coach Roy Wolfe, whose Ponderosa College teams have lost 13 of their last 14 games, dominated an hour of discussion in last night's meeting of the college's Board of Trustees.
> No action was taken, but. . . .

The story would go on to cite the highlights of the discussion and to quote the coach's reactions.

A Multiple-Action Story

The multiple-action story is similar to the multiple-viewpoint story, except that specific actions have taken place. The city council (we'll say) in last night's meeting (1) awarded a street-paving contract, (2) asked for a study of fire department financial needs over the next five years, (3) vacated two alleys at the request of property owners, (4) tabled a motion to buy five new fire trucks, and (5) accepted the resignation of the city street engineer. Again you have a problem in organizing such fragments into a coherent whole. (More about this type of problem later in the chapter.)

An Abstract Concept

An ancient newspaper expression wryly suggests that "if you can't score it, count bodies, count money, or get the governor to comment on it, it ain't there." The concept harkens back to days when news values were more incident-oriented and obtrusive than they are today.

Editors today certainly don't ignore major incidents, but they are more willing to consider story ideas that start with an abstract idea rather than bodies in the street. Of course, an incident often inspires the abstract idea.

A single case of child abuse, for example, might prompt a reporter to explore the psychological profile of the abusers. Who are the people who beat up or sexually molest children and why do they do it? The reporter then interviews the participants: police officers, social service workers, psychologists, the abusers themselves. Out of this comes a story abstract in concept but concrete in details (statistics, case histories, and so forth). And the beauty is that no one called a press conference to announce it; you did it on your own initiative.

A Hidden Drama

Many people get into journalism because they like to tell stories. Maybe they'd be short story writers if they could make a living at it. The elements of dramatic literature—such as character, action, suspense, irony—exist in real-life situations. The stories are abstract and often submerged, out of view except to reporters with a kind of literary imagination and the willingness to explore beyond the obvious.

We're talking here about human drama. If a crippled airliner, its engines trailing smoke, lands safely thanks to the skill and courage of its captain and crew, there's no story, right?

Wrong. The *real* story emerges in a suspenseful account of actions of the captain and others during those moments of terror in the skies—the courage, the heroics, the "drama in real life" to borrow a term from the *Reader's Digest.* You would not write a fictional account of the incident, of course. You would interview everyone involved and piece together a completely factual account filled with action and suspense. This is a severe test of your information gathering and writing skills, and that's what makes the story complex.

GETTING INFORMATION FOR COMPLEX STORIES

Sometimes information gathering isn't so different from that of simple stories—it's just that you're dealing with a lot more of it. It's easy to become engulfed by the enormity of the project. You consult documents and background clips from the newspaper library. You talk to lots of people. You follow your professional curiosity. You attend meetings. You observe. All of these things you do to arrive at an understanding of the true nature of the situation. And when you have it you try to illustrate your understanding with the facts.

One major task is to keep track of matters as you go along—to organize your story even as you are assembling the information. You listen, for example, to a rambling discussion of the city council. They are talking about building a new city hall, and you envision the headline: COUNCIL APPROVES NEW CITY HALL. It seems simple at first. But then the opposition starts talking, and you have to dream up a new head: COUNCIL REJECTS CITY HALL. Rancorous arguments ensue. "It's time we dragged River City kicking and screaming into the twentieth century!" "We're in it now," comes the pointed retort, "where have *you* been?" Then calmer heads try to enter. "Let's wait and see," they say. "We need an engineering study." "No we don't—what we need is some clear-headed thinking, not a bunch of carping." "*Who's* carping—this is serious business!"

Your headline totally evaporated. You're supposed to make some sense out of *that*?

Yes, and as you gain experience you will. Experienced reporters know that it all settles into compartments, three in this case: (1) views of the yes crowd, (2) views of the no crowd, and (3) views of the let's wait and see crowd. When you sort it all out, your story emerges. You might start with a question lead: "Does River City need a new city hall?" You relate how the issue came up, define the three predominant viewpoints, and quote a sample from each.

Simple.

It's easier if you "write" your story as you listen to the discussion. That is, you *prescreen* the debate as you listen, recording in your notes the comments that reflect each of the three viewpoints. At first you won't know what the views are, but

John Painter, local government reporter at brown-bag luncheon in city conference room. *(Photo by Randy L. Rasmussen.)*

eventually patterns will emerge. (On rare occasions they may fail to emerge, in which case *that* is what your story must say.) You will probably talk to the council members after the meeting to enhance your understanding. You needn't feel that you are intruding. Far better to ask than to make mistakes in print.

The information gathering also becomes easier if you keep three story components in mind as you work. They are: (1) the lead paragraph, (2) the major concepts or points, (3) the inverted pyramid.

The Lead

Thinking about your lead at this early stage helps you to define your newsgathering work as well as your writing, even if you consider and discard several possibilities in the process. If you neglect to think about the lead, you may be utterly confused when you sit down to write.

So you look for items that will make your lead. It may focus on what you perceive to be the most important element of the event or situation. Or it may be a succinct summary of several important elements. Sometimes an anecdotal lead helps to define a complex situation by illustrating it with a single, concrete example.

The Concepts

The principle of organization by concept will further direct your information-gathering efforts. If you are getting information about a big winter storm, for example, you might outline your concepts before you start and then you can use the outline as a guide for gathering information.

Transportation problems

highway conditions?
accidents?
stranded motorists?
hampered fire and emergency services?
stalled air and rail traffic?

Meteorological information

dimensions of storm, how much snow, wind, etc?
background: records broken? general trends? cause of storm?
forecast?

Casualties of storm

property damage?
power outages?
fatalities or injuries?

Digging out

rescue operations?
snow removal?

This is not merely a rhetorical process; it is a *thought* process. Reporters who are precise and orderly in their thinking will find this listing of concepts easier than those who merely rely on intuition and vague impressions.

Whether you literally write all of this down or keep it in your head depends largely on skill and experience. As you gain experience, you will tend to keep more in your head and rely less on written outlines. You may even devise ingenious methods for keeping things straight. One reporter uses colored pencils to take notes at city council meetings: red for budget matters, blue for capital improvements, purple for personnel, and so on.

The Inverted Pyramid

Not only do you categorize as you gather information but you rate the categories in order of importance. The ratings may change as new information comes in. Here are the ratings for a storm story.

1. Casualties and damages

at least 15 storm-related injuries
dramatic rescue of three men from sinking barge
power outages

2. Transportation problems

airport closed
rail transportation stalled

3. Digging out

snow removal equipment working
helicopter used to feed livestock

4. Meteorological data

"freak" unexpected storm
light snow tomorrow

The outline suggests that at the moment the reporter considers casualties the most important element, followed by transportation and digging out. Within the first category, casualties rate above the dramatic rescue. The ratings can change in an instant, of course, as new information comes in.

An exception to the inverted pyramid principle is the step-by-step recounting of an incident, usually a dramatic one such as the hazardous rescue of three men from a barge sinking in a howling storm. Here the chronology may build up to a climax rather than vice versa, starting with a distress call and ending as the chopper picks up the beleaguered trio just as the vessel slips beneath the water.

If you keep the three basic principles in mind from the beginning, not only will writing become easier but so will *understanding*.

HOW TO WRITE A COMPLEX STORY

If you are like most reporters, you probably find it hard to make the transition from information gatherer to writer. That's never more true than when the story is complex. Most reporters find their greatest pleasure in the "learning" aspects of their work: doing research, observing, meeting people, interviewing, discovering new ideas.

When you try to put on paper what you have learned—well, that's like taking a college exam. It's hard enough when you've done your "homework"; it's impossible when you haven't. However, if during the information-gathering stage you have kept in mind the three principles discussed above—leads, concepts, and inverted pyramids—you'll find the writing easier. But you have to start by facing up to one truth about writing.

That truth is that you can't say everything at once. Don't even try. Writing is linear. One thought follows another, word by word, sentence by sentence, right through to the end. Therefore you must learn to present one thought at a time. To see how this works, let's reexamine leads, concepts, and inverted pyramids in the context of *writing* rather than gathering information.

Leads

Although you present thoughts one at a time, you would not write about a storm snowflake by snowflake. Some information will be summarized; other information will be given in detail, often in support of the summary. The process is similar to the scoring of a football game. You don't report the game by starting with touchdown one, then touchdown two, then touchdown three, then the opponent's touchdown one, two, and so forth. No, instead, you say Ponderosa College beat Siwash 21 to 14. If you're a sportswriter, you probably incorporate into your summary a touch of color or information that suggests how the game was won.

> The Ponderosa Pine Cones rallied behind the strong passing arm of quarterback Rick Salter last night to come from behind and defeat a strong Siwash team, 21 to 14.

A sportswriter probably would follow this opening with highlights of the game: a spectacular 90-yard pass play that produced the first touchdown, a last-ditch defense that prevented a game-tying touchdown by the opponent. A storm story would start out with similar highlights.

> An unexpected storm dumped 10 inches of snow in River City last night, closing schools, halting air and rail transportation and sending at least 15 persons to hospitals in storm-related accidents.
> Residents can expect another four to six inches tonight. . . .

Here the lead to a complex story is essentially a summary of the "big picture." Sometimes, however, one aspect of a complex situation overrides all the others. Let's say the city council last night took action on several matters, but by far the most spectacular was the lively debate leading to a vote that asked for the resignation of the police chief. In such a case, your lead might run like this:

> The city council last night called for the resignation of River City Police Chief Darrell McManus.
> The council's decision came in a 5-to-4 vote after two hours of bitter debate during which the chief was accused of "arrogance" and "belligerence" in dealing with his officers and the public. McManus was defended with equal vigor by other council members who praised his "strong hand" and "vigorous leadership."
> Chief McManus did not attend last night's meeting. He said this morning that he will respond to the council's resignation request at a news conference at 9 a.m. tomorrow. . . .

Such a lead leaves the rest of the council actions to be handled later in the story. One way of doing that is to incorporate a flashby paragraph early in the story.

> . . . In other action last night, the council awarded a $300,000 paving contract, tabled a motion to buy five new fire trucks and asked for a study of fire department financial needs over the next five years.
> Discussion of the police chief's performance dominated the meeting, however, and. . . .

The second paragraph of the above fragment is a transition back to the main thread of the story, which is the debate about the police chief. The rest of the story would be organized by concept, including the following: (1) reasons for the problem as brought out in the debate, (2) sampling of comments against the chief, (3) sampling of comments favorable to the chief, (4) reactions of other city officials, such as the city manager, and (5) actions taken by the council on the other matters: the paving contract, fire trucks motion, and so forth. Some newspapers prefer to report such items in separate stories, with the police chief story on page one, the rest inside. In the front-page story, readers may find a boldface line, "Additional city council news on page 33." Some papers insert a boxed summary of council actions:

What the council did

1. Called for resignation of Police Chief Darrell McManus in 5-to-4 vote, Page 1.
2. Awarded $300,000 contract for paving a nine-block section of Circle Street, Page 33.
3. Tabled a motion to buy five new fire trucks, Page 33.
4. Asked for a study of fire department financial needs, Page 33.

But what if you lack a firm and important element of news for your lead? Then your best procedure is to combine two or three lesser elements into a flashby lead.

> The city council last night decided not to buy five new fire trucks this year, but it called for a study of financial needs of the River City fire department.
> In a four-hour session, the council also. . . .

What do you do if nothing in particular has happened—no motions passed, no police chiefs fired—just a lot of discussion? Often the discussion itself is newsworthy; it may be the first hint that something new is in the wind. Suppose, for example, that you have listened to an hour of "idle discussion" by the council on whether to build a new city hall. The council took no action and reached no consensus. Yet the fact that the council is thinking about new city halls is noteworthy.

Does River City need a new city hall?
The city council discussed that question last night for an hour without reaching any conclusions.
Councilwoman Martha McMurtry raised the issue, suggesting that the present city hall "is only a step ahead of condemnation by the fire marshal."
She added that "with a new city hall we can begin to drag River City kicking and screaming into the 20th century."
Two other council members, Alexander Burns and Donna Chu, agreed with her, but councilmen John Jencks and Charles Foxfire opposed the idea. The remaining four council members remained uncommitted. . . .

Your story would go on to give pro and con debate, quoting comments that represent what you perceive to be the significant arguments on either side. You may bring forth some background information obtained from news clips and interviews: history of the present city hall, comments about its defects and service-ability, information on what a new building would cost and how it would be financed. The story, as envisioned here, is no longer exclusively about the council meeting. It's about building a new city hall. Some newspapers prefer to write about the issues and ideas brought out at meetings rather than adhering strictly to the actions and discussions within the meeting. More interesting and significant stories are frequently the result.

Concepts

Once you have presented the opening summary of your story, you can deliver what you promised in the lead. The opening is a kind of "promissory note"; what you promise there is what you must deliver in the body of the story. If you opened with "an hour of lively debate," then you must provide samples of the debate that fairly and accurately represent the two or more sides. And you must capture the "lively" aspects of it, too.

So first you write your lead, then you present the basic concepts of the story (the city hall story in this instance) following a pattern like this:

1. how the issue was raised
2. comments of proponents of new city hall
3. comments of opponents
4. comments of noncommitted faction
5. history of present city hall
6. methods of financing new structure

You then write a story based on that outline. Some newspapers label their sections with boldface subheads or other typographical breaks that make it easier for the reader. The use of these "literary signposts" is becoming increasingly popular. (See the sample story below.)

Inverted Pyramids

To accommodate the complex story, the inverted pyramid principle needs reexamination and modification. It worked fairly well for simple stories involving one major incident or situation. It works less well in complex stories. And more stories are complex than simple.

To explain this, let's sketch out a specific hypothetical story, the one about a storm that hit River City last night. The story below is fragmented and incomplete, but it contains sufficient detail for us to make some points about modifying the inverted pyramid.

An unexpected storm dumped 10 inches of snow on River City last night, closing schools, snarling air and rail transportation and sending at least 15 persons to hospitals with storm-related injuries.

> Flashby lead captures the essence of the situation.

Residents can expect four to six inches of new snow tonight, the National Weather Service said.

The storm also caused power outages in East River City and in scattered sections of rural Holcomb County.

No fatalities were reported, and most injuries were minor.

> Three additional flashby paragraphs elaborate on the lead, conveying in brief form the remaining elements the writer considers important. A reader could quit the story at this point and still have knowledge of the essentials.

Among those hospitalized were three men rescued by helicopter amid blizzard conditions from a sinking barge in the ice-clogged Chickahominy River.

> Here's a transition to a dramatic narrative.

A DARING RESCUE. Police were alerted to the sinking barge by a radio distress call at 3:10 A.M. today, and. . . .

> Here begins a narrative account of the dramatic rescue, presented early in the story because of its high reader interest.

OTHER ACCIDENTS. In addition to the three rescued men, police reported that storm-caused injuries put another dozen persons in hospitals. The most serious of these was the broken leg suffered by nine-year-old Johnny Aspen who fell from the roof of his home at 1010 Highland St., River City.

> After completing the chronological details of the rescue, the writer proceeds to recount other injuries.

Other reported injuries included. . . .

SNARLED TRANSPORTATION. Snow removal equipment worked through the morning, clearing and salting most major River City streets by noon today. U.S. Highway 123 was open to one lane of traffic in both directions. Many outlying roads in Holcomb County remained closed to motorists without traction devices, however.

> After casualties comes information about the problems of transportation and activities to dig out of the storm.

River City Municipal Airport closed at midnight last night, and flights were cancelled through tonight. . . .

WEATHER REPORTS. **The National Weather Service said the unexpected snow, which began falling around nine last night, resulted from "a poorly organized and highly erratic storm center."**

Temperatures will decline to a low of about 15 degrees again tonight and a high of 25 tomorrow. . . .

SCHOOL CLOSURES. **Although Ponderosa College continued to hold classes, most schools closed today and planned to remain closed tomorrow. Two exceptions are. . . .**

POWER OUTAGES. **Municipal Power Co. crews worked through the morning to restore power to some 500 residents of East River City. Officials said the outage was caused when falling trees and limbs broke transmission lines. . . .**

MISCELLANEOUS. **Through the storm, River City fire stations did not receive a single emergency alarm. Fire Chief Charles Pickering said. "That's unusual—in fact, that's darned near miraculous." . . .**

This and the succeeding sections give details in accordance with each of the major concepts.

Finally, the story ends with minor details including items too insignificant to include in earlier sections, even though they might properly have fitted one or another of the concepts.

230022

A close examination of the story suggests the need for viewing the inverted pyramid principle in a more sophisticated light. The principle remains sound, however, because it is based on the idea of giving the reader a quick summary of the essentials with the remaining details presented more or less in order of decending importance.

"More or less." This is the key to rethinking the structure of a complex story. If you follow the descending-importance principle literally, you run the risk of what seems like a helter-skelter organization—the kind of organization that is sheer madness to readers. They might find bits and pieces about transportation in a dozen different parts of the story instead of just one or two.

On the other hand, if you put *all* the transportation information into one section before going on to the next, you run the risk of making the readers go through a lot of trivia at the end of the transportation section before they can go on to the important parts of the weather section, as diagrammed in Figure 1.

Such a pattern does not represent what actually appears in most newswriting. The minor details of transportation will often be combined with the minor details of weather and other elements into a "miscellaneous" section at the end of the story. Further, the pattern in Figure 1 does not account for narratives (such as the rescue of the barge crew) that may be inserted into such a story. So the weather story sketched out earlier will actually follow the pattern shown in Figure 2.

Another reason for rethinking the inverted pyramid principle is that things do not normally happen in order of descending importance. People do not talk that

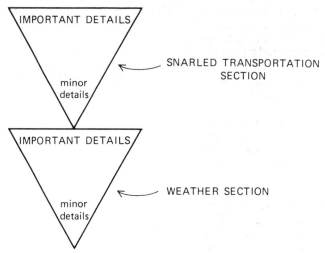

Figure 1   A complex story usually consists of a series of inverted pyramids rather than just one. It therefore runs the risk of awkward organization, as shown here: too many minor details in the snarled transportation section before getting to the important details of the weather section.

way. Rather, things happen chronologically. Therefore newswriting has loosened up in recent years to permit reporters to "tell stories" rather than just present facts.

POINTS TO REMEMBER

1. Complex stories require more information from more sources, and writing them takes more thought in deciding the essence of the story and in selecting factual details.
2. Common types of complex stories include roundups, multiple-viewpoint stories, multiple-action stories, stories with abstract concepts, and stories containing hidden drama.
3. Reporters should organize their stories even as they are gathering information, with particular attention to leads, concepts, and the inverted pyramid principle.
4. Lead paragraphs require summarization, sometimes the way you would cite a football score. Flashby and question leads are also useful.
5. The bulk of the complex story contains a series of concepts or points organized like chapters in a book.
6. The inverted pyramid concept requires some modification to accommodate chronology as well as to organize concepts or points into chapter-like units.

EXERCISE

Around 5:30 last night River City experienced a 20-minute ice storm. It was caused by freezing rain that briefly glazed streets and highways and played havoc with homebound traffic. It is now the following morning, and you are writing for

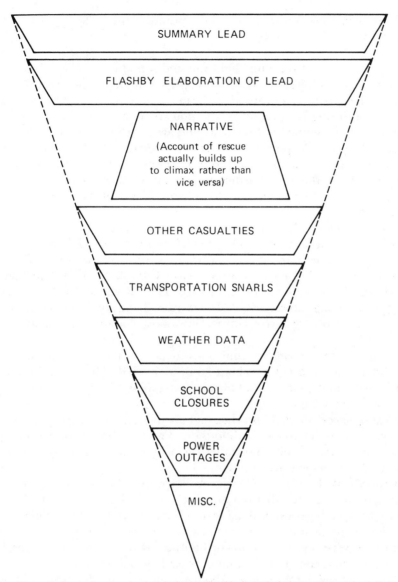

Figure 2 A complex story tends to look more like this. It can include narrative accounts that actually build in interest and importance rather than diminish. Unimportant details of each section are left out for possible inclusion in a catchall section at the end of the story.

the afternoon paper. Write a story incorporating the following fragments of information.

1. *Weather forecast.* Continued light rain today and tomorrow. Clearing trend starting tomorrow afternoon. Warmer. Predicted high for tomorrow 48, low 36. Last night's icing conditions caused by the oncoming warm rain after several days of clear, subfreezing temperatures: the rain froze on contact with the ground. Condition appears limited to River City and areas east of River City. Here at the River City Municipal Airport (located six miles west of River City) icing conditions were not present: the rain did not freeze. That's because the warm weather front, approaching from the west, warmed the terrain sufficiently before it started to rain. (Source: Fred Denny, chief meteorologist, National Weather Service, River City Airport.)

2. *Holcomb County Sheriff's Office.* About six or seven accidents occurred on slick roads in certain rural areas of Holcomb County, mostly to the east of town. All of them were minor accidents and no injuries were reported. A car driven by George T. Henry, 1173 Eastway Street, River City, skidded on Pine Tree Road about eleven miles northeast of River City. The car sheared off a power pole, causing power outage about 5:40 P.M. yesterday. Icing conditions cleared quickly as temperature rose. (Source: Gloria Dinwoody, community relations officer, Sheriff's Office.)

3. *Municipal Power Company.* Only one outage occurred: the one on Pine Tree Road. Due to the car accident, about 50 residents (i.e., 50 homes) were without electricity for about 90 minutes. Power restored about 7:15 P.M. (Source: James Harrington, general manager.)

4. *State Highway Patrol.* This office had about eight or ten accidents reported, almost all of them due to icy conditions on Highway 123 east of River City. The serious accident was a truck and trailer rig jackknifed on the eastbound lanes of Highway 123, blocking traffic for about an hour. This occurred about four miles east of River City. Driver was Charles A. Petrie, age 44, of Los Angeles. He was not hurt. Both of the eastbound lanes were cleared about 6:50 P.M. allowing traffic to proceed. No count was made of vehicles delayed by the stalled truck, but they had to be in the hundreds. No injuries were reported in any of the accidents. No accidents were reported on major highways south, west, and north of River City. (Source: Sergeant Karl Manning, State Highway Patrol.)

5. *River City Police Department.* About ten minor "fender bender" accidents reported. One injury reported: Cecil Arlington, age seven, of 2020 River Avenue (son of Mrs. Jane Arlington of that address) treated at Mercy Hospital for broken arm and lacerations. The boy was crossing the intersection at River and 18th Street when he slipped and fell in the path of an oncoming auto. Car swerved to avoid boy and hit a fire hydrant, which burst, releasing a large spray of water. Car did not hit the boy; his broken arm apparently caused by the fall. Driver of the car was Louis A. Weltzer, age 56, of 85 Salmon Street, River City. Several brief traffic tieups occurred around the city during the icy conditions, but the freeze was of

such short duration that the problems were not serious. The major problem was traffic attempting to negotiate three or four of the on-ramps to Highway 123. Icy conditions made if difficult to get up the inclines to the highway. This problem was complicated by traffic stalled on the eastbound lanes due to the truck accident four miles east. They no sooner got on the highway than they ran into the stalled traffic. (Source: Lieutenant Hiram Hefty, River City Police Department.)

6. *Fire Department.* No fire runs during icing period except repair of broken fire hydrant at River and 18th.

7. *River City Street Maintenance Department.* This department had salt truck ready to go, particularly to get the on-ramps salted, but by the time the trucks got there the freeze was over, so we didn't apply any salt. That doesn't mean traffic was moving—we still had that jam-up on Highway 123 because of the truck. But at least the problem wasn't ice on the ramp. (Source: Alfred A. Espinosa, director, Street Maintenance Department.)

8. *Mercy Hospital.* No storm-related injuries reported except Cecil Arlington's broken arm.

Suggestions. Try to summarize conditions rather than reporting separately what each agency said. Emphasize those aspects that seem the most serious. For your information, the police agency jurisdictions do not overlap. The River City Police Department is limited to the city itself. The State Highway Patrol covers the state and federal highways. The Sheriff's Office covers the rural areas in Holcomb County outside the incorporated municipalities. When you've finished your story, turn to Appendix C for a sample story.

8

Interviewing

The scene was a Kansas City hospital where the former President, Harry S Truman, was failing fast. The *Kansas City Star* established a "death watch" at the hospital, stationing reporters there in shifts around the clock. One young reporter spotted the frail President, assisted by a nurse, walking down a hospital corridor.

His big opportunity to get an interview, he thought to himself.

He approached Mr. Truman, introduced himself, and asked if they could talk for a few moments.

"Young Man," snapped the President, "get a haircut!"

And those were among the President's last words of public record, for he died a day or two later.

Mike Fancher, formerly with the *Kansas City Star,* later managing editor of the *Seattle Times,* tells the story to illustrate a point about interviewing: Nonverbal communication often is a more effective gateway, or *barrier,* to communication than what is said.

You can't always predict the reaction to nonverbal communication, however. Consider another incident, this one involving a college journalism student named Ann Curry. Ann, who later became a television reporter in Los Angeles, received mostly perfunctory and stilted answers as she interviewed a businesswoman across a big desk in the executive's office. Ann, seeking to change to a more informal setting, suggested that they move to a coffee shop across the street. They sat side by side at the counter, and the conversation improved a little. Then Ann, in a wild

Seattle Times reporter Mary Ann Gwinn interviews a high school student for a story on teen-age slang. *(Photo by Matt McVay.)*

gesture to emphasize a point, swept her arm across the counter and spilled her coffee.

Mortified, Ann assumed that she'd blown the interview.

To her astonishment, quite the opposite happened. From that point on, the conversation became more human: It was less stilted, more candid, and more anecdotal. Why the change? Perhaps because of Ann's unwitting demonstration of human vulnerability. The other woman, relieved of the need to show her own facade of perfection, began to talk more openly about herself.

Two other important points emerged from these stories.

The first is the unpredictable nature of the interview. Sometimes the reason for success or failure seems almost capricious. Who could have predicted that spilled coffee would lead to better conversational rapport? With another person it might not have.

Second is that we must try to understand the psychological dynamics of the interview. Most inexperienced reporters naively assume that interviewing merely involves asking questions and getting answers. Some eventually learn instead that the success of an interview depends largely on "people chemistry." Specifically, it means allowing people to be themselves.

"The key to a good news interview," says the *Seattle Times'* Mike Fancher, "is to make it possible for the source to say what he really thinks rather than having to think about what he says."

Journalists agree that good reporting is about 80 percent interviewing. A major problem in journalism education is that many a fine writer—fine in the craft sense—is thwarted by the reluctance or inability to talk with people and learn from them. Some people consider themselves too shy or reclusive to be effective at this. And yet countless insecure students have found inner powers they didn't know they possessed. They found these powers when they crawled out of their shells and started meeting people. If you doubt that, flip back to Chapter 2 and read the comments of Scott Martell, the young Florida reporter. He's the one who showed up in T-shirt and blue jeans for a black-tie interview. It was surprisingly successful, and from that point on Scott didn't worry so much about meeting new people.

Interviewing does, of course, require a certain courage when you are meeting people you don't know and talking about subjects of which you have little knowledge. You run the risk of having your ignorance exposed—or of being criticized for your hair.

But *not* asking questions is worse. You run the risk of remaining forever ignorant of matters that could well fascinate you. You also miss the opportunity to meet interesting people. A special kind of reward awaits the person who asks questions. *You learn.* You learn not only facts and opinions you'll use in your story, but you also add to your reservoir of knowledge.

"He who asks is a fool for five minutes. He who does not is a fool forever." So goes a Chinese proverb.

SOME PRINCIPLES OF INTERVIEWING

First a definition. An interview is a conversation, usually between two persons, to elicit information on behalf of an unseen audience. It is often a conversational *exchange* of information that can produce a level of intelligence that neither party could achieve alone.

The second part does not mean reporters should do a lot of talking—quite the opposite is true most of the time. It does suggest, however, that the reporter has a serious responsibility to do homework in preparation for the interview so that the level of conversation is beyond kindergarten. It further suggests that reporters, with an eye toward the needs and interests of an unseen audience, will ask the kinds of questions that will get answers suitable for the readers. And, finally, it suggests that sometimes reporters literally are the experts after having explored a topic exhaustively. In such instances, people are more candid if *you* are open and candid.

Some other principles to consider:

1. Be open and interested. Reporting, said the late A.J. Liebling, "by and large is being interested in everyone you meet." You don't have to *like* everyone you interview. Could you interview a convicted rapist for a story on how women can protect themselves against violence?

2. You get out of an interview what you put into it. Dumb questions equal dumb answers. Trickery and deceit elicit trickery and deceit in return. Sincerity begets sincerity.

3. People talk more freely when they are having fun. Call it the pleasure principle. You can make an interview fun by careful listening, by your appreciation of people as fellow human beings, by laughing at their jokes, by asking questions based on advance preparation and on your listening to what they're saying.

4. An interview is successful when the interviewee *feels free to say what he or she really thinks and feels*. This means nonjudgmental listening. It means trying to understand the message from the other person's point of view. Doing so can wash away the insincerities, defensive exaggerations, lies, and false fronts that, in the words of psychotherapist Carl Rogers, "characterize most failures in personal communication."

5. You must mine tons of raw conversational ore for each ounce of gold. Most people just talk. They answer your questions as best they can. They do not necessarily talk in perfect inverted pyramids for your story. It's your job as a professional reporter to fashion their sometimes-rambling and wayward comments into a cohesive news story or feature.

THE INTERVIEW STRUCTURE

After you know the principles, the best way to learn to interview is to interview. The typical structure of an interview comes in ten stages. We are talking here about a major face-to-face interview. Many interviews, to be sure, are quick phone conversations in which the process is not nearly so elaborate as indicated here.

1. Define a purpose. Interviews without a clear-cut purpose tend to wander aimlessly. The purpose must be known to *both* parties.

2. Conduct background research. Study news clips from the news library about your person or topic. For many stories, perhaps most, you will or should talk to several people, not just one. Many times you'll interview family, friends, colleagues, even rivals of the person who is your main interview.

3. Request, usually by phone, an interview appointment. Explain the purpose. Be prepared to "sell" yourself and your story idea if your person is less than enthusiastic.

4. Plan your interviewing strategy. Draw up questions in the order you plan to ask them. With background research, you should know the best ways to approach a topic. If the person is known to be evasive or taciturn, find out what you can about hobbies, opinions, interests, and so forth so that you can sweep the conversation along on topics of particular interest.

5. Meet your respondent. Repeat the purpose. "Sell" yourself and your

ideas again. Be enthusiastic about what you're doing. Use "icebreaker" comments.

6. Ask your first serious questions. Start with topics that reinforce the ego of the person being interviewed. Establish conversational rapport.

7. Proceed to the heart of the interview. Listen. Use "probe" (follow-up) questions.

8. Ask "bomb" questions if necessary (potentially sensitive or embarrassing questions). Save them for late in the session.

9. Recover, if necessary, from the effect of "bomb" questions.

10. Conclude the interview.

AN INTERVIEW CASE HISTORY

To illustrate these principles, imagine yourself assigned to write a news story about a police incident. Seems that one Mary Ann McQuillan was found lying unconscious near the Mercy Hospital emergency room bleeding severely from a stab wound. She was taken inside and given a blood transfusion. She's recovering satisfactorily this morning.

The police reporter might normally write this story, but that person is off on another case and the city editor—your boss—has turned it over to you.

Ms. McQuillan is a young writer who works as an unpaid volunteer in the emergency room to gather information for a novel she is writing about hospital emergencies.

So you have an interesting twist: She becomes an emergency case herself. What irony. Here is a step-by-step case history of the information gathering and interviewing processes involved.

Step 1: Define a Purpose

You can probably think of reasons *not* to do this story. It might exploit the victim. It might embarrass her. She might be hypersensitive. People are getting stabbed in River City all the time—why single out this one? Who cares, anyway? Why is it anybody's business but that of Ms. McQuillan and her hospital insurance agency?

Besides, how do we know she *wants* to be interviewed? (We never will, of course, unless we ask.)

All good points. All represent ethical considerations faced daily by reporters. The best reporters seem to be the ones who have thought about such matters and have come to the conclusion, with Oscar Wilde, that "there's only one thing worse than being talked about, and that's not being talked about."

To be effective, you have to believe that sincerely. That is, the more people know about each other the better humankind is served. We are journalists because we believe in free and open exchange of information. The fewer secrets the better. The more we are involved with each other—the bad and the good—the better.

Public knowledge is salutary; lack of knowledge is unhealthy. And, yes, even reports about incidents of crime are, by and large, useful to society. If we know that muggers inhabit the hospital parking lot—indeed, if we have it dramatized to us—we will be wiser for that knowledge. Knowledge is power and security. Lack of knowledge is weakness.

Some people will insist that what happens to people is of no concern to others, that people really don't care about anybody but themselves, that people are totally unwilling to share their ideas and experiences so others may learn, and that the less said about anything the better.

Those who hold such views would be wise not to become journalists.

But maybe Mary Ann McQuillan has ideas of her own. Her reaction should be respected. She has a right to say no to an interview. She does not have a right to keep her name out of the paper simply because, through no fault of her own, she has been thrust into the public arena by getting her name on the police blotter, a public record. This is the point where public authority—and the journalists—enter the picture.

Student journalists spend too much time worrying about what they *imagine* will be someone's reaction to being interviewed ("She probably won't want to talk about it"). That attitude tends to project itself in self-fulfilling prophecy. If you go in and say, "You wouldn't want to be interviewed, would you?" chances are you'll get your expected result.

The opposite is also true. Have you thought about the possibility that she might actually *want* to talk about it—at least to a reasonably sympathetic person?

It may depend on the approach. If you go to her hospital room arrogantly demanding, "Okay, Baby, you'd better come clean with the facts," she may balk. But if you come in and say something like, "I'm really fascinated with what you're doing—how you're researching your novel, why you work in the emergency room, whether the incident will impede your progress . . . ," you'll probably get along fine.

With that approach she may even welcome being singled out.

Call the approach "salesmanship." To sell, you must sincerely believe in your product.

So what's your purpose? Here's a possibility: *Ask her to describe her book and her research methods, particularly discussing the impact of last night's incident on her writing in general and her novel in particular.*

Think she'll "buy" that? Be optimistic. A reporter should be flexible, however, and review the purpose in mid-interview if facts and circumstances suggest a different kind of story.

Step 2: Conduct Background Research

For a news story, background research means reading documents and perhaps conducting preliminary interviews before going to the main interview. A good daily newspaper invariably has a library that contains clips of past stories indexed by topic. It also contains numerous reference books such as *Who's Who in America, Facts on File, Celebrity Register, Biography Index, Statistical Abstract of the United States,* encyclopedias, and many others. Sometimes an important and complex story will require extensive library research, including books and journal articles (more about that in Chapter 10). Your story on McQuillan is simpler; you can wrap up the background research with a few phone calls and a visit to the newspaper library.

The police reporter gives you these notes off the police record.

> Victim: Mary Ann McQuillan, age 30, 444 Eastway St., River City.
> Found unconscious by Dr. Douglas M. Duncan abt 40 feet from emergency room entrance. Time: about ten last nite.
> Purse with $20 and credit cards missing.
> Police report quotes her as saying, in substance, that she'd finished her work and walked to her car about 9:40. She fumbled for keys and suddenly "the world turned upside down." She was not aware she'd been hurt but felt dizzy and nauseous. Tried to walk/crawl back to hosp. "blacked out." Unable to provide description.
> Distance from her car (a VW Rabbit) to E.R. entrance: 175 yards.
> Contact: Sharon Oyama, E.R. Nurse. States that McQuillan works as Red Cross Volunteer as means of gathering material for novel, *Emergency!,* on hospital work.
> Treated for stab wound in left side. Underwent surgery & blood transfusions. By 11:15 vital signs stable.

Your next step is the *City Directory* where you find this entry:

> McQUILLAN, MARY ANN, emp Holcomb County, 444 Eastway, 277–8700

Next is the newspaper library. You ask the librarian for clippings under McQuillan's name. You also ask for a directory of county employees.

The county employees directory identifies her as a county extension agent in home economics.

The librarian hands you 30 clips of news stories in which McQuillan's name is mentioned. Almost all of them are stories about nutrition. She recommends that consumers buy local apples in the fall when they're inexpensive. She advises filling your freezer with chicken when it comes on the market at especially low prices in the spring. One memorable clip quotes her expressing outrage at the diets of Ponderosa College students she meets in the markets: "I just want to *scream* at them," she says. "For heaven's sake, put back the potato chips and the cupcakes and the soda pop. Fill your cart with fresh fruit, vegetables, and meat. But I know they won't listen. No wonder college students are always sick. Listen to me—I'm not even 30, and here I am, a meddlesome old lady."

One clip, dated 18 months ago, announces her joining the home extension staff. It gives some biographical information.

She was born in New Rochelle, New York. She's a graduate of Vassar College. She worked with Vista for a year in rural Kentucky. She worked for two different health agencies in Florida and North Carolina. She later got a master's degree in nutrition from Iowa State University. She joined the Holcomb County extension staff in home economics, her first job after graduation.

You do *not* find any information about her writing. That means you'll have to talk to someone. Two possibilities come to mind: the hospital and nurse Sharon Oyama. You call the hospital and talk to the director of community relations, Dixie Miller. Here are notes on the conversation.

1. The hospital's board of administration intends to discuss problems of hospital security as a result of the incident. Meeting scheduled for 11 A.M. tomorrow. There have been two previous instances of purse snatching in the parking lot in the past four months. This is the first injury.

2. McQuillan is a Red Cross "Gray Lady," hospital volunteers who perform nonmedical tasks such as comforting patients and running errands at busy times.

3. Miller knows nothing about the book *Emergency!* other than the fact that McQuillan asked for and received permission of hospital management to be in the hospital and observe medical procedures as research for her book.

4. The hospital has no objection to your approaching McQuillan for an interview. She cannot be reached by phone. She's in room 640, in good condition, and due to be released tomorrow. Miller says she'll tell McQuillan you're coming.

You make one more phone call, this one to nurse Oyama. You reach her at home. Unlike Miller, Oyama is not paid to talk to the media, and so your approach is different. You explain more. You "sell" more. Note the expressions of human concern in the following dialogue. Take note of the approach because you may find yourself using it a lot.

A. Hello.
Q. Sharon Oyama?
A. Yes.
Q. Hi, my name is Sam Dillard, a reporter for the *Express.*
A. Yes?
Q. I'm calling in regard to Mary Ann McQuillan. Do you know how she's getting along in the hospital?
A. Well, I understand that she's okay this morning. She's just fine.
Q. Oh, good. I'm glad to hear that.
A. Yes, well, she had quite a time of it.
Q. Yes, that's certainly true. I was sorry to hear that she was hurt. Anyhow, the purpose of my call is to find out a little more about her before I go to talk with her later this morning. The hospital is making it possible for me to talk with her about her work and her book. I'm curious and fascinated

by what she's doing. I understand that she is planning to write about her hospital experiences. Could that be true?

A. Yes, and she's. . . .

Yes, it's true that you already knew some of the answers. You are merely expressing a human kind of concern. You are also asking questions that are routine and easy to answer. These questions not only doublecheck your previous information (which could, after all, have been in error) but they help to put the other person in a "talking mode." In a good interview it's sometimes hard to tell where the small talk ends and the interview begins. If you're wise, you'll keep it that way. Never ask, "May I *interview* you?" That word is too formal and intimidating. Try asking, "Could we chat for a few minutes?" or "Would you mind answering a few questions?"

Better yet, don't ask for permission. Just start asking questions (but only after you have explained your purpose), starting with innocuous and pleasant ones. Let *her* decide when, if ever, you've gone too far. Do this gently, easily, and informally. Call people by their names (learn to pronounce them correctly), preferably their first names unless you sense that propriety dictates otherwise. Telephone interviews require that you "talk with a smile" since you can't smile in person. Respond with "uh-huh" or "hmmm" or chuckles or even humorous remarks when appropriate—all of these help to keep the conversation pleasant and informal. It also helps to ask questions that are provocative or challenging, but not threateningly so. Thus:

Q. Mary Ann's book sounds like a fascinating project. I wish I were writing it. I understand that novelists draw characters from real life—may I ask, are *you* in the book by any chance?

A. [Laughs.] Well. . . . Mary Ann did say that she had developed a character that sounds suspiciously like me. I'd been an Army nurse in Vietnam and I told her of some experiences that she found interesting, and so she's fictionalized all this and developed a character—and I do mean *character* [laughs]—who'd been an Army nurse.

Q. Character?

A. Well [laughs], let's just say this character in her book is a lot more amorously reckless than the real life prototype.

Q. Wow! I'll look forward to reading that book. I gather you've read some of the manuscript or she's told you about it?

A. Yes, she made quite a few candid admissions about this one character. . . .

Note how the interviewer carries the conversation along, picking items out of nurse Oyama's remarks to inquire about with follow-up questions. The reporter doesn't just read off a perfunctory list of questions and record the answers—a computer could do that. A preliminary interview such as this one helps you learn things that will assist in your main interview. It also offers bits of information that you might never hear from the main subject. Your story will benefit from observations from nurse Oyama such as these:

A. Mary Ann likes to be where things are happening. Just the other day she said a writer has got to be where the action is. You can't just sit in an attic and make up things out of your head.

Q. Sounds like good advice.

A. She also says a writer shouldn't be afraid to get a little mud on her boots or blood on her hands to get the *feel* of what she's writing. So that's why she works in the emergency room even though she hates it.

Q. *Hates* it?

A. She's too sensitive. She cries whenever there's a hurt child brought into the emergency room all bloody and pulpy. She'd make a lousy nurse. We had a little four-year-old girl who died in the emergency room a few months ago—a child abuse case. We all felt bad about it, but Mary Ann was literally sick for a week.

It is worth noting that nurse Oyama is talking quite candidly at this point—surprisingly so, it may seem, yet typically so whenever a reporter approaches an interview with sensitivity and sincere interest.

Steps 3 and 4: Request and Plan Your Interview

Normally you would request an interview first, then plan it. This case is different because you're simply going to show up at her bedside and hope she'll agree to talk with you.

Requesting the interview means "selling" her on your purpose. All the things said earlier about sensitivity and sincerity and gentle persistence apply here. It is highly unlikely that she will fly into an uncontrollable rage and scream at you to leave immediately. Simple social courtesy will cause her to invite you to talk for awhile, even if she's less than enthusiastic. If she's willing to take that first step, chances are that you can make the conversation so pleasant and interesting that she'll warm up within a few minutes.

Planning your interview means mapping out the areas you want to explore. Beginning reporters tend to write out their questions; experienced reporters usually prefer to jot down the areas they'd like to cover and to rely more on improvisation for the actual phrasing of questions. Often the first questions—the ones you thought up before the interview began—are not the important ones. A first question often elicits an answer that leads to a second question and then to a third and so on until you get to the heart of a situation. A good interviewer therefore will depend less on prepared questions and more on the ability to listen carefully and ask follow-up or "probe" questions based on what has already been said in the interview. All questions should be kept short and simple, also conversational and informal.

"Conversational" often means using your own experiences and feelings in the interview, though not to excess. Maybe you've always wanted to write a book yourself. Don't be afraid to say so. It will enhance the level of communication between you. But *do* avoid the common tendency of some people to ramble on about themselves. Keep your questions short and simple, and let the respondent do most of the talking. Here's one way you could bring yourself into the picture.

> Q. I've always wanted to write a book myself but I've been scared away by people who say it's a lot of hard work. Do *you* find it hard?

Planning your interview also means you'll build a basic pattern for the sequence of questions. They should be asked in a logical succession rather than helter-skelter. One good way, not always possible in time-limited news interviews, unfortunately, is a chronological sequence: "Start at the beginning and tell me what happened. . . ." Both interviewer and respondent can follow such a pattern, permitting the conversation to flow easily. A good reporter looks for adaptations of that structure. Here is a possible pattern of questions for your interview with Mary Ann:

Introductory questions

background of writing interests
connection between writing and hospital work

Substantive questions

describe novel
how balance writing with job in home ec
"mud on boots" philosophy

Possibly sensitive questions (save until late in interview)

use of stabbing incident in novel
lessons learned, if any, from incident

These areas represent the heart of your interview, not the start. The most important part of the interview is the first few minutes. Those minutes comprise a warm-up period during which you establish yourself as (1) a competent professional reporter, (2) a sincere and open-minded human being, and (3) a curious and interested person. A good interviewer gives thought to how the other person might feel. So before you can begin asking the important questions, you must go through the normal social amenities: How are you? How do you feel? You express sympathy for her plight; you comment on any personal effects you see in the room such as flowers or a book by her bedside.

Step 5: Meeting and Icebreaker Conversation

The dialogue that follows is hypothetical but it follows the actual course of many similar interviews. You arrive at the hospital room where Mary Ann McQuillan is sitting up in bed, her knees drawn up to support a loose-leaf notebook in which she is writing. She looks up as you enter.

Q. Hello. Are you Mary Ann McQuillan?

A. Yes.

Q. I'm Sam Dillard, a reporter for the *Express*. I believe somebody from the hospital told you I'd be coming by.

A. Yes. Come in. Sit down.

Q. How do you feel?

A. Surprisingly good, considering.

Q. Well, I'll bet the flowers cheer you up.

A. They certainly help. The chrysanthemums are from the people I work with, and the roses are from my fiance.

Q. You work with nice people. I was just reading about you this morning— about your job in home extension.

Step 6: Your First Serious Questions

Once this icebreaker phase is passed—it can run from a few moments to several minutes depending on circumstances—you can proceed with the business at hand. You start with a thorough explanation of purpose.

Q. Mary Ann—I hope it's okay if I call you by your first name—

A. Sure.

Q. May I take a moment to tell you what I'm doing?

A. Okay, uh, I don't know if I can be of much help, but—

Q. When I first heard about you, I felt sorry that you were hurt, then relieved to find that you were getting along pretty well this morning. Our paper's policy normally is to report briefly, if at all, these kinds of incidents. But your case is different. Fascinating, really. The thing about the book you're writing—is it really true that you're writing a novel about your experiences here at the hospital emergency room?

A. [Smiles.] Well, I'm trying.

Q. That's interesting, the way you try to get out and *experience* the things you're writing about. This is what really interests me: your book and your research methods. So if you're up to answering a few questions, I'd like to do a story about that for today's paper. By the way, your friend Sharon Oyama says hello. She also quotes you as saying a writer has got to be where the action is. Is that why you went to work in the emergency room?

Note that the reporter did not really ask for an "interview"; he did not even pause for a response to the phrase, "If you're up to answering a few questions." He merely explained his purpose and moved quickly to his first question. But examine closely that first question, for it is an important one, carefully calculated to accomplish two things.

First, it enters on the strength of a mutual acquaintance, the nurse, Sharon Oyama.

Second, it gives an example of the kinds of questions she might expect through the interview. So it is contrived to be a shade on the provocative side—an interesting and pleasant question to answer. Yet it in no way threatens her self-esteem. Even if she were toying with denying the interview, she might take the trouble to answer "just this one question." By the time she's done with that she may decide that she's having so much fun that she'd like to continue for "just one more." Reporters frequently encounter a source who flatly refuses an interview but answers "just one" question, then another, and then proceeds to talk for an hour, telling you everything you wanted to know—and then concludes with this apology: "Sorry I didn't have time for an interview."

Step 7: The Heart of the Interview

There's a lot of nonverbal "feel" in a good interview. The interviewer gauges the questions in accordance with this nonverbal response. A flushed face, raised eyebrow, averted glance, fidgety hands—all these indicate anxieties that should be coped with. Sometimes you speed up, or you slow down. Or you change the subject. Or sometimes you actually *increase* the anxiety, because anxiety can bring about revealing comments that might not appear when no emotional pressure is present. All this is people chemistry, and no formula exists for it.

One aspect of interviewing technique is the need to obtain both *general* and *specific* information. An article or essay or news story is built of generalizations supported by specifics. An example:

> *Generalization.* Mary Ann McQuillan believes writers cannot merely make things up out of their heads but must experience life to write about it.
> *Specific 1.* She works in the hospital emergency room two nights a week in search of experiences to write about for a novel.
> *Specific 2.* She cries when she sees an injured child brought into the emergency room.

An interview generally weaves back and forth between the concrete specific and the abstract generalization. Most interviewers have no difficulty with the generalizations, but sometimes they forget to ask for the specifics; the result is a vagueness and dullness in their writing. Therefore a good interviewer will ask for specific examples whenever a generalization comes up.

In any event, an interview is not always a smooth conversation. Sometimes you encounter resistance that you must try to overcome. Or you "negotiate," as the following segment suggests.

Q. Can you describe what your book is about?

A. Well, I've always considered it bad luck to talk about what you're writing before you've written it—an old superstition.

Q. Okay, I respect that. I wasn't thinking so much of a complete plot outline—I just wanted to get a general notion of how your experiences in the emergency room are showing up in your work. Sharon Oyama tells me, for example, that it contains one character she describes as a "recklessly amorous" Army nurse. [Note how introduction of the third party helps ease the interview over an apparent hurdle.]

A. [Laughs.] Yes, well, that's true. Of course, that character is *not* Sharon, but I did manage to use some of the wartime experiences she had told me about—not amorous experiences, mostly wartime medical emergencies.

Q. Is she the main character of the book?

A. No. The main thrust of the book is an emergency room situation that is quite tense and dramatic and goes on to involve a series of medical-legal problems. I don't want to be any more specific than that. In fact, I'm not sure I can be. I don't know myself how the book will turn out.

Q. That's interesting. You mean you just start your characters down a pathway without knowing precisely where it will end?

A. Exactly. You've discovered a terrible truth about me. All of my short stories have been that way. I figure if the endings surprise me, they'll surprise the reader.

Q. Will you actually incorporate into your book quite a bit from your emergency room work?

A. As background, yes. I see this as a kind of semidocumentary about hospital work. I detest novels that deal exclusively with intense personal feelings and leave out context. The reader ends up feeling he hasn't learned a thing except 37 ways to make love. I want to get my characters out of the bedroom once in awhile and into the emergency room. After all, that's where their work is supposed to be.

Such comments are interesting—unpredictable, in fact, and that's good. Already you can envision how your story is changing. Perhaps it will contain more about how a writer works than you had foreseen. Now that Mary Ann is talking about her philosophies of writing, this would be the time to bring up some questions about the irony of the situation in becoming an emergency case herself.

Q. Mary Ann, I'm interested in your views on research for a novel. You apparently told Sharon that a writer shouldn't be afraid to get mud on her boots and blood on her hands. Did you in fact say that?

A. Yes, but I didn't really have in mind my own blood, frankly. [Laughs.]

Q. And that is in fact your philosophy of research for fiction writing?

A. Yes.

Q. So that's brought you to the emergency room. Where else has it taken you? You've worked in coal mines, maybe, or shipped out on a freighter? [The citing of two specific examples is a means of both explaining the question further and soliciting specific examples in response.]

A. [Laughs.] Certainly nothing as exotic as that. But I once worked as a cocktail waitress one summer when I was in college, and I wrote a short story that was published in a little literary magazine about the guys who frequented the place, mostly truck drivers. It was kind of a rough joint and the way those guys *talked* to you—well, I'd never heard talk like that before. But after two months of that, *nothing* shocks me anymore.

Q. So your stories are based on those kinds of specific experiences?

A. Yes. I worked with Vista in Kentucky and published at least half a dozen stories based on that experience. My main subject is health and medicine—that's what I know best—and I've published both fiction and nonfiction.

Q. About how many articles and stories? [Always remember to get specifics lest the resulting article be unduly vague.]

A. About twenty. All but three were fiction, appearing mostly in little literary magazines like *Southern Review, Sewanee Review,* and *Fiction International.* I also wrote a factual piece for a now-defunct magazine called *Femme Fatale,* but frankly I'm not proud of that and would just as soon forget it.

Q. I gather your novel will use some material from the emergency room. Sharon mentioned a little girl who died.

A. In a way that's true, in another way not. There were five child abuse cases brought into the hospital during the time I was here. I know because I kept track. I keep a journal. It's true that I devoted some space to an episode of a little girl whose father abused her. But I didn't depict any one case. The girl in my story doesn't die—she merely ends up with a gimpy leg she'll have for the rest of her life.

Q. I'm curious—you said earlier that a writer must experience life, even blood and pain. Then you said you didn't really have in mind your own blood. Does that mean you see and use in your own writing only the pain that *other* people endure?

A. Not necessarily. I can experience real pain myself, such as when seeing a child hurt or killed, and I can write about that pain—

Q. But what about your own *physical* pain—hurt as you were last night? Is that particular experience usable in your book?

A. In theory, yes. But it's strange about that. I've shed buckets of tears for other people who have been hurt. Yet I spent an hour this morning trying to scribble notes about what happened to me last night. It just won't come. I don't feel anything at all. Nothing. Just numb. Empty. You know?

Q. You mean if somebody else had gotten hurt as you did, you could talk to that person and get a good grasp on how that person might feel, but you can't do it when that person is you? [Note how the reporter often paraphrases and clarifies the statements, partly to ensure that his understanding is correct and partly to carry the conversation along.]

A. Exactly. Strange, huh?

Q. No, I don't think it's strange, really, but it *is* interesting. A very *human* kind of reaction, I'd say. What do you suppose it means? [Note the ego reinforcement the interviewer provides at this point.]

A. Well, at the very least it's a fascinating touch of irony.

Q. Do you think it may take time for a kind of perspective to set in?

A. Maybe. I certainly hope it comes *sometime.* Not only do I *not* feel anything now, I didn't feel anything at the time. I didn't know I was hurt. I just felt sort of dizzy. I didn't even feel fear—it all happened so fast. I almost feel cheated.

Q. Cheated?

A. Yeah, like I ought to ask for my money back. I didn't get any usable material out of the experience.

This unexpected turn provides another, deeper element of irony for your story. Some inexperienced interviewers complain that they "never know what to do when an unexpected answer is given." The solution to that happy plight is quite simple: *treasure it!* It will add freshness and zest to your story because it portrays an interesting and unpredictable sidelight to human nature.

Step 8: The "Bomb"

"Bomb" means that in most major interviews you'll need to ask potentially sensitive or embarrassing questions, "tough" questions. A public official has made an embarrassing mistake, and you must inquire about it. Or you are writing about divorce and must interview people emotionally troubled by their marital breakups. Or you are writing a personality profile and need to explore the dark side of your subject's character. In these instances you'll have better success if you approach with caution, as you would a bomb.

The term does not mean that an explosion will inevitably occur when such questions are asked. Quite the opposite. By handling sensitive questions gently, so as not to jar feelings, you stand less chance of having the interview blow up in your face.

So *be gentle;* that's the first principle. A second one is *have a good reason for asking your sensitive questions.* Do you really need to ask them? If you have a good reason for asking, then you'll be able to explain it and thereby sell the need for it to your respondent.

The third rule is *wait until the mood is right.* A young man does not say "Will you marry me?" to a person he has just met. The same is true of a sensitive question.

When the mood is right, you should go ahead and ask your sensitive question, gently and in a sincere tone. The sincerity is hard to effect unless you *are* sincere, which means having a noble purpose for asking.

So sensitive questions are usually saved for late in the interview after good rapport has been established. Once the mood is right, however, don't pussyfoot. Don't show embarrassment with awkward preambles like, "Er, well, ah . . . I'm not sure how to ask this, but. . . ." For heaven's sake, just *ask* it.

Professional experience suggests several commonly accepted methods of getting into sensitive areas in interviews. Here are some of them:

Ask permission. A common conversational device is, "Mind if I ask you a personal question?" It works for interviews, too. Once permission is gained, you have a license to enter into the respondent's personal life. It helps if you accompany your request with an explanation: "Our readers need to understand more intimately the emotional trauma of divorce, and they can learn from your experiences. Your story will help people cope with their own emotions."

Attribute belligerent statements to someone else. You won't gain much asking of, say, a police chief, "Why are you such a hard-nosed, authoritarian so-and-so?" That will only result in defensive closure of communication. The question could be put more tactfully this way: "Chief, some of the city council members say they feel your methods are authoritarian and hard-nosed. Do you think they are fair in saying that?" If the chief gets angry, his wrath will be directed at them, not you.

Cruise to within striking distance and wait. Often you can approach a topic by indirection. If, for example, you want to ask a woman about a traumatic divorce, start by asking or talking about somebody else's divorce. The chances are quite good that she will volunteer to talk about her own divorce and you won't even have to ask questions. (You really aren't fooling her. When you start to talk about the other divorce, she'll realize that you've actually come to talk about hers. But the discussion of the other divorce gives her a chance to collect her thoughts and her emotions and thereby pick her own time and circumstances to bring up her own experiences.)

"Drift" into the sensitive area. In this instance the conversation under your subtle guidance casually drifts toward the sensitive area. Each succeeding question gets a little closer. If no resistance ensues, then you drift still closer. To illustrate, suppose you have reason to believe that Mary Ann McQuillan might not like to talk about her supersensitivity to the pain and suffering that she observes in the emergency room: She cries, she gets sick, indeed, "she'd make a lousy nurse." Here is one way a conversation might drift in that direction.

Q. I'm interested in a writer's *feelings.* I gather that you think it's especially important for a writer to *feel* things acutely.

A. Yes, the important thing in fiction writing, and a lot of nonfiction, too, is to try to convey feelings and how these feelings show up in your characters' actions.

Q. Is it possible for a writer's feelings to get *too* intense?

A. Oh, yes.

Q. You, for example, talked earlier about shedding "buckets of tears." [Note how the interviewer uses the respondent's own words, giving the impression that *she,* not the interviewer, introduced the topic.]

A. Yes, and I have, too.

Q. [Silence.] . . . [Silence is often the best question of all. A pregnant silence suggests the expectation of elaboration and willingness to listen.]

A. I mean, you can't very well see a four-year-old girl die a totally senseless and unnecessary death and not be affected.

Q. But you've observed nurses and doctors working in the emergency room. Have you thought about how they control their feelings?

A. Yes, I think it's a professional facade, almost like a surgical mask. I don't think a writer can do that and still be a good, sensitive writer.

Q. Nurses would make lousy writers, you feel?

A. And vice-versa. I would have great difficulty being a nurse. I'm interested in health and medicine, but the sight of blood makes me ill. . . .

From the above example it's clear that Mary Ann is talking quite candidly about herself, with only minimal defensiveness. This may not be due solely to the questions asked. Mary Ann may be answering to the nonverbal questions as much as or more than to the verbal. The nonverbal cues are signs of sympathetic and nonjudgmental listening and sincere interest. They are conveyed by eye contact, smiles, nods, erect and alert body posture. The opposite can just as easily dampen a conversation: averted glances, deadpan expression, slumped or back-leaning posture, and nervous mannerisms such as drumming fingers, doodling on notebook, or fondling your pencil.

If all else fails. If none of these suggestions works and you still feel that the "bomb" questions are important, then your only recourse is to go ahead and ask them. Do so with gentle persistence. Don't beat around the bush. If an explosion does result, try to be philosophical; you're still better off than a bomb disposal technician who experiences a similar failure.

Step 9: Recovery

Sometimes an exploding "bomb" so devastates the interview that it's useless to go on. You merely slink away as best you can. If, however, the rapport is not severely damaged you can make repairs by a little human reassurance. "You're only human," you tell the other person. "We all have problems like that. . . . You couldn't be a good writer if you didn't have those kinds of sensitivities. . . . What seems like a weakness is a strength in disguise. . . ." These comments may seem trite and platitudinous reading them here, but you'd be surprised how they ease you through a tense situation. Keep in mind one teacher's definition of a successful interview: a conversation from which *both* parties emerge with their self-esteem intact.

Step 10: The Conclusion

Many beginning interviewers are surprised to learn that they have more trouble ending an interview than starting one. How do you wind up a conversation that has become pleasant and stimulating?

You can start with a hint that you're about ready to close. One way is to ask permission. "It's beginning to look as if I have most of the answers I came for—may I take just a moment to go over my notes to see if there are any loose ends?" This gives both parties a chance to consider last-minute thoughts.

A second step is to ask if she has any final thoughts: "Mary Ann, I think I have the answers I want—but do you have any final thoughts on what we've talked about?" This often elicits answers to questions you didn't think to ask but probably should have.

It is prudent to ask permission to call back (by phone usually) if you need additional bits of information. You may have forgotten to ask an age or the spelling of a name or some other detail.

Finally, you should expect a pleasant afterglow at the end of a successful session. The notebook has been closed or the tape recorder has been turned off. The "ordeal" is over. Now Mary Ann feels she can just "chat" like normal people. It is here that some of the most unguarded quotes and anecdotes emerge. Do not try to write them down—why spoil the mellow mood? Just commit them to memory and write them down after you've departed.

POINTS TO REMEMBER

1. Interviewing is based on "people chemistry"; you can't always predict how people will react to situations or to certain nonverbal signals.
2. A good interviewer makes it possible for people to say what they really think, rather than feeling they must be on guard.
3. Reporting is four-fifths interviewing.
4. The best interviewers are open, sincere, nonjudgmental, good listeners.
5. You must believe in what you do, even "sell" yourself and your ideas if necessary.
6. A reporter must have a firm purpose in mind for the interview and must make the purpose clear to the source.
7. Preinterview research is vital.
8. Small talk at the beginning of an interview usually builds conversational rapport.
9. Approach sensitive or embarrassing ("bomb") questions with caution, patience, and sensitivity.
10. A pleasant afterglow often follows a successful interview; your respondent becomes unusually candid as you're standing at the door saying goodbye.

PROJECT

Interview a news source, someone who has been quoted in a recent newspaper story, and write a report on how this person feels about being interviewed and written about. *Purpose:* Gain experience in interviewing; also learn how the reporter-source relationship looks from the other side. *Suggestions:* Clip a local story from a newspaper and identify the person who appears to be the main source of information. Most sources will be public officials or civic leaders, and they are usually experienced interviewees. A few—subjects of feature stories or witnesses to an event—will be inexperienced. So your questions may be different depending on the experience.

Please make clear who you are when telephoning for an interview appointment. Explain why the interview is desired, what types of questions are likely to be asked, and why the interview is important as an educational project for the entire class. You could also suggest that the source may welcome a chance to comment on the performance of the news media. Management personnel at the newspaper might also be interested in seeing the results, so constructive criticisms might have some positive impact. It's important in any interview request to suggest *subtly* some ways in which the source might be "rewarded" for the time expended. Your source may derive satisfaction in being both an educator and a critic. Here are some questions that could be explored:

1. Generally speaking, was the experience of being interviewed and written about a positive or negative one? Why? What are some specific examples? (Positive experiences might be such things as pleasure in being interviewed by a sympathetic reporter, pride in having comments in print, favorable reactions of family, friends, neighbors, colleagues, and so forth. Negative experiences might include brusque or arrogant behavior of the reporter, frustration at inability to give good answers, misquotations or inaccuracies in the published story, unfavorable reactions.)

2. Describe the interview. (Please include background information based on the clipping.) Was it done by phone or in person? What were some of the questions and answers? Did the reporter take notes, use a tape recorder? Did the source feel comfortable with the interview? What problems, if any, were present (such as reporter asked dumb questions or loaded questions, failed to listen carefully, etc.).

3. Was the published story accurate, fair-minded, balanced, and complete? What specific problems can the source identify in the story? Can source suggest a cause of the problem (for example, reporter didn't seem to listen carefully and, sure enough, got the facts wrong). Did the story enhance or hinder any goals of the source or his or her agency?

4. What, if anything, would the source do differently next time?

5. In general, what has been the *continuing* relationship between the source

and all the news media? (This would not apply to inexperienced, one-time respondents.) On balance, has it been favorable or unfavorable? What kinds of items are not being covered by the news media but should be? What differences are apparent in the techniques and products of print media vs. broadcast? What suggestions can be offered for improvement? In all cases, please cite *specific* examples.

EXERCISE

From the details given through this chapter, write a story for today's newspaper about Mary Ann McQuillan. Here are some background details. She expects to finish *Emergency!* in about six months. It is her first novel. It is *not* under contract with a publisher, however. "With a first novel," she explains, "you have to write the whole thing first and *then* negotiate with a publisher." Does she plan to continue work in the emergency room? "Of course!"

Suggestions: This should be treated as a news story rather than a feature. Therefore the assault and its relation to her literary activities should be the main focus of the story. However, the distinction between news and features has become blurred, so a "feature" lead—the kind that focuses on a human interest angle—certainly would be appropriate here. You might practice writing a variety of leads. How about one that incorporates both the assault and the research for a book into the first paragraph? Or how about a short narrative, two or three paragraphs, that sets events into a chronological perspective? How about a lead that focuses on the "irony" of the writer's wanting to be "where the action is"?

9

Reporting from Observation

Reporting is more than attending press conferences and interviewing official sources. Some aspects of it are similar to the work of our fictional heroine, Mary Ann McQuillan. She, you will recall, is the fiction writer who, in Chapter 8, worked as a hospital volunteer to gather background for a novel. If a fiction writer will go to such extremes to inject reality into a novel, then "reality" writers should take note.

Reporters, too, can report from observation. Your press credentials entitle you to visit the athletes in the locker room, the cowboys in the horse barn, the beauty contestants backstage—all places the general public seldom sees. But you can move beyond mere observation. How about entering a beauty contest yourself? Or posing as a skid road derelict to see what the experience is like? Or serving time in the county jail?

When a new county jail opened in Eugene, Oregon, a woman reporter, Gail Bullen, arranged to have herself locked up overnight so that she might write a story about the experience. Her anxiety verged on panic the next morning when, by prior arrangement, she was scheduled to gain her freedom.

They didn't let her out at the scheduled time. None of the jailers that morning seemed to know of the arrangement.

The release did come eventually—within minutes, in fact—but not before the young woman was about to scream in anguish. Seems that some "friends" in the police department—where she had once worked in radio dispatch—had con-

Seattle Times sports columnist Steve Kelley watches
fans in the stands as the Seattle Seahawks
shut out the opposition. *(Photo by Matt McVay.)*

spired to give her a few uneasy moments, just to make sure she got an interesting
story.

In times past the writing of news was more rigid than it is today. It got so bad
that reporters complained that they couldn't even include a description of a
sunset—as in the governor driving off into a vermilion sunset—unless they could
get the governor himself to comment on it. The only descriptions commonly used
were cliches. Female murder victims were invariably "blonde, attractive," beauty
queens "shapely," fires "raging infernos," and young children "bright-eyed mop-
pets."

Today much writing contains better-considered description woven in as part of
the fabric of the story. Editors have come to expect it. Here is the opening of a
comprehensive story in the the *National Law Journal,* where the quality of news-

writing rivals that of any city daily. The article deals with the unique problems of prosecuting child abuse cases. The story's opening depicts an experiment to solve the problem of terrified children having to testify in open court:

> The witness box was empty. Instead, the packed Los Angeles courtroom audience watched a 5-year-old girl testify on a large TV screen placed before a podium from which lawyers asked her questions.
> The tiny witness could have been at home, or even in another state. She was in the next room.
> Washed in the glare of floodlights, the child was demure until questioning turned to details of her alleged molestation by an elementary school principal . . . charged with sexually assaulting seven students. The little girl, seated beside her mother, stared into space, then froze. "Your honor, we'll need a little more time," came the voice of the bailiff as the sound of sobbing arose. . . .

> —Mary Ann Galante, National Law Journal

WAYS TO USE OBSERVATION

Clearly, a good share of information gathering comes from observation. When we attend a meeting or a speech, we are reporting from observation. When we interview, we look for descriptive touches such as mannerisms or how the respondent fits the ambience of a scene. Does the famous actress, in the privacy of her home, look and act as she does on screen? Is she calm and relaxed in contrast to her on-camera pyrotechnics? Curious readers want to know.

Perhaps television has goaded print reporters into being more colorful nowadays. Speakers are permitted in news accounts today to pound the podium, pace the floor, perspire freely, or otherwise display some signs of life other than the words pouring out.

You can go from those descriptive touches all the way to full-fledged features based on extensive observation. The ultimate may be a dramatic personal experience such as having yourself locked in the county jail. One enterprising young woman even had herself hogtied to a telephone pole in San Francisco, just to see if anyone would come to her rescue. Someone did, but not until 110 cars had passed.

Observation lends a new dimension to reporting. No longer are you confined to delicate little events like press conferences and ribbon-cutting ceremonies. The whole world—big and dirty and even a little dangerous—awaits your literary imagination and your courage and energy.

* In Cincinnati a reporter hired out as a bar-girl, hustling drinks at a strip joint in nearby Covington, Kentucky. She claims she learned a lot about men in the process—mostly about what suckers they are for subtle come-ons that would keep the drinks flowing.
* In Chicago a woman posed as an ex-con looking for work (with little luck).

* In Portland, Oregon, a reporter spent two days alone on skid road. She panhandled for money, slept in a flophouse, even ate food from a garbage can.
* And in a classic Chicago example, the *Sun Times* purchased and operated the Mirage Tavern as a means of documenting the demands for payoffs by city inspectors.

Little has been written about these kinds of journalistic observation. It is to academic fields such as anthropology and sociology that we owe much of our knowledge of observation techniques. A standard procedure in anthropology, for example, is to live with the group under observation: Stay with it, adopt as many of its customs as possible, and try to fit in to where you are no longer a novelty. Most journalists lack the time and motivation for such a project. But journalism has produced some classic examples of reporting from observation.

George Plimpton's book, *Paper Lion,* is one example. The author trained with the Detroit Lions football team, and he ran five memorable plays as quarterback in an exhibition game (running the team backward instead of forward). "Participation," he concluded, "puts you in a privileged position which gives you a more acute view than if you had been up in the press box."

Other examples abound. Among them are Tim Crouse's *The Boys on the Bus,* about reporters on a Presidential campaign bus; Gay Talese's *Honor Thy Father,* about a Mafia family; and John Howard Griffin's 1961 classic, *Black Like Me,* where a white man posed as a Negro and traveled the South in the pre-civil rights era.

And feminist Gloria Steinem first gained fame when she posed as a Playboy bunny and wrote an article about her experiences for *Show* magazine in 1963.

Both Steinem and Griffin kept their identities secret so that their experiences would be equivalent to the people they claimed to represent. Griffin went to great lengths to darken his skin through drugs, ultraviolet lamps, and stains so that he could gain acceptance as a Negro.

Other reporters, making no secret of their identity, have slogged through the jungles of war with foot soldiers, jumped with paratroopers and smoke jumpers, bivouacked with troops on maneuvers, even traveled with bands of renegades (as, for example, Hunter Thompson's travels with a California motorcycle gang, depicted in his book, *Hell's Angels*). In Eugene, Oregon, reporter Mike Thoele was working on a series of articles about the local economy. His explorations led him to a group of unemployed drifters. When they said they were on their way to hop a freight train, Thoele decided to join them for a colorful account of what it's like to be on the road.

Traveling incognito is a delicious prospect for many reporters, but using your true identity can usually open more doors. You could visit an Army base by posing as a recruit, perhaps, but you wouldn't have much time to ask questions. But with your press credentials on the table, you can get around more easily, talk to more people, travel in all echelons of military rank. Naturally, your presence changes matters when people know they're being watched.

But people often talk more candidly when they know you're a reporter. That's because you have credentials for asking questions. As a bogus Army "recruit," your role is more likely to obey orders and keep your mouth shut.

Besides, people like to talk. They may not have all that much to hide. A reporter from the now-defunct *Oregon Journal* came to a college campus in 1968 amid much student strife and violence. She looked young, so she decided to pose as a student and nose around the student union. She discovered that students talked just as candidly when they discovered she was a reporter. Often more so. In such circumstances people often wonder why the questions. When they realize the questioner is a reporter, they *know* why. They'll speak candidly to a trusted interviewer.

Traveling incognito poses ethical questions, too. How much should you write about a situation when you've gained information by false identity? Reporters screamed bloody murder in Oregon when police posed as television reporters to extract an armed fugitive from a house. The cops promised not to do it again. Is it somehow more ethical when reporters strike similar undercover poses? Is it fair to quote people saying things they would not have said if they'd known you were a reporter?

Like all matters of ethics, the answers are neither simple nor clear-cut. Often they come down to weighing the public good against an individual's or agency's right of privacy. Your own sense of fair play must reign paramount.

Keep in mind that observation is merely *one* of the tools of information gathering (along with interviewing and documentary research). It is seldom a case of observing versus not observing. Rather, you incorporate observation into your daily work, keenly and systematically observing elements of the events and situations you cover. Sports reporters do this routinely; all reporters should. Go out and cover personally the next big fire in your community rather than merely phoning the fire chief.

Some people tend to adapt better to observation than others. Some are natural voyeurs. They love to play roles incognito. Perhaps it's fulfilling a fantasy.

TYPES OF OBSERVATION

It is largely because vague impressions make dull reading that we turn to observation. You must get into your notes and ultimately into your stories the most graphic and precise information possible. From what we know about observation through the literature of sociology and anthropology, we can draw some principles useful to journalism. Observation, most of all, must be systematic. First, consider the three basic types of observation: (1) participant, (2) nonparticipant, and (3) unobtrusive.

Participant Observation

In the purest form of participant observation, the reporter becomes a full-fledged member of the group or scene under observation. This was the technique used by John Howard Griffin in *Black Like Me* and Gloria Steinem in "A Bunny's Tale." In almost all such cases the purpose is to gain a journalistic insight into a culture group through membership in that group.

Here the ethical problems are the stickiest. Here, too, the rewards are highest. You can be the closest to the reality of any situation. In *Black Like Me,* Griffin dramatically discovered the reality—the anger, the hate—of the pre–civil rights South. You wonder, though, whether a talented black writer could have written that book. The answer is probably not. A writer who grew up white has a certain set of social expectations as a basis for comparison. This heightens the drama.

This purest form of participant observation poses difficulties for journalists because of time limits and because of stringent requirements for membership. Chances are you won't be accepted on a professional football team if you're a 90-pound weakling. Sometimes, though, the journalist's presence truly makes the story. So it was with George Plimpton's book, *Paper Lion.* He started incognito, but the team soon discovered his identity, perhaps because members wondered why someone so lacking in athletic talent could remain on the team. As it turned out,

Seattle Times reporters ride an "alternative" bus line for travel feature. *(Photo by Matt McVay.)*

the discovery didn't matter. It even made it easier for him to move freely among the players and ask questions.

In practice, then, the reporter's participant-observation techniques will likely fall somewhere between full participation and low participation.

If you're good enough to make the team with no quarter given—and that seemed the case with Steinem and Griffin—then you have full participation. Plimpton was kind of a half-participant. If he'd merely hung around the locker room, turned out for practice, and so on, he would have been a low participant.

Your own attitudes can make a difference no matter what the level of participation. Suppose you pose as a bar girl in a tawdry strip joint as a means of learning more about men. In the first place you meet only the kind of men who frequent such places. Second, you get one set of reactions if you behave as a temptress, a different set if you behave as a matron.

Participant observation, then, can be powerful and dramatic, but it has the potential for misuse.

Nonparticipant Observation

Most observation practiced by reporters is nonparticipant. Reporting from the scene of a fire is an example. So is watching brain surgery or standing by at the emergency room Saturday night waiting for the car wreck victims. So is attending a school board meeting or watching a football game from the press box. Or maybe you want a behind-the-scenes scenario, so you watch the game from the team bench complete with locker-room intermissions. You stay with your person or situation, openly asking questions and leaving no doubt about your journalistic status, even capitalizing on it.

You need to be careful, however, that you don't intrude too heavily on the scene, or worse, start to direct it. So enthralled are people at the prospect of publicity that they will do almost anything to accommodate a journalist. So what you get is a staged media event that bears little resemblance to reality. Then the whole point of observation is lost.

To be effective you must have as little impact on the course of events as possible. Do not make a nuisance of yourself with incessant questions and note taking. Suppose you are writing about scenes at the emergency room. Several nurses find a moment to talk candidly about their problems, their feelings, their ideals. They've accepted your presence by now. You no longer inhibit their conversation. This would be a poor time to whip out a notebook and start writing down everything they say. Learn to commit things to memory. Here, too, ethical concerns emerge. Use discretion on what you quote. You might quote directly the comments related to professional concerns—they're delighted that they managed to save a badly hurt patient, or they're downhearted to have lost one. But you'd be more discreet and circumspect in quoting purely personal comments about spouses, family problems, personal relationships, gossip, and so on.

Unobtrusive Observation

In the two preceding categories, people are aware of your presence though not always your identity. Unobtrusive observation, by contrast, operates on the mouse-in-the-corner concept. You are there in the singles bar listening to the conversations to pick up color for your article on single life. Or you're in a western bar frequented by cowboys, and you're picking up all kinds of colorful remarks about horses, gambling, and women.

Some observers—again, mostly those in academic pursuits—have developed methods to tally the results of unobtrusive observation. In one classic example, a social scientist tallied conversations overheard among people walking along Broadway in New York City. He found, among other things, that "talk of the opposite sex" occurred in 44 percent of woman-to-woman conversations but only 8 percent of man-to-man conversations.

Unobtrusive observation is particularly useful for background color: the spectators at the football game, the fraternity crowd at the kegger party, the rodeo cowboys at the bar. By careful listening you can pick up bits and pieces of talk that can be written up as a collection of conversational snapshots. With a system to tally what you hear, you can even pin it down with percentages: Talk at fraternity keggers is about sports (33%), beer (16%), women (24.6%), and so on. (Those percentages are pure fiction. Wouldn't it be interesting, however, to find out for real?)

PARTICIPANT OBSERVATION: A CASE HISTORY

An interesting example of participant observation is a young woman's role as "undercover student" at a 3,100-student high school in Albuquerque, New Mexico. In 1983, Leslie Linthicum, then 24, dyed a few strands of gray in her hair and spent eleven days sitting in classes, observing the drug scene, tuning in on student conversations, and, gaining a whole new youth vocabulary:

"He's so O.T.S. that she blew him off."

"Oh, wow, get real!"

Translation: (1) He's so "Out There Somewhere"—absentminded or otherwise vacuous—that she got rid of him, broke off the relationship. (2) Gosh, I'm having trouble accepting what you say.

Linthicum learned that the student body roughly divided itself between the Freaks and the Jocks, and that "Freak Wall" was a place outside the vocational building where the drug culture gathered to hang out, smoke, and talk of heavy metal.

She wrote a candid and provocative series of articles for the *Albuquerque Trib-*

une. Her accounts focused on indifferent teachers, on smoking in the girl's bathroom, on the ease in getting drugs such as ten hits of low-grade speed for seven dollars. She included many vignettes of student life such as this:

> Back in the English classroom of bubblegum chewers, the students are settled down and the class is told it must read the short classic, *To Kill a Mockingbird,* by Harper Lee.
> A dark-haired girl slumped in a desk at the back of the room mutters loudly enough for the class to hear:
> "You mean we have to read?"

A five-part series emerged from Linthicum's eleven days of participant observation. She described a videotaped lecture on rape (the advice was "go along with the attacker or you may end up dead"). She recounted a minor student-teacher conflict: A boy throws something across the room. The teacher orders him to move to the back of the room, and he responds, "Who pissed in your cornflakes this morning?" The teacher ignores the remark but later confides to Leslie, "This would be a good class if it weren't for about four people." A serious, college-bound senior remarks: "People talk so much, I just want to tell them to shut up." Teachers seldom lectured. They showed videotapes, filmstrips, or movies. They brought in guest speakers or gave exams or monitored "silent reading."

The series focused largely on the kinds of things that students seldom tell their parents. High school is a joke, some students said. A rigid social structure prevailed—you were a jock, a freak, or a "nothing." The series graphically portrayed drugs, drinking, lack of discipline, Mickey Mouse assignments, and general indifference toward education. She graphically dramatized some scenes.

> During SSR (Sustained Silent Reading) one morning, a slim, dark-haired senior—a frequenter of the drug-oriented Freak Wall outside the Vocational Building—discusses his experiences with "chocolate mescaline," a brown strain of the hallucinogen.
> "I took it and I was walking home and I saw my whole house melt," he tells a shaggy, sweatshirted classmate.
> The other student—also a senior—says he and a friend tried the drug recently and "just sat there on the beds staring at each other all night."
> "I don't like that," the first student responds. "You just sit there like a vegetable." After a bit of thought, he decides psychedelic mushrooms give the best high.
> "With mushrooms it's a body high," he says. "Mushrooms must be my favorite drug."

The series proved most controversial in Albuquerque. Critics charged that its vision was narrow and that its undercover methods were unfair. Why single out one high school among the several in the area? Linthicum got lots of phone calls, many of them obscene, a few even threatening.

Yet the articles prompted considerable discussion, even a spontaneous demonstration seeking to break down the social barriers cited in the article. Some teachers vowed to clamp down on classroom discipline, and several parents expressed gratitude for the candid portrayal of the school's problems. Linthicum became a minor media celebrity with eight radio and TV appearances, even though she was not admired in all quarters. One caller suggested the paper send an "undercover child" to the homes of students to investigate the home conditions that lead to problems in the schools. It's the homes that create the problems with wayward students, not the teachers, the caller said.

Some critics said that Linthicum could have gotten largely the same story by identifying herself as a reporter. Linthicum, who had changed her name and entered school with fake ID, disagreed. She and her editors thought that the known presence of a journalist would have produced a skewed picture of student life.

"Education is an important story but one that is usually bathed in rhetoric," she said later. "Taxpayers and parents, it seems, no longer have a clue about what goes on in the institutions they fund and trust with their children daily. I think the public deserves to have the doors opened for them, and that sense of responsibility as a reporter outweighed the skittishness I had about lying to get the story."

WHAT TO OBSERVE—AND HOW

Leslie Linthicum says she found the experience as "undercover student" emotionally draining. She wouldn't jump at the chance to go undercover again unless she felt the story was worth it. Reporting from observation, however, need not be limited to occasional special features. You can use it daily in your work. What, precisely, do you look for?

Detail. "Massive details dramatically employed make for a readable story," Associated Press reporter Hugh Mulligan wrote in an anthology titled *Reporting: Writing from Front Row Seats*. It is lively detail, he said, that makes a story "move off the page and into your mind and emotions." A St. Patrick's Day parade in New York City is an example.

> The drums coming through that canyon of office buildings made an echoing sound that you wouldn't remember later when you sat down to write unless you had written it down in your notebook. There were details that the eye could supply, too, and the nose as well as the ear. Was there enough breeze to make the flags flap? Was it so cold that the Cardinal had to sit under the blanket on the steps of St. Patrick's Cathedral? Could you smell the flowers just put out in the boxes above the Saks Fifth Avenue awning?

The best way to learn to observe is to heed Shakespeare: "All the world's a stage, and all the men and women merely players." A good writer can use the techniques of dramatization in writing about reality. To produce more systematic observations, separate them into four elements.

The elements are *setting, character, action,* and *meaning* (that is, purpose or plot). They form the acronym SCAM.

Let's look at the four elements in the context of a story titled "The Inside Job," by Robin Cody, in *Northwest,* the Sunday magazine of *The Oregonian* in Portland. The story portrays electronic surveillance methods used to catch dishonest employees in a department store. The job often requires them to play "burglar." At night, unseen, they must break into an attic or loft and set up video cameras to scan a cash register station or wherever suspicious activity takes place. They remain hidden there for hours, sometimes days, watching TV monitors whose cameras are trained on the suspects.

Setting

Descriptive touches of the scene provide a context for your story. Ben Miller and Susan Pafko, the surveillance team, find themselves in a dingy attic above the sales floor. These touches help set the scene:

> It's cold, dark and deathly quiet up here among the steam pipes, wires, vents and insulated ducts. Miller has set up his camera and monitor 50 feet or so from Pafko. A sneeze, or the creak of a piece of plywood spanning the joists could burn them.
>
> The anemic glow of the VCR monitor has a hypnotic effect in the dark and still surroundings. Pafko remembers emerging from one of the attic snoop coops to find herself amazed, *thrilled,* to see people and objects in real live color.
>
> Because of her build and agility, Pafko gets assigned to the toughest coops. Once they stuck her alone in the hollow metal oval above a shopping center entrance, a place in which nobody else could fit. The sound of automatic doors opening and closing vibrated right up her spine, and it was so cold that she had to take along a sleeping bag. . . .

A major feature story tends to employ more description than a simple news story, of course. Yet even straight news stories can benefit from touches of description—the flames and black smoke shooting skyward in the warehouse fire, the somber murder scene, the plush, carpeted board room where the details of a corporate merger were worked out.

And as a trained observer you will look for details that others may miss. At the scene of the big fire, run your eyes across every aspect and record everything in your notes. How high are the flames? The smoke? What color? How high is the ladder to the fourth floor? What equipment is in use? What do you hear and smell? Zoom in like a camera on specific details, such as the icicles forming on a firefighter's helmet or the battalion commander barking orders into the handset radio.

Descriptive detail is particularly useful in articles about people. The setting of, say, an important executive can speak volumes about character. He drives a ten-year-old car to work or, conversely, rides in a white limousine. He has trophies, plaques, posters, or particularly expensive furniture (or particularly cheap) on display. He wears a button that says, "It isn't creative unless it sells." All are clues to character.

Keep metaphors in mind. Figures of speech can add zest to your descriptions. What's it like? What's the person like? She's a bubbling brook, lively, energetic, talkative. Or he's Old Man River—deep, slow, placid, powerful.

Too much descriptive detail can get tedious, of course. Too little produces flat, colorless prose. So description comes more in touches than in long passages, and the touches help to set the scene and provide clues that graphically illustrate the topic or the personality. Here, for example, is how the *Wall Street Journal* opened a feature, published in 1984, about a salesman who travels through rural Idaho selling Apple computers.

> POCATELO,Idaho—A 1965 Ford Falcon rumbles down the road past grazing cows, muddy rivers and old wood fences. The car has 300,000 miles on it. Upholstery is ripped; the cigarette lighter, a radio knob and the interior light are missing. The needle on the broken speedometer bobs back and forth.
> "I get it down pretty close," says the driver. "I can usually tell I'm going 55 by how fast the telephone poles go by—except in places like this, where there aren't any telephone poles."
>
> —*Carrie Dolan, Wall Street Journal*

Such description alerts you to character. The salesman—whatever else he may be—certainly does not try to impress his rural customers with automotive glitter. Perhaps this tells us something about the nature of rural Idaho, too.

Character

Most articles involve people. So your observations will tell how they look and act. Here's what Robin Cody's article says about Susan Pafko, the store detective:

> Slender and agile, Pafko is wearing jeans, a plaid flannel shirt and oversized glasses. She might pass for a hip young single looking for a special on yogurt, except that she could get to milk products later today only by crashing through an acoustic ceiling tile. And she won't. Pafko does not make mistakes.

Observing character does not end with physical description. Mannerisms, habits, outward signs of character—all these help bring your person alive. In Cody's description of the two detectives we find contrasts:

> Miller, a gentle, dark-bearded fellow with soft, chocolate eyes, spends words reluctantly, as if each one were a collector's item.
> She talks; he listens. She worries; he reassures her with a nod. She makes the decisions.

Look for small details. How does your character walk? With a bounce? Briskly? What does he do with his hands when talking? How is he dressed? What about rings, tattoos? How about hair? How people feel about themselves and their world often shows in the way they fix their hair. Unconscious mannerisms can also illustrate character: She drums her fingers, bounces her foot while seated, pats her hair, paces the floor, grips the telephone with a choke hold, strokes her left elbow with her right forefinger, and so on.

Eventually you pick up clues to character. He is shy, indecisive. At the lunch counter he doesn't look at the waitress as he orders dessert, and he has difficulty making up his mind between cherry pie and cheesecake. He's anxious: Note the way he keeps looking at his watch. He's preoccupied: Several times people have had to shout to get his attention.

Often description accompanies action. Here's an example from the store detective article:

> In a couple of trips out to the dark parking lot, Pafko and Miller have loaded their equipment into Pafko's car, a dusty and cluttered 8-year-old heap that looks like a mobile shed.
> Pafko drives. Stopped at a light, she maneuvers her thin left wrist so that the streetlight hits her watch. 2:20 A.M.

Always be alert for specifics: times, numbers, colors, temperatures. How many cigarettes did the detective smoke? How many times did the speaker pound the lectern or use a certain cliche? How many miles a night does the cop walk on his beat?

Development of character, as both fiction and reality writers will confirm, is the most difficult aspect of writing. It's hard enough to understand the character, her motives, her goals; it's harder still to illustrate her on paper. The outward manifestations that you catch through observation certainly help. But the development of your character comes largely through action—what she does and says. Show your character and you allow her to speak for herself.

Action

Action tests the observation skills and also the insight of a reporter. Things happen all the time, but it's up to you to determine which actions truly help to characterize a person or situation. To do this you must understand the character, usually through research and preliminary interviews. You must understand well enough to recognize the significance of everyday happenings as they pass before your eyes. You say your celebrity character is insecure in ordinary situations? Then his indecision in ordering dessert is a scene worth recording in detail.

Tom Wolfe, author of *The Right Stuff,* uses the term "saturation reporting" to describe the act of observing people and events in action. You don't "fictionalize." You are present when revealing scenes occur.

Often the small, everyday happenings illustrate best, not the major crises. Here the store detectives plan their late-night break-in.

> Pafko is a meticulous planner, note-taker and list-keeper. "Jigsaw," she says.
> "Jigsaw," he answers. She checks it off her list.
> "Screws, ⅜-inch, flathead, 12."
> "Screws." Miller counts them. "12."
> For want of a single screw, Pafko knows, a job can be muffed.

How dull and flat the story would have been if the writer had merely alluded rather than illustrated: "Pafko and Miller ran through a checklist of equipment and made sure all equipment was present." Some scenes, because they vividly illustrate a person or situation, deserve to be lingered over. Others can be "flashed": summarized quickly through a flashby.

Meaning

Sometimes your observation can add to an understanding of your person or topic; sometimes it works the other way. Your understanding makes it easier to know the significance of illustrative scenes. Whichever way it happens, deriving meaning from observation is like arriving at a lead paragraph of a news story. Somehow you have to try to capture the essence.

The understanding of meaning operates on two levels.

The first is to make sure that any given scene clearly illustrates *something*—a shy, indecisive celebrity, the relentless quest for a certain personal goal, or anything else that's definite. The checklist scene cited earlier, for example, illustrates the precision by which the detectives plan a break-in, and the writer makes clear why: For want of a single screw a job can be muffed.

The second level of meaning is an overall thematic unity—the thing that ties all the elements together in your story. This is where you as a writer make some overall sense, some message, out of the account. It's where you try to answer the reader's question, "so what?" It will, of course, be based on more factors than observation alone.

And it's never easy. But it's a mark of a reporter who's gone beyond the simple news stories and is ready to cope with—and understand and write about—the complexities of reality. When you read some of the forthcoming chapters, notably the ones on features, comprehensive newsfeatures, and powerful writing, you'll gain further understanding on the uses of observation.

POINTS TO REMEMBER

1. Newspapers are using more vivid descriptive details in articles than ever before.
2. Reporting from observation ranges from touches of description in news stories to full-fledged "participation" stories such as having yourself lodged in jail overnight.
3. Observation produces vivid detail, color, and drama in news and feature stories.
4. "Undercover" observation poses problems of narrow vision and questionable ethics: getting information through subterfuge.
5. Observation is divided into three categories: (1) participant, in which the reporter actually

becomes a member in the activity; (2) nonparticipant, in which the reporter observes an activity; and (3) unobtrusive, or "mouse-in-the-corner" eavesdropping.

6. A New Mexico reporter who emerged from an 11 day "undercover student" assignment concluded that the experience was traumatic but worthwhile to get a valid picture of the culture.
7. Observation is not confined to "big" projects but can be used every day by reporters.
8. The main task of observation is to gather graphic, dramatic detail, which leads to colorful writing.
9. Details being sought in observation come in four categories (1) setting, (2) character, (3) action, and (4) meaning or "plot," all of which form the acronym SCAM.

PROJECT

Write a narrative feature for a campus or community newspaper about a person or group intensely involved in some activity. Base your article on both observation and interviewing. *Purpose:* Practice skills of observation. *Suggestions:* Choose a person who is so intensely involved in the activity that your presence will not affect anything. Here are some possibilities:

1. A colorful teacher in action in the classroom or leading a discussion.
2. An athletic coach or player in action during a game.
3. A police officer on patrol.
4. A cheerleader in action.
5. An aircraft controller at an airport control tower.
6. A theater director with actors backstage or in rehearsal.
7. A geology student or teacher on a field trip.
8. A student leader in action, such as presiding over a meeting of the student senate.

When you approach a person with a request to do an observation interview, explain precisely what you plan to do and the time you'll need. Success depends on your ability to fit in—to establish an easy, informal relationship with the person and others who are part of the scene. In short, this is not a typically brief question-answer session. The project normally encompasses four stages.

1. Preinterview research.
2. Preliminary interviews. You must learn enough about the topic and person to know what scenes may be significant.
3. The see-it-in-action stage: the game, the field trip, etc.
4. Follow-up questions, the ones you couldn't ask while the action occurred. Sometimes, of course, you can ask during breaks in the action.

10

Using Documents and Numbers

The faintest of ink is superior to the best of memories. Wherever you turn as a news reporter, you constantly confront the past. In doing so, particularly the distant past, nothing beats recollections written on paper. To illustrate, consider the prospect of once again writing about Mary Ann McQuillan. Remember her from previous chapters? She's the nutritionist and part time author who got mugged in the hospital parking lot.

Even as a hypothetical character, she plays an important role in this book. She demonstrates the repetitive nature of news—the way people and situations recur frequently in public affairs. Often ordinary people get caught up in news events through circumstances over which they have little control. Reality is like soap opera.

McQuillan's role as a journalistic guinea pig demonstrates another point central to this chapter: Newsworthy people and agencies invariably leave behind them a "trail of paper." All of us leave some paper—records of birth, marriage, employment, education, real estate transactions, voter and tax activities and, ultimately, death. Newsworthy people leave more paper than most of us.

THE NEWSPAPER LIBRARY

Take Mary Ann McQuillan, for instance. Already your newspaper has several clippings on file in the news library, the department once irreverently called the morgue: the file of dead stories. Today we call it a library, and we treat it with more

(Photo by Randy L. Rasmussen.)

respect. A good library is invaluable to reporters because it keeps track of the paper—clips from prior stories along with other useful documents—on countless thousands of persons and topics.

If the mayor of River City suddenly toppled over dead—thus unavailable for an interview—you'd turn to the library. There you'd find biographical background. There you would look for the clips recounting the problems and highlights of the mayor's career. Some newspapers even plan ahead; they've already written obituaries on important people and stored them in the library against the possibility of sudden demise close to a deadline. If the library is a good one, it will have other research materials on hand: encyclopedias, books of quotations, indexes, and other reference works useful to journalistic research.

Suppose now that Mary Ann McQuillan becomes nationally famous. Suddenly her paper trail becomes a superhighway. Assume for the moment that her novel, *Emergency!,* has been in print for four weeks and has just made the *New York Times* best-seller list. She's become the toast of the literary world. She's appeared on *Good Morning America* and has even traded quips with Johnny Carson. *Newsweek* hails her work as a "significant new form of documentary drama." *Time* insists that she is a writer worth watching. The *New York Times* and the *Washington Post* have written profiles on her. Paperback publishers are bidding on the reprint rights, and movie makers are debating whether Alan Alda or Robert Redford will play the main character. McQuillan herself, meanwhile, is on a 30-city promotional tour.

Wow. Such things do happen—success stories that make great news copy. That it should happen to a River City author is truly splendid for the hometown paper.

THE USE OF DOCUMENTS: A CASE HISTORY

Let's assume that you're going to write a story about McQuillan's success as an author. You'll start with the clips. They will remind you of what she has done and said in the past. That in turn will suggest what to ask in a new interview.

In Chapter 8 of this text you can discover a few of the items the library clips would reveal. You can review the parking lot incident, her work on the novel, her concern about the eating habits of college students. You'll even find comments about her philosophy as an author—the "blood on your hands, mud on your boots" remark. In the real world, she would also turn up in reference works befitting her new status as a national celebrity. Consider what this has done to the trail of paper.

1. More clips in your own news library.
2. Numerous promotional releases from the publisher, not to mention the book itself and its promotional dust jacket.
3. Clips and tearsheets from hundreds of book reviews and articles in national magazines and newspapers in other regions.
4. Excerpts of book reviews from the reference work, *Book Review Digest.*
5. Eventual if not immediate listings in such standard references as *Who's Who in America* or *Contemporary Novelists.*
6. Biographical references such as *Current Biography, New York Times Biographical Service,* and *Biography Index.*
7. Listings of articles published about her in such indexes as *Readers' Guide to Periodical Literature, New York Times Index, Business Periodicals Index,* and others.

New journalistic installments invariably build up from the documents of the old. That is, the new, celebrated Mary Ann McQuillan can be interviewed more effectively if you tap the issues from the past and inquire as to how they fit in the new circumstances. How does she feel about "blood and mud" today? Has she compared notes with other authors? Does Norman Mailer agree? How about John Updike?

Sometimes you may write extensively from the documents themselves. A biographical profile might probe into what the literary critics are saying about our heroine, what she has said about herself in previous articles, and perhaps—with her permission—even what she has said in private correspondence or her journal. If you had no opportunity to talk with her personally, you could still write a good piece about her from these sources alone.

THE WIDE WORLD OF DOCUMENTATION

The foregoing account barely taps the vast reservoir of documents. Consider these additional sources.

Annual reports. Just about every agency and organization puts out an annual report. They range from glossy reports published by corporations for their stockholders to simple statistical recountings of a year's activities in a local governmental agency such as the sheriff's office or the fire department. They often make a good news peg for writing about that company or agency. Collecting them year by year in the library can produce useful trend stories as you compare the most recent report with those of earlier years.

Court records. With few exceptions, papers that accompany court proceedings are open to the public. They usually are scanned by journalists on a regular basis, for they bring news of major lawsuits, criminal indictments, grand jury reports, judicial opinions and decisions. Some enterprising reporters have tallied several years of records for interesting trend stories and investigative reports.

Police records. They're the source of most crime stories. As shown in Chapter 4, much police reporting starts with the police daily activity records, proceeds through incident reports, arrest reports, and, ultimately the court records. Police records are also the source of crime statistics that show up in annual reports and in national records. They can be used by enterprising reporters working on special projects such as identifying high crime areas or assessing highway safety (finding the ten most dangerous intersections in the city, for example).

Research reports. Much research data pours out of government agencies, colleges and universities, private research organizations, school districts, special-interest organizations, political offices, associations—the list could go on. The federal government is among the all-time great publishers, with a backlist of some 50,000 titles on all topics imaginable. Academic and professional journals can enlighten you on esoteric topics ranging from range management to sexual behavior, and most of them are probably in your college library. Even graduate student theses provide a little-known but rich source of research. One reporter, seeking to explore the rate of progress of college athletes toward their degrees, was surprised to find that precisely the same topic had already been taken up by a former UCLA fullback in his doctoral dissertation.

Real estate records. You can find out, usually through the county clerk's office, who owns what property, what it's worth, what mortgages or liens exist, and, in the case of land sales, who's selling to whom.

Tax records. These include information on tax valuations and actual taxes paid for individual properties, also statistical compilations of tax rates. The information is a little tedious but important for taxpaying citizens. Such documents are often the source of trend stories, such as higher taxes or the existence of wide disparities among taxing districts. In most states, individual property tax records are open for public inspection. Federal income tax records are not open, however.

Business records. Building permits, licenses, assumed business names, reports of safety and health inspections, articles of incorporation or dissolution, partnership registration, securities registration, product liability insurance claims, energy facility site applications, solid waste landfill permits—all these and more are on the public record.

Vital statistics. Birth, marriage, divorce, and death records are kept by various agencies, and they're compiled annually by each state.

Campaign spending. Most states require candidates for public office to file such information as the names of members of the campaign committee and details of campaign contributions and expenditures. Political action committees and lobbyists must likewise file statements.

Personal records. A reporter need not be limited to public records, of course. Authors write book-length biographies of people long dead largely through the paper trail. That trail includes personal journals, private correspondence, memos, news articles, tape recordings, and similar sources. Dramatic news articles have been written from journals of deceased persons: a teenage drug addict who died of an overdose but kept a journal depicting his private torment, a high school girl who committed suicide but left a trail of letters and poetry sent to friends. Stories based on such documents can be most revealing, particularly when supplemented with interviews with friends and relatives. These personal documents are usually not open to the public, however. Permission of the author—or the family of a dead person—must be obtained to quote from them.

The list could go on—military records from the Pentagon, the Veterans' Administration, vehicle records, charity records, books, school and college yearbooks, manuscripts of speeches, preliminary drafts, committee reports, petitions, advertisements, videotapes, pamphlets, handbills, flyers. On one college campus, an archivist kept all the radical literature from the era of student revolution. Chances are that journalists and historians yet unborn will be glad he did.

DATA-BASE RESEARCH

A few electronically advanced newspaper libraries have the paper's previously published articles in computer storage. Enter the name Mary Ann McQuillan into a computer search function and you get a list of all the stories in which her name appears. Maybe you want just the ones that discuss her writing, so you ask the computer to locate the stories in which both the name and some other key word ("novel" or *"Emergency!"* or "writing") appears.

A major advantage of computer research is the astonishing speed and flexibility of the equipment. It can scan thousands of documents in mere seconds, fishing out material that might take months if done by reading. You are not limited to the holdings of the hometown newspaper, for the search can be nationwide.

If the newspaper subscribes to a national data-base such as Nexis, Vu/Text, or CompuServe, you can ask for stories in which McQuillan's name appears and pick them up from all over the country. We know that she has appeared in the *Times*, the *Post*, and several magazines. Nexis, the so-called Cadillac of the data-base industry, contains the full text of 25 newspapers, including the two cited above, plus 100 magazines and newsletters. Sitting in River City, you can quickly pull up exotic kinds of information unheard of in the more traditional methods of research.

Use of imagination in selecting the key words can lead to exotic results. One researcher entered the words "Hamlet" and "skull"—and found several instances where people had bequeathed their skulls for theatrical productions of Shakespeare's *Hamlet*.

In 1984 about 1,300 data-base subscription services were available, most of them specialized in areas ranging from agriculture ("AgriStar") to state legislatures ("Legislex").

WRITING FROM DOCUMENTS

Documents are but one of the three sources of newsgathering (the others are interviewing and observation, Chapters 8 and 9). Normally you will combine documentary material with information from the other sources and then begin a process of synthesis, that is, putting it all together, determining the essence of the material, assembling it into a coherent whole. You still have to provide a good lead, paring it all down into a few words, even if you have assembled an astonishing amount of trivia.

It's never simple. These suggestions may help.

1. *Synthesize.* Seems as though nobody writes "short" these days. Reporters have to learn to read fast and glean the essence of the document quickly. A 500-page engineering report can be scanned in mere minutes, however, if you turn to the "Summary and Conclusions" statement at the back. You can then seek out material that supports the summary. Often the two news essentials in this type of document are *money* and *service* (or maybe *impact*). How much will it cost? Who pays? Where's the money coming from? What will it accomplish? How many people will it serve, how can it help, what problems will it solve? Who, if anybody, will be hurt, disadvantaged, or otherwise bothered by it?

2. *Supplement.* Should you not understand something, ask questions of its author or some other expert. A controversial document might require interviews covering many points of view.

3. *Avoid jargon.* Documents are invariably steeped in the jargon of the profession or trade from which they derive. Lawyers talk of writs of mandamus, doctors of postmyocardial infarctions, and English professors of Joycean epiphanies. It's fun to show off your knowledge when you first learn the meaning of these terms, but your readers will be served better by translations into ordinary English.

4. *Use quotes sparingly.* Using long stretches of material in direct quotation may make your job easier, but it will make your readers' job harder. Used judiciously, quotes can add life and color to your story. But long quotes tend to bore, even confuse, your readers. Use caution in quoting copyrighted material without permission; short fragments quoted in support of your own concepts are usually okay, but extended quotes may require permission of the copyright holder.

5. *Use numbers*—graphically but sparingly.

6. *Attribute.* Quote documentary sources just as you would interview sources.

7. *Add people to your statistics.* Good reporters seek out flesh and blood examples of what the statistics show. If the figures suggest that a certain percentage of high school students are alcoholics, show your readers a live example, even if you can't reveal the name.

8. *Remember the "bottom line":* how the material relates to your readers' lives. Don't say the school board passed resolution 311-C calling for a tax levy of $16.37 per thousand dollars of assessed valuation of real property in the City of River City—say that citizens will be paying higher taxes next year.

INVESTIGATIVE REPORTING

Think of the term *investigative reporting* and you envision reporters getting the goods on crooks, shady dealers, scams, and coverups in high offices, starting with the Watergate scandal of the early 1970s. Perhaps this branch of journalism has matured in subsequent years. Today it has broader meaning: major journalistic projects involving lengthy paperwork and multiple interviews, perhaps by a team of reporters rather than just one. And the topics no longer focus on catching crooks. It was a three-person team that in 1980 produced a monumental report on Philadelphia's ailing public school system.

This project, published by the *Philadelphia Inquirer,* consumed fifteen months, involved hundreds of interviews with school patrons, teachers, and administrators. It even provided statistical analysis of such materials as the 7,200 contracts let by the school board over a five-year period, a project so complex that it took two months just to enter the data into a computer.

Investigative reporting often means the newspaper itself produces the documents rather than depending on possibly self-serving industries or public agencies. With its own computer, the newspaper can reevaluate statistical materials. In both Philadelphia and Fort Lauderdale, Florida, newspapers gathered thousands of court records and ran them through computers to show the justice system's biases. In both cases the statistical analyses suggested that the justice system clearly favored the white and the wealthy—and in Florida it also favors those on drug and sex charges. In Philadelphia, statistics showed that certain judges with reputations for leniency were actually strict. And Republican judges gave longer sentences than Democratic judges.

USE OF NUMBERS

Central to your use of documents is the ability to understand numbers. Documents increasingly take the form of vast tables of statistics. A lot of routine news today comes as numbers. We no longer say it's going to rain tomorrow; we call it an "80 percent chance of rain." Inflation is up 3.5 percent, crime down 2.8 percent. You also can make your reports more definite by inserting numbers. Samples:

> *Weak:* There were a lot of people at the concert.
> *Better:* Some 5,000 people attended the concert.
> *Weak:* John Smith, retiring police officer, figures he's worn off plenty of shoe leather in walking his downtown beat.
> *Better:* John Smith . . . calculates he's walked 80,000 miles in the 40 years that he's patrolled downtown River City. (Ten miles a night, 200 nights a year—figure it out for yourself.)
> Better yet: Smith figures he's walked the equivalent of 26 times across the United States—80,000 miles . . . (or a third of the way to the moon, or three times around the world at the equator, etc.)

Sometimes, though, numbers can confuse rather than clarify.

> In Precinct A, Jones leads Smith 4,567 to 2,355, while in Precinct B, Jones leads Smith 2,331 to 1,599.

It's clear enough that Jones leads Smith in both precincts but too many numbers get confusing. Reducing the numbers to a common point of comparison—a ratio, for example, or a percentage—the point becomes more clear: Jones has 66 percent of the vote in Precinct A and 59 percent in Precinct B.

Journalism newswriting instructors report that their students are a little paranoid about numbers, which is unfortunate. The dimensions of news invariably comes in the form of numbers—budgets, taxes, inflation rates, crime statistics, public projects, engineering reports, economic progress (or lack of it), sports statistics. You can hardly find a segment of a reporter's work that doesn't get reduced to numbers. One reason is that, used boldly but sparingly, they convey impressions in less space than the other devices such as the quote or the anecdote. In the hands of a number-savvy sports writer, exciting sports events emerge graphically. Note how clearly the statistics convey the dominance of one football team over the other in this report:

TAMPA, FLA.—The Philadelphia Stars routed the Arizona Wranglers 23–3 Sunday night in the second United States Football League championship game.

The Stars, 19–2 this year and 35–6 for two seasons, gained 414 yards against the league's best defense and dominated in every phase. Philadelphia led the Wranglers in first downs, 23–7; rushing yards, 256–72, passing yards, 158–47, and possession time, 43:19 to 16:41.

—Gordon Forbes, USA Today

Note how we tend to characterize people through statistics. Athletes are, of course, among the prime candidates: Running back O.J. Simpson has a lifetime rushing total of 11,236 yards, 4.7 yards per carry. Babe Ruth had a lifetime record of 714 home runs, but Hank Aaron beat that with his lifetime tally of 755. And so on. Even in describing a writer we often cite numerical references such as "author of ten books and 1,000 magazine articles." Descriptions of business tycoons often speak of their millions of dollars of net worth, their six-figure salaries (averaging $419,250 in 1983), the dimensions of their domain (18,000 employees, 30 branch plants worldwide, etc.).

What You Should Know About Numbers

A reporter with little or no knowledge of numbers will be seriously disadvantaged in journalism today. Courses in elementary statistics, college-level algebra, and the rudiments of computing would seem to be the minimum for getting along in today's journalistic arena. Take even more math and science courses if you plan to report on technical subjects such as science, medicine, business, economics, and engineering.

Probably the first thing a reporter needs to know is the use of simple numerical designation, such as percentages, averages, medians. If a community's population increases from 500 to 600, what's the percentage of increase? If you have five people whose ages are 3, 5, 7, 9, and 33, what's the average ("mean") age? What's the *median* age? (Answers: 20 percent, average age 11.4, median age 7).

Those are but a start. Heed meanwhile the prophetic words of H.G. Wells, the early science-fiction writer: "Statistical thinking will one day be as necessary for efficient citizenship as the ability to read and write." Perhaps that day has come.

Misuse of Numbers

As noted, numbers are so specific and graphic that they tend to have a powerful and convincing effect on your readers. Numbers are a little like great fiction—so graphic that they create a suspension of disbelief. Journalists sometimes misuse them either through ignorance or—on rare occasions, perhaps—by deliberate attempts at deception. It was Benjamin Disraeli, the nineteenth-century British prime minister, who identified three kinds of falsehoods as "lies, damned lies, and statistics." The lesson is that journalists must use caution when supplying numbers and statistics. Do not fall unwitting prey to those who would misuse figures to further their own biases. Politicians may well be the worst; notice how the opinion polls released by the candidates always favor their side.

A classic example of misuse of statistics occurred in 1966 when a newspaper reported that an unusually high number of births had occurred during a 36-hour period in New York City hospitals precisely nine months after the city had suffered its major power failure—millions of people without electricity for as much as 12 hours. The implication was that, deprived of TV and similar diversions, residents had simply retired to bed in heterosexual pairs. But the newspaper had checked only seven hospitals. Later 100 area hospitals were tallied, and the new figures showed the number of births slightly lower than normal.

Similarly, a typical mistake is to call a few people and present those few as representative of a larger group.

"People in River City favor gun control legislation," suggests the lead to your story. But you called only 15 people—friends and acquaintances, perhaps—and you made no attempt to select people who represent various economic and social segments of the city's populace. About the best you can say is that the conclusion represents the collective view of the 15 you talked to. Don't be too sure even about that. Some reporters find that an astonishing number of the people they interview agree with the reporter's own view. Reporters are only human, and they are not above subtly, perhaps even unconsciously, telegraphing their own views by the way they ask the questions or listen to the answers.

Two books, both slim paperbacks, are particularly useful for reporters who deal with numbers. One is called *Newsroom Guide to Polls & Surveys*, the other *How to Lie with Statistics*.

"The magic of numbers brings about a suspension of common sense," suggests *How to Lie*, which proceeds to document the many ways in which figures can be manipulated to show what an interest group wants to show and hide what it doesn't.

It may be impossible in just a few paragraphs to provide the level of sophistication needed to cope with numbers. Perhaps most important is to exercise a healthy skepticism about granting a scientific validity to horseback number crunching, that is, informal manipulation of statistics. An example would be a newspaper that runs a coupon in its pages asking readers to "vote" or express opinions on some civic issue such as capital punishment. From among the (let's say) 100,000 subscribers, 1,500 coupons are mailed in (at the readers' expense), and the tally shows that 898 favor the death penalty for anyone convicted of first-degree murder. So along comes a big headline.

59.8% OF RIVER CITY RESIDENTS FAVOR DEATH PENALTY

Another spurious statistic is on the loose. The problem is that the opinion is valid for only the 1,500 who took the trouble to respond—a "self-selected sample" of people interested enough in the issue to clip the coupon, fill it out, and spend 22 cents postage to send it. In other words, it's a group of people who have strong opinions about capital punishment.

Here are a few of the most common ways that the reporting of numbers can lead to inaccurate reportings.

Statistical error. Several possible sources of error exist in a poll, including such things as sampling error, biased questions, faulty interviewing, and inaccurate recording of answers. Most polling organizations report a sampling error estimate along with the poll's findings.

For example, a research firm may report that a political poll shows candidate A ahead of B "50 percent to 47 percent, with 3 percent undecided," and that sampling error is 3 percent. This means the chances are remote that the reported percentage for a given candidate is off more than 3 percent in either direction. Even so, candidate A's true percentage may be anywhere from 47 percent to 53 percent and candidate B's may be anywhere from 44 percent to 50 percent. Obviously, the reported lead of candidate A may be more apparent than real, and a reporter should make readers aware of that fact.

Cause-effect inferences. A college student once ran a statistical comparison between weather and violent crime. The student found an interesting and statistically valid comparison: In U.S. cities where it snowed the most, rates of violent crime were the lowest. Can you therefore conclude that snow prevents or dampens violent crime? No. Other sociological factors are involved.

Errors in math. A lot of journalism students are notoriously deficient in the rudiments of arithmetic. One student insisted that an increase from 50 to 60 was a "10 percent increase" (it's actually 20 percent). Another figured that a price increase from 10 cents to 15 cents was a "five percent markup" (it's a 50 percent).

The anecdotal approach. Case studies can be a powerful device for getting your readers interested, but don't assume that a small set of experiences adds up to a valid statement. If you interview a dozen convicted murderers and find that seven of them hated their mothers, it would be unwise to assume, in the absence of supporting scientific evidence, that most murderers hate their mothers or, worse, that hating your mother makes it more likely that you'll commit murder. Scientists call this the "anecdotal approach," and they quickly dismiss its validity, no matter how dramatic the material.

POINTS TO REMEMBER

1. Documents are essential to newsgathering, one reason being that "the faintest of ink is superior to the best of memories."

2. Everyone leaves a "trail of paper"; documents trace our very existence and the major events of our lives.
3. The newspaper library itself is an important source of journalistic research materials.
4. As people become celebrated, they show up in important reference books such as *Who's Who in America.*
5. An important new research tool is computer access to national data bases that contain full files of many newspapers, magazines, and newsletters.
6. As documents tend to be plentiful and lengthy, skills at synthesis are necessary when writing.
7. Investigative reporting involves tracing and assembling numerous documents, even tallying such things as judicial decisions to discover trends.
8. Journalists today need to understand statistics, percentages, averages, and similar uses of numbers because of their extensive use in documents.
9. Caution must be used to avoid misuse of statistics.

NUMBERS QUIZ

Pass this quiz and you won't qualify as a math wizard, but at least you'll have taken the first step. Calculate the following and then check your answers in Appendix C.

1. A city's population has increased from 566,876 last year to 603,119 this year. What's the percentage of increase?
2. Another city's population went down from 109,788 to 101,400. What's the percentage of decrease?
3. A city with a population of 550,000 had eight murders last year. What is the crime rate for murder (number of murders per 100,000 population)?
4. In a city tax levy election, 45,000 voted yes, 38,976 voted no. What was the percentage of yes vote?
5. Ages of the employees at XYZ Company are 21, 21, 24, 54, 19, 21, 34, 62, and 18. What are the mean, median, and mode?
6. A baseball player has been at bat 34 times and made 11 hits. What's his batting average?
7. An airplane is 38 feet long with a wingspan of 47 feet. A scale model of the airplane has a wingspan of 33 inches. How long is its fuselage?
8. An environmental lobbyist figures Senator A voted "correct" (in accord with the lobbyist's views) on 7 out of 18 issues. Senator B voted correct in 6 out of 13 issues. Senator C voted correct in 18 out of 27 issues. Rate the senators from "most correct" to "least correct."

11

Cultivating News Sources

Where does news come from? How do you get it? Do you just wander through the streets until you happen across it, or what? Whom do you talk to? What do you ask? Do you just ask, "Got any news today, sheriff?" And what is it, precisely, that you're looking for, anyway? How do you recognize it when you see it?

These are questions students ask in newswriting classes. Most reporting students are insecure about the mystique of newsgathering. What they see of it on the six o'clock news does not soothe them—the thrust and parry of a Presidential news conference, the clamor of the impromptu news briefing on the front steps of the federal court building, the jostling and shoving of reporters trying to outdo each other in arrogance with their questions. "Is there any place in journalism for a reporter who is not a loudmouth?" a student once asked.

The answer then and now is "yes." Emphatically so. The glimpses of news reporting seen on the evening news constitute but a small portion of the reporter's work. The daily work of most reporters is that of quietly but persistently keeping in touch with the newsmakers and other sources who are familiar with the major events and issues of the day. Far from requiring loud, pushy types, reporting requires men and women of intelligence, discernment, and enthusiasm—*listening* reporters whose job is to observe, ask questions, and report the swirling crosscurrents of public affairs.

Swirling crosscurrents? It does seem that journalists often resort to watery figures of speech when speaking of newsgathering. It was Edwin L. James of the *New York Times* who compared newsgathering to "casting a net across a salmon

Reporter Debbie Cafazzo talks to a minister helping to coordinate Christmas baskets to the poor *(Photo by John Froschauer of the Walla Walla Union Bulletin.)*

stream." And A.J. Liebling, the late press critic for the *New Yorker,* once said newspapers reminded him of modern fish canneries—gigantic, gleaming, expensive—but dependent on a meager number of hand-line fishermen in leaky rowboats for their raw material.

On most papers, newsgathering is not as efficient as the salmon net nor as haphazard as leaky rowboat fishing. Even so, "fishing for news" is an apt comment. It means getting around, talking to newsmakers and news sources, asking questions, observing, learning, trying to balance a youthful enthusiasm with journalistic skepticism. Most of this is done on "newsbeats."

A newsbeat is a group of agencies entrusted to the coverage of one reporter. As that reporter, you make periodic contact with news sources, mostly public officials, to learn what's going on. What progress is being made toward meeting their objectives? What new trends and activities are under way? What problems have emerged to get in the way? How are these problems going to be resolved? What is the outlook for the future? How will the problems, trends, and changes affect your readers?

Beats vary, of course, as do the methods of coverage. A police reporter gets tips on stories from a radio scanner tuned to police frequencies, by examining the police logs each day, and by frequent contact with the police chief and other major officials. A labor reporter calls frequently at the offices of labor leaders, establishes contacts among the rank and file, and tries to catch the top people informally over coffee or at a favorite cocktail bar. A business reporter keeps in touch with bankers, chambers of commerce, the leaders of business associations, and top executives—sometimes also with consumer groups and even with ordinary people with extraordinary vision. A *Wall Street Journal* bureau chief, for example, has lunch periodically with a representative of the black ghetto—just to keep in touch with the people affected by the economic tides and the executive decisions made in plush board rooms.

Even the lifestyles of reporters vary with the beats. Education and court reporters enjoy a regular nine-to-five schedule for the most part, while the police reporter often gets called out at all hours as police emergencies occur.

In a typical community, the list of beats usually includes police and fire services, the county courthouse (courts and county government), state agencies (which would comprise several beats if the community is also the state capital), city hall, labor, business, education, sports, science and technology, agriculture, transportation, culture and entertainment, social services, federal agencies, politics.

Some beat reporters adhere rigidly to a particular set of offices—on government beats, for example. Others, such as "lifestyle" reporters, may range widely into most any field of human concern. Some beats depend on geography—the military in Hawaii, the marine beat in seacoast cities, oil in Oklahoma, entertainment in Southern California. And some papers work in specialties. *Education Week,* a Washington-based national weekly, concerns itself only with education news. It separates its beats into such highly specialized areas as the federal beat (Congress and federal agencies dealing with education), science, vocational education, special education, private schools, the courts (as they deal with education), and so forth.

Newspapers also employ general-assignment reporters to cover stories that don't fall within beats or to supplement the work of a beat reporter. A major crime story, for example, may originate with the police reporter but be assigned to one or more general-assignment reporters for completion. Many news stories do not confine themselves to a single beat. An impending labor dispute might start on the labor beat but spread quickly to other areas such as business, city hall, the courts, state and federal agencies as it goes to arbitration.

ANATOMY OF A PUBLIC AGENCY

Most news reporting deals with public agencies. An overview of just what a public agency does, as seen from a journalist's viewpoint, will help you understand the ways in which news emerges from these agencies. Agencies have seven characteristics in common. Each of them can stimulate ideas for news stories.

1. *A purpose:* goals to be achieved. We have a need for an educated populace; public schools are established for that purpose, complete with school boards, teachers, superintendents, and tax levies. A need exists to protect people against lawlessness; police, courts, and jails serve that purpose. If you know the agency's purpose, you'll be able to monitor its progress (or the lack of it) toward meeting the goals. News stories can come at such milestones as having met a goal, having new goals estab-

lished or proposed, having missed a goal, being "halfway there," exceeding a goal, and so forth.

2. *Money:* from taxes, fees, or other sources, used to carry out the purpose. Stories emerge from such considerations as where the money comes from, where it's going, overspending, underspending (rare), controversies over misdirecting of funds, and so on. "Go where the money goes," advises one veteran reporter. The "nose for news"—the supposedly uncanny ability to sniff out important stories—may be little more than following that advice.

3. *People:* the staff that spends the money to achieve the purpose. People are your sources, of course, and also can serve as the focal point of feature stories or persons behind the news. Don't ignore the people affected by the agencies—patrons, clients, opponents, and others. For a story on the juvenile department, focus on one or more examples, a success story about a rehabilitated juvenile, for instance, or even a meaningful tragedy, such as a juvenile whose death from drug overdose may contain a message for the living.

4. *Power:* who controls what. You'll soon learn who runs what, who controls the money, who makes the important decisions. The leaders, the power sources, will be your news sources. Their manipulations may produce important stories. The power struggles of opposing factions often involve issues worthy of public attention. The views, activities, and backgrounds of the powerful—or the would-be powerful, such as candidates for elective office—can produce stories.

5. *Action:* programs, projects, policy-making activities, enforcement of standards, and so forth. The more action that occurs, the more news you have. Ongoing activities of police and courts produce news regularly. New trends, projects, changes in viewpoint, new policies—all are reportable.

6. *Issues:* philosophical questions and political differences over any and all of the above characteristics. Public bodies are constantly confronted by issues. A school board must decide whether a school play should be banned because it's too sexually explicit or has a religious theme that may violate separation of church and state. Or it must decide whether to ask for more tax support, whether to enhance the kindergarten program, whether to grant a new wage contract demanded by the teachers union, or whether to ban a controversial book from the school libraries —the issues are endless.

7. *Obstacles:* problems to be overcome, issues to be resolved, hazards, emergencies, and so on. The obstacles can come in any form and involve any of the areas listed above: changed goals, unattainable goals, lack of money, people problems (workers threatening a strike, for instance, or attempts to dismiss a wayward executive), power struggles, backlashes to actions taken (such as court suits or protest demonstrations), major political differences over the issues. Some obstacles are inherent in the work of an agency (criminals will always be an obstacle for police, and vice versa), and sometimes they are unexpected (the juvenile detention

center burns down). An old journalistic maxim says an agency off track is more newsworthy than one on track.

GETTING ESTABLISHED ON A BEAT, STEP BY STEP

Success in covering a beat depends on your ability to recognize news. Your sources will tell you things, but they do not necessarily tag them as "news" and relate them to you in inverted pyramid form. They merely tell you what they know. Do not expect a shaft of golden sunlight to burst forth the very instant that the words of a bureaucrat constitute news. The only light that's going to shine is the figurative one in your head, and then only if you've done your homework in learning to recognize news. If you have any lingering doubts about your ability to do so, review Chapter 3 and ask for help from your instructor.

In the suggestions that follow, we are assuming that you have been newly assigned to cover the county beat. That means you're responsible for county government, including such agencies as the sheriff's office, county roads department, county clerk's office, tax assessor's office, elections department, health and sanitation department, planning department, juvenile department, and board of county commissioners, and probably many more, depending on the size and nature of the county. Although the discussion focuses for convenience on the county beat, you can of course adapt the suggestions to any other beat that concerns you.

Step 1: Collect Materials

This may seem like elementary advice, but it's too often overlooked. Before you can plan systematic coverage, you must know what agencies constitute your beat, where they are located, who runs them, what they do, and whom they're responsible to. You start with paper work, as follows:

Get documents. Ask for brochures, memoranda, organizational charts, county employee directories, job descriptions, employee handbooks, budget reports, annual reports, position papers, clip books, scrapbooks, county maps, in-house newspapers or newsletters, news releases, building codes or other regulatory documents, bulletin board notices. The best place to find such documents is the office of the community relations director. If no such person exists, try the county manager or the chief administrator. What you can't get from central offices you may have to get from individual agencies.

Read clippings. You'll get clippings from your own newspaper library. These clippings give you lots of ideas because much news is either ongoing or recurring. Last year's clipping about an outbreak of measles will prompt you to inquire about the possibility of a similar outbreak this year. Last year's political campaign promises might be pursued to see which of them, if any, have been accomplished by the elected officials.

Start a futures book.   Buy an appointment book, preferably one small enough to carry in pocket or purse. In it write the dates of all scheduled future events, even the approximate dates of tentatively scheduled events. Suppose the sheriff tells you he expects new radio communications equipment to be ready "in about six months." You'll make a note to check back with him in, say, five and a half months. Also log into your book all the recurring events you can think of: the beginning of road repair work in the spring, construction of new picnicking and camping facilities in the summer, communicable diseases in the fall. Also include regularly scheduled events, such as the commissioners' meeting every Wednesday or the planning council's meeting the second Tuesday of each month, and so on.

Acquaint yourself with the literature.   Almost every field of endeavor has a trade magazine, such as *Law & Order* for police, *County Government* for county officials, *Media and Methods* for educators, and so forth. You'd be wise to subscribe so that you can keep abreast of national issues and thereby talk the language of the officials you contact. Similarly, the public library may yield special books and reports pertinent to topics you cover on your beat.

Make a list of sources.   Perhaps all you need is a directory of county employees if one exists. You should have a full list of names of important officials and their phone numbers at your fingertips so that you can get in touch with them in a hurry if necessary (and it often is necessary in the daily rush of newspaper work). The numbers should include both office and home, with notes on how to reach persons by extraordinary means if necessary (such as radio contact with the roads superintendent as he travels). For officials with unlisted home numbers, try to obtain the numbers after you have become acquainted with them and gained their trust.

Prepare a list of potential issues.   As you pore through the mountain of documents that you have collected, you'll begin to grasp the major issues in various departments. Many are recurring issues, and you'll make a note to check on them at the proper season. Some are ongoing issues such as a political controversy between two factions, and you'll tap into this issue as appropriate events occur. Some are philosophical issues, such as controversy over the use of chemical sprays for roadside brush control. Some are financial issues; money is scarce and so you constantly encounter differences of opinion on spending priorities. You can also see news stories in the making by reading documents such as annual reports. For example, the county tax assessor says in an annual report that plans are underway to reassess property values in the county next year. "Next year" is here, and so you put appropriate questions on your list: Has the program been started yet? What is being done by whom? What progress has been made? What obstacles have been encountered? What does it mean to taxpayers in the county? If it hasn't been started yet, why not? If you make this list, you'll have plenty of things to talk about when you first approach your sources in person.

Prepare your own documents. All of the foregoing are intended to prepare you for your first personal contacts with the officials who comprise the bureaucracy. One further step is recommended. Many newspapers prepare calling cards for their reporters to leave with sources so that if something newsworthy occurs the source will be able to get in touch with the reporter. If this is not the practice, you might consider producing a duplicated statement on your own—one that not only lists your name, phone number, and background, but also suggests the kinds of stories you are looking for and what to do if one turns up. You can leave copies with various officials as you visit them.

Step 2: Get Acquainted With Your Beat

"What's new? . . . Got any news today?" Asking such questions of public officials is a singularly ineffective way to get news. A good reporter learns as much as possible about the agency first so that specific questions can be asked. Once you have done your homework, the next step is to make the rounds of the agencies on your beat to get acquainted. One good way to start is to write letters to all the important officials—introducing yourself, outlining the kinds of stories you are interested in, and promising to call on them personally in the near future.

Public officials and their staffs tend to fall into three basic categories: the friendlies, the neutrals, and the heavies.

The friendlies are invariably open, gregarious, and helpful to a new reporter. They'll give you ideas; they'll call you when something comes up that they think you might be interested in. Sometimes, of course, they have something to gain from helping you—better public understanding of the work of their departments. But often they will offer suggestions about other agencies, too. In general, they are public spirited and committed to the principle that the public has a right to know what's happening in their respective agencies, both good and bad. (Human nature being what it is, they will tend to emphasize the good and downplay the bad.) They usually have a good concept of what makes a news story or feature, and they do not carry grudges if a reporter must explore situations that don't portray the agency in a favorable light. They ask only that you be fair and accurate. This group comprises about one-third of the people you normally contact on a beat. But if you are friendly yourself—and honest, fair, and accurate—you may be able to increase that proportion to around half.

The neutrals are usually honest, and they will answer your questions truthfully, but they seldom volunteer anything. They'll never call you. They seem indifferent to publicity; they can take it or leave it. If they have anything they want in the paper, they'll usually issue a press release or call a press conference. They are not usually skilled in handling press relations, but if they come to trust you they can be good sources.

Finally, you have the heavies, sources who are suspicious of your every action, who read political manipulation into your every question, and who are convinced that the public should know only what they choose to say. Some seem outwardly friendly but will attempt to manipulate the press in overt ways, the most common being gushing, platitudinous rhetoric served up with a smile for TV but accompanied by a polite refusal to give specific answers to questions. They often have you on the defensive. They accuse you of being devious or manipulative when in fact it is *they* who are devious. And they constantly accuse you of misquotation, of overemphasizing a view opposed to their own, and of failing to be "objective."

A second type of heavy is the one who simply refuses to say anything at all—"I can't comment on that at this time"—and hides behind a bureaucratic fortress: "This is an ongoing investigation of an allegedly criminal action, and we are precluded by departmental policy from giving public testimony that could jeopardize. . . ." You won't get much out of them unless you prod them or apply leverage (charm seldom works).

Much depends on the nature of the job as well as the person. Homicide detectives are secretive largely in the light of legal limits on pretrial publicity. The same officers suddenly transferred to traffic safety may turn out to be the best of friendlies, simply because they need the media to accomplish their goals, which are essentially public education.

Getting established on a beat normally starts with contact with the friendlies. You can identify them by talking to other reporters or by reading clippings of past stories. The friendlies are the ones most frequently quoted, often with the most colorful remarks. Some of them have jobs that require a friendly attitude, such as the director of community relations. Many of these are excellent sources—the best ones are more likely to scold a bureaucrat for being too secretive than a reporter for being too nosey. Therefore the community relations office may be your first stop, and may continue to be a productive source of information, depending on the skill of the director.

Whatever office you call on, the procedure is largely the same. It starts with knowing three basic sources of news.

The first source is based on your own ideas (or those of your editors), perhaps ideas you've picked up from your reading of documents or ideas passed along by the city editor: Ask the engineer when they're going to start repair work on the Center Street Bridge. Ask the elections office what they're doing to get their computers to run more efficiently.

The second source is the ideas originated by the agency itself, events or situations the department would like to see publicized. They may be presented conversationally to a reporter or they may be in the form of press releases or news conferences. They consist of announcements, personnel changes, new policies, forthcoming public events, and so forth. In addition, you will have a number of meetings to cover regularly.

The third and probably the most important source is the exchange of ideas between a reporter and a source. Some reporters call this "coffee cup reporting." Over coffee, in the hallways, during recesses in public meetings, reporters and sources talk of the events of the day. Sooner or later ideas drop out of the conversation—at least they do for a reporter who listens carefully and who recognizes news.

The coffee cup phase of reporting comes later, of course, after you've become acquainted. Your first meeting with an agency head may be relatively formal, and you approach it much as you would an interview. You've probably phoned for an appointment, explaining that you're new on the beat and would like to drop around to "chat informally" about ideas for news coverage. The friendlies and the neutrals invariably invite you to drop around. Suddenly you find yourself in the office of a department head. What now?

You probably start by dropping off your calling card. Next comes small talk—the weather, the high price of coffee, or perhaps a news event recently in the paper. When you get down to business, you might explain your mission along these lines:

> As I mentioned on the phone, I'll be covering county government, including your department, on a regular basis starting Monday. I'm taking Charlie Griffin's place—he's off on a research project on Egyptian mummies . . . I'm taking this week to get acquainted with people and maybe get a handle on the kinds of activities that are taking place—accomplishments, projects, problems, and so forth—anything that the public should know about. I've been reading about your department, and I have a few ideas for stories already, such as following up on your plans to build a new jail or the development of wilderness parks around the county. Perhaps you have some ideas, too . . . To start with, were there any problems in the news coverage our paper has provided in the past—anything you think we can work to improve in the future?

You should say this informally and in your own words, not recite it from memory or read it from a card.

Your first few stories from an agency probably will show it in a favorable light, as in a honeymoon period. Plenty of time later to follow up those rumors about shady dealings. And if the agency head does choose to complain about past news coverage, you'll keep an open mind, naturally.

Here are some other ideas for getting started on your beat:

Ask for names of other persons who would be good sources of news.

Ask for ideas for future stories.

Ask to be put on mailing lists for materials regularly sent out by the department: minutes, reports, news releases, agendas, and so forth.

Ask for names of books, magazines, and other documents that might be useful in understanding the work of the department.

Ask for specific dates of forthcoming events. Write them in your futures book.

Ask to inspect projects that are underway or facilities that might one day be in the news, such as the state penitentiary or a military base.

Ask to meet other staff persons, including secretaries, receptionists, and clerks.

Attend public meetings, either for news coverage or to get further acquainted with issues and personnel.

Ask for names of persons who can help you understand bureaucratic, legal, or technical jargon.

Be specific with questions. Don't ask, "What's new?" Ask, "How are plans for the new jail coming along?" "What became of the proposal made three years ago to reorganize the health and sanitation department?"

Remind sources to keep you in mind. Set up a regular schedule of visits, such as every Monday. Ask people to call you with ideas. Tell them the kinds of items you want: forthcoming speeches, meetings, or conferences, new projects started or concluded, surveys or research projects, policy changes, visiting dignitaries, new trends, personnel changes, budget requests or changes, or "anything out of the ordinary," such as incidents that are amusing or ironic or "revealing of human character," as the *Reader's Digest* says.

And when people come through with story ideas and assistance, don't hesitate to express your appreciation. Try sending a brief note to say thanks for help on such-and-such a story. Don't neglect the "little people," such as the secretary who put through your urgent call to a busy boss. She could just as easily have brushed you off. Don't make a big thing of it; just a word of thanks will do.

Step 3: Fishing For News

Fishing for news, like casting for trout, is largely a matter of skill, patience, and knowing where the fish are. It's not mysterious. You may start out being a little awed by high government officials, but then you find they're pretty much like everyone else: decent people trying to do a creditable job.

Helen Altonn, a reporter for the *Honolulu Star-Bulletin,* describes her beat coverage technique as an informal one. "There's a pot of coffee going all the time in the governor's executive offices and in most department offices. Once you've gotten established, you can go in and say 'Hi' and have some coffee and just chit-chat."

It is from the chit-chat that story ideas emerge, says Helen. A good reporter is constantly saying things like "Oh, that's interesting . . . I didn't know that! . . . That might make a story—I'd like to hear more about it."

To make the transition from scared beginner to trusted confidante, you start by being friendly. You're honest and fair-minded. But you're nobody's patsy. You have a professional obligation to find out what government is doing—the bad as well as the good—and to report it to the public.

To the *Star-Bulletin's* Helen Altonn these qualities add up to *professional integrity.* They also add up to a high level of professional performance. She is considered among the best beat reporters in Honolulu. Her editors say that; her sources confirm it. Even editors on the rival daily, the *Advertiser,* admit that she is formidable competition. Helen believes that if you want your sources to be honest and fair, you must be honest and fair yourself. Helen offers some other points, in an interview taped for this text:

Attitudes. "I try always to be fair and to take a positive, open-minded approach. I'm not looking primarily for dirt. A beat reporter with a predominantly negative attitude may get through the door once, but never again. Of course, I try to be alert for signs of shoddy administration and activities that are wrong, such as misuse of public funds, programs stifled by political wrangling, and so forth. But I try to be cautious and remember the power of the press. You can easily embarrass someone. If someone makes an absurd comment, I ask, 'Did you really mean to say that?' If they say, 'Yes, I did,' then, fine, I'll print it. I just want to make sure. I suppose I lean over backwards not to do anything to anybody that I wouldn't want done to me. I talked with a department head the other day who said, 'Helen, you give us a bad time every once in a while but at least you quote me accurately.' And I said, 'Well, if I'm going to hang somebody in print, I'm going to do it in his own words.' "

Techniques for beat coverage. "I approach public officials to find out what activities are going on that the public ought to know about. I'm concerned with programs that affect the taxpayers' pocketbooks or their daily lives or their way of looking at the world around them. Sometimes they're merely things that give people a chuckle or make them sad—human interest stories."

Objectivity. "When you try to be fair and objective, I don't think your sources can fault you. They can't say, 'She's only interested in sensationalism. She twists the facts. She's sneaky. You can't trust her.' I haven't lost any sources that I know of. I wrote a series about a housing project with stories that were unfavorable to both state and city administration. But I don't believe I lost any sources from it because the stories were true. I'm careful about that. You have to be factual, fair, and balanced and give people who are implicated a chance to respond to the story."

The foregoing comments confirm that fishing for news cannot begin, nor can it ever be effective, unless it is done in a spirit of sincerity and fair play.

Fishing also requires alertness. News tends to just slip out in bits and pieces. The better reporter you are, the sooner you will recognize one or more of the pieces as part of an important story and the sooner you'll start to ask questions. You will improve with experience, of course.

Here is a conversation between a reporter—an inexperienced one—and the county sheriff. It's hypothetical but based on actual conversations and events. See how many potential news stories you can recognize in the dialogue:

Q. Hi, Sheriff, how's it going?

A. Hi, Scribe. Goin' fine. How's it with you? Help yourself to a cup of coffee.

Q. Thanks. Well, things are fine except my wife and kids are down with colds this week. This is a bad time of year for that.

A. Well, I can understand that. If you think *you* have problems, you ought to take a look at the county jail.

Q. Oh? What's over at the jail?

A. The flu, that's what. They're jammed like sardines over there right now; it's pitiful. One guy comes down with the flu and it just spreads like wildfire. We had the county medical examiner over and he said conditions are bad, even had to send a couple over to the hospital. Now the *women* aren't so bad off, they seem to be tougher. But we cleared them out and put the men in the women's section. Now I'm afraid the whole sheriff's office is coming down with the flu. They get infected by the prisoners we keep transporting back and forth between the jail and the courthouse. That's damn well gonna stop one of these days, believe me! We spend half our man-hours running prisoners back and forth. We can't get out on patrol and nail those drunk drivers like I said in my election campaign I was gonna do. We've got to put our manpower where it'll have some effect. Of course, I should have said woman-power, too, since Saturday. That's changing.

Q. You're having trouble keeping up with drunk drivers?

A. Well, we nail 'em when we find 'em. I'd say our major trouble is keeping up with drunk husbands. But that's gonna change, too.

Q. Husbands?

A. Yeah, we're not gonna handle those darned family beefs anymore. That's one change. A man—well, a woman, too—could spend hours coping with a family argument. And it's dangerous. The old man gets liquored up and no telling what he'll do. And for all your trouble, the wife *never* signs a complaint against him. The other evening one of our deputies got clobbered with a baseball bat—lucky he ducked so it just hit him on the shoulder, not the head. And—would you believe?—as my man was hauling this slob off to jail the little woman was *screaming* at him to let him go! Well, we're just not gonna worry about it anymore, especially now that they're gonna build that new shelter home for battered wives. . . . Well, I gotta go—the Juvenile Department is having an emergency meeting about security in the juvenile detention shelter. Lots of problems over there.

Q. Okay, so long, Sheriff. Thanks for the coffee. By the way, you got any news today?

A. Nope. Everything's quiet. See you around.

Did you spot any potential news stories in that dialogue? If so, what do you do? It may seem incredible that not once did our hypothetical reporter stop the sheriff to check out any of the potential news story ideas that were falling out of that conversation. It takes only a few questions of the who-what-when-where variety. Here are some possibilities for stories that emerged from that dialogue (if you didn't notice them the first time you read it, take another look):

1. Possible overcrowding at the county jail.
2. Flu epidemic apparently resulting from overcrowding.
3. Possibly one or more women newly employed as sheriff's deputy.
4. Possible changes in personnel deployment.
5. Problems and possible policy changes in answering calls for domestic fights.
6. Security problems at juvenile detention center. Did someone escape or what?
7. "Cleared out the women" from the jail? What does that mean? Reporter should ask.
8. What's the new shelter home for battered wives?
9. Campaign against drunk drivers, if any.
10. Successes and problems of sheriff in keeping campaign promises.

Not all of those stories will pan out, of course. Fishing for news means recognizing a nibble of a news story idea and then attempting to reel it in. You won't always succeed. But let's look at how the reporter might land just *one* of the story possibilities.

Q. Sheriff, I'm interested in what you said a moment ago about deputies' answering calls about family disturbances. Do I understand correctly that you're considering a policy change on that?

A. It's more than considering—we're going to do it.

Q. When?

A. Zero six hundred hours Monday. At that time our radio dispatch people will no longer send officers to the scene of a domestic fight unless it's an extreme emergency.

Q. What would you consider an extreme emergency?

A. Shots fired. Clear danger to life and property. Serious injuries inflicted. That kind of thing.

Q. I think there's a story here.

A. Well, it probably wouldn't hurt to let people know.

Q. How did you arrive at your decision to change the policy?

A. By statistical analysis, actually. We put manpower deployment statistics into the computer and compared them with our priorities. We found we were neglecting some things we consider important and spending far too much time on items we considered of minimal importance. I'll admit that a wife in danger of being injured by a drunken slob of a husband may be important. But so is an innocent motorist endangered by a drunken slob of a driver. And drunk drivers we can do something about. Battered wives, we can't. It's as simple as that. So when the proposal came up to open a new shelter home for abused wives, we felt this was a time to make our change.

Q. What is the new shelter home?

A. A couple of women are renting a big house in River City that wives who are getting beat up by their husbands can retreat to when their safety is in jeopardy. They have some kind of foundation grant to establish this on an experimental basis. I can give you their names, if you want.

Q. Okay. Do you anticipate opposition from feminist groups?

A. We consulted with a couple of them. I can't say they're overjoyed but I think they understand our problem. . . .

It would appear that you have an interesting story here, particularly if you flesh it out with more details. A lot of readers will identify with your story because there's a quarreling family in every neighborhood.

This is but one example. You still have seven or eight possibilities to check out with just this one source on this one day. The techniques of landing the story are largely the same for all stories, though circumstances and personalities will differ, of course.

POINTS TO REMEMBER

1. Most news comes through regular contacts with groups of agencies that comprise newsbeats.
2. Newsgathering has been compared to "fishing"; the metaphors range from casting a net across a salmon stream to hand-line fishing from leaky rowboats.
3. Understanding a public agency—its purpose, funding, staffing, activities, issues, power centers, and the obstacles that confront it—must precede good beat coverage.
4. Typical bureaucratic sources come in three categories, friendly, neutral, and "heavy" (uncooperative).
5. Three steps are involved in starting on a newsbeat: assembling background documents, getting acquainted with sources, and regular contact, preferably on an informal basis.
6. Ideas for news stories come from three sources: reporters or their editors, from sources themselves, and (most important) from informal "coffee cup" conversations between reporters and sources.
7. Reporters should stay alert for possible ideas that drop out of informal conversations; they're easy to miss sometimes.

PROJECT

Interview a person who is a news source, either on a college campus (such as an academic department head or an administrative officer) or in the community (such as the sheriff or the city engineer). Through the interview, identify several specific ideas for news stories that could be written about the activities of that department.

Purpose: Practice interviewing. Practice identifying and shaping specific stories just as a beat reporter might do. The list of specific ideas might be shared with the campus or community newspaper for possible use, or might form the basis of assignments to newswriting students.

Suggestions: Prepare for the interview by learning something about the department and its activities. If possible, read clips or files in the campus information department. If it's an academic department, talk to students taking courses there: Who are the best teachers? What specific projects are underway? What are some of the department's problems?

Remember that developing news stories is a dual responsibility of the reporter and the source. Don't expect merely to ask for them. You may start out with more general questions: What are the source's views of the general quality of news coverage of the community or of the specific agency? When getting to specifics you may have to play hunches. What about research activities? Interesting books or dissertations underway by professors or grad students? Interesting classroom projects? Innovative teaching ideas? Field trips? Comments and opinions by experts on topics of the day (such as a meteorology professor commenting on unusual weather conditions): How about trips, conferences, speeches, meetings? Don't rely on just one source; try others within the department. Make sure your ideas for stories are *specific*. They should look like this:

> Starting Monday morning, the sheriff's office will no longer handle domestic disturbances unless there is an extreme emergency, such as shots fired, persons seriously injured, clear danger to lives and property. The decision was made on basis of statistical evidence showing that time spent by officers did not match the priorities the department had set—too much time spent on domestic beefs, not enough nailing drunk drivers, for example. Part of decision made on basis of new shelter home for "battered wives" to be established soon in River City.

Your list of ideas should *not* look like this:

> Mr. So-and-So believes papers should give more news to teaching activities.

(*What* teaching activities? List a specific activity. You have to "sell" your ideas more.)

12

Special Problems of Newsgathering

What do you do if someone you're interviewing is evasive or downright hostile? Should you use a tape recorder? How can you listen, think up questions, and take notes all at the same time? Is there any kind of special etiquette when asking questions on the telephone? These and many other questions stump reporting students—for a while, at least. Instructors also encounter problems of which the students themselves are not aware. Problems in listening, for example, or in making careless mistakes. Often, however, the problems can be cleared up quickly. Here are the nine most common ones:

1. taking notes
2. using a tape recorder
3. covering meetings and news conferences
4. using the telephone
5. handling hostile or evasive sources
6. handling off-the-record requests
7. being accurate
8. listening
9. gaining self-confidence

What follows are some suggestions for handling the problems, based on experience—that of the author plus about 100 professional reporters interviewed over the past decade for this book.

(Photo by Stan Wakefield.)

TAKING NOTES

Newswriting students say taking notes is one of the hardest parts of reporting. This is a surprise, for most college students have been taking notes in classrooms for years and should be experts. But the notes you take to learn a subject or pass a test differ from those taken to write a news story. Among the differences is the need for reporters to record specific details, including descriptions and touches of color, such as direct quotes and anecdotes. Reporters must be totally accurate on meanings, numerical data, and all details.

Professional reporters differ greatly in their note-taking procedures. Some take sketchy notes—writing down such things as exact quotations, dates, names, and numerical data—relying on memory for the essence of the material. They literally have trained their memories to retain much of the material long enough so that they can flesh out the notes afterwards or, if they get to the typewriter or VDT immediately, they can write partially from memory. Other reporters take copious notes no matter what. Some take detailed notes at speeches but take fewer notes at interviews, preferring to listen carefully and to clarify details before recording them. Many reporters take notes on the VDT, particularly in the office or in phone interviews.

The newest technique at this writing is to take your notes on a tiny, battery-powered portable computer-word processor. Computers have become so small—

Reporters taking notes. *(Photos by Dan Dillon and Randy L. Rasmussen.)*

some are hardly bigger than a woman's purse—that they can be hauled along to speeches, meetings, and interviews. They're particularly useful when working with documents—such as police or court records—because most reporters can type faster than they can take notes by hand. A police reporter, Gail Bullen of Grants Pass, Oregon, says she doesn't even take notes for the simple stories, the ones that come largely off the police records. She simply writes the stories on the spot and then transfers them onto the paper's computer system when she gets back to the office. She also uses the portable to take notes during interviews, as do many reporters on their VDTs when sources come to the newspaper office. The difference is that the portable computer is so small that it can be carried along to interviews and used unobtrusively (at least by a good touch typist) as the conversation proceeds. Many reporters are fast enough at touch typing to get quotes verbatim.

Indeed, the portable computer has the potential to revolutionize the way reporters take notes.

Lacking a computer, reporters normally take handwritten notes on paper, often on a small spiral notebook, a skinny one about half the width of a stenopad. Others use clipboards or big yellow-leafed tablets. A few even use the backs of old envelopes or whatever is at hand. Time was when most old-time reporters used a sheaf of copy paper—newsprint—but when VDTs came in, copy paper went out.

However you do it, note taking involves developing three skills. You will not develop them overnight but you can easily practice them every time you attend a lecture. Practicing in your classrooms can even help you improve your grades. The three skills are:

1. knowing what to take notes about
2. developing a shorthand, particularly for hand-written notes
3. training your memory to hold quotes, anecdotes, and details temporarily

Knowing What to Take Notes About

Most speakers, including interview respondents, seek to make a central point. They support that point with certain particulars. Therefore in note taking you listen and try to identify the main point first. The point is invariably an abstract generalization that is usually based on concrete evidence. Let's take an example. Suppose you are attending a speech on the subject of highway safety.

"Our highways are becoming increasingly dangerous," the speaker says. That's the point, or one of them, and you write it down. But by itself it doesn't mean much. So you listen for specific evidence to support the point and you write that down, too. If the speaker is any good, he or she will provide it. Thus:

> In the United States we kill about 55,000 persons annually in motor vehicle accidents. That's an average of 150 funerals a day.
> At the present rate of accidents, half of all the people born in the United States this year can expect to be killed or seriously injured during their lifetime.
> Highway accidents are the leading cause of death among people aged five through twenty-five, exceeding the next four causes combined.
> Property damage from motor vehicle accidents runs 16 billion dollars annually, enough money to replace all the college buildings in the United States, all the county courthouses, all the hospitals, with enough left over to replace most of the public libraries.

And so on. The more you record specific details, numbers, facts, dramatic comparisons, the better your story will be. You need not get them word for word unless you plan to use a direct quote, that is, precisely what the speaker said.

The speaker usually will go on to other points and provide similar specifics for each point. He or she may say, "Lives *can* be saved, and one way to do it is to rid the highways of the drunk driver." That's a second point. Again, specific supporting evidence is used to support it:

> If there were no drunk drivers, we'd have only 75 funerals a day—because half the fatalities are caused by drunk drivers.
> In this state, the State Highway Patrol conducted an anti-drunk driver campaign that has resulted in a 100 percent increase in arrests and a 25 percent drop in motor vehicle fatalities.

And so on. The reporter who listens for points plus evidence will be able to organize his notes for easy reference. One way to do so is to put the points on one side of a stenopad page, and the supporting evidence (including direct quotes) on the other. Thus:

Points	*Evidence*
Highways becoming increasingly dangerous.	55,000 killed annually.
	150 funerals a day.
	"Think about that—can you imagine attending 150 funerals a day?"
	At present rate of accidents, half the people born this year will be killed or seriously injured in lifetime.
	"The greatest enemy of highway safety is the drunk driver."
We *can* save lives.	One-half of all motor vehicle fatalities caused by drunk drivers.
	Get rid of drunk driver, have only 75 funerals a day.
	"75 funerals is a hell of a lot better than 150!"
	State drunk driving campaign—arrests up 100%—M.V. fatalities down 25%.

Developing a Shorthand

You can take a course in shorthand or the simpler briefhand, but this is time-consuming and difficult. As they gain experience, most reporters develop their own shorthand, using symbols and abbreviations to stand for common words. One reporter uses:

9 to mean "that"
= to mean "equals" or "is"
& or + to mean "and" or "in addition"
7 to mean any "ing" ending
hay (Spanish) to mean "there is" or "there are"
selon (French) to mean "according to"

A reporter will often improvise abbreviations on the spot to stand for commonly used words. If a speaker is discussing urban problems, for example, you can devise a whole new shorthand to adjust to the speech. "U" stands for urban renewal, "V" for crime and violence, ICG for inner-city ghetto, T for transportation. As you work on it, you'd be surprised how abbreviated your notes can become and still remain coherent.

"No hay enuf rd7, wr7 + A n skuls tdy" means "There is not enough reading, writing, and arithmetic in our schools today." Simple. It just takes practice.

Training Your Memory

Your mind can be trained to perform remarkable feats of memory if you work at it hard enough. The reporter may find it convenient to develop an ability to remember quotes and anecdotal stories for at least short periods. Numbers, by contrast, are harder to remember and should be recorded immediately. But if a quote is truly a "memorable" one, then you should be able to remember it. Story lines for brief anecdotes are also easy to remember if you work at it. A remark like "The greatest enemy of highway safety is the drunk driver" is not so long a quote that it can't be retained in mind long enough to get it down in note form. Often a reporter needs only sketchy notes to remember the quote, something like *grtst emy–dk. dr.* If you have that much down you may find times when you can go over your notes and flesh out the material word for word while your memory is fresh. Experienced reporters become so proficient at remembering, however, that they often write their stories without even referring to their notes. Then, when the story is finished, they may go to their notes to verify quotes or check facts.

If despite your best efforts your notes remain incomplete, don't hesitate to clarify the points in an interview or to approach speakers afterward. They may be able to give you a script. You can at least check the accuracy of your quotes with them or clarify anything you didn't understand. Experienced reporters have discovered that speakers welcome a brief conversation after the speech and certainly do not resent your taking the time to check with them. Often they will provide additional information so that your story contains details that are new even to those who attended the speech.

Note Taking During Interviews

Your note taking bothers no one at speeches and meetings, but interviews are different, particularly with inexperienced sources. They may find it unnerving to see you whip out a notebook and write down everything they say. It's even worse if you use a VDT or portable computer, as many reporters do. One way is to ease into the note taking in easy stages. First comes small talk, then routine, innocuous inquiries such as the names and ages of the source's children. When you ask sources how they spell their names or the ages of their children, this would be the time to take out the notebook and write them down. That's no more threatening than giving the same information to the people at the auto license bureau. Eventually most people become accustomed to the note taking.

It helps, however, if you maintain eye contact as much as possible—though some find it unnerving when a reporter looks them in the eye while at the same time taking notes. How on earth can they write without looking at what they're doing? Typing your notes during interviews, on a portable word processor, for example, is a little unnerving to some, even though a good touch typist can easily maintain eye contact. Another problem with the computer is that it's such a novelty that it sometimes gets in the way of the information flow.

Perhaps the important point is to make your interview as conversational as possible while at the same time accomplishing your purpose. Note taking can be a part of the conversation as long as it doesn't dominate. It is perfectly okay to slow down a conversation with comments like, "That's an important point—please give me a moment to get that in my notes" or "I love that quote. . . . I simply *must* write it down." That not only supplies the time you need to take the notes, but it also allows the source—who is often flattered by your comment—to think of other potentially quotable remarks.

In a similar vein, print interviews need not project the flawless nature of a broadcast interview. A certain amount of amiable fumbling is reasonable, particularly when you consider that three skills are involved: asking questions, listening, and taking notes. If you're having trouble juggling all three, then slow the conversation a little. One reporter claims that this "Columbo technique," unwittingly patterned after the fictional TV detective famous for his bumbling ways, actually seems to make him less intimidating to most respondents, thereby enhancing conversational rapport.

In short, careful listening—so that you understand and respond to what you hear—is more important than getting everything into your notes. Not much point in getting something into your notes that you don't really understand.

How you take notes in interviews will also depend on the experience of the respondent. Notes taken on a VDT during telephone interviews may disturb some if they hear the clacking keyboard. But experienced sources often are disturbed if they *don't* hear clacking; "Are you *sure* you're getting all this down?" they often ask.

USING A TAPE RECORDER

The pocket recorder, a miniature, transistorized machine small enough to fit into a coat pocket or purse, has become the darling of the reporting profession, both broadcast and print. It is small enough to be carried routinely to all assignments. You can use it in conjunction with note taking to assure word-for-word accuracy. Should you miss a quote, you can find it again on the tape if you note the number on the digital counter as you conduct your interview. It is especially useful for news conferences and speeches.

The pocket recorder is battery operated, usually with AA penlight cells or rechargeable battery pack; thus it needs no electric plug. It is useful in situations where note taking is difficult, such as recording a conversation where both parties are walking or running. The recorder, small as it is, records as much as two hours using both sides of a C-120 tape cassette. It costs between $50 and $200.

The usual objections to tape recorders come in three categories; potential mechanical failure, intimidation of respondents, and problems of transcribing the tape.

Mechanical Breakdown

A malfunctioning tape recorder is the most common problem, and the cause is usually dead batteries. Some people understand and appreciate machinery; others don't. The best advice is to get a high-quality machine, keep it in good repair, and check it out before each use, perhaps employing a checklist with the acronym CAB.

C means cassettes. Check to see that you have enough available. Check to see that they don't contain old interviews that you want to save. (Learn to remove the "accidental erase" tabs from tapes you want to keep.) See that the cassettes run freely, without entanglement, by running them forward and back for a few moments. Be wary of using thin tapes (C-120 cassettes) on cheap recorders; they tangle.

A means actuality. Actually record a "testing one-two-three" and play it back.

B means batteries. Check your batteries (good recorders usually contain a battery meter or warning light). Always carry extras with you; they wear out fast in pocket recorders. Rechargeable packs usually give three or four hours of service. They also have the nasty habit of *suddenly* running out of power, rather than gradually, as regular batteries do. This means you have to keep track of use time rather than depending on the battery meter, which can show your batteries in good condition one moment and useless a second later. Running out of power is like running out of gas: Common sense precautions can avoid both.

Intimidating the Respondent

Most experienced respondents *prefer* reporters to use recorders to ensure accuracy. They're used to recorders in broadcast interviews. Inexperienced respondents tend to take their cues from the interviewer. If *you* are nervous and apprehensive about the machine, they probably will be, too. So set the machine in an unobtrusive place—preferably out of the line of sight between you—and leave it alone. Let it record as you talk conversationally. Forget the machine, and they will, too. Don't even look at it. Don't check to see that the wheels are turning. When the tape ends, most good machines click off, at which time you can replace the cassette.

Sometimes a little preliminary reassurance helps with inexperienced sources. Tell them the tape will make the interview more conversational, that you'll take your notes off the tape later, that you don't plan to play the tape on the radio or at parties for entertainment.

Far from being intimidating, use of recorders often enhances conversational rapport. The reporter, freed of note taking, can get involved in the discussion, listen more carefully, ask better follow-up questions. Many reporters, though, still take sketchy notes, often just to keep track of the conversation: what's been covered, what still remains to be asked. It's easy to forget.

The recorder is also an excellent learning tool. Most reporters learn painful lessons about their conversational and questioning techniques by listening to the playbacks. The most typical flaws turned up by the experience are: (1) They talk too much, (2) they cut off the source, often at the point where an interesting revelation is about to occur, (3) they ask long, rambling, convoluted, often incomprehensible questions, and (4) they don't listen carefully, failing to catch subtle meanings and half-articulated points, and so don't ask good follow-up questions.

Problems of Transcribing

Who said you had to *transcribe* the tape? Typically, the tape is handled in one of two ways.

The first method is from the type of interviews in which you have relied primarily on the tape. You will listen to the entire playback, taking notes as you go, same as you would at the scene except you use a typewriter or VDT. You wear earphones—the earmuff type, not the single plug—which help to block outside noises such as your clacking typewriter. If you're a fast typist you can actually keep up with the conversation pretty well.

In the second method, you kept track of the recorder's digital counter as you taped a speech, meeting, or interview. This is an especially good technique at stand-up interviews quickly done with dignitaries you might meet briefly at an airport or in the lobby of a legislative hall. It's hard to take notes under such conditions, particularly if the source is in motion, walking to another appointment. When a quotable quote drops out of the conversation, you merely write down the number on the counter with perhaps a brief notation of what the quote is about. Back at the office, you can roll the tape to that precise point and play back the quote.

COVERING MEETINGS AND NEWS CONFERENCES

The prospect of covering a meeting such as the school board often intimidates a young reporter, and with good reason. Bureaucratic terms routinely used in meetings are hard to understand. The board often discusses an issue without explaining the background. "We've got to take action on that Roosevelt High situation . . . all in favor?" Now what was that all about? *What* situation? The reporter who failed to prepare for the meeting feels helpless and lost. You simply must learn to prepare beforehand and to ask a lot of questions.

Another problem is that meetings of public agencies are inherently dull. A legendary story tells of one reporter who, suffering through long hours of city council meetings, decided to write a novel. He settled on a sordid and bloody murder mystery. He wrote it on a big yellow pad during lulls in the meetings. With fiendish delight he killed off the fictional equivalents of the council members one by one, starting with the mayor. The councilman from Ward IV suffered a particularly unfortunate death, having mysteriously fallen into the very same sewage treatment plant he had promoted in tediously long-winded tirades through many months of meetings.

Reports of meetings are often dull to the readers, too.

Some newspapers, however, are working to solve the readership problem. The reports about, say, school board meetings are dull largely because editorial policies—or lack of reportorial imagination—force a reporter to write about agenda items, detailing the discussion and disposition of each. Readers are interested in the education of their children, not necessarily in the decisions of school boards. Sometimes the two coincide, which is splendid. But when they don't, you can supplement the board discussion with other interviews with teachers, administrators, parents, and students. A school discipline problem that seemed so dull in abstract board discussion becomes understandable, even fascinating, with the additional perspective.

Even with that principle in mind, the reporter still must attend meetings and report on them. Here are some suggestions:

1. Decide which meetings are important. Those bodies that have the power to affect directly the lives of citizens—to levy taxes, put a measure on the ballot, or rezone a neighborhood—would be the ones to attend regularly. Others can be attended sporadically or covered through sources.

2. Prepare for the meeting much as you'd prepare for an important interview. Call officials to determine what's on the agenda, and which of them are considered important. You may want to do premeeting research in the newspaper library or conduct relevant interviews. Ask for documents—reports, memos, position papers—that you can read beforehand.

3. Talk to people at the meeting. During breaks contact members with questions about anything you don't understand. Supplement the meeting discussion with private interviews.

4. Try to keep in mind the shape of your story as the meeting progresses. What's your lead? What's important? What can be downplayed or ignored? This will make writing easier, particularly if you have a tight deadline.

5. Pay special attention to members of the public who speak at the meeting. They, as much or more as board members, can give you clues to what interests the public. Talk to them after the meeting if necessary, for elaboration, clarification—or maybe just to spell their names correctly.

6. Use direct quotes to represent various sides of an argument. Particularly quote members of the general public—they often speak more colorfully, less guardedly.

News Conferences

Reporters typically see the news conference as less excruciating than the meeting, as well they might since it is staged for their benefit. At least it is short, seldom more than 30 or 40 minutes. Its purpose is to allow officials to convey messages of interest to the public and/or make themselves available to media questioning. It is often a necessary method for an official or a celebrity to deal with incessant media requests for interviews. If the official granted every request, no time would be left for anything else. At best the news conference efficiently and conveniently conveys legitimate news of public concern. At worst it is a media hype staged by a publicity-hungry person.

The conference format is simple: usually a statement followed by questions. Broadcast and print reporters see conferences differently, however. They give broadcasters an opportunity for "actualities" or on-camera comments. Television reporters tend to ask questions that elicit active responses, often incisive or irritating questions, as one TV editor expressed it. Print reporters tend to stay more in the background. A veteran *Chicago Sun-Times* reporter once told a Northwestern University student, "Son, stay as far away from the TV lights as you can. Someday those lights will explode and everybody will be killed except you and me. *That* would be a story."

USING THE TELEPHONE

The telephone is a quick and efficient means of doing business. Many reporters estimate that they do half their interviewing over the phone, including feature story interviews, particularly the kind that call for a lot of different comments from many people. In the time it takes to drive across a big city to conduct a face-to-face interview, you can talk to a dozen different people by phone. And people are surprisingly candid on the phone about their personal lives, at least to a sympathetic voice. Sometimes it's easier to talk into an impersonal instrument about these things than to talk face-to-face. Here are some basic considerations of newsgathering by telephone:

1. Start with a purpose that can reasonably be done on the phone—one that does not require extensive description, for example.
2. Start in a businesslike way. You are So-and-so from the paper; you're doing a story on such-and-such., and you're eager to get your source's ideas. A little flattery—emphasizing the source's importance to your story—can help.
3. Follow with a challenging or provocative—but ego-reinforcing—sample question or two, something you think your person will *want* to answer. Ask an author how she manages to write mystery novels while raising three children and driving a tractor on the farm or whether she ever creates a character whose opinions coincide with her own.

4. Move ahead. Often a provocative sample question will elicit an enthusiastic reply right on the phone. This would be the time to suggest that you'd like to talk now on the phone "if this is a convenient time." If not, offer to call back later, as you never know what you're interrupting with a call. Indicate also how long you think the conversation will last.

5. Read voices. Common courtesy will keep your respondent on for a few moments, and it is during this brief period that you must perceive the person's feeling and attitudes through the tone of voice. Anxious voices need to be reassured, hesitant voices given ego support, and so on. Telephone interviews seem a lot like kite flying—they may falter a little at first but soon catch the wind and take firm and enthusiastic flight.

6. Project your own voice. Other people read voices, too. Your voice should spell out professional confidence, sincerity, and, when necessary, sympathy. It helps if you are, indeed, confident, sincere, and sympathetic.

7. If the conversation is likely to be personal and sensitive, it may help to set forth the topic you've called about and then let it hang for a few moments while you get acquainted. Perhaps tell a little about yourself, or ask personal but nonthreatening questions, such as where she grew up, schools attended, her family, and so on. If you know a little about her or have been given her name by a mutual acquaintance, you can launch a conversation through those entries: "Your friend, Charlie Brown, says hello," or "Charlie says you enjoy mountain hiking—me, too; I just got back from a hike in the Desolation Wilderness in California. . . ."

8. In sensitive interviews, you must respond with sympathetic interest to personal revelations. Such comments say, in effect, "It's okay for you to come into my personal life now; I've come to trust you." *Not* to respond to such an invitation is an act of insensitivity.

9. Having started such a conversation, the major problem is how to end it. People love to talk candidly with a sympathetic listener (listening is the key). They know the price they may eventually pay is revealing more of themselves than they wanted or expected. Yet it feels so good that it's worth it, they say. Naturally a conscientious and sensitive reporter will exercise some discretion in choosing what to print. Often, though, it's not what's revealed in the article but the *way* it comes out. In a sympathetic article context, the traumatic revelations can be almost salutary.

HANDLING HOSTILE OR EVASIVE SOURCES

The best way to cope with evasiveness or hostility is to try to figure out the reason for it—or asking the reason if it's not apparent. A little sympathy and human understanding helps, too. If you were the police chief and three of your trusted lieutenants had just been indicted for embezzlement, how would *you* feel about the journalistic wolfpack howling outside your door? The "wolfpack"—the snide, snarling, kangaroo court type of mass interview you often see at airports, courthouse steps, and sidewalks—is one of the more unfortunate aspects of news-gathering.

Do not assume, however, that people won't talk with reporters just because they've suffered a traumatic experience. Bereavement is a case in point. A reporter interviewed a couple who had just lost two children in a house fire, and he found to his surprise that they almost welcomed a chance to talk to a sympathetic listener. People had been avoiding them, apparently thinking that's what they preferred, when in fact they seemed to yearn for human contact. Reporters who have had extensive experience interviewing bereaved families tend to agree: The families consider talking to the media an important task to make sure the story is accurate. Funeral homes, the source of most obituary material, are notoriously inaccurate and incomplete.

Beyond bereavement the reasons for evasion or hostility can range widely. Sources may be upset about the very crisis you've come to discuss. They don't trust the media. They're upset about last night's editorial. They're Democrats and the paper is Republican, or vice versa. Or perhaps they've never talked to reporters before—isn't *everyone* supposed to snarl at the adversarial, tricky, and deceitful news media the way you see it on TV? Sometimes your own demeanor brings the response—don't expect calm, rational responses to arrogant, loaded questions. (Some reporters seem to feel that excited, irrational answers make good copy, however, which is unfortunate because truth often gets lost in the confrontation.)

Some suggestions when you sense hostility or evasions:

1. Put yourself in the other person's shoes—how would *you* feel under similar circumstances? Proceed sympathetically based on that understanding.

2. Take extra time and care to explain your purpose and why the source is important to your story. Gentle, sincere praise for the source's role seldom hurts.

3. Try to identify the reason for hostility and work to defuse it if you can. If the source is angry about last night's editorial, you can easily dissociate yourself: "I don't write the editorials—oftentimes I don't even agree with them." If, however the anger stems from something *you* have done, perhaps you need to talk it over or try to set it aside while you work on the current project. Much depends on your own level of sincerity. A conscientious, sincere reporter typically has fewer problems of this type than a more cavalier one, and the problems that do exist can be handled more readily. Sources perceive huge differences in reporters, with the listening kind usually getting a better break from them than the arrogant reporters get.

4. If the reason for hostility can't be guessed at, then ask. Let your source talk about it. Usually it's something unconnected with you, something you can't do anything about, anyway, except listen. Listening does help. Relieved of the burden, and appreciative of your courtesy, the source

will often begin to talk freely in response to your questions, and the interview begins anew.

5. Ask for background and context. Allowing a hostile source to explain the situation thoroughly will drain away hostility or prevent its building in the first place. Conversely, curt, arrogant questions along with frequent interruptions—the sort of thing you often see in TV courtroom dramas—can cause hostility to build.

6. Dissociate yourself from the snarling journalistic wolfpack as a matter of principle. Don't be the reporter who shouts the loudest or asks the most loaded, hostile questions at the news conference. Sources have long memories.

7. Try to maintain your sunny disposition even when the response is gloomy. Most sources *do* respond even if you can't win them all.

HANDLING OFF-THE-RECORD REQUESTS

Most news articles name their sources in what journalists call "attribution." The practice of naming sources is in response to the logical question, "Who told you that?" People judge the validity of statements largely in accordance with their assessment of the source's credibility. And although named sources are always preferable, a reporter must almost daily cope with requests that certain information be "off the record." What, exactly, does that mean? Let's examine several such terms.

On the record. If you call a source, identify yourself as a reporter, and explain that you're writing a story for the paper, then the usual assumption is that anything said by the source in answer to your questions is for publication. In practice the term "on the record" is seldom used; it is merely assumed. If a source does not want a statement published, he or she has an obligation to say so—or else not make the statement at all. Sometimes you have to explain this to inexperienced sources so that there can be no misunderstanding.

Off the record. This term means that anything specifically identified as "off the record" is not to be quoted for publication. The information is intended for the reporter's ears only. You may ask, if the comment is not intended for publication, why should it be said to a reporter at all? A good question. Sometimes it's said because the source can't resist spilling a little juicy gossip. Sometimes it's because the source is relaying an unconfirmed rumor or venting a personal attack on someone such as a political opponent—an attack he or she would not want to see published. Often it's because the reporter is asking penetrating questions about a situation the source is reluctant to discuss publicly. Example: You've learned that the sheriff has called up his reserve deputies for tomorrow night. You wonder why. It turns out they're planning a raid on a gang of bootleggers. Premature publicity would obviously thwart their plans, but the sheriff, in order to stop your incessant questioning, lets you in on the secret but asks you to keep it off the record.

Not for attribution.   (Sometimes called "background" or "deep background.") This means that the source is giving you information that you can publish but without identifying the person it came from. This is the usual condition behind euphemisms like "it was learned" or "sources said." One example would be a story about juvenile crime in which you quote several juvenile offenders without identifying their names. Often, however, the not-for-attribution condition is bureaucratic manipulation. Let's say the governor wants to propose a new state tax on hotels and motels. He has someone "leak" this information to the news media on a not-for-attribution basis, quoting sources "close to the governor." It is really a trial balloon. If too much adverse reaction greets the proposal, the governor may drop it without ever really having said he was going to do it.

Such are the ways the news media are "used" by clever politicians. Although idealists may find it abhorrent, the fact remains that much good reporting is done under conditions in which naming sources is not possible—the Watergate scandal, for example.

Newspaper editors, however, have begun to examine the off-the-record phenomenon with an increasingly critical eye. Some are insisting that all off-the-record fragments be corroborated by at least one additional source, named or unnamed. They also ask that reporters refrain from reckless use of unnamed sources. Media credibility is none too high anyway, they say, and reporters meanwhile have themselves learned to be wary of off-the-record requests. "If you don't want it published," they tell sources, "please don't tell me." (Sources often tell anyway.) Many journalists have also learned that with prodding, sources can often find the courage to have their names used. This is especially so when they know that the information may end up in the wastebasket unless the source is identified.

Naturally, the reporter and the editors must use discretion and judgment on whether to honor off-the-record requests when important information is being conveyed. Sometimes negotiation is called for. If the information is vital, and if sources insist on anonymity, then the reporter may very well publish the material if it can be corroborated by at least one more source.

BEING ACCURATE

It hardly seems necessary to make a case for accuracy. Accuracy is vital. Period. Rather, let's try to identify points at which mistakes in accuracy commonly occur in reporting to see if some of them can be avoided.

1. Failure to check spelling of names, ages, addresses, and similar routine factual information. *Always* check the city directory, telephone book, or other reference sources for *every* name with which you are not familiar. Ask for spelling when interviewing. Spelling of women's names, in

particular, has become exotic in recent years. If she tells you her name is (phonetically) TAIR-ee, do you spell it Terry, Terri, Teri, or Tari?

2. Failure to understand meanings. Often reporters are so intent on getting every word in their notes that they don't listen carefully for meanings. To be sure you understand a point, learn to repeat it back ("As I understand it, then, you are saying that. . . .") You may feel a little foolish if the source says, "No, that's not what I meant at all," but you'd feel a lot more foolish if your mistake showed up in print. Sometimes you can hedge a little by putting your "understanding" in the form of a question ("Are you saying that . . . ?"). Repeating your understanding of a point has a curious but salutary effect on conversations. Quiet people realize someone is really *listening,* and they tend to open up with more candor. Garrulous people discover that people are having difficulty getting their meaning amid the torrent of words, and so they strive to make their points more succinctly.

3. Unwarranted assumptions. Suppose you get a police report that says a man was found dead on top of an apartment building. Drug equipment was found nearby. So you write, "So-and-so died of an apparent drug overdose." That's an unwarranted assumption. Don't make such assumptions unless quoting a person qualified to comment, such as a medical examiner in this case. Be especially careful in arrest cases. Never say, for example, that "John Doe was arrested for murdering Jane Roe." Instead, say "John Doe is accused of first-degree murder in the death of Jane Roe." Doe, after all, is only accused, not convicted, and thus must be considered innocent until proven guilty. Furthermore, he may be convicted of a less-serious charge, such as manslaughter, in which case the death is not considered murder in the legal sense.

4. Failure to understand context. You can be accurate in describing an event, but grossly misleading in identifying the news issue behind the event. This is a common complaint among public officials; reporters tend to focus on the superficial facts of an event—the shouting, the violence, the confrontations of a street demonstration, for example— without going to the trouble of searching for the deeper issues that cause the event.

5. Failure to report both sides. You can be totally accurate in reporting that politician A accuses politician B of mishandling a situation, but grossly inaccurate if you don't quote B's reply. Some newspapers have a policy of not reporting A's accusations until B's reply (or refusal to comment) is on hand.

LISTENING

Few human pleasures quite equal the ecstasy of being listened to. The authors of the book, *Are You Listening?* suggest that listening is one area in which "a degree of selfishness is even appreciated by others. If, by careful listening, you take what other people offer, they will like you for it. And the more you accept the happier will be the person speaking." (Nichols and Stevens, 1957.)

The point is confirmed by public officials who serve as news sources. In Hawaii 50 public officials were interviewed for this text on the subject of relationships with the news media. Their most frequent complaint was that reporters, particularly the inexperienced ones, do not have sufficient knowledge of government and business. The second was that some reporters don't listen.

Some reporters do listen, of course, and they have greater success. A city councilman in Honolulu explained: "I don't try to treat all reporters equally. Some get more than others, and the reason is because they *listen*." A Honolulu business leader divides reporters into two categories, the "dogmatists" and the "listeners":

> The dogmatic reporters always put you on the defensive. They seem to have all the answers and they merely want you to confirm what they have already decided. The listener *really* listens. He takes the issue from various angles, gets underneath and over it and around it. Then he wants to know who else he should talk to about it for still another viewpoint. You go after the listener. You seek him out because he can tell you important things he's learned. The dogmatist—you try to avoid meeting him in the hallway.

Listening means more than merely hearing what is said. It means trying to pick up ideas or feelings only hinted at or pointedly ignored. In interviews, listening means asking follow-up questions to probe into these half-articulated ideas. One public official in Hawaii, discussing the work of an unusually successful reporter, observed:

> She picks up your attitudes by your choice of words. She's really quite skilled at reading your feelings through your words. For example, in talking with her I'll say something like, "As an administrator, you're subjected to certain kinds of—" and she'll say, "What do you mean *subjected?*" She picks up these fine nuances of meaning, and she can tell where you're at very quickly.

This skill permits the reporter to open up whole new vistas, often getting information that is new and fresh rather than platitudinous. (The reporter's name is Helen Altonn, of the *Honolulu Star-Bulletin,* depicted in Chapter 11.)

By contrast, a reporter who seems oblivious to fine nuances is often dealt with cautiously and perfunctorily. Explains one official in Hawaii:

> The guy I worry about is the one who doesn't seem to understand what I'm saying. You can sense this kind. They don't ask the right questions; they don't seem to understand. And sure enough, their articles are not very good. The *good* reporters know what to look for. When they ask a question and get an answer, they know what to ask for the second question instead of merely accepting the answer.

All of the foregoing comments suggest that the nonlistening reporters' work is vastly harder. Sometimes they must conduct cross-examinations bordering on inquisitions to get information that is readily available to the listening reporter.

If you would prefer to be the listening kind of reporter, here are some suggestions:

1. Put aside any preconceived notions on what the story should be. Go to the interview or speech with an open mind. Avoid stereotyping people: All murderers are *not* cold-blooded psychopaths, for example.

2. Stay alert for the fine shades of meaning. Richard Meryman, who used to write for *Life*, says he goes into "training" for an important interview: No alcohol, sugar, or starch for several days prior to the session. He spends the day before in bed; he eats steak the morning of the interview—all to "clear my mind" to catch subtle meanings in the conversation.

3. Avoid distractions. These include noise and movements within sight and hearing. They also include getting emotionally sidetracked by what the speaker is saying or the speaker's appearance or manner of delivery (stuttering, for example). Avoid getting so emotionally hung up on a flagrant word or phrase (such as "sex," "mother," or "law and order") that you don't listen to the message.

4. Don't let the mechanics of note taking interfere with your listening.

5. Listen for the main point or series of points the speaker is trying to make. Find the speaker's central theme or idea, then listen for supporting data: facts, illustrations, examples.

6. Evaluate what is being said. The good listener will appraise the speaker's comments in comparison to what has been learned from other sources. In an interview, for example, you need not accept everything at face value, particularly if you have prepared for the session. Often you find yourself asking follow-up questions based on several sources: "If this is so, and that is so, then what you just said a moment ago seems to add up to. . . . What do you think?"

7. Listen with your whole body. A speaker or interviewee can usually tell when the audience (or an interviewer) is listening. The telltale signs of failure to listen include slumped body posture, absence of eye contact, preoccupation with note taking, and nervous mannerisms.

GAINING SELF-CONFIDENCE

"I'm just a student." No question but that a conspiracy exists against college students, most of it unwittingly conveyed by the students themselves. It's too easy to say that you're "just a student," and that therefore people shouldn't expect much of you. Or that you've suffered from lifelong shyness so that when you talk to a source you just hope that the source will do all the talking so you won't have to ask any questions.

All of this comes under the heading of self-confidence as you prepare to face the professional world. It's hard to discuss it here without its sounding like a sermon. So let's just talk about Kaye.

Kaye Larson was a student in a class taught by Professor Lillian (Lee) Wilkins at the University of Oregon. Professor Wilkins announced to a newswriting class one day that thence forward the students would cover campus newsbeats and write real stories to be distributed to the news media.

"You mean we have to talk with *real* people?" one student asked. Students soon learned that they had to figure out how to "harvest" news—define it, find it, process it.

That's what they did. Student-written articles, distributed through the university information service, appeared in numerous papers, on broadcast stations, and the AP and UPI. Getting published, sometimes with a byline, was a real ego booster. An interesting byproduct of the experience, however, was the increased self-confidence it imparted to students, especially Kaye.

Kaye had found it so difficult to meet new people that she could hardly bring herself to contact the people on her beat, the university's dance department. Professor Wilkins pushed her a little: "Ask them about the phenomenal growth in enrollment over the past few years—they'll enjoy talking about that." It took four or five weeks, but Kaye gradually got more interested. Soon she found the dance department "fascinating," and the increasing flow of copy began to reflect her new attitude. Kaye was a changed woman, as she admitted when she wrote an evaluation of her experience.

"I didn't really want to go out and do this stuff, meet those strangers and expose my weaknesses," she said. "But once you get started, you find that they are all people and that you are doing all right. They like what you are doing. You act professional and try not to infringe on their time—and all of a sudden that old, creeping, nagging fear is gone, and you wonder why you ever suffered from it in the first place."

The experience, said Kaye, had given her new confidence in her professional abilities. Professor Wilkins, later a teacher at the University of Colorado, observed that Kaye's self-confidence probably began growing the day she got so interested and involved in gathering and writing stories about the dance department that she forgot that she was supposed to feel nervous and insecure.

POINTS TO REMEMBER

1. Reporters' note-taking practices vary from sketchy scribbles on scratch paper to use of portable word processors.
2. Note taking requires recognizing main points to be recorded along with supporting data.
3. Developing shorthand and training one's memory help both listening ability and note taking.
4. Tape recorders probably intimidate sources a lot less than they do interviewers.
5. Transcription of tapes is unnecessary; just take notes off the tape.
6. Taping interviews can be a good (painful) learning experience.
7. Meeting coverage is more readable when reporters go beyond the agenda and explore issues through supplementary interviews.

8. The telephone is an especially efficient way to gather information, particularly for stories requiring input from many sources.

9. Hostile sources can often be disarmed by empathy, candor, courtesy, and sincerity.

10. Sources will sometimes give information only under certain restrictions: "off the record" or "not for attribution."

11. Reporters should recognize typical causes of inaccuracy, such as failure to check details or to clarify meanings.

12. Sources don't necessarily treat all reporters alike: "listening" reporters usually get more material than "dogmatic" ones.

13. Getting out to interview real people for publication can help you gain self-confidence, even boost your ego.

PROJECT

Interview by phone one or more reporters about their "tricks of the trade." Ask about the kinds of things the reporters learned on the job as opposed to textbooks and classrooms. *Purpose:* Gain experience in telephone interviewing, also gain practical ideas from reporters that can be shared with the class and put to use.

13

Features: Beyond Straight News

If reporting is fun, then feature writing is the most fun of all. It's also the hardest. It requires skills not needed for straight news reports, such as the ability to think through the point of a story when traditional news values provide little guidance. Features require the ability to show things happening, rather than merely talking about them, and to organize a story on a pattern distinctly different from the inverted pyramid.

Most definitions of a feature story range from insipid ("It's not straight news") to banal ("It's people-to-people reporting"). Journalists typically describe features in words like "imaginative," "creative," "unpredictable," "human," "entertaining," and even "literary." A feature story has "unity, focus, and purpose." All the terms are appropriate, yet the definition remains elusive. Even so, most people seem to know what it is, if only by example. They know it when they see it.

One problem in finding a definition is that newswriting has changed so much in the past two decades that distinctions become blurred. Straight news often emerges in the form of feature writing. Take, as an example, the famous tumble that U.S. distance runner Mary Decker took after tangling with Britain's Zola Budd in the 1984 Olympics in Los Angeles. Somehow the straight news approach seems inadequate—"Mary Decker tripped and fell in the women's 3,000-meter race yesterday." Here, on the other hand, is an example of melding the feature approach with spot news.

Stan Federman at the Tacoma Zoo with whales at feeding time. *(Photo by Randy L. Rasmussen.)*

LOS ANGELES—Fate had brought them together on this day, to this race. All season long they had been on a symbolic collision course.

Theirs was a rivalry with a 0–0 record, until last night. It was Mary Decker, perhaps the most acclaimed distance runner in the world, against Zola Budd, the tiny, reticent teen-ager who left South Africa for Britain so she could legitimize her athletic standing.

Olympics fans couldn't have asked for more. But then, before a crowd of 85,159 dumbstruck spectators and millions more on television, the race of the games was cut short by controversy, injury and bitterness.

With a little more than three laps to go in the final of the women's 3000-meter race, Decker tripped over Budd's legs and fell to the infield. She injured her hip and lay writhing in a sobbing heap on the grass, unable to rise. . . .

—*John Crumpacker, San Francisco Examiner*

CASE HISTORY OF A FEATURE

Examine a hypothetical case history for what it shows about defining the feature and distinguishing it from straight news.

Let's say that around seven this morning a man named Alexander Bridlington, 67, called the sheriff's office to report seeing a body floating in the Chickahominy River. He'd been walking along the river bank, and he saw something in the river about 50 yards offshore. Deputies responded with a boat and retrieved the "body," which turned out to be a store mannequin, female, wearing black panties and a bra. "Guess my eyes aren't so good anymore," said an embarrassed Mr. B. "That's okay," a deputy reassured him. "You shouldn't feel bad. You did the right thing, calling us. We'd rather go on a dozen wild goose chases than miss the real thing." The deputies even presented the dummy to Mr. B., who said, "Well, I guess I'll keep it in my closet as a symbol of my own foolishness." So they drove him and his dummy home where his wife, Ellen, was unimpressed. "Get that thing out of here," she demanded. "Either you take it to the garbage dump or I'll take *you* to the dump!" The argument raged on as the deputies left.

How do you write a story with those facts? Frankly, a straight-news approach might look absurd.

> A semi-nude store mannequin was rescued from the Chickahominy River this morning by sheriff's deputies. . . .

Sounds pretty silly, doesn't it? Yet a touch of irony exists here: The good citizen called the authorities only to be embarrassed by the outcome. It may not be news by the usual definitions, but it's interesting because it's human. It calls for different handling:

> Alexander Bridlington, 67, was walking with his dog along the bank of the Chickahominy River this morning when he spotted something in the water about 50 yards offshore.
> A human body, thought Bridlington. He called the sheriff's office, and two deputies responded with a boat.
> They fished from the water a female store mannequin clad in black panties and bra.
> "Guess my eyes aren't so good anymore," said Bridlington, chagrined.

We now have what newspapers call a "suspended interest" bright (often spelled "brite"). The story's purpose is not to convey news, only to give readers a light touch, a chuckle over the unexpected outcome. Or, if written differently, it could serve to remind readers that they need not feel afraid to call authorities whenever they see anything amiss. (In that case, you'd add the quote from the deputy: "We'd rather go on a dozen wild goose chases than miss the real thing.")

But other approaches are possible. Consider this:

> People who commit indiscretions have a common problem.
> What do you do with the body?
> Alexander Bridlington, 67, faced that question today and decided to keep the body—a semi-nude female form—in his closet at home "as a symbol of my own foolishness."
> His wife, Ellen, was not enthusiastic when he came home with it, however.
> It came into his possession this morning after he discovered it floating in the Chickahominy River. He called the sheriff's office, and deputies responded with a boat.

> The deputies "rescued" a life-sized store mannequin.
> "Guess my eyes aren't so good anymore," Bridlington said, taking the manne-quin home with him.
> "Get that thing out of here," Ellen Bridlington demanded. "Either you take it to the garbage dump of I'll take you to the garbage dump."

This version could end here or the reporter could determine by a quick phone call the outcome of the drama. If, as one suspects, the body ended up in the dump, that fact could be added to the end of the story.

Toward A Definition

Although the Bridlington saga does not tell the full story of features, it does illustrate one of the principles, and it even suggests a definition.

A good feature story is a creative work of art. It does not record reality so much as it offers an artful, *but still factual,* rendition of it, largely through the selection of facts by the writer and the interpretation placed upon the facts. The feature story never fictionalizes. It taps into some event or situation and weaves information into a coherent story designed both to entertain and to make a memorable point—a statement about reality. It could be, as here, a whimsical point or it could be serious. Usually it is some variation of the theme: *This is the human condition . . . This is what people are really like.* Often the feature will make a reader laugh or cry or say, "Well, I'll be darned" or "It could happen to anybody."

Success in feature writing depends largely on a writer's ability to *see* the significance of people's actions and to make sure the reader sees it, too. To do this effectively, the writer must have precise control over the content of the article. And that, in the end, may be the only possible definition of a feature story:

A feature story evolves when to make a point the writer controls the facts—by selection, structure, and interpretation—rather than the facts controlling the writer.

This places a big responsibility on the writer. Controlling the facts does not mean expressing opinions. It certainly does not mean fictionalizing. Nor does it imply a sinister omission or manipulation of facts in order to advocate a point of view or present a skewed view of reality. Rather it means trying to give a *clearer* view of reality as seen by a skilled and unbiased observer.

Some Distinguishing Characteristics

A feature story, even if it can't be defined precisely, does have three distinguishing characteristics.

1. It readily identifies with the reader, usually on an informal or conversa-tional basis. It covers topics carefully calculated to relate to most readers' concerns.
2. It makes a point. Unlike the news story, the feature story must justify its existence to the reader, sometimes in explicit terms. It says in so many

words. "You'll learn something about your own health by reading this story about heart attacks." Sometimes the point is implicit; the reader infers the point without having it spelled out.

3. It is interestingly written. It is well-organized and to the point. It may cover a frivolous topic or a serious one, but even the serious one is laden with humor, drama, suspense, irony—all literary characteristics that make a piece of writing come alive. This is done largely by showing people in action, thus *demonstrating* the humor, drama, and so on in their lives.

In sum, the essence of a feature story is the drama of human endeavor. You show people, often ordinary people, striving to improve themselves, coping with troubles and obstacles, sometimes reaching beyond their grasp in quest of a worthwhile goal.

It almost seems a cliche: "An appealing character struggles against odds to reach a worthwhile goal." That it may be a cliche should not deter us. The basic elements of drama—human against nature, human against human, human against self—are also the elements of good feature writing. All human endeavor is a symbolic mountain climb, a struggle toward the top, sometimes to reach it, sometimes not. Often the best features come out of struggles to avoid being carried down the mountainside away from your goal by avalanches beyond your control. Such was the Mary Decker tumble in the 1984 Olympics.

A feature story, then, can record reality in a way calculated to interest readers and even show them something about people, possibly even themselves. Consider a tiny example, a story out of Salem, Oregon.

> Because of a scheduling mixup, the boys' softball team failed to show up for Garfield Elementary School's traditional game with arch-enemy Highland yesterday.
> But eight Garfield cheerleaders were there, and one of them, Penny Nelson, said:
> "What the heck—shouldn't we play Highland ourselves?"
> They did. And they won, 10 to 7.

In its microcosmic way, this storiette fits the pattern of many features. It's a simple pattern. You start with a problem or goal. You propose a solution (or define a goal). You show the struggle to solve the problem or reach the goal, and you finally record the outcome. (The inverted pyramid, by contrast, would record the outcome first, then provide the details.)

Thus:

> *Problem.* Boys didn't show up for the game.
> *Solution (goal).* Cheerleaders decide to play Highland themselves. Appealing, plucky characters.
> *Struggle.* "They did."
> *Outcome.* "They won, 10 to 7."

The drama of the underdogs emerging victorious gives this a classic, suspenseful quality, even in its short length. In its tiny way it makes a point about the human condition: the indomitable human spirit.

Not all feature stories portray in narrative form a struggle to reach a goal, however. But most at least allude to it, even if it's only a "view from the top' interview with a celebrity. Most features portray some kind of quixotic "Quest."

TYPES OF FEATURES

Whatever a feature is, it has certainly increased in popularity among newspaper editors. They are using more and more features, and they are even establishing special sections of the newspaper for them: magazine sections, "people" sections, service departments, and special feature sections. The following categories suggest the wide range of features used in a typical newspaper.

Bright.   Already described, a "brite" is a tiny human interest featurette, usually written in anecdotal style with the climax at the end (suspended interest).

Sidebar.   This is a feature story that accompanies a main news story. A story about a major flood, for example, may include such sidebars as an interview with a refugee family, a background story on what caused the flood, or a color piece on the work of rescue units—perhaps even a narrative account of a single dramatic rescue.

Personality sketch or profile.   A sketch is usually short and treats only one aspect of a personality, such as Ms. Jones' hobby of collecting models of antique sailing ships or Mr. Smith's work with handicapped children. A profile is longer, more detailed, and psychologically deeper. It tries to depict what the individual is *really* like down deep.

Organization or project profile.   Similar to the personality sketch or profile except that the organization/project article deals with groups or agencies rather than individuals. An example would be a story about a group of women who form a committee to secure better treatment of battered wives and take their case to courts, legislators, police officials, and so on.

Newsfeature.   This is a news story written in feature style. Instead of a straight, unvarnished account, it will use feature techniques, such as opening with an illustrative anecdote, even though the story's major purpose is to convey news.

Comprehensive newsfeature.   This kind of story depicts trends and ongoing news issues rather than specific news events. It is better researched than most daily news stories because it comes from a wide variety of sources. It is usually more analytical and interpretive; it tries to depict not only what the news is but what it means. More about this in Chapter 14.

Personal experience article.   Editors increasingly allow first-person accounts, particularly in magazine and feature sections. They are usually written by a reporter or ghost-written for a person who has undergone a unique experience such as crossing the country alone by hot air balloon. Sometimes a reporter will arrange a unique experience to write about, such as having herself committed to the county jail overnight. (See Chapter 9 on participant observation.)

Service feature.   This is a "how-to" story, describing anything from how to fix a meal to how to build a log cabin. Such features are becoming increasingly popular as newspapers strive to get closer to the needs and interests of their readers. They are treated separately in Chapter 15.

Interview.   Although most features are based on interviews, the special interview feature portrays a dialogue between a reporter and another person, often a public figure or celebrity. Sometimes it runs in question-and-answer format.

String of pearls.   This is a "collective" feature, such as a series of anecdotes on a common topic. "Person on the street" interviews fall into this category, as would a Valentine's Day feature depicting "the ten greatest love letters of all time."

Narrative.   Some observers see the narrative as another category of feature, and in its pure form it probably is. It is like a short story, even though it treats material factually. It depicts events unfolding scene by scene, utilizing description, characterization, and plot. However, the narrative is also a writing technique that can be used in any of the above categories of features. In such forms as anecdotes and case histories, narratives can be inserted into traditionally structured articles.

GETTING IDEAS FOR FEATURES

Nobody ever called a news conference to announce a feature story. The first place to look for feature ideas is in the drama of everyday life. Especially look for situations in which ordinary people face extraordinary events. Look for them on the police beat, in the courts, at athletic events (there's perhaps no more dramatic Quest then the athlete seeking to win; that's why the personality story is popular on sports pages).

Look for features in social or cultural change. You find them, for example, in the drama of women, newly liberated, adjusting to their new and uncertain status—girls seeking places on athletic teams, women seeking to become police officers or fire fighters, and mothers seeking to adjust to their daughters' new and exotically liberated ideas.

Look for feature story ideas in ordinary conversations. Suppose somebody remarks, "I had the strangest experience yesterday—I was arrested for speeding by a petite female cop! How can a woman that small cope with police work?" How, indeed? Your answer may come in the form of a feature story about that woman or about female cops in general.

And most important, look for feature ideas inside your own head. It is in your mind that feature stories are discerned. They seldom merely "happen"; rather, they emerge from a writer's ability to see significance in everyday circumstances. Consider connections in events or circumstances that might at first glance seem to have nothing in common. In them a writer might recognize human drama that has meaning for other people. Let's look at some examples.

- A writer heard his eleven-year-old son remark that the most memorable thing he ever did in his "youth" was climb a 10,000-foot mountain with his dad at the age of nine. This surprised the father because the climb seemed to be quite a struggle for the boy. The writer mentioned it to other youngsters, and they often echoed the idea: Kids like to respond to physical challenge as a means of proving their oncoming adulthood. He did research (mostly interviewing youngsters and their parents) and wrote a story containing the elements of a feature. *Problem:* grow up. *Solution:* test one's physical abilities. *Struggle:* the long, arduous trek upward; pain; momentary self-doubt. *Outcome:* reach the top, look at self with new respect.

- A writer was curious to know how a seventeen-year-old girl views life after having just witnessed a court trial in which her father was sentenced to death for murdering her mother. So he arranged an interview and asked her. (Life must go on, she said. Now she's planning to get married and move on to whatever the future holds.) *Problem:* cope with traumatic experience. *Solution:* build a tougher shell, move on with life. *Struggle:* shed a lot of tears, wake up screaming at times, but gradually learn to cope. *Outcome:* uncertain at the moment, but in sight—a return to normal, plans to get married.

- A man died a skid road derelict, yet a Phi Beta Kappa key was found on his body and $100,000 was in his bank account. A feature story explored the reverse of the typical pattern: Goals may be set, but problems are *not* overcome, solutions *not* found—therefore a tragic outcome.

Getting Information

Once you have an idea in mind, the next step is getting information. This is important. You cannot cover up for lack of information by clever writing or fictionalizing. The success of your story depends on your ability to get significant and lively material. An orderly pattern for doing so comes in three steps: *see, define,* and *illustrate.*

See means getting the preliminary facts, starting with background reading of news clips and preliminary interviews. You have to get sufficient information to get a clear idea where the story's going—which leads to the second step.

Define means that the point of the story has now become clear to you. You have gained the slice of the human condition that is to become the focal point of your story. Now your information gathering shifts into the third stage.

Illustrate means that you will find the quotations, the anecdotes, scenes, descriptions, and case histories that support your points. The task is not forbidding; we do it every day in conversation. A doctor who says that it's been a rough day in the emergency room may illustrate that point with graphic descriptions of some of the most interesting or bizarre cases.

Above all, a good feature story requires skill and empathy in asking questions. You are usually dealing with ordinary people, not newsmakers. Most of them have never been interviewed before. So the interviewer's job is to make the session seem like ordinary conversation—like friendly neighbors chatting. You'll find no formula for it. However, a University of Nevada professor, LaRue Gilleland, has devised a simple pattern for asking questions that seems uniquely suited to the quest-struggle-outcome nature of the feature story. He calls it GOSS, the letters representing *Goals, Obstacles, Solutions, Start.*

> *Goals.* What is the person or agency struggling to achieve?
> *Obstacles.* What stands in the way of achievement? What problems exist?
> *Solutions.* What is being done or proposed to surmount the obstacles?
> *Start.* How did it all begin? Understanding beginnings is often helpful in understanding fundamentals. Beginnings often make interesting anecdotal stories in themselves.

If your interviews focus on those elements, you can obtain the material for your feature stories. If you start by having the respondent identify goals, you will learn the direction of that individual's quest. Knowing the obstacles, and how those obstacles were overcome, will give you the dynamic pattern of the appealing character struggling against obstacles to reach a worthwhile goal. Of course it's not that simple. To *show* the struggle, you must in your interviews press for graphic detail, particularly specific examples and anecdotes.

Getting Anecdotes

You need anecdotes for your feature story, but when you ask for them your sources never can think of any. Right? One solution may be to avoid stilted, formal kinds of interviews, the kind where you have to ask for anecdotes. How? Have you thought of spilling your coffee?

You may recall (Chapter 8) that a journalism student did that once—unwittingly, to be sure—and found to her astonishment that it enhanced conversational rapport rather than damaging it. From that point on the source began talking more anecdotally.

Anecdotes are important to writers, for they have a unique ability to illustrate points that are hard to put across any other way. The spilled coffee story is a case in point. Would you really believe a generalization? Try this: "If you want human candor from your sources, first display some of your own human vulnerability. Maybe even do something kind of dumb, like spilling your coffee." Not very convincing unless dramatized by the story. The anecdote, which by definition is a factual storiette that illustrates a point, gives drama to your writing.

To a skilled interviewer, anecdotes are not hard to collect. The spilled coffee story just dropped out of an informal conversation. The student was so excited about her ironic experience that she simply had to share it. Many anecdotes arrive just that way. They come from people who enjoy talking about their experiences to an enthusiastic listener. They're eager to share what they've learned from life's experiences.

A few suggestions may help in your quest for anecdotes:

1. Make clear at the start of an interview that you seek illustrative stories: "I want to talk about your *experiences*." You might also add, "And what you've learned from them." Avoid using the term "anecdote." People tend to freeze up when pressured to produce one on demand.

2. Keep the conversation informal, and tell stories yourself. In your interview with a Montana cattle rancher, for instance, tell the story about tough financial times that you picked up from an Oregon logger: If he had a million dollars, he'd go into logging for a living, and he'd have the time of his life for a few months until he had it all spent. Your story will challenge any self-respecting cattle rancher, and he'll top it: "I figure there are three great ways to lose money. The fastest is to bet on the horses. The nicest is to play around with women. But the *surest* way—the surest damned way to lose money—is to raise cattle!" These are tall tales, of course, but the use of them to illustrate financial difficulties gives them journalistic validity.

3. Get anecdotal information via preinterview research. Often you can get stories by interviewing family, colleagues, and friends of your subject. Spouses often like to spill favorite stories: "Ask her about the time she ran out of gas en route to meet the President." You can find stories by reading articles about a topic that you plan to discuss. An anecdote picked up from the *Reader's Digest* may prime the pump. Conversely, if *you* don't know any stories related to your topic, why do you expect another person to surrender stories on demand?

4. Interview for "crossroads." Fiction writers salt their stories with "willy-wonties": crossroads where a character faces a crucial decision. Will he fight the villain and rescue a beleaguered partner or won't he? Reality also has its melodramatic moments. You can recreate tense factual situations by tracing a person's pathways of life. Look for the specific crossroads that led to a present predicament. Ask the businesswoman about crucial decisions she has had to make in her climb to success. To quit a dead-end job, perhaps? To fight a boss? To take on a project with a

high risk of failure? To pursue a career instead of marriage? Everyone confronts such decisions. When you find an important one, you probe for enough detail to write an anecdotal narrative.

5. Look for "surprises." Ask your sources to share their unexpected pains and pleasures. Passing along the story of a surprising experience may surprise your readers, too. The spilled-coffee story illustrates the point.

6. Interview for "epiphanies." Epiphanies are nuggets of learning—sudden insights that fall out of everyday experiences. If you ask a female executive what she's learned along the pathways to success, she may cite points that are educational for others. Suppose she says, "One thing I noticed is that among executive equals, the pecking order is largely based on who has the fastest wit and best sense of humor." Try next to uncover the specific experiences that led her to that conclusion. One woman who was asked such a question explained that she had gained acceptance into the "wit club" the time she arrived an hour late for an important meeting. She had overslept. She wryly explained, however, that she was actually testing a hypothesis: "My theory was that it is impossible to leave home at eight, drive 100 miles to this meeting, and arrive by nine. You know something? I was right!" The tension eased, and the late arrival was quickly forgotten.

7. Be enthusiastic. Nothing rewards a source more than an appreciative audience. A young writer, upon hearing an interesting story, exclaimed, "Wait—I've got to get that marvelous item into my notes." The source replied, "I didn't know you wanted *those* kinds of stories." During the ensuing silence, as the writer put the information into her notes, the source remembered three more anecdotes, each a little better than the one before.

8. Make sure you can recognize a good anecdote when you hear one. A newspaper writer, interviewed by a journalism student, reported that he had had the student laughing uproariously at accounts of his blunders as a beginning reporter. But when the reporter read the student's report of the interview, he was amazed. Not one of his stories appeared. One good rule is, "Whenever you hear anything that makes you or others laugh, put it into your story, recounting it the same way you heard it." Maybe you can make the reader laugh, too.

Getting Good Quotes

Like anecdotes, colorful quotations can add zest to your feature story. The quest for them starts with knowing the five variations of quotations commonly used in news and feature stories.

1. *Direct quotations* represent word for word what the speaker said, and they are enclosed in quotation marks. Some minor deviations from the exact wording are considered okay by most newspapers, provided the meaning is not changed. Suppose councilman Jones says:

> Well, what I'm trying to say is, like, maybe we ought to, ah, I mean we ought to consider, ah, whether we have, you know, the money to build a new city hall.

People do talk that way—you, too, probably—when speaking off the top of the head. Would any purpose be served in quoting verbatim? Probably the quote would be cleaned up to read, "We ought to consider whether we have the money to build a new city hall."

2. *Indirect quotations* represent what the speaker said and more or less the way it was said but with changes. Quotation marks are not used. Example: Jones said the council should consider whether funds are available for a new city hall.

3. *Paraphrased quotations* represent what the speaker said but are presented in the *writer's* words. No attempt is made to preserve the wording of the original statement: Jones raised the question of financing a new city hall.

4. *Fragmentary quotations* are combinations of paraphrased and direct quotes. They are especially useful when the speaker has incorporated a few colorful words into an otherwise routine comment.

> Smith opposed rebuilding city hall as an "extravagance that even Fort Knox couldn't support."

5. *Dialogue* is used when two or more speakers are quoted in a conversational exchange, such as in a court trial. Dialogue often makes a news article more readable.

> The cross-examination was brief.
> "Did you in fact pick up the gun and shoot the deceased?" asked District Attorney Johnson.
> "No, sir," the defendant replied.
> "Then how does it happen that on the morning of June 5, when the officers came to arrest you, they found blood all over your room and your clothing?"
> "I don't know."
> "No more questions," snapped Johnson.

The hardest part of using quotations is recognizing them in the mass of verbiage in people's conversation. People don't normally talk in succinct little packages suitable for quotation; rather, they merely converse. You must learn to recognize a quotable quote much as you might separate gold from raw ore.

Here are some suggestions for getting good quotations during interviews:

1. Develop an ear for them. They should represent the unique character of the speaker, something pithy, succinct, authoritative, epigrammatic, perhaps metaphorical. Use quotes that contrast with your writing. In formal writing, for instance, seek breezy, informal quotes.
   "A good quote is an amiable kick in the pants," says one editor.

2. Ask your questions colorfully and informally. Dull questions elicit dull answers and vice versa. Formal questions tend to bring out noble public posture instead of candor.

3. Don't be afraid to joke with your respondent. Your subtle wisecrack may produce a juicy retort and establish a tone of informal candor. Use common sense, but don't be grim.

4. Use metaphorical questions to elicit metaphorical answers. "Should a quote be a kick in the pants?" you ask, and the reply might well be, "I'd prefer it to be a dash of spice or a barrel of laughs."

5. Use interesting quotes yourself. Browse through books of quotations. Preface your questions with comments like "as Oscar Wilde [or Mark Twain or Aristotle] once said. . . ."

6. Show enthusiasm when you get a usable quote. You'll encourage more of the same.

7. Represent opposing viewpoints, not by arguing but by indirection ("*Mr. Blank* disagrees").

8. Probe, probe, probe, that is, pursue points vigorously and enthusiastically with follow-up questions.

9. Seek analogies: "What's it like?" Asked what job hunting was like, a college woman said it was "like sorority rush," and a young man said it was "like asking my wife for money."

STRUCTURE OF THE FEATURE STORY

The feature story offers considerable freedom to the writer, but a structural pattern does exist and should be learned. It is roughly equivalent to that of other forms of communication: a college theme, a speech, an essay. It starts with a central theme or central point. The theme is supported by factual data, quotes, ideas, observations, and so forth, that can be separated into the major supporting sections. The overall pattern of the feature, then, looks like this:

1. An opening calculated to gain reader attention and interest, also to indicate what the article is about. Often it is an illustrative anecdote or a descriptive scene to set the stage.

2. A general statement of theme in which you orient the reader *specifically* to what the article is about and perhaps what it means to the reader or how it ties in with some news event or trend. This orientation section— some writers call it the "establishing section" or the "nut paragraph"— may be brief or it may be explicit, taking several paragraphs.

3. Two or more main supporting points for the theme. These are like topic headings for an essay or speech. They comprise the body of the article. Let's say you are writing an article whose main theme is, "Thousands of River City residents have taken to bicycle riding for inexpensive transportation and for exercise." The major supporting points could run like these:

    A. Statistics show a fivefold increase in bike riding in the last five years.

    B. Examples show men and women riding bikes for specific health reasons such as losing weight, toning their muscles, improving their heart and circulation.

C. Statistics show how some families save money riding bikes to and from work.

D. Problems and precautions to be taken with bikes, such as theft or traffic safety.

E. Future of bicycling in River City, plans of city officials to build bike trails to accommodate the expected increase in bicycling.

4. Ending. Your ending should be strong. If your feature is well written, many readers will follow it all the way to the end. They deserve a reward, like dessert after a meal. Do it with a colorful anecdote, a touch of humor, a worthy quotation, or a food-for-thought comment. Many endings try to tie together with the beginning, so that a question raised in the opening paragraph is answered to the reader's satisfaction in the end.

Although the above pattern fits most features (not always precisely), you will find exceptions. One exception is the narrative, the kind that reads like a short story, depicting a series of incidents involving a central character.

Be careful of narratives.

Like a short story, the nonfiction narrative must have a purpose. That purpose essentially is to make a statement about reality. To do this it must be more than a mere stretch of linear chronology. For instance, you could not tape-record a conversation in your living room, have it transcribed, and expect to publish it as either a short story or a nonfiction narrative. A nonfiction narrative, like a short story, must be a statement *by the writer,* shown through selection of detail, interpretation, and structure. It must have a central theme supported by documenting points, even if the points come within the narrative.

THE PERSONALITY FEATURE

A final observation must be made about that special genre of article, the personality feature. People like to read about people. Many newspapers have replaced the old society page with a feature section on people. Instead of the big pictures of brides, you now see pictures and stories about coal miners, divorcees, single parents, and beachcombers.

Most of what has been said in this chapter applies to the personality feature. But two further points need to be made.

First, to write about people you must try to understand them. Not to judge them, but to understand them. This requires skill, experience, tolerance, and a special interest in psychology. It is never easy to understand the reasons for a person's behavior, let alone write about them. For example, why does the police chief you are interviewing get so irate whenever he hears an adolescent say, "Life is boring"? The chief himself might not know the reason. Or he may give you platitudinous reasons. It often takes the observations of other persons—parents, a spouse, children, colleagues, even enemies—to give you a more plausible set of reasons. (His mother, for example, may suggest that the reason for the chief's behavior is his own difficult struggle during adolescence amid impoverished surroundings; he can't understand how a child who has not had that kind of struggle can possibly be bored.)

The second point is that you must capture the essence of a personality by presenting scenes, examples, anecdotes, and quoted comments. The more informal and offguard these scenes are, the closer you'll come to revealing the real person. By presenting scenes and examples, you also "stay out of the readers' way" and allow them to make their own generalizations. If you show the police chief kicking the wastebasket and pounding the desk after a difficult conversation with a "bored" juvenile, it probably is not necessary to say the chief was angry. You allow your characters to speak for themselves through their actions and comments.

This approach definitely precludes the passive kind of feature, the one that involves no action but is a mere compendium of miscellaneous information about a person: birthplace, education, degrees, honors and awards, and so on. You can write page after page of such material and still not capture the personality.

Note, on the other hand, how skillfully the author brings out some amiable personality characteristics of Olympic athlete Edwin Moses in the opening paragraphs of this 1983 portrayal:

> Edwin Moses: "My mother says I was a natural on the saxophone."
> Myrella Moses: "Your mother? What do you expect your mother to say?"
> Edwin: "She wouldn't make up something like that. If she says I was a natural, I was a natural."
> If Edwin Moses had it all to do over again, he would be an astronaut. No, he would be a doctor. Or maybe he would be an aerospace engineer. Or a television weatherman. Or a musician—a saxophone player.
> While his German wife, Myrella, rolls her eyes playfully, Moses says in all seriousness, "I could have been (sax man) Grover Washington Jr."
> Instead he has had to settle for being Edwin Moses—without question the greatest intermediate hurdler ever and one of the most successful track athletes of all time. . . .
>
> —Randy Harvey, Los Angeles Times

The Edwin Moses article and the following article about a corn geneticist both make a transition from an opening to an orientation or "establishing section." This is the most important part of a feature story, for it sets the stage. It tells the reader what to expect. In the above example, it's the paragraph that says he has to settle for being Edwin Moses and goes on to say who Moses is. In the article below, the establishing section is the paragraph that introduces Mr. Galinat as the University of Massachusetts geneticist. Note how the lead paragraphs flash several unique accomplishments before establishing the story with his identity. Citing the accomplishments tends to define the character and attract reader interest.

Walton Galinat invented a square ear of corn when he learned airlines don't serve corn on the cob because it rolls off the plate. He figured square corn would be perfect for a plane, but so far no one seems interested.

He bred the longest ear of corn in the country, 18½ inches, in a US Department of Agriculture contest, and to celebrate the Bicentennial in 1976 he bred red, white and blue corn with stars on the kernels.

Galinat has bred more than 30,000 pedigrees of corn, including an ear with an edible cob and a variety that does not stick to your teeth. He credits his research with helping to keep down food prices by increasing corn yield and he said it could lead to agriculture without pesticides.

Galinat says he relates to corn; colleagues concur, and some add that he's different.

A corn geneticist at the University of Massachusetts Experiment Station in Waltham, Galinat is an internationally known scientist and authority on the corn plant. The 60-year-old professor, farmer, and inventor has spent 10 hours a day, seven days a week for the past 45 years researching the origin and evolution of corn. . . .

—*Elizabeth Karagianis, Boston Globe*

Finally, let's examine an entire article. In the following story about a college president, note how the opening anecdote and the quotations lead to the theme of concern about matching job and family relationships. Indeed, the entire article narrowly focuses on the theme of balancing an important job with family responsibilities. The narrow theme actually produces a better article. Too broad a theme—the "everything you wanted to know about a Radcliffe president" approach—would tend to be superficial and dull. This story, by contrast, zeros in on the career-family dilemma effectively and identifies with the concerns of younger women.

BY DIANE C. MANUEL
CHRISTIAN SCIENCE MONITOR

BOSTON—Shortly after she became president of Radcliffe College, Matina Horner, 44, found herself dashing about the house one evening, changing clothes and saying good night to her husband and children before she left to make yet another campus speech. As she was going out the door, one of her sons stopped her with a quiet plea: "It's not like you're my mommy anymore."

Even though it happened 12 years ago, Matina Horner still values that incident as a turning point in her approach to her family and career responsibilities.

"It was then, with those big brown eyes flashing up at me, that I realized that raising those three kids really meant a lot to me," she says. "I decided that when I couldn't get home until late at night, I was going to wake them up if I had to, to talk with them.

"The rest of my family thought I was nuts, but it worked. When the children had something to say, they woke up and were ready to talk. And when nothing much was on their minds, we'd have a hug instead.

"I think you find ways to maintain the relationships you want to maintain," she adds, breaking out an incandescent grin. "But they're not the ordinary ways."

Relationships are at the core of Matina Horner's prismatic world. In her often overlapping roles as wife, mother, teacher and administrator as well as clinical psychologist and pacesetting researcher in the field of achievement motivation in women, she is finely tuned to the needs and aspirations of others.

"I guess my biggest thrill in life is watching things grow," she explains somewhat shyly. "I've loved watching my own children grow, watching students develop, and watching Radcliffe take shape as an institution, too."

When she was selected as the youngest president ever of the prestigious women's school in 1972, Horner was a popular assistant professor at Harvard, teaching a precedent-shattering course in feminine psychology. Since then, she has almost single-handedly created a new and independent sense of identity for Radcliffe. Undergraduate women now have equal access to all resources available to Harvard students, and a kaleidoscope of programs specifically designed for women has also been established, including lectures, colloquia and internships. Largely as a result of Horner's continuing interest in women's lives, the Arthur and Elizabeth Schlesinger Library on the History of Women in America and the Henry A. Murray Research Center: A Center for the Study of Lives have become preeminent resources for research on women in the United States.

When her family and students are asked about her impact on their lives, however, it is her sincerity that appears to count most. Tia, who was 7 when her mother was appointed president and now is a sophomore at Princeton University, wrote in a recent issue of the alumnae quarterly, "Her love of life and human beings is contagious," adding, "She's so 'unpresidential,' so unaffected that I can't think of her in formal or official terms."

Students interviewed for the same periodical recalled a presidential wink in the midst of otherwise solemn commencement ceremonies. They cited the annual Christmas tree-trimming party at Horner's home and even opined that she must be "more popular than breakfast" with classmates who have taken advantage of the open office hours she holds two days a week from 8:30 to 10 A.M.

Not surprisingly, Horner says she gets plenty of questions from undergraduates about her personal experience. They want to know how she and her husband shared child-care responsibilities while they were both in graduate school, how potential tensions were resolved when he found himself out of work for six months while she was teaching at Harvard, and why he encouraged her to interview for the Radcliffe position when she felt she was too young and too inexperienced for the job.

But the questions that most frequently come up in her office and in the classroom where she teaches "Women and Social Change: Family, Work, and Children" have to do with how students can balance their own personal and professional objectives.

"In the late '60s, we encouraged women to have a career instead of children," she begins, "and the dominant pressure is still to pursue a career and one's own self-development before deciding to think about having a family.

"But the big difference now is that the younger women are questioning whether that's right. They're getting messages from the generation just before them—the women who are now in their mid-30s, who chose what was essentially the new stereotype of the early '70s. Today that group is beginning to say that it's lonely out there, that the rewards of having a high-paying profession are not as terrific as one might think, that if you postpone marriage, the quality of men available gets pretty negligible."

Although she tells her students that there are no simple answers to their questions about how they can successfully combine marriage, family and career, Horner contends that society has an obligation to help.

POINTS TO REMEMBER

1. Features are not easily defined, given the merging of feature style writing into straight news stories.
2. Think of features and you envision terms like *imaginative, creative, human, entertaining,* and others.

3. In features the writer controls the facts, not by fabricating or fictionalizing, but by selection, structure, and interpretation, to make a point.
4. Features are pointed, they identify with reader interests, and they are entertainingly written.
5. Nobody ever called a press conference to announce a feature; ideas must come from the writers themselves.
6. Research for a feature comes in three stages, labeled *see, define,* and *illustrate.*
7. GOSS—*goals, obstacles, solutions, start*—is a useful pattern when interviewing for features.
8. Anecdotes are the lifeblood of features and require special interviewing techniques.
9. Quotes can be made more colorful through interviewing techniques such as phrasing your questions more colorfully.
10. Features are organized in three parts—opening, establishing section (theme), followed by elaboration in two or more main points.
11. Writing about people requires the ability to (1) understand the person, and (2) illustrate your understanding.

PROJECT

Develop an idea for a feature and conduct the appropriate research and interviews to write it for a local newspaper such as the campus paper or a community paper. Below are a few ideas to get you started. Obviously the best features are those uniquely adapted to your community and your own interests. In short, these are only suggestions; the best features are the ones you think of yourself.

1. Depict a counselor's work coping with alcoholism or drug addiction among students. Try to make the feature detailed enough to be helpful to students, that is, to those who have a problem or know someone who does.
2. Write an article on student stress as seen by doctors and counselors.
3. If ROTC exists on your campus, write a feature depicting the work of one officer or cadet in maintaining military programs. Does an antimilitary feeling still persist?
4. Show the work of an employment recruiter who comes to your campus to recruit students as prospective employees.
5. Show the struggle of one or more students finding employment as graduation nears.
6. Show the work of employment counselors in teaching job-finding skills such as how to be interviewed, to write a resume, or to "sell" yourself.
7. Portray the work of a campus official who finds housing for students (particularly if housing is tight in your community).
8. Depict the work of a researcher on your campus in an area of current interest (such as consumer affairs, nutrition, solar energy).

14

Comprehensive Newsfeatures

One major criticism of the news media is that they report the news in fragments. Typically defined, news means that you report events that have obtruded themselves. In an earlier chapter we differentiated between news events and news issues. Some critics suggest that media report too many events and not enough issues. Reporting meeting after meeting of the school board without touching on major educational issues is like a doctor treating pimple after pimple instead of the underlying cause: chicken pox. The comprehensive newsfeature is one way to get at the issues and the underlying causes.

Consider an example. In the State of Washington one of the most catastrophic events in natural history occurred May 18, 1980. Mount St. Helens, a 9,677-foot volcanic peak exploded with a force equivalent to 500 Hiroshima-type atomic bombs, devastating an area of 156 square miles, and leaving the mountain about 1,300 feet shorter than it was the day before. Sixty-two persons were listed as dead or missing. The *Seattle Times* reported the story day by day, of course, in bits and pieces as new information came in. Then the paper decided to publish a special section for the Sunday edition a week after the explosion. Richard Zahler, a veteran journalist, was placed in charge of writing the main story—a comprehensive newsfeature that would somehow come to grips with the awesome sweep of events.

Out of this came a unique journal of that fateful day. The story won a distinguished writing award from the American Society of Newspaper Editors. It was reprinted in the book *Best Newspaper Writing 1981*, whose editor, Roy Peter

Seattle Times reporter Richard Zahler watches a video of a NASA/FAA experiment at Edwards Air Force Base in California. *(Photo by Matt McVay.)*

Clark, called it "Micheneresque" in its grand scheme, a novel-like but factual account reminiscent of the work of James Michener *(Hawaii, Centennial)*. More about the story after some definitions and explanations.

WHAT IS A COMPREHENSIVE NEWSFEATURE?

The comprehensive newsfeature is the journalistic form that allows you to report the chicken pox rather than the individual pimples. The term really embraces a wide variety of journalistic practices. They go by such terms as *depth reporting, investigative reporting, precision journalism, saturation reporting,* and *interpretive reporting.* Although each of these has a specific meaning (see Glossary), they all fall roughly into the broad definition suggested here. A comprehensive newsfeature is "comprehensive" in that it draws from a wide variety of sources. It is "news" in that it reports new things, sometimes-subtle trends. It is a "feature" in its theme and structure, which are under tight control by the writer.

It differs from the simple feature described in the previous chapter in three ways: (1) It is usually longer and more complex, (2) it is more newsy in conveying major trends and changes as opposed to the simple feature's focus on an individual's quest for accomplishment, and (3) it is more thoughtful in evaluating the meaning of the situation being conveyed. In short, it tries to convey the disease, not the pimple.

The comprehensive newsfeature need not always depict what we traditionally consider public affairs, however. A trend toward getting married at a later age can be news just as much as a spiraling cost of living or rising taxes. So can a trend toward (or away from) the growing of beards. An article on a personal problem, such as shyness, could be news, too, especially if it presents new insights derived from psychological research. Not only are all of these examples news, but they have the further advantage of being close to the readers: their personal problems, their family relationships, their immediate environment.

To summarize, here are six basic characteristics of the comprehensive newsfeature:

1. It's topical. If it doesn't relate to a specific news event, it at least deals with matters that concern large numbers of people.
2. It identifies with the reader, not only in choice of topic but in readable style of writing.
3. It explores the essence—the why—of an issue or problem.
4. It relies primarily on a reporter's ability to *understand* a problem or situation— often through open-minded and diligent research.
5. It relies on a wide variety of sources.
6. It makes a point.

All of this may sound intimidating to the student journalist. Nevertheless, you can learn to write comprehensive newsfeatures first by studying them and then by starting with the elementary varieties.

Here's an example of a comprehensive newsfeature depicting the aftermath of a college's decision to ban fraternities on the campus. The story grew from many sources as the writer worked to depict the various facets of a complex and controversial situation. When it came time to write the story, the author elected to flash three brief scenes that represent three reactions to the decision and then to move along to a general statement of the essence of the article. Here are the opening paragraphs:

BY THOMAS J. MEYER
CHRONICLE OF HIGHER EDUCATION

AMHERST, MASS.

Saturday night. John M. Blasberg wanders down to the Amherst College parking lot to see how bad things are.

The lot is nearly empty. Things are pretty bad. "It used to be," the Amherst senior says later, "on Saturday night the lot was packed with people coming to Amherst. Now people are going away." Going to find parties elsewhere, he says—at Smith College or Mount Holyoke. Or just going away.

Mr. Blasberg sighs. "Everyone used to say Amherst was a great social school."

■

Homecoming weekend. Every year since Peter J. Weidman graduated, he's partied here with his fraternity brothers at Delta Kappa Epsilon.

Someone always orders a few kegs from the same local package store the Dekes have patronized for years. And Mr. Weidman and his buddies put on their tweeds, gather round the bar, and remember the good old days.

This year, it wasn't so easy.

Mr. Weidman, a New York City lawyer, ran into a few snags when he tried to organize the annual bash this month. The first was a call from an Amherst administrator who told him, in no uncertain terms, the party was off.

"To me, not having the frat to go back to is like not having the homecoming game," Mr. Weidman says. "It's like saying, 'Hey, alumni, come on back. We'll welcome you with open arms. By the way, there's no football game this year.' "

Thirty of the fraternity's members—alumni and undergraduates—ignored the college's new policy forbidding fraternity activity, and spent the weekend carousing at the house.

■

Wednesday night. The officers of the Psi Upsilon fraternity have planned a meeting off campus. They cancel it, but still have a keg to finish off. They invite the members of Delta Chi Psi over to the dormitory room where they're having the impromptu party.

"Everyone there was there because they were in one of those two fraternities," one member says. "But it wasn't a fraternity party."

That is a subtle but important distinction these days at Amherst College, which this fall banned any fraternity activity on the campus. Last spring, the college's trustees abolished its eight fraternities. A year ago, nearly half of the college's 1,500 students—including more than 200 women—were fraternity members. Even for those who weren't affiliated, the fraternities were the focus of social life here.

Now they are gone, and though the group that requested their abolition called the fraternities, "sources of hurt and humiliation for many Amherst students," their absence has led to bitterness and indignation among students here.

Many simply resent that the change had to come during their college years.

"We're here now," says Chuck O'Boyle, a junior and an outspoken advocate of Amherst's fraternities. "It seems the administration is writing us off in terms of commitment to the college."

$100,000 for Entertainment

Amherst has hardly ignored its students' need for social activities. Earlier this fall, the administration turned over $100,000 to a student-run committee charged, basically, with the entertainment of undergraduates.

The college's long-term plans are more ambitious. A committee of advisers to Amherst's president has already planned for a new dormitory and the renovation of a campus center. This spring, the committee—whose members include students, administrators, faculty members, alumni, and trustees—will recommend a comprehensive plan to restructure residential and social life.

But this fall has been a season of transition on this pastoral New England campus, and the promise of an exciting future isn't adequate compensation for some of the current students.

"No transition is easy," says Erwin Nussbaum, Amherst's dean of housing and one of the highest-ranking administrators. . . .

The story goes on to depict the college's attempts to restructure the students' social life sans fraternities. The story also shows additional reactions to the ban, such as off-campus social bashes. This is but one example of the comprehensive newsfeature. Obviously a reporter is limited only by lack of imagination in the kinds of topics to be covered. Here are some other examples.

* Josh Getlin and David Reyes assembled a seven-part series of articles for the *Los Angeles Times* on the newest slums—the suburbs. The articles focused on a community named Buena Clinton, located just three miles from Disneyland. When it was fashioned out of a soybean field 23 years earlier, it typified California's "suburban dream." By 1983, the date of the articles, it had become a troubled, lawless nightmare. The authors quote an expert on urban-suburban problems: "It's a myth to think that the American suburb remains a haven with green lawns for middle-income people. In many cases these neighborhoods show symptoms that are as bad as, or worse than, the slums of central cities."

* Andrew H. Malcolm wrote in the *New York Times* about a significant trend toward growing legalized gambling around the country. The story is datelined Bellevue, Nebraska—a far cry from Las Vegas but one of the many places where certain kinds of gambling are legal. Sixteen states and the District of Columbia have instituted state lotteries. In Bellevue, some officials suggest that taxes on gambling could one day replace property taxes.

* Lawrence Biemiller wrote in the weekly *Chronicle of Higher Education* that the nation's 140 agriculture schools have changed markedly—"the old cow college ain't what it used to be." Among the changes are the increased percentage of women students, the decreased percentage of graduates who go into farming (they work instead for banks, chemical companies, government agencies, commodities markets, and food processors), and the astonishing ignorance of students who enter agricultural schools with little or no farm background (they don't know how to tell a bull from a steer, as one incredulous professor expressed it).

GETTING IDEAS

You get ideas for comprehensive newsfeatures by listening and observing, by asking questions, by reading, and by putting things together in your own mind. Ideas seem to drop out of ordinary circumstances. Perhaps the essential ingredient is a high level of curiosity. Writers who continually wonder what makes people behave as they do—and who are willing to get out and ask questions—probably will come up with more ideas than their more indifferent peers. Here are some typical examples.

You read a magazine article about the relative unimportance of college grades as a measure of success in later life. A study shows that the connection between high grades and success is tenuous at best. So you decide to interview ten of the most successful persons in your community about their college grades.

A fellow reporter tells you that a girl no older than fourteen has a record as the most incorrigible juvenile in the state, at least in terms of the number of times she's been in the juvenile detention center, mostly for running away from home and getting into fights. About that same time you learn that for the first time, your state is recording more girl runaways than boy runaways. See any possibilities there?

A man who graduated a dozen years ago from college tells you that he got only a C-plus average in college. He was a general ne'er-do-well in college, he says, yet he was hired for a high-paying position at a soap manufacturing company that seems to appreciate independent thinking. Now he's an employment recruiter visiting campuses. He tells you that good grades are way down the list of his priorities as far as prospective employees are concerned. Somehow this ties in with your earlier reading about grades as a relatively minor contribution to later success. Perhaps you should interview employment recruiters.

You read a piece in *Time* about people seeking out physical adventure in their recreational pursuits these days. Not content with lying on the beaches, they are sky diving, hang gliding, whitewater kayaking, rock climbing, and wind surfing as never before. You wonder if the same holds true in your community, and you set about to find out.

All of these ideas are real, and some actually produced articles. They have one thing in common: They come largely from contact with people, through listening or reading or observing. In essence, the ideas came from exposing oneself to a wide spectrum of human knowledge and experience.

So rule one is you can't get ideas in a vacuum—or in an ivory tower. But what's rule two? Rules and principles are scarce. The elements of news discussed previously certainly help: principles such as prominence, proximity, consequence, change, or conflict. News pegs help. And you always look for the unusual, the whimsical, the ironic—for the things you know will make readers laugh or cry.

But what may help most is a creative mind that puts bits and pieces together and detects a pattern. Things just fall into place for the alert journalist as the fragments of information flash forth and become pieces of a potential pattern.

GETTING INFORMATION

It's important to draw your information from a wide variety of sources. Where you might have interviewed two or three people for a news or feature story, you could easily talk to twenty or thirty for a comprehensive story. You may talk informally with many people: neighbors, fellow employees, or those you meet at social gatherings. Much of your work depends on informal contacts rather than official sources. One reporter, seeking anecdotes for a story on divorce, let it be known at a social gathering that he was looking for divorcees. Word quickly got around and the fellow was besieged by women he claims were eager to tell their stories. Informal conversations are only part of the standard procedure. Here are the usual steps.

1. *Background research as usual.* (Review Chapter 10 on documents and research procedures).
2. *Selection.* Find the people and groups who know the most about your subject. They may be experts in the field, such as high school counselors or police officials who can be interviewed about juvenile runaways, or they may be the people who are involved in the subject, such as the juveniles themselves.
3. *Interview, interview, interview.* The domino theory applies at this stage—if you ask, people will suggest others you could talk with. Ask them to recommend people who are outstanding: the most adventurous of your physical adventure enthusiasts, for example. Seek personal experience anecdotes: They help breathe life into your prose.
4. *Observe.* Perhaps even participate. If you are going to interview a circus high-wire performer, perhaps you'd like to try high-wire walking yourself? Not very likely, you say? Yet journalism is full of examples. One classic instance involved John Muir, the great naturalist. He once climbed to the top of a tall tree in California during a raging windstorm—swaying back and forth "like a bobolink on a reed"—so that he might write about the experience.

EVALUATION AND WRITING

The structure of the comprehensive newsfeature is the same as that of the simple feature described in the preceding chapter. It starts with an opening, often a quote, an anecdote, a flashby, or perhaps a descriptive passage. The opening leads into a general statement of theme, the "establishing section." The theme is then supported by two or more supporting points, just as in the simple feature.

But writing a comprehensive newsfeature is never easy. If you've done a good job of research, you'll probably have ten times more material than you can use. This is good.

It's good because you have to select the best material, the top 10 percent. It's good because the other 90 percent will help you understand your subject so thoroughly that you'll know *which* 10 percent best tells the story. It's like picking the cashews out of the mixed bag of nuts.

And the over-research is good because it will help you to find the essence of your material: the theme. The process of doing so is called "synthesis" or "research evaluation."

"Evaluation is the heart of the interpretive writing process," says Andre Fontaine, former editor of *Redbook*, in his book, *The Art of Writing Nonfiction.* "It is also the most difficult part for the writer, for it is here that he must finally make a judgment, here he must identify truth. It is not only a rigorous intellectual exercise, it is the nub of the creative part of this kind of writing."

Evaluation means not only identifying the theme of your article but also ensuring that the material you have gathered does indeed add up to your stated theme. You must face the possibility that the information you've assembled does not really support the conclusions you have drawn. What then?

Let's say you started out to develop a story showing that grades are unimportant to employment recruiters and also are largely unconnected to success in later life. Your preliminary evidence certainly pointed in that direction. Now, after having interviewed a dozen or more employment recruiters from big firms, you begin to have serious doubts.

The recruiters are telling you that grades are not important if—. It's a big "if." If low grades can be explained satisfactorily—her grades weren't especially high because she was editor of the college paper, president of her dormitory unit, and she earned money for college expenses by working at McDonald's—then the grades won't prevent her getting the job. Conversely, you find that a near-perfect scholastic record may not mean much unless combined with outside interests and campus activities. Students who have done little but assemble a high grade average are seen by recruiters as untested in the crucible of professional life. The best combination, according to the recruiters, is high grades *and* a record of activities.

If that is what you find (and, indeed, it's what one campus reporting team did find), then that's what your theme—your establishing section—must say.

The evaluation process never follows a precise formula. It comes closest to the academic pattern of starting out with a hypothesis (that is, a possible explanation for a pattern of things observed—a "tentative theme"). You then test the hypothesis or, if necessary, change to another hypothesis and start over. Eight steps are involved:

1. You start with a topic—grades, in this case.
2. You start preliminary research—reading, observing, talking to sources.
3. You develop a hypothesis: Grades don't mean much to recruiters and in later career success.
4. You continue research, directed toward supporting your hypothesis. You may never really support it in the statistical sense, but you are likely to get a pretty clear idea from your work whether you're on the right track. You keep an open mind.
5. Being open-minded you assemble your research and think through whether your original hypothesis is correct.
6. You make the necessary modifications if, as usually happens, your original ideas are not 100 percent correct. In the grades example, your modification runs along the lines suggested earlier: Recruiters will forgive mediocre grades if they can be satisfactorily explained by other achievements.
7. You organize your material into an outline (preferably on paper or on file cards). Your story has an introduction, a main theme, and two or more supporting points.
8. Using your outline as a guide, you begin writing. It is often in the writing, by the way, that you're led to rethink your ideas and, if necessary, make changes in thematic direction. What seemed so logical in your mind simply doesn't work when committed to paper.

THE MOUNT ST. HELENS STORY

Richard Zahler studied English at Whitman College in Walla Walla, Washington, and at Stanford University. In 1984 he returned from a year's leave at Stanford and became the *Seattle Times'* writing coach. His background in English literature—including the writing of short stories and one so-far-unpublished novel—has influenced his perception of newspaper writing, he believes, particularly long articles such as the one he envisioned on the eruption of Mount St. Helens for the *Times* in 1980.

"I'm a strong believer in storytelling," he says. "The thing has got to move and develop. It's got to have detail and real people and feeling and emotion."

He worked with a team of about a dozen reporters. He deployed them to search for the kind of factual material that he might use in a short story: graphic, detailed accounts of ordinary people involved in extraordinary situations—the raw material from which dramatic literature is fashioned.

Yet this was to be a totally factual account, every word depicting something that really happened.

But where do you find those people stories? You play hunches, says Zahler.

How about a minister in some small town about to conduct Sunday services on that beautiful morning, only to have them disrupted by an exploding mountain? Here was symbolism reminiscent of divine intervention in Greek tragedy—if the right person could be found. Where would you find such a preacher? Probably to the north, they concluded, because the mountain's major zone of devastation lay to the north. Poring over a map the reporting team spotted Morton, a tiny mountain community 30 miles north of the volcano. Somewhere in Morton, they guessed, would be a preacher with a story, and so a reporter started calling parsonages in Morton.

Hunches prompted other reporters to seek out a family who took in refugees from the awesome ashfall east of the mountain; a service station attendant with stories to tell about stranded motorists whose cars became clogged with ash; a lumber executive whose logging crews had worked in rolling country once clothed with stately trees now denuded and blown askew like matchsticks.

Some hunches paid off; some didn't.

Zahler also wanted to capture the geological and historical background; the story, after all, had actually begun millions of years earlier.

The reporting team worked almost entirely by phone and delivered extensive notes to Zahler's desk. Zahler himself worked 24 hours straight to meet the Friday morning production deadline with a 7,500-word story.

By then the team had found the preacher, the refugee scene, and the geological sweep. The lumber executive and the service station attendant somehow eluded them. "They're probably still out there today," Zahler remarked four years later. "We just didn't find them."

Space precludes our reprinting the entire story, 7,500 words being about half again as long as this entire chapter. But here are some excerpts, starting with the beginning.

BY RICHARD ZAHLER
THE SEATTLE TIMES

Residents of the Pacific Northwest like to think they are blessed by nature and a benign deity.

There was no reason to think otherwise early Sunday, May 18, 1980.

A bright sun rose in clear skies from the border of Eastern Washington to the Pacific Ocean beaches. In succession, its life-giving light bathed the young wheat stalks of the Palouse and the crops of the broad Columbia Basin. The sun shone on the blossoms and buds of Wenatchee's orchards, and hastened the ripening of another bountiful cherry crop in the Yakima Valley.

The sunrise glimmered off the snowy mountains of the Cascades, sparkled in a thousand crystalline lakes, caught the color of new wildflowers in the high meadows.

Rising above the Skamania County foothills, the sun illuminated the east slope of 9,677-foot Mount St. Helens. It did not reflect so brightly there, for the volcano in the past seven weeks had awakened from a century and a half of slumber. The snow on its slope was dingy with ash.

Under the bright Sunday skies, barely broken here and there by high cirrus clouds, temperatures across Washington would climb into the 70s and 80s. Visibility was clear for dozens of miles.

With the region's long and damp winter clearly and finally behind them, thousands of Washington residents had set off for the weekend, driving across the state, camping, taking photographs. At home, others planned to spend the weekend working in their gardens, and others planned to do nothing at all but enjoy their weather and their land.

As the sun shone Sunday morning, Ron and Barbara Seibold and their two children were in the middle of one of the weekend outings they loved, watching deer, looking at the trees and flowers.

Not far away, Michael and Lu Moore were backpacking in the beautiful high country north of Spirit Lake with their 4-year-old daughter, Bonnie Lu, and their baby, 3-month-old Terra.

To the north, in the little logging town of Morton, Pastor Thomas Slate had warmed up the Sunday School rooms in his United Methodist Church, made sure the church bulletins were in place, then returned to the parsonage for breakfast.

In Yakima, it was Police Chief Jack LaRue's day to manage the Yakima Valley Sportsman's Association's trapshooting club, and he loaded shotguns, ammunition, scorecards and other equipment into the trunk of his car.

In Spokane, for Mayor Ron Bair there was levity in a relaxed Sunday schedule heavy with receptions and parties ending the annual Lilac Festival.

For each of them, and for thousands and thousands of other Washington residents, it was a million-dollar morning, full of spring and full of promise. Within hours—in some cases, minutes—the promises all were broken, and the day couldn't be traded for a few cents.

Mayor Bair's levity soured when he discovered sludge in the bottom of his beer cup, and when he drove through his city and found it as dusty and deserted as a ghost town.

Chief LaRue and his trapshooting friends didn't spend the day firing at clay pigeons in Yakima. They couldn't have seen the flying targets if they had wanted to.

In Morton, Pastor Slate rose to give his 11 o'clock sermon and, for the first time in his life, found every pew empty. Not a soul was in church.

For the Moore family of Castle Rock, the day became a nightmare that they didn't escape for more than 24 hours.

The four members of the Seibold family didn't escape the nightmare at all.

The lead is a long one, a novel-like description and introduction of characters whose fates would be determined later in the story. Clearly a sense of foreboding creeps in. In succeeding paragraphs, Zahler weaves in geology, history, and the mountain's ominous rumblings over the previous seven weeks. Then a man named David Johnston, a geologist stationed in an observation post named Cold-water II, north of the mountain, speaks cryptically on his radio as Zahler's story speeds up.

"Vancouver! Vancouver! This is it!"
"Vancouver! Vancouver! Is the transmitter still working?"
The message wasn't heard in Vancouver.
A ham-radio operator picked up the call.
It was 8:32 A.M.
The mountain was exploding.
Johnston's outpost was directly in the path of what geologists later said was a completely unexpected horizontal explosion of superheated gas and debris from the mountain, a planetary cannon blast.
The concussion of that explosion leveled tall evergreens for miles, stripped them of their branches, left them stacked and aligned on the ground like cordwood.
Where there had been a bulge on the mountain, there grew a crater as millions of tons of rock and ice—the top 2,000 feet or more of Mount St. Helens—was demolished.
The boulders and rocks sprayed to the north. The part of the mountaintop that was pulverized into pebbles and dust rose billowing 9 or 10 miles into the air, first rolling like the black smoke of an oil fire, then broadening in a frightening mushroom cap as the gases and ash poured higher.
Far above the mountain, the ash was caught by southwesterly winds to become disaster in another form as it blew north and east, darkening the Sunday sky over thousands of square miles. The ash landed in the orchards and bowed the fragile wheat stalks of Washington's farming heartland. It stranded thousands of people.
At the mountain itself the explosion created what scientists said would be the volcano's most destructive force if it blew—a "pyroclastic flow," a descending wall of hot gas and water and ashen mud. It roared off the mountain obliterating and burying whatever was standing in its path, slamming into the once-pristine waters of Spirit Lake.
The hot mud and gas plunged into the forks of the Toutle River, gouging out wider valleys. Displaced by the mud, water in the river rose instantly, creating its own wall of destruction. Timber, roads, bridges and cabins were swept from the map. Trees torn from the banks tumbled into a mile-long logjam that crashed toward the Cowlitz and Columbia Rivers. . . .

The story recounts some of the casualties, the missing persons, including the most famous of them all, the grand, eccentric owner of the Spirit Lake Lodge, Harry Truman. Then on to the long-sought minister.

The other property owner with permission to be at the lake was Harry Truman, the 83-year-old lodge owner who became a folk hero by virtue of his stubborn refusal to leave his home of 54 years. The mud and rock and gas flowed over the shore, leaving no sign of Harry Truman, his lodge, his 16 cats or his player piano.
Pastor Thomas Slate's mind may have been on Heaven early Sunday morning. His thoughts decidedly were on the heavens by late Sunday morning. Mount St. Helens' first explosion spewed dark clouds of ash and mud in a mighty roar to the north. In the logging town of Morton, 30 miles away, a parishioner called Mr. Slate at the United Methodist Church and told him to look to the south. The minister did and saw the dark volcanic cloud looming above the foothills.

"It was, of course, glowing with sunshine on the east face of the cloud. Underneath there were flashes of lightning. There was a good deal of lightning. I didn't hear the sound of the eruption, but I heard thunder rolling in the distance as the lightning crackled."

Observing that display, Mr. Slate didn't forget practical matters. From newspaper accounts, he knew he should expect ash fallout from the volcano. He carried a tank-type vacuum cleaner to the vestibule of his church to help clean any members of the congregation who might arrive for services. The sky over Morton turned black by 9:30 A.M. Seven people showed up for Sunday School. Half an hour later, they walked outside into a town that Mr. Slate remembers being "as dark as midnight on a moonless night."

Mud rained from the sky in balls the size of pencil erasers. It coated everything. Ash drifted in, and five people went to the hospital with breathing problems.

At 11 o'clock, no one from Mr. Slate's 160-member congregation had arrived for the regular worship service.

"I played the organ and sang some hymns by myself and when, at 11:20, no one had arrived, I simply made a prayer and closed the church up, closing all the doors and sealing it as tight as I could." Then he sealed up the Sunday School rooms and returned to the parsonage and sealed it up.

By 12:15 P.M. the sky began to lighten again.

That evening the police called and asked Mr. Slate to put up stranded travelers. Nine of them, in two families, joined him at the parsonage, and he retrieved the vacuum cleaner from the church so they could clean the ash off themselves.

By week's end, Thursday and Friday, the heavens sent rain. The dust settled. Some of the mud washed away. The people of Morton took the eruption well, Mr. Slate said. There seemed to be no fears of disaster.

"On the contrary, the people I've been in contact with have reminded me of the promises of God to watch over us and have also reminded me that we don't have any real security in this world and we should be prepared under all circumstances for such things as the shaking of the earth and pouring out of these destructive energies.

"And, of course, I have agreed with them."

The article recounts the fates of the other characters. Yakima Police Chief LaRue never made it to the trapshoot because ash rained down through the day on the hapless city. Campers Michael and Lu Moore and their two children were rescued by helicopter after a 24-hour ordeal. The four-member Seibold family died in the heat and gas exploding through the Toutle Valley, becoming the first identified victims of the eruption. David Johnston, who had radioed the first alarm was missing. Mayor Bair and his wife drove through downtown en route to a cocktail party in the ash-covered city of Spokane and found the scene desolate and eerie "like the city had been empty for 100 years and had been gathering dust." Zahler's story concludes:

Until two months ago, in the memory of every living person, Mount St. Helens, shimmering across Spirit Lake, stood as a ready symbol of benign and beautiful nature in the Pacific Northwest.

The mountain never will symbolize that again to those who have seen the destruction that has been wrought, or to the thousands whose lives have been wrenched in the days since that bright, peaceful and deceptive Sunday morning of May 18, 1980.

POINTS TO REMEMBER

1. Comprehensive newsfeatures involve multiple interviews to get at issues and causes of news rather than the events—reporting the chicken pox rather than the individual pimples.
2. Ideas come from being alert to change, new trends and customs, new ideas.
3. Sources of ideas include reading, talking, listening, observing, and also putting wide-ranging elements together in your mind to deliver new insights.
4. A good comprehensive feature requires massive research and interviewing.
5. Research evaluation is essential in going through the masses of material; you must synthesize to arrive at the main point, the essence of your article.
6. Like a scholar, you propose hypotheses and then set about getting the material to support them.
7. You must remain open-minded enough to abandon unsupportable hypotheses.
8. Comprehensive, coherent, well-researched articles, such as Richard Zahler's report on Mount St. Helens, relay vivid images to the reader.
9. Writers can develop story-telling techniques—showing people in action—that lend great strength to articles.
10. To find "people" stories, try playing hunches.

PROJECT

Here are some suggestions for comprehensive newsfeatures you can do on your own campus for publication in a campus or community newspaper. Not all of them will fit your campus, obviously; they are merely suggestions to get you started.

1. Write a story about employment trends among students. Are more working today than before?
2. Write a story about employment opportunities for students after graduation. What are students doing to make themselves more employable? Talk with employment recruiters.
3. Write about the health problems of students.
4. Interview campus disciplinary committees and professors about cheating among students. Is the trend up or down?
5. What changes are being made in campus cafeterias to accommodate the changing dietary habits of students (for example, more health foods, vegetarians, and so forth)?
6. Write about the security problems on the campus, burglary, petty theft, personal attacks, and how one copes with them.
7. Widespread changes are reported on some campuses in career orientations—toward computer training, for example. Explore the trends on your campus.
8. Interview teachers, deans, and others about trends in teaching. Is there a resurgence of interest in good teaching on your campus as there is on some?

9. Interview coaches and athletes about their superstitious beliefs going into competitive performance. Is the trend toward more or less superstition? You may find interesting examples.

10. Attendance and participation in campus affairs, social events, and extracurricular activities is said to be returning to some campuses. What about yours?

11. Colleges have traditionally been confined to a straight four years. Now students are taking six or seven, with time out for work, travel, internships. What's the situation on your campus?

12. Explore the trend toward more litigation over campus problems—student suing over grievances on financial aid, grades, admission, and so forth.

13. Explore how your college or university recruits students in an era of declining enrollment. Many colleges have become very promotion minded.

14. Interview psychological counselors about the kinds of emotional problems students face these days.

15. Interview professors about how they sometimes are unwittingly cast into pseudoparent roles. Some professors complain that students bring their emotional problems to them, ask for personal advice, even try to borrow money.

16. Explore the changes in some traditional campus departments to find what surprises you can uncover. Note this chapter's reference to agriculture schools, for example. One law school reports that its students are older and more idealistic than they were a dozen years ago.

15

Service Journalism

The questions that preoccupy people day by day are not necessarily the ones that make big headlines. They are personal questions like these: What shall I wear today? What shall we have for dinner tonight? Where can I get ideas for decorating my apartment? How can I get the city to repair the potholes on my street? How can we make our food dollars stretch? Where can I take an inexpensive vacation away from the crowds? Life is dull—where can I find adventure? Should I try wind surfing or rock climbing? How can I meet somebody new, make new friends, enjoy new relationships? How can I make more money, or save the money I have, or invest it wisely? How can we make sure our children are getting the best education?

Often the answers come in an expanding branch of reporting known as "service journalism." The term means simply the reporting of information that helps people cope with their daily lives.

In truth, all journalism is supposed to do that, more or less. But service journalism does it more directly and personally. Regular journalism may report that the economy is down and that jobs are hard to find; service journalism tells you what to do if you get laid off or how to find your first job out of college in a tough economy. Regular journalism may report that food prices are up by 11.3 percent this year; service journalism tells you how to make your food dollars stretch by such devices as relentless pursuit of "loss leaders" sales in grocery stores, or buying chicken at low prices when the market is glutted and keeping it in your

Seattle Times Sunday Magazine assistant editor Tom Stockley (left) works on a food photo with photographer Ben Benschneider in a studio. *(Photo by Matt McVay.)*

freezer. Regular journalism may report a new study in alcoholism; service journalism makes it more personal: what to do about the alcoholic in your family.

Service journalism is not new. It is, indeed, the bread and butter of magazines. Newspapers have carried food, home, and garden sections for years. But newspapers have pursued service journalism with new vigor since the early 1970s, a time of general decline in newspaper readership that many publishers found worrisome. They surveyed reader interests and discovered the service features rated high on the list, particularly among the young people that newspapers were trying to win away from TV.

Pollster Lou Harris, whose opinion surveys effectively trace the changes in public attitudes, expressed in 1976 the view that news coverage would have to "move where the people are, not necessarily where the surface action is, not necessarily where wizened news hands have always thought it was."

A survey released by the American Newspaper Publishers Association in 1977 asked readers what they'd like to see added to the regular coverage of newspapers. "More consumer information" stood at the top of the list. It was particularly important to the younger (21–35) of the two age groups studied.

And the younger group showed more interest in how-to-do-it stories, feature stories, and movie reviews than the older (35+) group. The young showed less interest than the older group in the traditional fare of newspapers, local news, national news, and editorials. A 1984 study by the American Society of Newspaper Editors reiterated the desire for more consumer information, also for more stories on health and business.

Out of this has come what one researcher, Joe Belden, has described as a "revolution in newspaper editing." In one speech Belden said:

> What we are finding is that space might well be devoted more to information, hopefully but not necessarily news pegged, than to details of the latest sensation already reported ten days in a row—let's say information such as:
>
> How to shop more intelligently in your town.
> How to save a marriage.
> Where to get free medical aid.
> Who the best preachers in town are.
> What the latest utility rate increase means to *me*.
>
> Or, just information on movies, music, bowling, good food, investing, camping, exercise, people, money, practical psychology—there are hundreds of such subjects.

Indeed so. The thinking in the mid-1980s has changed but little since the crises that brought service journalism out of the closet. In the 1980s, researchers are finding that people want hard news as never before, but they *don't* want to give up the features, the people stories, and the service features that expanded through the 1970s and early 80s.

TOWARD A NEW DEFINITION

Service journalism, though it has expanded, tends to be thought of as "utility" journalism—how-to-do-its on leisure, fashion, food, home and garden, child care, family health, and the like. But something has been added to the definition of late.

That something might be called *the spirit of service*. It means a change in attitude among reporters and editors. In essence the attitude has changed from mild arrogance ("Here's today's news; take it or leave it!") to a more modest, audience-oriented approach ("Here's the news we think will interest *you*—we hope you like it"). Arrogance won't work in this era of intense media competition.

The spirit of service, moreover, means greater attention to how the news will affect readers personally. The reporter who thinks "service" will often have different criteria for what is news. The selection of stories may be different, or the story angles will focus more on personal impact.

Given the dedication to reader service, the education reporter may find a school board decision that kids will attend school an hour longer next fall more important than a minor but dramatic personality squabble between two board members. Similarly, the budget story that starts out, "Next year the owner of a $50,000 house will be paying $20 more in school taxes" has service more in mind than the story that merely reports a new $30 million budget.

Attention to service in everyday reporting, then, can produce what some call a "usepaper." Consider these examples:

* A famous author comes to town to talk about her novel, but you decide to ask about advice to authors—how she got started and how others might follow suit. Just about everyone dreams of writing a novel, so readers will enjoy your story.
* You interview an expert on gerontology (study of aging). Don't ask him the usual questions about political power of oldsters or about federal funding of anthropological research on geriatric lifestyles. Get information readers can use, such as "What can people do now to help them enjoy life more fully after 60? What can you do today to ensure good health later? What about investments? Insurance?"
* You've written an article about violent crime. Now write another on "Five especially dangerous places to avoid after dark."
* You interview one or more psychiatrists, not about trends in psychiatry, but to develop some self-help theme, such as what to do about depression or shyness or "how to get over a broken heart." (The *Los Angeles Times* published just such a story, noting that what we used to call a broken heart is now called a "loss-distress syndrome.")
* You've written about the disaster that struck your community—the flood, the tornado, the earthquake—now write stories calculated to help people put their lives back together: about filing insurance claims, how to clean up, where to get advice and help, how to cope with emotional problems.
* At income tax time you interview experts on ways to reduce your tax load. Not all service pieces are serious, by the way; the *Washington Post* once ran a tongue-in-cheek article on the "ultimate income tax dodge—earning very little money."
* The next time you interview a computer expert, ask why average families should invest in a microcomputer rather than asking abstract questions such as, "Are computers getting too intelligent?"

TYPES OF SERVICE ARTICLES

Service articles generally fall into four categories: the straight how-to, the case history, the feature with how-to emphasis, and the list.

The how-to. This is the most common service feature, the staple of the food, home, and garden pages. You address the reader directly, and the headlines are equally direct and to the point: "How to guard against termites" or "Plant now for spring daffodils" or "Ten ways to save energy by winterproofing your home."

The case history. Here you write about someone who has already done something that others might try. The basic theme is "they did it, and so can you."

Suppose, for instance, that you interview a young couple who have just returned from a four-week bicycling trip in Europe. Your story is about them, written in third person, but the content is definitely how-to. That is, your questions and your story focus on the traditional how-to elements: How do you plan such a trip? How much does it cost? Where do you stay nights? What are problems to watch out for? What advice have you for any who might follow your path?

The feature with how-to emphasis.   Two types are involved here. One is the straight news story that happens to deal with how-to information. The tax assessor develops a new form for use in paying one's property taxes and calls a press conference to tell the public, step-by-step, how to use it. The second type is the story in which the writer consciously includes service information.

Lists.   They've become ever more popular in the media of late; they're both fun and utilitarian. They're often controversial, which enhances reader interest. What are the ten best weekend vacation spots within a two-hour drive of your community? What are the ten most dangerous intersections in your city (measured by police tallies of traffic accidents)? Some other possibilities:

> Ten uplifting things to do when you are feeling low. (It could be nine or eleven, of course, but ten seems to be a comfortable number.) Interview psychiatrists and others for suggestions.
>
> Ten most spellbinding professors on your campus.
>
> Nine outdoorsy things to do on a rainy day. (Take a walk with your best friend under a big umbrella. Roast hot dogs from under a tarp adjacent to a bonfire. Take refuge in a phone booth and call someone you like. That's three—you think of the rest.)
>
> Five great viewpoints for watching the sunset.
>
> Five equally great spots for watching the sunrise.
>
> What career-minded college women should know about business. Interview successful businesswomen for their advice.

COVERING THE SERVICE BEAT

Some reporters make service their full-time beat. But instead of covering city hall, they keep in touch with experts in their fields of interest. A "shelter" writer, covering homes and gardens, would keep in touch with college nutritionists, architects, home economists, agricultural extension agents, and similar sources. A reporter specializing in people problems would develop sources from among counselors, doctors, psychologists, and the like.

Ideas also come from ordinary circumstances. A journalist once remarked that ideas come from the most tenuous of sources: "There's an idea in what keeps you awake at night." If worrying about money keeps you awake, perhaps writing about it—how to save it, how to make it go farther, how to get more—will help you sleep better. Ideas come from the people who deal with the public. What are the most frequently asked questions of the tax assessor's office, for example? If lots of people are asking a certain kind of question, perhaps it's time to write an article that would share the answers with everyone. Ideas come from ordinary conversation. A chance remark by your neighbor—"I wish I knew whether that tree is dying or not"—can prompt you to write an article, "When to get rid of a dying tree."

WRITING THE SERVICE ARTICLE

Many service articles are written the same way as regular news or features. One exception is the list, but probably no advice is necessary on preparing a list. The other major exception is the how-to article.

A how-to starts with a good idea, even a novel one, backed up by good research. Research is vital. You must have sufficient detail to tell the readers how to make that bicycle trip through Europe, anticipating all their insecurities: things like taking enough money, speaking the language, finding safe places to spend the night, protecting health. Many of the details are strictly utilitarian. For a building project you include such elements as what materials are needed, their cost, where to get them, how to assemble them step by step. The writing itself must be simple, clear, direct. No room exists for purple prose.

The structure of the how-to is similar to that of the feature. You usually start with a statement of the problem or an anecdote that illustrates the problem. You then propose a solution (which becomes the theme of your article). You then take the reader through the solution in chronological order, an easy step at a time. When you have delivered your last bit of information you summarize quickly and stop.

Here is an excerpt from a typical how-to article. Note how the opening anecdote leads to a general statement of theme—indeed, the same kind of establishing section cited in earlier chapters on features. Following that comes the main body of the article with the actual suggestions to parents.

BY NANCY J. STOHS
MILWAUKEE JOURNAL

The toddler was shopping with his mother.
"Mommy, I want that puzzle," he said.
"I don't have enough money," she replied.
"It's OK. You don't need money. Just write a check," the little boy said.
All right, parents, what do you do now?
First you probably chuckle. Kids are cute, aren't they?
But then, something should click: It's a perfect opportunity to explain to the child the purpose of checks.
Checking accounts are but one of a multitude of money matters these little future adults will need to deal with someday. How can parents prepare them?
Teaching a child to save pennies in a piggy bank is still a good lesson, but in an

economy marked by inflation, unemployment and uncertainty, it's not enough anymore.

Not according to Chris Snyder. Not according to Milwaukee-area financial experts who were interviewed recently.

Snyder, president of a financial counseling and planning firm in Toronto, is the author of "Teaching Your Child About Money" (Macmillan of Canada, 1982), a succinct, clearly written manual for parents.

Yet complex as the economy is today, you don't have to be an accountant or economics professor to teach your children sound, up-to-date money management, Snyder asserts.

Although specific advice on how to do that varied, several common themes ran through the experts' recommendations:

Look constantly for opportunities to encourage good habits and attitudes—in family conversations, while shopping, when paying bills, etc.

Expose your children to the banking system early in life.

Resist the natural temptation to just give your children everything.

Set a good example.

Preschoolers aren't ready for a lecture on the supply vs. demand theory, but they are intrigued by coins.

Let them spend a few pennies when you shop. Show them that a nickel buys less than a dime, although the nickel is larger. Confusion of size and value is common at this age. . . .

An important aspect of the how-to is the need to get quickly to the point of the article. This one moves quickly through the illustrative anecdote and on to establishing the need for teaching children about money. Note the use of direct address—the word "you," meaning you, the reader, is an important one in service reporting.

So is the word "now." It means that the article should deal with something the reader can do now. Clearly, money can be explained to children most any season, but garden articles, to cite a different problem, must be timed to match climate patterns. An article on planting daffodils probably will run in the fall, when you can actually plant the bulbs, rather than spring when the reader can do little but admire the spring-flowering bulbs in someone else's garden.

Many service articles contain a none-too-subtle "sales message." They often incorporate a sense of urgency almost as direct as a nagging parent. You often encounter phrases such as "Now's the time to plant those daffodil bulbs if you want spring color" or "Interviews with architects and home builders suggest a *new urgency* in checking your fire insurance coverage." (Emphasis added.)

Finally, the development of a good how-to piece suggests the inclusion of such practical details as the phone numbers of sources of information, or books, pamphlets, and other materials that would help the reader.

POINTS TO REMEMBER

1. Service journalism has gained respect and popularity in newspapers since the early 1970s when newspapers sought to gain back lost readership.
2. The spirit of service increasingly infuses journalistic thinking so that many routine kinds of stories have more of a "service" angle today.

3. Main type of service article is the "how-to," followed by case histories, features with service emphasis, and lists.
4. Reporters cover "service beats" just as others cover city hall, except the sources are different; many are experts in specialized fields, not public officials.
5. Structure of a service article is similar to that of a feature.

PROJECT

Write a how-to feature for the campus newspaper on a topic of interest to college students. Some possibilities:

1. How to appeal a bad grade.
2. How to be interviewed for a job. Advice from counselors and employment recruiters.
3. How to take an exam (lots of students don't know).
4. Ten spellbinding professors.
5. Ten quiet places to study.
6. How to get along with your roommate (counselors' suggestions).
7. Books you ought to have read before graduation.
8. How to listen and take notes during lectures.
9. When to argue in class (professors say there's a time to argue, a time to keep still). interview your favorite professors.

16

Toward More Powerful Writing

The best writing contains power. It moves compellingly toward a clear goal: to get an idea off the page and into the reader's mind, to paraphrase *Time*'s late publisher, Henry R. Luce. Powerful writing is like a four-engined airliner. The four rhetorical engines that lift your message off the page are called *purpose, organization, detail,* and *drama.*

Each will be described in turn, but first let us examine a case history that illustrates the potential for powerful writing when a reporter goes beyond the routine style of newswriting.

"COLLISION COURSE": A CASE HISTORY

Tom Hallman, Jr. had been the police reporter for *The Oregonian* in Portland, Oregon, for more than two years when he came across a story from the sheriff's office about a fatal auto collision.

The story was strictly routine, of course. Human tragedy and suffering fill the daily work of police reporters in every city. Hallman had seen it all before, many times.

Hallman quickly pounded out the requisite story for such occasions, enough to fill three column inches. And it was strictly what Hallman calls formula writing. "You know how they go," he says. "So and so was charged with . . . de-dah,

Tom Hullman on the job in Portland. (*Photo by Randy L. Rasmussen.*)

de-dah, de-dah." The story showed up on page 6-B, pared by the copydesk to a mere two inches, 50 words.

But the story gnawed at the reporter. Something—fate, circumstance, whatever—had brought two parties together on that dark street that night and then, in one grinding, terrible instant, changed their lives forever. Hallman sensed a cruel irony in the fact that the story *was* routine. He began to toy with a different kind of story, a detailed recounting of the incident. Perhaps this would bring a new dimension to the journalistic treatment of highway carnage.

But such a story would require scrupulous attention to detail, much of it painful to the parties involved. Would they want to talk about it, have the ordeal spread out in print for all to see? Hallman decided to give it a try.

Over the next several months he interviewed more than 50 people connected with the accident. Hallman was only mildly surprised to find that most of the people involved seemed almost eager to discuss it with him. Such is frequently the case with those who have endured traumatic experiences.

"It's strange," he says. "People who are in those situations often want to talk about it to somebody who's neutral, who isn't immediately involved."

Out of it came a 4,200-word story titled "Collision Course" that ran in *Northwest,* the paper's Sunday magazine. The story traces the lives through that fateful day in gripping detail. The readers see the Griffiths—28-year-old Tom, 23-year-old Shana, 3-year-old Tiana—through the routine of that fateful day: Tom off to work as a self-employed painter, Shana out to ride her beloved horse, an Arabian gelding named Prince Halani. The tension builds as we see Peter Cavallero, 21, off work early as a handyman, working on his 1972 Oldsmobile Cutlass, having dinner with friends, buying a bottle of bourbon for a party at one of their homes, then a second bottle of bourbon.

Later that evening, the Griffiths are returning home from a visit with Tom's mother and have turned onto a darkened route called Harold Street. Pete Cavallero has been arguing with his friends off and on through the evening, and he's also upset about a $40 loan a friend hadn't yet repaid. Note how the suspense builds in this excerpt:

> Pete Cavallero stretched out across the front seat of his car in a lethargic stupor. His car keys lay somewhere on the dark floor. . . .
> He sat up and fumbled for his keys. When he finally found them he squealed onto Harold Street.
> He didn't even see the oncoming car.
> Susie Karsten slammed on the brakes and veered off the street. Her windshield shattered from the rocks thrown up by the Cutlass. Pete headed eastbound on Harold Street—in the westbound lane. His headlights were off, and he swerved on and off the shoulder.
> Karsten followed, flashing her headlights and honking her horn, hoping she could warn oncoming drivers.
> But Pete pulled away. First 45, 50 and then nearly 60 mph.
> Karsten continued to honk. Beyond Pete she saw the headlights of a westbound car.
> Tom Griffith turned onto Harold Street, his car's headlights on low beam. Usually he used the high beams when he drove the dark street. But a fuse had blown.
> Shana, her eyes closed, dozed in the seat next to her husband. Tiana slept in the back seat. In the trunk was a large, sealed can of yellow paint. . . .

The article may read like detective fiction, but it was painstakingly crafted from reality, that is, from the research Hallman had put together from the more than 50 sources he interviewed. And that becomes the first major point to be noted here: The four rhetorical engines won't do you much good unless you have a good story to tell.

START BY FINDING SOMETHING POWERFUL TO SAY

Tom Hallman conceived his "Collision Course" because he wanted to elevate at least one case history beyond the routine. Consider for the moment a different kind of story. A reporter was assigned to cover a speech, and he found the speech pretty boring. He let his mind wander.

Isn't this *interesting*? he thought to himself. It's actually interesting that this guy is so dull. Why so? Is it in the delivery or the message or the fact that he repeats everything three times, or what? Why does he have so little rapport with the audience? Does he realize how dull he is? Is he trying to do anything about it?

If he could come up with some answers, the reporter thought, perhaps he would not only have something interesting to write about, but he might not have to listen to so many dull speeches. So he began exploring the phenomenon of dull speeches, mostly by asking college students. He assumed that they were experts at listening to boring lectures.

From a series of interviews, a whole treasury of campus folklore came to light. Far from sleeping through the lectures, the young collegiate minds were wide awake. But they were not listening to the lecture. They were indulging in fantasy. Or playing games.

One young woman said she often fantasizes on what it would be like to jump off a 100-story building. "It would be interesting to see the looks on the faces of the people through the window as you whizzed by the 46th floor," she said.

A young man always had his notebook open to a tally sheet: He was counting cliches uttered by professors. He'd been doing it for almost four years. High on his list were such phrases as *viable alternative, it seems to me,* and *in my judgment.* But the all-time winner was the phrase *in the final analysis.*

And the reporter found irony. In one class it was the *professor* who fell asleep. Lecturing from a desk, he put his head down to peer at his notes, dropped his head down on his arms, and promptly dozed off.

The reporter learned that not all professors were insensitive to the problem of dull lectures. One made a practice of watching his students carefully. When he spotted three yawns in unison, he'd immediately drop in mid-sentence whatever he was saying and shift to a more anecdotal style of lecturing. That worked fine until one of his students caught on to his practice. She arranged with two of her friends to yawn on cue.

"The first time that happened, I fell for it like Pavlov's dog," said the professor. "By the third time my only thought was, 'What a remarkably perceptive young woman!'"

These findings suggest that to a reporter with imagination, interesting material somehow emerges even from boring situations. All of the above material came out of interviews on two campuses in Oregon, but no doubt could be done on any campus.

So you start with good material—interesting, even novel material. It could be life-and-death material, as Hallman had, or whimsical material as in the dull lectures folklore. But how to make a story out of dull lecture folklore? What would be the *purpose* of writing about that? This leads to the first of the four rhetorical engines.

1: PURPOSE

Finding a purpose for an article is really answering the question, "So what?" What is the significance of your article? Its essence? What does it mean to the reader? Can you state the purpose in just a few words in the manner of a topic sentence for a theme or class speech?

A specific purpose is not always necessary for straight news. A tornado strikes, Congress passes a bill, a football team wins or loses. All of these are specific, timely events that interest a significant number of readers. Thus, they are news, and no further purpose is necessary. It's the feature stories, service reports, investigative articles, and comprehensive newsfeatures that require an explicit purpose.

So now you plan to write an article based on the material on dull lectures. Here are some possibilities for purpose.

1. *Look at the strange, funny things students do to tune out boring lectures!* Your purpose is largely entertainment here, plus maybe an insight into the inner workings of the college student mind. Yours would be a light-hearted, fun kind of story, designed largely to give readers a chuckle.

2. *What their fantasies during boring lectures reveal about the character of college students.* Here you work to develop a story that is psychologically revealing. You concentrate more on the kinds of insights the material provides about the character of young men and women. You interview psychologists to explain what it all means. This purpose will actually *limit* the direction of your interviews because some things (the professor falling asleep at his desk, for example) simply don't fit in.

3. *How to avoid giving a dull lecture.* This approach, directed more toward professors than students, is even more confining. The bulk of your story would be suggestions from students and teachers about ways to make lectures less tedious.

4. *How to keep your teachers from being dull.* Perhaps the episode in which the young woman engineers three yawns in unison to force the professor to lecture anecdotally contains a message for all students. With additional research you could point your story in this direction, and you could provide a feature that has both reader interest and strong purpose.

In defining your purpose four terms are useful.

The first is *reader involvement.* The more you direct your purpose to the interests of your readers the better. If your audience is students, for instance, purpose four has more involvement than purpose three.

The second is *simplicity.* The simpler and more limited the scope of your article the better. Take a narrow subject and write in depth. Broad, superficial writing is dull.

The third key word is *explicitness.* It means the more the reader *understands* your purpose the better. Make it clear, either in the lead or in the establishing section.

Finally, *originality* is important. Don't wait for a news conference to be called before you can write about dull lectures, student fantasies, or play-by-play accounts of tragedy.

2: ORGANIZATION

A sense of coherence is vital to powerful writing. Each statement must be in its proper place, must lead logically to the next statement, and so on to the end. Consider an elementary example. You're in unfamiliar surroundings and you ask directions to your destination.

Here the purpose is clear, and the organization should be equally clear. *First,* you go down Bodoni Street four blocks, *then* turn left on Caslon Street, *then* watch for a big green house—and so forth. The simple one, two, three chronology takes you from where you are to where you want to go.

But suppose you ask: What are the most interesting sights in this city? With a different purpose comes a different organization. Were you to write an article about it, you might organize it like this.

1. State the topic, perhaps in the form of a question: What are the most interesting sights in town?
2. State a theme as part of an establishing section. River City is big on outdoors and history, so it is in these areas that you would look for the best sights.
3. Add some preliminary support to your theme: On hot days residents flock to the river to swim and boat, or to Rocky Butte Park for picnics and kite flying, or down to Fort Baskerville to poke around the ruins of a 200-year-old blockhouse.
4. Then you would list the top sights one at a time, almost like chapters in a book, perhaps arranging them in some order—such as east to west or from downtown outward to suburban areas.

So you have the two most common patterns, by chronology in the first instance, and by concept (traditional feature story organization) in the second. Let's examine these and some others more closely.

Chronology. This pattern seems simple at first but leads to difficulty if followed too literally. Suppose you were describing a cross-country bicycle-camping trip. It would get a little boring if on each of 100 days you described the same routine, getting up, eating breakfast, breaking camp, loading your gear, and taking off. Most chronologies are (or should be) organized *both* by chronology and by concept. So you show planning in the first part of your bicycling article, camping in the second, physical fatigue in the third, and you don't bring them up again in subsequent segments.

Concept. This is the basic pattern for most stories except the straight news inverted pyramid. The concept pattern actually embraces most of the others mentioned here. As noted, the pattern involves a lead, an establishing section, and supporting points. The supporting points make up the bulk of the article.

How the supporting points are arranged, however, can vary. Here are some possibilities.

Simple to complex. The pattern is similar to a teacher's lesson plans. Start at a level your reader can understand readily and lead into more complex material as you proceed.

Geographical. If you were describing Manhattan Island you might start at the Battery at the south and work your way uptown. Or you might discuss urban problems by starting with inner-city slums and working your way outward to the suburbs.

Numerical.   Listing points that involve numbers or quantities is easier if you do so in an orderly manner, least to most, perhaps, or highest to lowest, shortest to longest, and so on.

Cause-effect.   You can run the cause-effect structure in either direction. One is to start with the effect and work toward the cause like a detective starting with a murder and working to locate the killer. Or you can start with, say, insensitive professors as the cause and proceed to the effect: dull lectures and fantasizing students.

3: DETAIL

As the third engine powering your writing, *detail* is easy to overlook. A phrase such as "there were a lot of people at the stadium" tells the reader little, whereas "85,000 people jammed the stadium" draws a much more graphic picture. It is vague to say that the Mississippi is a crooked, muddy river. It is much more powerful and graphic to say—as Mark Twain did—that the river takes 1,330 miles to cover a distance a crow could fly in 675 and that each year it carries enough mud downstream to form a block of land a mile square and 241 feet high.

Detail comes in many forms. One is the *choice of words,* particularly nouns and verbs. The more specific and precise, the better. Never say flowers; say yellow daffodils or red roses or white chrysanthemums. Never say "going" when you could say walking or running or flying or driving a 1968 Ford Mustang. Avoid using terms like "there is" or "there were" as in "There was a man in a green suit who ate green apples." (How about, "A man in a green suit ate green apples"?)

Another form of detail is numbers (see Chapter 10). Seek to use them dramatically through comparisons. An Associated Press writer, describing the power of the Boeing 747 airliner's four jet engines, said they totaled 174,000 pounds of thrust. But that figure has little meaning to most readers. So the writer also said the four engines had power equivalent to 87 diesel locomotives, thereby giving a much more graphic picture.

A third form of detail is *documentation,* which simply means backing up generalities. If you write about the grizzled old hermit spinning tall tales, then document the generalization with one of his favorites: "Have you heard the one about the wooden-legged farmer? He got bit on his wooden leg by a rattlesnake one day, and the leg began to swell. Got so big he began selling off slices to a lumber mill. Eventually the mill sawed the leg into thousands of boards, which helped to build dozens of homes. But now the swelling is going down, and those houses are getting smaller every day."

The final use of detail—*narrative detail*—is best demonstrated by a segment of

Tom Hallman's story on the fatal collision. Interviewing for vivid detail is painstaking but necessary for effective writing.

> The oncoming car, like something out of a nightmare, was there so suddenly that Tom didn't have time to scream. He cranked the steering wheel hard to his left, but the reflex came too late. Shana never saw what hit them.
>
> In the memory of the neighbors up and down Harold Street, the collision sounded like a bomb. It rousted them from beds and distracted them from televisions.
>
> At impact, in the middle of the dark street, the Volvo and the Oldsmobile performed a macabre dance of horror. Their rear ends rose off the pavement together, for a moment defying gravity, before slamming violently back to the ground.
>
> The right side of the Volvo collapsed, and the steering wheel broke. The can of paint in the trunk literally exploded, and paint gushed into the passenger compartment through stereo speaker holes. A front tire blew, and the car hit the street with such force that it gouged the asphalt. The hood of the Oldsmobile flew 30 feet down Harold Street. The battery tore loose and sailed 20 feet beyond the hood. The windshield ripped out of the frame.

The foregoing example contains descriptive detail but refers only fleetingly to the actors in the drama. Here we see the characters at the scene.

> Tom shook uncontrollably with cold. Slowly he realized what had happened. Harold Street filled with neighbors. One wrapped Tom in a blanket. He asked about Shana and Tiana, but no one would answer him.
>
> A woman told Tom she had seen the accident. Tom told her to call his mother, and gave the woman the telephone number.
>
> Keep calm, he told himself. Keep calm.
>
> Shana hadn't made a sound. Not a moan nor a cry. Tom couldn't see the Volvo, but he heard someone trying to pry open a door.
>
> "Help me up," he pleaded to Linda McIntosh, one of the first neighbors on the street.
>
> "My wife and daughter are there," he said, pointing to his car.
>
> McIntosh told him not to move. She would check on Shana and Tiana. McIntosh walked through the debris and looked in the car.
>
> The interior was dark, but she could see Shana. Her shirt had been forced open, and her stomach was exposed. McIntosh reached in the car to touch her.
>
> Shana's skin was very dry; scared, McIntosh quickly withdrew her hand. Tiana tried to crawl out of the car and McIntosh saw her. She picked Tiana up and walked back toward Tom. She stopped to check on Pete, but as she knelt beside him, McIntosh showed Tom that Tiana was alive.
>
> Suddenly, Pete groaned. He lifted his head and plopped it into MacIntosh's lap. He was bleeding from a bad cut to his temple. Pete's warm blood quickly soaked through her dress and ran down her legs. Someone took Tiana from her.
>
> The witness walked over and yelled at Pete, telling him he had hit a car with a woman and child inside.
>
> Pete started to yell.
>
> "I killed a kid. I killed a kid."

The kind of detail noted here leads us into the final engine that makes your writing powerful: drama.

4: DRAMA

Drama essentially means demonstrating something so that it leaves a vivid word-picture with the reader. You'll generally employ two ways to do that. The first is "narration," which is the technique used by Hallman in depicting the traffic accident. The second we'll call "graphic presentation."

Narration

To one extent or another journalists are "story tellers." Some even say we live in a story-shaped world, with discernible beginnings, middles, and endings. Our job is to identify the stories and to find the details that flesh out the stories.

Those conversant with the techniques of fiction may find it easier to find stories amid the raw material of reality. Certainly the Hallman story is a fine example. Finding such a story, one might be tempted to fictionalize rather than going through the difficult task of interviewing witnesses for detail, indeed, rather than putting the witnesses themselves through the pain of retelling their stories.

Hallman, however, worked to ensure the accuracy of every detail. This is burdensome yet necessary. It can also be exciting, particularly when an extraordinary piece of writing comes out of a "routine" story.

So the rule is, don't fictionalize. A good reporter doesn't have to. "Truth is stranger than fiction." Yet many techniques of fiction writing can be used by journalists to convey those strange truths of reality without making up facts. The technique—something we used to call "new journalism"—now has emerged under a new umbrella: *literary journalism.* It means packaging factual stories more or less in the form of creative short-story writing. Techniques of description, dialogue, narration, characterization, and even plot are no less possible just because the story is factual.

Some of the rigid requirements of fiction—the hero's resolution of the final "darkest hour" conflict must come precisely three minutes before the last commercial, for instance—don't make sense in reality, of course. But others work fine. Maybe that's because art imitates life. Here are a few examples of ways fiction techniques can be adapted.

Using elements of dramatic literature. Aristotle defined these elements as *tension, unity, action,* and *irony.* Tension means suspense, and Hallman uses it effectively in the accident story; indeed, the story may be even more suspenseful knowing that it's real. Hallman keeps you in suspense about who died until toward the end. Unity means organization, and we've already discussed that. Action means putting characters on a literary "stage" and showing them acting out their own story, as Hallman does. Irony means an unexpected outcome or an unintended meaning (the classic example being the husband who praises his wife's virtue while we, the audience, know her lover hides under the bed). Clearly, all of these can and should apply to nonfiction or "reality" writing.

Foreshadowing.   An effective device hints at things to come, often things that the characters are not yet aware of. Example: "Charter pilot Steve Laing didn't notice the tiny oil leak during his preflight check of his Cessna 180. This time Steve was in a hurry. The weather was deteriorating on his proposed route across the snowy Sierra Nevada range in California, and if he didn't take off in the next 15 minutes. . . ." Thus, the author gives the reader something to worry about.

Flashing back.   One maxim of short-story writing is, "Get into the story at the last possible moment." That heightens the drama. A sample would be a story that depicts a mountain climb. You show the heroine nearing the top of Killer Mountain just as an avalanche roars ominously above her. Having thus gotten your reader involved, you can flash back to an earlier time and explain how she came to be on Killer Mountain this day: "Smith had always wanted to climb Killer Mountain, and she began to prepare for it three years earlier when. . . ." Caution: Clumsily handled, the flashback can be confusing.

Using interior monologue.   Hallman's story shows Tom thinking things as, for example, these lines: *Keep calm, he told himself. Keep calm.* That's interior monologue, which can be used effectively. You might ask: How does the writer know what the person thought? Answer: You ask. (Or you have documents such as letters and memos.) Some editors might insist on attribution reminders (such as "as he told a reporter later," and so forth). It depends a little on how the story is structured and whether it is a feature or straight news.

Using characterization.   As the Hallman story illustrates, people acting on specific events add power to your story. That's not only because of reader identification but also because most drama needs people to act out the situation being described. Writing about auto accidents in the abstract is not nearly so powerful as showing real people involved in tragedy.

Many other kinds of articles can benefit from characterization. Suppose you are writing about education. First you must narrow it down to a theme: *What* about education? How about ghetto schools in big cities? *What* about ghetto schools? How about writing what it's like to teach in one?

Now you can employ the techniques of dramatization. Find one teacher whose character—whose personality, activities, and thoughts—speaks for the subject. To do this effectively you must select the right person, say, a teacher of English whose personal characteristics will appeal to your readers. She is dedicated, attractive, personable, enthusiastic, progressive. She is not perfect, but even her faults are appealing: She's forever stumbling over things, falling off her bicycle, hurting herself (not too seriously), which is why her friends call her Calamity Jane. She has a dangerous habit of becoming so engrossed in literature that she does not watch where she's going. Once, while reading Wordsworth, she stumbled down a flight of stairs and cracked a rib.

By focusing on such a person, the writer can add color and personality to a story. You can *show* her crying in the privacy of her apartment after a trying day. You can show her trying to reason with a troubled seventh grade girl. The girl attacks the teacher with a knife and pushes her down a stairway (another cracked rib). Through such scenes you give the reader a graphic picture.

Although your story will focus on one central character, it probably will include background material drawn from many sources, such as principals, other teachers, students, parents, counselors. Their information will give your story strength and substance—like the symphony orchestra behind the guest soloist.

Plot. Defined broadly, plot simply means a planned course of action in a short story or play, and this is a suitable definition for nonfiction plots. You are actually *retracing* a course of action. It probably will have a beginning, will run through a middle consisting of several episodes, and will end. The teacher mentioned here (a true story, by the way) went through several crossroads decisions ending with the big decision: Should she continue teaching or get into something else? The teacher decided to quit. She became a venereal disease investigator for the health department—an even more dangerous job, as it turned out. The job required her to visit bars in tough neighborhoods in Oklahoma City seeking individuals who might be spreading VD through sexual contacts. A man shot at her with a rifle one day, barely missing her but putting a hole through her auto windshield. Even so, she preferred it to the ghetto school.

Graphic Presentation

Graphic presentation is the other form of drama. It means expressing yourself in a manner as to draw vivid word-pictures for the reader. The techniques for doing so include figures of speech, dramatic comparisons, and structuring for emotional impact. Let's examine each one.

Figures of speech. The most common device to make your material more graphic is to use a figure of speech. Take this example: "If that dam bursts, the water's gonna go spilling over like Niagara Falls." The speaker uses a "simile" to create a more graphic and powerful image in the reader's mind. One is limited only by lack of imagination: Speakers can blow their tops with the explosive power of a Mount St. Helens, people can stand straight and tall like a western pine tree, crowds can roar like the ocean's surf, a worried mother can pace the living room like a restless pony, and so on.

Three noteworthy kinds of figures of speech are the *simile,* the *analogy,* and the *metaphor.* All three compare something unknown or abstract with something specific and concrete.

The simile does it by making a comparison. *The finances of X Corporation are as solid as Mount Rainier.* (Or for an ironic meaning, *The finances are as solid as Mount St. Helens.*) *When he gets angry he talks like a string of exploding firecrackers. Jane's life moved along slowly, peacefully, like Old Man River.*

The analogy is an extended simile, making several points of comparison. Example: "Gaining professional success in writing is like climbing a killer mountain. The writer encounters many a steep and rocky trail, many a dangerous glacier traverse, many a threatening avalanche between the bottom and the top. And the top is a lonely place to be."

The metaphor suggests that the comparison is real—sort of. To say "She broke her mother's heart" is to employ a metaphor whose meaning is readily apparent: She caused her mother some kind of emotional upset. The meaning is not to be taken literally. The same goes for such remarks as "He stole a kiss" or "She has a chip on her shoulder." These have become idiomatic expressions in the English language. With a little thought you can make up your own *original* metaphors because being a writer is to be awash in the creative juices.

You must, however, avoid overworked figures of speech—*deader than a doornail, fast as greased lightning, quick as a flash*—otherwise known as cliches. Also avoid mixed metaphors—"He drove an iron spike into the seas of circumstance"—and similar nonsense.

Dramatic comparisons. These have been discussed from time to time through this book, so only a reminder is necessary here. To describe a Texas ranch as containing 350,000 acres is not nearly so dramatic as saying it's half the size of Rhode Island. Similarly, the Boeing 747 airliner not only has the power of 87 diesel locomotives, but it would fill a football field, its length is twice the distance of the Wright Brothers' first flight, it weighs as much as the *Mayflower* sailing ship, and so forth.

Emotional impact. Often the way you structure a story can produce an impact on the emotions of your readers. The Hallman story does this effectively at the end.

> The neurosurgeon walked around Shana, testing her body for any response. Nothing.
> At 1:18 A.M., the nurse stopped squeezing the respiratory bag. The neurosurgeon left to tell Tom that Shana was dead. Then he went to tell Pete. One by one the nurses filed out of the room until only two remained.
> The heart monitor was on, but the sound turned off. Shana's young, strong heart struggled on. After the artificial respiration stopped, it beat once every 15 seconds. Then once every 30 seconds. Finally, once a minute.
> The two nurses did paperwork and reports, keeping one eye on the monitor. The electrical graph showed the heart activity grow more and more faint. There was no pulse, no pumping, but the heart fought on.
> At 1:45 A.M. the monitor stopped. Flatline.
> Shana Griffith was dead.

OTHER WAYS TO IMPROVE YOUR WRITING

Writers use other devices to get their message into the reader's mind. Here are a few noteworthy ones:

Subheads.   You literally identify your points, as we are doing here, by naming them. This not only helps to present the points effectively but also makes them memorable.

Gentle nudges.   Sometimes you do not need a literal signpost as much as a gentle kind of guidance to make sure the reader gets a point or slows down to catch a change in the direction of thought. A suggestion at the beginning of a complicated passage or a sudden change of thinking tells the reader what to expect. In the following examples, the gentle nudges are italicized.

> Smith sees *three reasons* why River City needs a new city hall. *The most important of them* is. . . .
> It was after the earthquake that Smith *began to change his views* about city hall.
> Jones takes a view *almost diametrically opposed* to Smith's ideas.

Stop sign.   You can literally stop the readers—or at least slow them down—to press attention to an important point. One way is to funnel the writing toward the point. You lead up to it breathlessly. You use short sentences. Perhaps you put a phrase by itself. Put it in its own paragraph. Repeat it for emphasis.

By itself?

Yes, by itself. Now it has the attention it deserves. Don't belabor such points, and don't use them too often lest they lose impact.

Transitions.   The need for transitions between paragraphs has already been discussed (Chapter 6). The need for transitions within paragraphs may not be so clear. Consider how confusing a paragraph can be without them.

> Coach Harry Jones was in a mellow mood. The thought of his team angered him. He maintained his mellow mood. He thought of George, the quarterback. If he ever got hold of George, he'd wring his neck. The team was a marvelous group of boys.

The material seems contradictory unless the proper transitions are inserted. Note how these transitions (shown in italics) help to make things clear even though they add little of substance.

> *Even though* Coach Harry Jones was in a mellow mood, the thought of his team angered him. He maintained his mellow mood, *however, at least until* he thought of George, the quarterback. If he ever got hold of George, he'd wring his neck. The *rest of* the team, *by contrast,* was a marvelous group of boys.

POINTS TO REMEMBER

1. Powerful writing means that it moves compellingly off the page and into the reader's mind.
2. Powerful writing starts with having something interesting and worthwhile to say, backed by good, detailed research.
3. A routine story—a traffic fatality, for instance—can gain awesome power with good research and attention to detail.
4. A powerful story starts with a strong sense of purpose.
5. The purpose can vary widely, even on the same topic.
6. The best stories focus in depth on narrow topics; broad, superficial topics tend to be dull.
7. Working with purpose is organization; articles must have a sense of unity to fulfill the purpose.
8. Attention to detail is vital, and too often overlooked. Good writing is specific in factual detail and also word choice.
9. Drama is the fourth rhetorical "engine" to lift writing off the page; it means fictionlike narrative and also graphic ways of expression such as figures of speech.
10. Subtle signposts can be used to guide the reader effectively, such as subheads, "stop (or slow) signs," and transitions.

17

Journalistic Teamwork: The Big Story

At 7:48 on a chill, windy November morning, the red phone rang on the cluttered desk of Tom Jackson, veteran city editor of the afternoon daily, *River City Express*, circulation 87,443.*

The red phone was the "hot line," an unlisted number reserved for urgent calls from reporters to the city desk. Because Jackson was away from his desk at the moment, Cynthia Louise Johnson—or Cindy, as she preferred to be called—picked up the extension at her own desk, the "rewrite desk."

"Cindy Johnson."

Her voice was brisk, businesslike.

"Fire—maybe a big one," the caller said.

It was Ron Mason on the phone. Ron covered police and fire for the *Express,* and he sounded excited. "Fire department's a little nervous about this one—it could be big. Better get Jackson on the phone. Tell him I want to go have a look myself."

The next four hours would represent one of the reasons Cindy Johnson got into journalism. Drama. Excitement. A sense of accomplishment. Satisfaction in helping to provide vital information to the public. Being part of a big story that

*This hypothetical case history is based on an actual fire that destroyed a car dealership in the author's home town. I gratefully acknowledge the assistance of Tom Jaques, former city editor of the *Register-Guard* of Eugene, Oregon (subsequently assistant managing editor), in preparing this chapter.

Seattle Times reporter Greg Heberlien telephones a breaking news story on an FBI fugitive manhunt back to the city desk via mobile telephone. *(Photo by Matt McVay.)*

everyone will be reading in the paper that evening and talking about through the week.

The dramatic moments of a big story with its banner headline tend to etch themselves into the minds of a newspaper staff—to be discussed, rehashed, exaggerated, maybe even lied about, for years to come whenever *Express* staff members assemble.

And if you've never witnessed a daily newspaper newsroom mobilize for action for the big story—well, this chapter is dedicated to you. Covering the big story is like running a well-executed football play, with each player having his or her own assignment from the coach. At least it's supposed to be.

Tom Jackson, who as city editor supervised the newspaper's staff of reporters and photographers, was the coach.

And Cindy Johnson, on rewrite, was the quarterback, sort of. She would plan the story and call the plays. But Jackson as coach would be the overall supervisor. And he might even send in a play himself occasionally.

A fair amount of newspaper reporting used to be done through rewrite. From various locations reporters conveyed by phone information to be assembled by the rewrite person. In recent years, however, most of the rewrite function has been replaced by remote VDT terminals. Reporters out in the field often write their stories on portable word processors and then send them electronically by phone line directly into the newspaper's computer.

But on complex stories, tight to deadline, editors still deploy whole teams of reporters to gather information from widely dispersed sources and report it to one person who puts it all together into a coherent whole—the rewrite person. In theory, journalistic teamwork works like a well-executed football play, although fumbles and miscues remain ominous possibilities.

Cindy's work on rewrite lacked the glamour of the old days before the electronic revolution. The old line, "Hello, Sweetheart, give me rewrite," something out of *Front Page* era movies, has yielded to log-on commands, passwords, and similar computer jargon. Still, the *Express* maintained a rewrite desk, staffed by a general assignment reporter whose work tended to range from writing the daily weather report to rewriting handouts and fielding phone calls from the public. Part of the job, to be sure, was just being on hand, in case something big occurred.

The prospect of the big story always seemed a little intimidating to Cindy. Writing a complex story against a harsh deadline requires concentration, organization, and some luck. Cindy hated making mistakes. "Nobody wants to fumble where the ice is the thinnest," as she once expressed it.

A 27-year-old woman from Jasper, Alabama, Cindy was noted for charm, horseback riding, culinary arts (fried chicken especially), feature writing, mixed metaphors, and a kind of homespun grits and 'taters philosophy—not necessarily in that order. Eight years had elapsed since she left the South, first to go to Carleton College in Minnesota, then to the University of Missouri for a degree in journalism, finally to River City and the job with the *Express*.

YELLOW ALERT

The term "yellow alert" is not commonly used in newsrooms, but it does suggest the first step toward handling certain kinds of big stories—the kind where you're not sure you *have* a big story. City Editor Tom Jackson guessed that for every ten yellow alerts, only one story might turn out to be big beyond the routine, big enough to call for newsgathering teamwork.

But the call from reporter Ron Mason about the fire brought a reaction conditioned by fifteen years of experience as city editor. Jackson, in fact, had his first-string varsity team already in mind—at least the two or three key people.

His key quarterback would be Sam Wyman, 53, veteran writer who could turn out a column of flawless copy in 20 to 30 minutes.

His key reporter would be Al Romanoff, 43, a tough, persevering kind of reporter. If you needed information in a hurry under difficult conditions, Romanoff was the man to send.

And his key sidebar person—the writer who would produce a secondary story about the human dimension—would be Sam Dillard, 33, a feature writer. Dillard had an uncanny ability to find the people stories, the human drama, the color, the irony, in any situation.

Around that nucleus, Jackson would add whoever was available in the newsroom. Jackson, after all, had hired most of them, and with maybe one or two exceptions any of them could fill out the rest of his emergency team.

And a coach can always improvise with the material at hand. Cindy Johnson sat at the rewrite desk that day, and in Jackson's eyes, Cindy was okay. A fast writer, accurate, painstaking. She didn't make many mistakes—probably because making a dumb mistake was a devastating blow to her self-esteem. In Jackson's view, she worried a little too much about getting everything right, but how could you fault her for that?

So if Cindy were on the rewrite desk when something big came along, Jackson's instincts would be to keep her there. You can't call on Wyman, the old pro, all the time. You have to bring the young ones along, give them experience. But if something big came up, Jackson would want Wyman on hand—just in case.

And so, on this cool, windy day, Jackson would put his team into action.

Police reporter Ron Mason was calling from fire department headquarters. He said a call had come to the fire station at 7:46 A.M. A man named Larkin said thick smoke was pouring out of several windows at Continental Motors, a Ford car dealership and repair shop at 3200 River Avenue, about two miles west of downtown River City.

Tom Jackson, hastily summoned by Cindy, told Mason to hustle out to the fire and have a look.

"Call me the moment you know something."

Jackson's emergency coverage plan had been well-rehearsed in discussions with the staff.

1. Alert the photo desk. (The photo editor dispatched one photographer to the scene and told another to stand by.)
2. Put your team together. (Jackson tapped six reporters on the shoulder, including Romanoff, Dillard, and Wyman. "Sit tight," he told each. "We may have a big fire going. Don't leave the office without checking with me.")
3. Alert other editors in the newsroom.
4. Get the rewrite desk prepared. Clear your rewrite person of all nonessential activities.

"Cindy, stay cool until we see what we've got. If it's big, you're in charge. Get ready, just in case."

Cindy, as it turned out, had her own emergency plan in mind.

Her biggest problem, she knew, would be organization.

A writer has to sort things out quickly, because once the material starts coming, a writer can quickly lose track.

Cindy made a quick outline of possible categories, based on her earlier experiences in covering small fires.

1. How the fire started
2. How it was fought
3. Damage and casualties, if any
4. Consequences (layoffs, public inconvenience, etc.)
5. Future plans (repair damage, etc.)

As always, Cindy would take notes on the reporters' calls on her video display terminal, then get "hard copy" (computer printouts) that she could separate into the five categories. She learned this by watching veteran reporters—Wyman, Dillard, and Romanoff especially—at work. Over the years she'd synthesized her observations into six points valuable for covering the complex, fast-breaking, ever-changing kinds of stories.

1. Keep cool.
2. Work as a team. Follow orders precisely.
3. Organize, organize, organize. Keep things sorted out.
4. Keep your lead paragraph in mind at all times—changing it, of course, as new information comes in. Be ready at any moment to write your lead on the screen. For a truly complex, rambling story, consider using a flashby lead.
5. Assume that your newsgathering is complete only when (a) your deadline is at hand, or (b) your sources tell you nothing you don't already know.
6. Use short sentences. Also short paragraphs. It speeds writing, and it allows easier inserting as new information comes in, as it inevitably does in a fast-breaking news event.

Cindy Johnson wondered if the feeling in the pit of her stomach represented excitement or apprehension. A little of both, she decided, like a nervous pony in a cement mixer.

RED ALERT

The general alarm sounded at 8:01 A.M. via an air raid siren that could be heard all over the city. A "general alarm" meant that the city's entire fire department was on call, including off-duty and reserve fire fighters. By prior arrangement, nearby communities began sending equipment into River City for standby in case another fire broke out somewhere else.

City Editor Tom Jackson sent Al Romanoff and Sam Dillard exploding out of the office to the scene. He asked the photo desk to send a second photographer.

He asked Jim Alexander, 29, general-assignment reporter, to phone the emergency agencies during police reporter Mason's absence—just to make sure nothing important got overlooked. "If you pick up anything more on the fire, give it to Cindy."

He asked Charlie Boggs, 33, business writer, to monitor the city's emergency radio frequencies on a radio scanner and to report anything noteworthy.

He asked Ruth Pucinsky, 26, a feature writer, to put aside her story about sexual child abuse and sit tight to await further instructions.

He asked Sam Wyman, the old pro, to stand by.

The red phone rang on Cindy Johnson's desk.

"Hi, Cindy, this is Ron. We've got a hell of a fire out here—flames a hundred feet high. Tell Jackson."

"He knows. Dillard and Romanoff are on their way. Also two photographers—anybody there yet?"

"Hope they get here okay—traffic's a mess on River Avenue. I see one photographer on the job, and she ought to be getting great stuff—this thing's a roaring inferno. You can feel the heat a block away. It's even cracking the plate glass windows in the library across the street." Mason dictated a few more random notes. Cindy, wearing a headset with earphones and a mouthpiece like a telephone operator's, took notes on the VDT.

> flaming debris being carried north on a stiff breeze across river ave & dropping burning material on the roofs of buildings across the street, posing major threat. buildings incl river ave branch of city library.
>
> fire battalion cmd Walter Jacobs says the fire may spread to other blds if more equipment doesn't arrive soon.
>
> IT'S "touch and go," sez jacobs.
>
> Continental mtrs is "totally involved," says jacobs, no hope of saving bldg or contents, main job is to save other bldgs.
>
> lots of cars inside cont mtrs bldg.
>
> occasional explosions heard inside bldg.
>
> first fire truck arrived here 7:50 & immediately called for assistance. two more trucks came abt 7:55, general alarm at 8:01.
>
> Jacobs sez "we got at least a half-million-dollar fire on our hands—probably more."

"Wow," said Cindy. She imagined a lead—"A half-million-dollar fire raged out of control at Continental Motors this morning. . . ."

"Ron, how about calling me back with some quotes—like maybe from the people who first saw the fire? Okay?"

"Right, Cindy. Back in 15 or 20 minutes."

Cindy Johnson was in charge now, directing the coverage. Not that veteran reporters like Romanoff and Dillard—and even Mason, the young police reporter—needed much direction. They knew what to do. But Cindy called the plays because she knew what information she needed for a well-rounded report.

Tom Jackson saw to it that Cindy got what she needed.

"I want background on big fires in the past," said Cindy. "Also, Ron mentioned traffic tieups."

"Okay," said Jackson, "and I'll get someone checking power and gas for possible problems."

Working in concert, they put Charlie Boggs to work in the newspaper library, looking up clips of big fires in the city's history. Jim Alexander talked to police about the traffic problems. Ruth Pucinksy called power and gas companies.

Jackson transferred a call to Cindy. "Something about somebody inside the building screaming," Jackson said. "We'd better check it out."

The woman said she'd been standing in a crowd of bystanders, and she overheard a man saying he'd heard screams within the building—sounded like a woman's screams.

The red phone rang. Cindy was not good at handling two phones at once.

"Got another call," Cindy explained. "We'll investigate the screams. Thanks for the tip." She picked up the hot line.

"Hi, Sweetheart, this is Dillard."

Sam Dillard picked the damnedest times to get familiar. Dillard was rather a good-humored character who called any woman under 60 "sweetheart." When he said it to Cindy, she couldn't help noticing, he seemed more inspired. It was just his way of talking. She thought he might even use it as an interviewing technique to elicit colorful quotes out of his feature sources. It worked with her. She never failed to respond with a sharp retort about his rotten, chauvinistic behavior.

"Sam, you turkey, you're barking up the wrong rainbarrel. So what's up?" In truth she not only enjoyed the repartee with Sam, but she learned a lot about information gathering from his almost cavalier informality with people. Mostly she learned not to take people too seriously, Sam Dillard especially.

"We got stuck in a traffic jam a good half-mile short of the scene," he said. "Romanoff took off on foot and I think he'll set a new record for the half-mile. Just wanted you to know that we're on the job."

"Okay, Sam. And Sam—how about calling me with some touches of color? Don't save them all for your own story."

"Sure, Sweetheart."

Ron Mason called again and dictated some more notes.

> Witness to fire: Peter L. Larkin, age 37, address 3400 Harlow Ave. He first reported the fire to authorities. Direct quote: "I caught a glimpse of something bright orange out of the corner of my eye. I pulled off the street and about that time I heard a muffled explosion inside the building. Then a window blew out and this thick gray smoke started pouring out. That's when I called the fire department."
> Larkin is a lawyer, works downtown, was en route to work as he passed the scene.

"Ron, did you hear anything about a woman's screams inside the building?"

"No. Did someone tell you that?"

"Yes, someone phoned and said a woman's screams supposedly were heard inside the building."

"Okay, I'll check it out."

"Also, Ron, can you find a company official to talk about things like laying off employees, plans to rebuild, amount of loss—all the little nitty-gritty stuff?"

Cindy hung up and looked at some notes: printouts other reporters had delivered to her desk.

> Cindy: River City Power & Light sez abt 30 residents in area of fire are without power due to broken hot wire resulting from fire. Crew enroute to make repairs. I'll check again for update before deadline. Hang in there, kid!—Ruth

Cindy: Dillard called with a feature idea. He'll call back, as you were on the line. But, hey, remember, play this one straight, and let Sam do the color sidebar. Okay?—Tom

Memo to Cindy
From C Boggs
Re: big fires of the past
Here's a list of biggies of yesteryear, culled from the libe. I'm writing a separate story abt same but thot u'd like look for ur story.

1. Food Mart Shopping Center, August 28, 1981. Loss $1.1 million.
2. Acme Manufacturing Co. plant July 7, 1972, $1.8 million.
3. River City Elks Lodge, Dec. 14, 1962, $390,000.
4. McKenzie Hotel, Jan. 2, 1944. $250,000. Worst fire in history of river city for loss of life. Five persons died, three men and a woman who were guests of the hotel, plus one employee, a maid.
5. FYI, the *least* costly fire on record in the history of River City probably was Mandy Baker's tree house fire, July 2, 1957, caused when Mandy's little brother, Nathan, threw a firecracker into the house and it, the house, started smoldering. Fire dept. called and used hand extinguisher. Damage estimated at $4.87.

Al Romanoff came on the phone with a quote from the River City fire chief, Charles Pickering. Cindy took notes on the VDT.

Pickering: "This fire is one of the worst in the history of River City. There's a good half-to-three-quarters of a million dollars in the building, plus who knows how much inside. The building's totally involved in the fire, and our job is to keep it from spreading to other buildings."
About 60 fire fighters on the job, plus 9 or 10 fire trucks. Pickering doesn't know how it started: "it could be any one of a hundred different reasons."
Pickering again: "We're fighting a hell of a lot more than just a fire. We're fighting wind and we're fighting traffic and we're fighting bystanders."
General notes: about 2,000 bystanders around. Bad traffic tieups. River Ave blocked. About 20 fire fighters and two firetrucks are diverted to protecting three buildings downwind from the fire—that's north across River Avenue from the fire. They are (1) River Ave branch of city library, (2) the OK Tavern, and the Oakway Building, which houses five small businesses, including the Beeckman Fire and Casualty Co.

Cindy picked up the phone again moments later—"Hi, Sweetheart"—and Sam Dillard reeled off a few color items.

"First, at eight o'clock the library opened across the street from the fire. It closed at 8:05 when they evacuated all those buildings. But in those five minutes, one patron came in to check out a book. Would you like the name of that book?"

"Oh, Lord, if it's *The Fire Next Time,* I'll simply die."

"How about *The Witches of Eastwick,* by John Updike? Will you die for that?"
"No."

"Good. Now listen up while I fill your wondering mind with additional gems. First, groups of teenagers will be late getting to school today. That's because they're pushing several new cars, parked near the burning building, to safer locales. They saved about 30 cars. In some cases they had to break windows to get inside the cars because the keys were inside the burning building. And now, Cynthia, are you ready for Number Two?"

"Ready like a train waiting at dockside about to sink from overloaded circuits."

"Write down auto horns. Auto horns have been blowing voluntarily as the fire reaches the cars inside the building. I guess the fire short-circuits the wiring. So the horns go off, they blow a mournful wail for two or three minutes, and then they die out like the last cry of some dying monster."

"Sam, that's good. Let me get that in my notes. You really have a way of expressing yourself."

"Cindy, be serious. Have you considered the possibility that the automobile may be a dying species, going the way of the dinosaur and other anachronistic phenomena? Anyhow, I counted at least six horns going off in the last ten or fifteen minutes, sometimes two at once."

"In harmony?"

"More like lovestruck hounds howling at the moon before the witching hour."

Ron Mason called the moment Dillard finished. Mason dictated a quote from one Harry A. Lovelace, age 69, 433 Abby Lane, which is a block from the fire.

> "I was walking by the fire scene and I couldn't believe my ears. There was kind of a sharp scream, a woman's scream. Then I didn't hear it anymore."
>
> Ron asked, "Could you be mistaken about its being human?"
>
> Lovelace: "No, I know what I heard."
>
> Assistant Fire Chief Red Britton, commenting on screams: "Yeah, I'd been told that. But by the time the first equipment arrived, that part of the building was totally involved. There was no way anyone could get in to check."

"Ron, what time did Mr. Lovelace hear those screams?" Cindy asked.

"Maybe three or four minutes before the first truck arrived. He's not sure. Maybe around a quarter of eight."

"Okay, Ron. By the way, I—"

"Good God!"

"What's the matter, Ron?"

"I just heard a loud rumbling crash, and now I hear people screaming. Something's happened. Talk to you later."

Cindy shuddered as the line went dead. City Editor Tom Jackson told her, "Just sit tight by your phone. I'll get people checking fire and police to see what happened."

For the first time that morning, Cindy grew conscious of passing time. It was 8:37. One hour and 53 minutes to deadline for the first edition.

Cindy calculated she could write the story in an hour, or even 45 minutes if necessary. During the momentary lull, she even wrote a couple of paragraphs, including the quotes from Larkin about spotting the fire and from Lovelace about the screams. She stored them in the computer for recall later—like money in the bank for a rainy day.

Charlie Boggs yelled across the newsroom: He'd picked up a call on the police radio. Three ambulances had been dispatched to the fire.

"Three!" said Cindy.

Ruth Pucinsky learned that Mercy Hospital had been alerted to expect casualties.

"Get to the hospital, Ruth," said Tom Jackson.

Cindy turned to her VDT and wrote a lead to her story, just for practice.

Fire raged through Continental Motors this morning, sending XX persons to the hospital. . . .

Dillard was on the phone. When he didn't say "Sweetheart," Cindy knew something was frightfully amiss.

"Romanoff and Mason are both on the job, and they'll be calling in. Here's the situation. A major portion of the north wall—the one facing the street toward the library—of the Continental Motors building collapsed at 8:36 this morning. It fell on top of four or five firemen who had been manning one of the fire hoses up close to the building. Witnesses said three of the firemen saw the wall about to collapse, and they tried to run but were felled by falling debris. That's about all I know now. Romanoff will call momentarily."

Jackson sent Jim Alexander to the central fire station. "Get names and backgrounds of the injured," he said. "And find out how many in the past have been killed or injured on duty."

Another call from Ron Mason via the switchboard. "Background stuff. It can wait."

"Go ahead, Ron. If Romanoff calls, I may have to cut you off." Cindy took notes.

Asst. Police Chief Jim Parsons says crowd of onlookers to be 3,000 to 4,000. 20 officers have been deployed for crowd control and traffic.

Traffic backed up for three miles on River Avenue on the west side, and for a mile on the east side, toward downtown. Traffic being detoured on side streets.

Parsons says crowd behaving well except for two men arrested for disorderly conduct and resisting arrest. They fought with police when cops tried to push back the crowd.

About 500 witnessed collapse of wall. Many spectators tried to surge forward to help the injured, but were restrained by cops. They finally allowed about a dozen to go through to help.

Manager of Continental Motors William Harrison (also interviewed by Mason): says building is worth about $700,000 and contents (cars, equipment, office facilities) about $750,000. About 55 cars inside building, 30 of them new, the remaining 25 customers' cars in the repair shop. All were destroyed. Most of the loss covered by insurance. The firm employs about 120 persons. Plans for rebuilding must await return of Alexander Winthrop, of River City, who holds most of the stock in the company. He's vacationing in Hawaii but is returning immediately. Some employees may have to be laid off temporarily.

Al Romanoff called a little after nine.

"Sorry it took so long," he said. "I had a terrible time getting names. Everybody's tensed up.

"So far, five people have been taken by ambulance to Mercy Hospital. One of them is a woman. Nobody knows her name. She was found unconscious on the south side of the building. She's middle-aged. A real mystery woman."

"Wonder if she's the screamer," said Cindy.

"Don't know. I'll get back to that. Ready for the names of four injured?"

"Go!"

"First we have William A. Kennedy. [Spells out names.] Then we have one Al Lindley, or Lindsay it might be. Third is Charles Larson. The fourth fireman has not been identified yet, but I can tell you unofficially the name is Felix Doerner. He was the man on the nozzle. He's probably dead, but no one will say so officially."

"Okay, Al. Ruth is at the hospital so we'll check."

"And here are some more details from Fire Chief Pickering. Twelve trucks are on the scene, with 75 fire fighters. The fire is considered 'under control' as of 9:20 A.M. Here's a quote from Pickering: 'I could see the structure about to give way, and I yelled to them but they couldn't hear me. A moment later it all came down.' "

Sam Dillard called moments later with a quote from another witness: James Englemann, 18, who lives with his parents at 1818 Spruce Street, about three blocks from the fire scene. He was among the 500 spectators who saw the collapse. He said, "There were four men on the hose, and one of them went back into the street to pull more hose. The other three remained right up close to the wall. Then the fourth man began hollering to the other three when the wall began to crack. They all turned and two of them started running back, but the man holding the nozzle couldn't seem to get out in time. He threw up his hands like he was trying to stop the wall. He just crumpled up and went down."

About 25 men helped to free the injured from the rubble, Dillard said. He quoted Fire Chief Pickering about the cause: "It's still too early to tell. We'll have a man down from the State Fire Marshal's office, probably late this afternoon, to help us look through the evidence to find the cause."

Cindy asked Dillard for an overall description that she could use in her story. She learned that the building was a two-story cement and brick building occupying a quarter of a city block. Sales rooms were in the front and repair facilities in the back (south) side of the building. Offices were on the second floor. The building was set back about 30 feet from River Avenue and was surrounded by a large paved parking lot where about 250 new and used cars were parked.

"Is the building a total loss?" asked Cindy.

"Yes."

"How high were the flames?"

"Eighty feet at least. They could have been higher except for the wind."

"And the flames were going out the roof?"

"Yes, except eventually there was no roof. Little by little it all collapsed in on the fire."

"The roof first, then the wall came down?"

"Right."

"Are other walls still standing?"

"The outside shell of the building is still there except for a good portion of the north wall, the one that collapsed."

"Are any other walls in danger of collapsing?"

"I don't know."

"Are any precautions being taken—like fire fighters being told to stay away from the other walls?"

"I don't think so—they're still working in close."

"Okay. Sam, you know I have to ask these questions because I need descriptive material. They don't have pictures for me yet. Okay?"

"The TV people are here, so maybe you can catch it on the tube. You'll want to know the color of the smoke, right? Dirty gray-brown. It's all floating northward on the wind. Firemen have been hosing down the buildings across the street to prevent the fire from catching there. The danger is past now. But the big plate glass windows in the library building, the ones facing toward the fire, are all cracked and warped from the heat."

"Okay, Sam. Anything else? Touches of color?"

"You might mention the frequent explosions inside the building. Things have been exploding all morning long inside, which Pickering identified as drums of flammable goop, gas tanks on the cars, and so forth."

It was 9:35. Cindy knew she'd have to start work to meet the deadline. She set about checking names of the injured in the *City Directory*.

"The desk is giving the story a 96-point banner headline," Jackson said. "What should it say?"

"How about 'Rewrite woman drowns in a sea of gray-brown smoke'? Just kidding. You know how I am when I get nervous."

"What's your lead?"

"I was thinking of something like 'River City's worst fire since 1972 destroyed the Continental Motors Building this morning sending five persons to Mercy Hospital.' "

"Sounds good. What about the collapsing wall? Should that get into the lead somehow?"

"Um, okay, how about 'A collapsing wall sent five persons to Mercy Hospital this morning in River City's most disastrous fire since 1972'?"

"The wall sent only four persons."

"Hmmmmm." Cindy started nibbling on a fingernail.

"I'm sure you'll work it out, Cindy," he said. "Just give it a try on the tube."

"Right. Like my Daddy always says, 'Ya don't get the soap less'n ya boil the hawg.' "

"No kidding. Your Daddy always says that?"

"An old country saying. You should hear Daddy when he *really* gets nervous."

Cindy turned to her VDT and wrote:

> Fire raged out of control this morning, destroying the Continental Motors Building on River Avenue, sending five persons to Mercy Hospital, causing $1.45 million in property loss, and for a time threatening th.gfhjkl/88. horsefeathers!

"Well, let it stand for a moment," said Tom Jackson. "Let's sketch out the rest of the details." Together they produced a tentative outline.

Lead
Flashby with additional important details
Names of injured
Details of wall collapse
Assessment of damages
Details of fire alarm, witness reports, mysterious screams
Narrative of fire's progress, details of fighting it
Plans to rebuild, plus miscellaneous

Cindy knew that she wouldn't follow the outline precisely, but she would use it as a general guide, like a road map. As she wrote sections of the story, she punched them into the computer so that Jackson could call them up on his screen for editing before sending them along to the copydesk for further editing. She turned to the screen for another try on the lead, but Ruth Pucinsky was on the phone from the hospital.

She gave a rundown on each of the fire victims, most of it obtained from the hospital's spokeswoman, Dixie Miller.

Felix Doerner, age 38, 1836 Circle Lane, River City. A fireman. Dead on arrival at the hospital. Doctors said he'd probably been killed instantly by the falling wall.

Elbert A. (Al) Lindsay, also a fireman, age 46, of 1234 Elkay Drive, River City. He died about five minutes after arrival at the hospital. Doctors said his injuries were minor, and they suspect a heart attack, though that's off the record pending autopsy.

William A. Kennedy, fireman, age 35, of 12 Dorsey Drive, River City. He is in good condition with only minor injuries. Pucinsky talked with him at the hospital for this account of the collapse of the wall: "I could see it coming and it was like a nightmare. I yelled at them to get out, the wall's going, and Charlie and Al started running, but Felix just seemed to stand there frozen, and he just crumpled up in the middle of a ton of cement and brick. It was awful."

Charles T. Larson, age 31, whose home is Rural Route 7, River City, a fireman, in satisfactory condition with a broken leg and two cracked ribs.

A fifth person, a woman about 40, identity unknown, in serious but stable condition, still unconscious. She had marks on her body that look like electrical burns, the doctors said.

As Cindy began work in earnest writing the story, Tom Jackson told her: "Jim's going to write a separate story about the background of the firemen, but here's something you might want to put in your main story—these are the first River City firemen killed in the line of duty since 1928."

He also rolled up a portable TV set. "Channel 13's running fire stuff between soap operas," he said. "Want to watch?"

"Sure. Just turn down the damned sound."

Cindy turned to the VDT and in 50 minutes wrote the story. It was not the best thing she'd ever written, but it was all right. She met the deadline. She got an extra ten minutes beyond deadline to review the editing job done by Jackson and the copydesk. She tinkered with the copy a little, splitting long sentences into two short ones, replacing a couple of passive verbs with active ones, touching up an occasional awkward sentence. Around two that afternoon she stopped at a coffee shop for lunch—and saw three people reading *her* story. And when she got back Tom Jackson said she'd done a good job. "Now let's talk about tomorrow's follow-up. What are some of the loose ends? By the way, how do you feel?"

"Great. Tired. But I'm on a real high. Like buried treasure floating on the wings of a hot air balloon."

POINTS TO REMEMBER

1. Some stories—big, complex ones written close to deadline—require several reporters to work as a team.
2. Though such stories are rare, they're exciting and important.
3. In teamwork, reporters are deployed widely and call their reports in, usually by phone, to a rewrite person.
4. The city editor, who is manager of the newsroom, selects a team with care, placing the most skilled and dependable reporters on the varsity squad.
5. The big stories center around the rewrite person who takes all the diverse elements and weaves them into a coherent story.
6. Lots of yellow alerts occur—where you *think* you might have a big story going—but many are false alarms.
7. Organization—outlining and keeping information sorted out—is the key to writing big, complex stories close to deadline.

EXERCISE

You write the story from the material presented in this chapter. Read it over carefully, take notes, prepare an outline. Give yourself a deadline. When you've finished, examine Cindy's story (as edited by the city editor and the copydesk) in Appendix C.

18
Media Law

You're at police headquarters early in the morning and you're a little sleepy. The cops bring in two men for booking, John Doe and James Roe. Roe's charged with first-degree murder, Doe for reckless driving.

"No question about it," says the police booking sergeant. "Doe's our man, all right. A cold-blooded killer if I ever saw one. Another one of them drug-crazed hippies. Gave us a full confession. Admitted everything. Ran down his best friend, probably in a fit of doped-up frenzy."

You sense a story here so you press for details.

"Where's this guy live?" The sergeant glances down at his papers and replies, "I guess it's out on Western Avenue."

You begin writing a story for the paper.

> John Doe, a drug-crazed hippie who lives out on Western Avenue, was arrested this morning for cold-bloodedly murdering his best friend, apparently in a fit of doped-up frenzy, River City police reported.
> "No question about it, Doe's our man," said the police booking sergeant. "A cold-blooded killer if I ever saw one."

Slow down. If you drove a car the way you're writing that story, you'd be arrested for reckless driving. Maybe you can't be arrested for "reckless reporting,"

The author gratefully acknowledges the assistance of Professor Jeremy Cohen, of Stanford University, in preparing this chapter.

Covering the police beat requires painstaking accuracy. Here Gail Bullen consults with Lt. Dave Jimenez about the day's police activities in Grants Pass, Oregon. *(Photo by Dan Dillon.)*

but you can be sued for libel. And you might think of the laws of libel—along with invasion of privacy—as equivalent to a set of rules against reckless reporting.

Consider some of the legal implications of your story.

First, Doe is not the man accused of first-degree murder. It's Roe. Doe's accused of reckless driving. An innocent mistake, easy to make. But lawsuits have been filed and damages collected for just such mistakes. You have damaged Doe's reputation, and he's entitled to compensation for that. True, you heard the sergeant say "Doe," but he seemed to be indulging in a lot of careless talk—and that alone should alert you to be careful. It's one thing to carry on about drug-crazed hippies down at police headquarters, quite another to put it in the paper.

Second, your identification is vague. A lot of lawsuits result from vagueness. Maybe several John Does live on Western Avenue, and every one has been injured by your story. That's why editors insist on having precise identifications on crime stories. Make it read, "James Roe, 23, of 123 Western Avenue" so that readers will know which person you're talking about.

Third, you must be careful to report only what you can prove. That Roe was arrested on a charge of first-degree murder is safe enough, being a matter of record. But to suggest that he in fact committed the crime is both dangerous and prejudicial to Roe's chances for a fair trial.

Finally, the loose talk about "cold-blooded murderer" and "doped-up frenzy" is excessive and reckless.

So certain kinds of restraints—some legal, some ethical—limit what you can say in news reporting. But, interestingly enough, the law provides some freedom to report reckless remarks that you might not have considered. Suppose a witness at a court trial blurts out, "Roe's a cold-blooded killer!" That would be safe to print because it's protected by "privilege."

The scenario suggests, if nothing more, that the laws governing mass communications are not simple. They undergo constant change so that anything said today may be out of date tomorrow. Yet the work of a reporter must somehow continue. What kinds of legal guidelines can we use? Here are a couple:

First, the law does not restrict the reporting of truth, except in some kinds of "invasion of privacy" cases (to be discussed). Usually, though, the truth must be provable in court should it ever come to trial.

Second, the law grants the right to publish statements suspected to be false and libelous if the statements are privileged. That's the case in the court trial, for example. What goes on in an open meeting of a government agency—namely, the public's business under the concept of self-government—is protected by what the law calls *absolute privilege.* The same protection applies to such sources as public records, open meetings, governmental bodies, and *official* actions and pronouncements of government officials. The newswriter's report of these governmental activities is covered by *qualified* or *conditional privilege,* which means that comments covered by absolute privilege can be reported in a balanced and reasonably accurate account. Note the term *balanced.* If you quoted a witness calling Roe a cold-blooded killer and didn't report comments that defended his good name, then your qualified privilege would not protect you.

But if someone got on a soapbox in city park and called Roe a killer, the statement is *not* covered by privilege. It would be dangerous to report. Not only would the person who said it be liable for damages, but so would the reporter who wrote the story and the paper that published it.

FACT REPORTING

A single chapter cannot tell you all you need to know about media law. For adequate preparation, read a book that specializes in law such as Don Pember's *Mass Media Law,* or Gillmore and Barron's *Mass Communications Law,* both standard texts. (See Bibliography for full citations.) Also useful is the law section of the *AP Stylebook and Libel Manual.* The *Seattle Times* publishes a 69-page handbook titled *Newsroom Legal Guidebook* especially designed to assist reporters in their daily work. A course in mass communications law is the best way to keep up to date. You can't just take it once and forget it, though, because the fine shadings of media law keep changing as the courts decide new cases.

It will be easier, in any event, to absorb these legal complexities if you think of ethical and legal limits at the same time. The two are intertwined. You might even consider the legal restrictions as reinforcement of conscientious reporting. The law of "torts" (a legal term meaning "civil wrongs") tends to reflect what society considers fair and just. The law tends to discourage incompetent or blindly biased reporting—the kind you might even call "reckless reporting."

So the key to avoiding legal problems is accurate, fair-minded, factual reporting. That, indeed, is what this book is about. The important ethical principles of reporting can be summarized in four words, as suggested by a veteran newsman and former professor, Dean F. Rea:

Fairness. Accuracy. Completeness. Temperance.

The four principles add up to the acronym FACT. FACT reporting is the surest way to keep you and your paper out of the courts.

Fairness

Fairness means that you will be honest and aboveboard, that you will not engage in trickery or deceit. It means you will not accuse (or quote someone else as accusing) a person of wrongdoing without evidence and without giving the person a chance to respond or explain. It means that your reporting will contain no personal bias. Granted, everyone has personal opinions, but a good reporter can rise above personal leanings. Be tolerant and open-minded. You certainly don't have to agree with everything you quote people as saying. By allowing people to say what they really think and feel, you depict a broader, more varied world—also a more interesting world. Difference of opinion is not only what makes horse races, as Mark Twain suggested, but also adds color and zest to the reporter's professional life.

Accuracy

Being accurate is not easy. It requires you to take great pains to be correct in every detail, checking and double-checking the small details as well as the large concepts. Names, addresses, ages—these are where mistakes most frequently happen. If you can't even spell a person's name right (when you have city directories, telephone books, and other sources available), can your reporting of other facts and ideas really be trusted?

Accuracy is more than just factual details, however. "Balance" is also essential. Your account of, say, a city council meeting could conceivably be accurate in the details you chose to report, but dreadfully inaccurate if you chose to report only one side of a controversy and not the other. Quoting out of context is another hazard. Consider a statement like this by a councilman we'll call Jones.

"Smith is a terrific used car salesman 95 percent of the time, completely honest and aboveboard. I'd send my aging mother out to buy from him. But once in a blue moon we get that dark side, that five percent facade that strikes me as slightly shady and slippery."

If you quoted Jones calling Smith "shady and slippery" without noting the 95 percent honesty quotient, you'd be quoting out of context.

Paying close attention to such problems is not just good reporting; it is a test the courts give in the reporting of public discussions covered by the legal concept of privilege. If in the heat of discussion, a council member calls someone a "crook," you'll be safer in reporting that epithet if you also report that several other members rose to the person's defense.

Completeness

Your story should include not only a balanced account but a complete one. It means going to special pains to get the other side of the story. It means seeking out replies from those whose good name might be ruffled in the heat of public discussion in a privileged agency such as the city council.

Temperance

Temperance does not apply here to abstinence from alcohol or drugs, though that's good advice to follow while on the job. Rather, the term means restraint and common sense. It means not going off the deep end. It means good taste. It means avoiding the pitfalls of sensationalism such as elevating petty gossip to banner-headline status or blowing minor details grotesquely out of perspective.

These four principles are the benchmarks of good reporting. On the whole, they go beyond what the law requires. With these principles in mind, let's look at the major legal considerations one by one. They are (1) libel, (2) invasion of privacy, (3) access to open meetings and public records, and (4) potential conflict between the freedom of the press and an accused person's right to a fair trial.

LIBEL

Libel is the foremost hazard in day-to-day reporting. Libel is defined as defamation in writing as opposed to defamation by the spoken word (slander). However, defamation that comes from broadcast news is considered libel rather than slander.

The term *defamation* means an untrue and unprivileged statement that tends to hold a person up to public contempt, ridicule, or hatred, or to injure a person's reputation, or to cause a person to be shunned or avoided, or to injure a person in business or professional pursuits.

A person who claims to have been defamed may bring a civil (as opposed to criminal) lawsuit into court. Upon winning the suit—not always a sure thing, of course—the defamed person may collect monetary damages running into many thousands of dollars. Indeed, in the 1980s some libel judgments have run in the millions of dollars.

So it's important to avoid lawsuits in the first place. Step one is to recognize libel when you see it. Suspect libel whenever someone or some agency is accused of any kind of wrongdoing, such as a crime or a moral indiscretion. Some statements are so recklessly extravagant that they should ring alarm bells the moment you hear them. For example it's dangerous to call (or quote someone as calling) a person any of these terms:

Adulterer, murderer, cheat, blackmailer, racist, embezzler, gangster, and a host of similar terms. Here are some other clearly libelous statements, safe to report only if they are *provably* true or are privileged.

> John Doe is a Communist (or Nazi, fascist, Ku Klux Klanner, etc.)
>
> Jane Roe is a streetwalker (home wrecker, whore, call girl, unchaste, syphilitic, unclean, etc.)
>
> Jane Roe is an alleged streetwalker. (The "alleged" is no protection.)
>
> Jane Roe is a streetwalker, said John Doe. (Quoting another person is no protection.)
>
> John Doe is a rapist (bastard, grafter, swindler, seducer, child molester, pimp, drunkard, drug addict, etc.)

All of these are so reckless that a journalist ought to recognize them immediately. As noted, quoting another person's libelous statement does not protect you from liability.

Someone suing you for libel must establish four elements: *defamation, publication, identification,* and *fault.*

Defamation has already been defined as an injurious statement about another person or agency.

Publication means the defamation has been disseminated to other people.

Identification means that the person or group bringing the suit must be specifically identified. This does not always mean the defamed party must be named. To refer to "a certain butcher on Park Street who sells adulterated meat" is cause for action if only one butcher operates on Park Street. If two butchers operated there, you might even be sued by both because the innocent butcher may have suffered injury as well as your intended target. However, statements like "all politicians are crooks" are so vague as to preclude libel actions.

Fault means that the defendant—the reporter and the paper—has done something wrong which brought about the libel: what the law calls "negligence." States vary in the way they define negligence, but in general it boils down to this question: Did the reporter exercise a reasonable care collecting and writing the information?

This "simple negligence" applies to libel suits brought by private citizens. A different standard applies to public officials and what the courts call "public figures." They must prove "malice," which is a higher level of negligence. The legal definition of malice is that the reporter or paper either knew the information was false or acted with "reckless disregard" to whether it was true or not.

The mere filing of a lawsuit against a journalist does not, of course, mean that the journalist always loses. Far from it. A study published in 1983 by Marc Franklin has shown that juries rule against media defendants in 85 percent of the libel suits brought to trial, but that most of those cases are overturned on appeal to a higher court. The significance of this is that juries tend to decide against the media, but that higher ("appellate") courts, looking at the finer nuances of media law, tend to overturn the jury decisions. It's small solace to media to win the case ultimately in the appellate courts, however, because of the enormous expenses involved in defending a case.

Four standard legal defenses against a civil libel suit are available to the media—*privilege, truth, fair comment,* and the constitutional *First Amendment defense,* sometimes called the New York Times Rule or the "actual malice defense."

Privilege

Privilege is the first line of defense. Privilege is based on the principle that public debate on public issues should be uninhibited, even "robust and wide open," to use the words of one jurist. Therefore the legal concept of absolute privilege protects statements made during the official conduct of the three branches of government: executive, judicial, and legislative. This is true at all levels of government, national, state, and local.

The defense of privilege is, however, a little shaky at the lower echelons of government, such as an ad hoc subcommittee of the school board or informal statements made by, say, an administrative assistant to the governor or a deputy sheriff (or the police booking sergeant). What it does protect are statements made in formal and official proceedings of Congress, the legislature, the school board, the city council, courts of record, the official statements of the President, the governor, cabinet officers, and the heads of important branches of government. All of these are protected by *absolute privilege.*

Thus, libelous statements are safe to say in the conduct of official government business. And under the protection of *qualified privilege,* a journalist may report it in a balanced and reasonably accurate account of the proceedings.

A similar privilege applies to most government records that are open to public inspection.

However, police incident reports and witness interviews are *not* privileged. Court documents in most states are not privileged until they are acted on by the court. These include pleadings, complaints, indictments, replies, and other such documents that have merely been filed with the court clerk. Reporters are generally safe to report the fact of filing of the document and the general nature of the content, but they should refrain from quoting the more flagrant allegations until after the court has acted (for example, heard an indictment read to the defendant in open court).

Truth

Truth is, of course, a defense against libel, but it may not be as solid a defense as you think. Knowing something to be true and proving it in court are two different things. You must have documentary proof or a string of witnesses willing to testify in court before you are on safe ground. This means that a reporter, particularly an investigative reporter, must know the rules of evidence just about as well as a prosecuting attorney before proceeding to publish.

One major landmine to be avoided is "hearsay" evidence. If John Doe tells you that Jane Roe embezzled $500 while treasurer of the church welfare fund, you must be prepared to prove in court that she did in fact commit the act or an act close to it (proving that she embezzled $250 is sufficient). It is not enough merely to prove that John Doe told you that. He could put it in writing and sign it, and you still would be liable for damages unless you have proof of Roe's guilt (such as a court conviction) or unless the statement is privileged (such as having been said in open court or at a legislative hearing).

Fair Comment and Criticism

Although fair comment, as applied to public officials, is superseded by the *Times* Rule, it still has validity when applied to artistic or literary endeavors put out for public display.

"Fair comment and criticism" is the term applied to an honest expression of opinion on a matter of public concern. The opinion may be vigorous, even satirical, sarcastic, or vitriolic, but it must be based on facts correctly stated. It must concern itself with the public aspects of the work, which is to say that you may pass judgment on the literary merits of an author's work, but not his or her private morals.

A misstatement of fact, of course, would be treated like any other libel case. You can voice the opinion that the author's work is "dull, worthless, trashy, unworthy of thinking men and women," and so forth, but if you add that the author plagiarized the work, you'd better be prepared to prove it. Similarly, you must avoid questioning the artist's motives with remarks like, "He's obviously a racist or he wouldn't have written such trash."

For three-quarters of a century the classic textbook example of the right of fair comment has been a case involving a newspaper review of an act by the Cherry Sisters. In 1901 the Iowa Supreme Court held that a newspaper had the right to publish without malice fair comments about matters presented for public consumption. The review in point is excerpted here.

> Effie is an old jade of 50 summers, Jessie a frisky filly of 40, and Addie, the flower of the family, a capering monstrosity of 35. Their long and skinny arms, equipped with talons at the extremities, swung mechanically and anon waved frantically at the suffering audience. The mouths of their rancid features opened like caverns, and sounds like wailings of damned souls issued therefrom. They pranced around the stage with a motion that suggested a cross between the *danse du ventre* and a fox trot,—strange creatures with painted faces and hideous mien. . . .

More recently a reviewer labeled a musician a "tone-deaf mediocrity," and a politician called his opponent "a horse's ass, a jerk, an idiot and paranoid." In both cases courts ruled that the remarks were opinions protected by fair comment under the First Amendment.

First Amendment Defense: The New York Times Rule

Just as comments by public officials are privileged, a certain kind of privilege, based on the First Amendment to the Constitution, offers protection to comments said *about* public officials. This is based on a famous U.S. Supreme Court decision in 1964. L.B. Sullivan, a police commissioner in Alabama, had sued the *New York Times* for libel in connection with a civil rights advertisement protesting harsh treatment of blacks in 1960. The ad contained some factual errors and exaggerations. An Alabama jury awarded Sullivan $500,000.

But the U.S. Supreme Court ruled in 1964 that public officials could not collect damages for defamation unless "actual malice" was proved. Justice William Brennan wrote:

> The constitutional guarantees require, we think, a federal rule that prohibits a public official from recovering damages for a defamatory falsehood relating to his official conduct unless he proved that the statement was made with actual malice— that is, with knowledge that it was false or with reckless disregard of whether it was false or not.

Subsequent court decisions have broadened this concept to include persons who are not public officials but are considered prominent enough to be "public figures." These have included cases involving a retired Army general, a famous athletic director, a well-known coach, a candidate for public office, and a former officeholder (in which the defamation concerned performance in office).

The term "malice" does not carry the usual meaning of "ill will," but refers to the publication of statements known to be false or with "reckless disregard" of their possible falsity. In 1968 the Supreme Court defined the term (*St. Amant* vs. *Thompson*). To prove malice the public official or public figure who brings the suit must show "sufficient evidence to permit the conclusion that in fact the defendant entertained serious doubts as to the truth of the publication." The Court explained further:

> The finder of fact must determine whether the publication was indeed made in good faith. Professions of good faith will be unlikely to prove persuasive, for example, where a story is fabricated by the defendant, is the product of his imagination, or is based wholly on an unverified anonymous telephone call. Nor will they be likely to prevail when the publisher's allegations are so inherently improbable that only a reckless man would have put them in circulation. Likewise, recklessness may be found where there are obvious reasons to doubt the veracity of the informant or the accuracy of his reports.

One notable example of a suit successfully brought by a public figure was the 1969 case in which Senator Barry Goldwater sued publisher Ralph Ginzburg for publishing defamatory material about him during the 1964 Presidential campaign. Ginzburg had sent hundreds of questionnaires to psychiatrists asking them to analyze Goldwater's mental condition. Goldwater's attorneys presented evidence that Ginzburg had published in his now-defunct *Fact* magazine only those comments from the questionnaires that conformed to a predisposed view that Goldwater was mentally ill. The attorneys also showed that Ginzburg had actually changed the content of some replies. A federal appeals court concluded that Ginzburg had published the defamation knowing that it was false.

The line between public and private figure is hazy in the light of Supreme Court decisions subsequent to the 1964 New York Times decision. In one example, a lawyer involved in a controversial court trial was deemed by the Supreme Court *not* to be a public figure (*Gertz* vs. *Robert Welch, Inc.*, 1974). So was a socially prominent woman involved in a divorce proceeding (*Time* vs. *Firestone*, 1976).

Reporters must exercise caution, therefore, in writing about a person who is prominent but not a public figure. Out of the 1974 *Gertz* decision came a definition of a public figure as a person who (1) has open access to the media, (2) thrusts him or herself into the vortex of public controversy, and (3) attempts to influence the outcome of the controversy.

Out of the *Gertz* decision also came the requirement that "fault" must be proven in order to bring a successful libel suit. Fault comes at two levels: "simple negligence" by the media defendant in the case of a private person, "actual malice" in the case of a public official or figure.

So the fault requirement has become a standard defense as the defendant tries to prove that he or she was not negligent in a suit filed by a private person or that no actual malice occurred in a suit filed by a public official or figure.

Partial Defenses

A written waiver of liability would, of course, relieve the publication of responsibility. You may think it seldom happens—why would anyone waive away the right to collect damages? But in one instance, a writer joshingly criticized another writer with the comment, "The only thing he's written successfully is bad checks." A wary editor sent it to the victim, asking (and receiving) permission to publish the libel. Joking and satirical commentary are a special problem on college campuses with April Fool's editions of the campus paper or a fraternity magazine's "celebrity roast" issue. Usually it's all taken in good fun, but some caution might reasonably be exercised.

The typical newspaper practice of calling people for a response to verbal attacks on them is a good one, though it is by no means a complete defense. People who respond with "no comment" when called still have the right to sue and try to collect damages if they feel they've been libeled. But the fact that they failed to respond when given a chance could influence a jury's decision or reduce the amount of damages.

A retraction of the defamatory comment, made promptly and completely, is at least a partial defense against libel, particularly the unintended (honest mistake) kind. Laws in some states severely limit the amount of damages that can be recovered in a libel suit (usually to specific monetary losses), unless a retraction is demanded and refused. Similarly, permitting the defamed party the right to reply is a partial defense.

PRIVACY

Privacy is not the day-to-day problem that libel is, but it has its own peculiarities, largely because it's a vague area of law. Navigating the channels of privacy law is like cruising through shipping lanes laden with mines. This suggests the need for a wary attitude. In general, the law of privacy boils down to the right of a citizen to be left alone. The more a person is in the limelight—celebrities and public officials particularly—the more privacy one surrenders. Even celebrities and public officials are entitled to protect some private facts of their lives, however.

Privacy law generally comes in four categories:

1. *Appropriation.* You cannot appropriate another person's name or image for commercial gain. You can't use a name or photo of a person, celebrated or not, in an advertisement without that person's permission. How did the celebrated nude photos of Miss America of 1984, Vanessa Williams, get into *Penthouse?* The publisher claimed she had signed a "model release," which is a written waiver customarily used for advertising purposes.

2. *Intrusion.* You cannot intrude unreasonably on another person's seclusion. This precludes electronic eavesdropping or going to unreasonable lengths to photograph a person in seclusion, such as using a helicopter and a telephoto lens to get a picture of the mayor sunbathing nude in a secluded backyard. Similarly, you cannot trespass on private property in the quest for information, such as following the police or fire fighters into a private home to photograph a crime or fire scene. You cannot use false identity to gain access to a private area, such as posing as a cop. However, a person gives up the right to privacy when going into the *public zone:* the streets, sidewalks, parks, public auditoriums. Observes one authority: "On the public street, or in any other public place, the plaintiff has no legal right to be alone; and it is no invasion of his privacy to do no more than follow him about and watch him there." (Prosser, 1971.)

   A journalist may not pursue this principle to the point of harassment, however. In the celebrated case of the photographer who followed Jacqueline Kennedy Onassis on virtually her every outing, the court held that while she was the legitimate subject of news coverage, the photographer's "obtrusive and intruding presence was unwarranted and unreasonable."

3. *False light.* You may not cast a person in a false light such as ascribing

views he or she does not hold, or describing the person as having done things the person has, in fact, not done. This is true even if the description is highly laudatory, as was the case with an unauthorized biography of Warren Spahn, the baseball player. The author said Spahn had won a Bronze Star (not true) and that he was involved in other World War II heroics, which the court found to be in error.

The defendants said, as a defense, that they had "used the literary techniques of invented dialogue, imaginary incidents, and attributed thoughts and feelings."

One scene, which the court quoted, depicted Spahn's return home after a long and mysterious absence. His wife is just sitting down to dinner when the doorbell rings.

> "Now, who can that be?" she said aloud to herself. She strode briskly across the room and opened the door. A startled cry escaped her lips.
> "Warren!" she gasped.
> "Surprise!" Spahn cried. He swept Lorraine off her feet and carried her into the room. "Surprise! Surprise!" he kept shouting as he swung her around in his arms.
> "Warren! Warren!" she laughed and cried at the same time. "Put me down."

The court pointed out that the author had never met Spahn and had done little research beyond reading magazine articles and news clips about Spahn. Despite its highly complimentary nature, Spahn found it embarrassing because it had cast him in a false light.

In another celebrated case, the *Saturday Evening Post* published a photo of a child almost struck down by a careless motorist to illustrate an article titled, "They Asked to be Killed." The court held that the photo falsely depicted the child as a careless pedestrian. False light cases are becoming increasingly important as writers experiment with "new journalism" or "literary journalism," which means using the methods of fiction to depict factual materials. To some careless or unscrupulous writers, however, it means "fictionalizing": creating fictitious events and dialogue of conversations involving real people without a scrap of evidence that these things ever occurred. Celebrities, long the target of careless and distorted reporting, have been striking back at the gossip papers, and juries are sympathetic to the celebrities.

4. *Embarrassing facts.* Use caution when writing about a person's private life, particularly when revealing embarrassing or unduly intimate facts. This is an unpredictable area of privacy law. Consider the following examples: (1) You write about a former child prodigy years later, depicting the highly idiosyncratic lifestyle of a person attempting to live in seclusion. (2) You write about a well-known athlete, going beyond the public side of his character and delving deeply into his private life. (3) You depict, years later, the earlier activities of a former prostitute involved in a sensational murder trial who has since assumed the identity of a respectable matron, putting her past life behind her. (4) You use without permission a photo of a woman emerging from a carnival fun house, her skirt blown above her waist by a jet of air. (5) You write about a person

who had committed a crime years earlier but has since been living an exemplary life following his release from prison.

These are actual cases. The courts ruled for the defendants (publishers) in Examples 1 and 2, for the plaintiffs in Examples 3 and 4. In the numerous cases represented by Example 5, the courts have usually held for the defendant.

But the variety of rulings suggests the need for caution in dealing with truthful but potentially embarrassing details of a person's private life.

Defenses

Unlike libel cases, truth is not always a defense in privacy cases. Your account can be totally factual and true and yet be subject to privacy litigation. Two legal defenses are commonly used in privacy suits.

1. *Newsworthiness.* This is the defense particularly suited for litigation in Category 4, the depicting of intimate facts. This means the information provided is truly a news event or concerns a person, particularly a famous person, in whom the public has a legitimate interest. By and large this includes people who were once infamous in the public eye but have since retired to oblivion. Legal definitions of newsworthiness tend to be even more vague than our own journalistic definitions. The courts, however, have tended to side with the publishers in most cases: If the media publish it, it must be newsworthy. But note that the decisions went against the publishers in the cases of the billowing skirt and the reformed prostitute cited earlier.

2. *Consent.* Clearly you need consent—usually in writing—to use someone's name or likeness to be used for commercial gain. Consent, however, is not required for news reports or news photos dealing with public activities such as public meetings or automobile accidents on the public streets. The photo of the girl almost struck down by the motorist needed no consent for publication in the newspaper where it originally appeared because it was a newsworthy incident. It was only when its use in the *Saturday Evening Post* cast the child in a false light that the absence of consent was meaningful.

"Implied consent" can also be a defense in cases where revealing facts are published in, say, a newspaper interview. If the person has invited you to her home, agreed to be interviewed, and spoke candidly about her personal life while you took notes, raised no objection to their possible publication, then she has *implied* consent so long as the proposed story was not misrepresented and is a balanced account of the interview.

"False light" suit defenses are to prove the truth of the published statements and to show the absence of actual malice—knowledge of falsity or reckless disregard of truth.

"Intrusion" suits—the telephoto shots of the nude mayor in the backyard—are also hard to defend other than to convince the court that the activities complained of do not constitute "intrusion." Failing that, no legal defense exists for intrusion.

Confusing as the privacy laws are, FACT reporting can help—particularly the self-imposed restraints of fair play and temperance. They may in the long run be your best protection in coping with the uncertainties.

ACCESS TO INFORMATION

Newsgathering must precede newswriting, otherwise reporters would have nothing to write about. To do their job, however, reporters must have access to the machinations of government: the meetings, the paperwork, the decisions, the records.

Not everyone agrees with that principle, of course. Some secretive bureaucrats insist that it is in the public interest to make decisions in private and announce them (if at all) after everything has been concluded. This limits public knowledge and debate on an issue, thus severely crippling the concept of self-government. For that reason, such secrecy is illegal in most governmental jurisdictions in the U.S. State legislation and court decisions have generally opposed the view that secrecy is in the public interest. You'll find occasional exceptions, such as military activities or court orders closing certain hearings or trials to the public and media.

Sunshine Laws

In concert with the open-government principle, almost all states have passed "sunshine laws" specifying that all meetings of government agencies shall be open to the public, including special and emergency meetings, and that they must be announced to the public through the media before they take place.

Some exceptions must be noted. Public agencies can hold meetings closed to the media and public ("executive sessions") when discussion turns to one of four areas:

1. Individual personnel matters, such as hiring, firing, or discussing performance or allegations of misconduct
2. Real estate transactions
3. Lawsuits, actual or threatened
4. Labor negotiations

Open Records Laws

Similarly, the federal government and the states have passed laws that make records of public agencies open to public inspection, with some exceptions.

Laws vary from state to state, but many are similar to the federal Freedom of Information Act (FOI) of 1966. It makes specifically requested records available within a short time upon payment of a search and copying fee. The federal law exempts information in nine categories where information is not generally available:

1. Records exempted by executive order as being secret in the interests of national defense and foreign policy
2. Records related to personnel rules and practices
3. Records specifically exempted by statute
4. Records containing trade secrets and financial data provided by individuals and firms on a confidential basis
5. Inter- or intra-agency communications
6. Personnel or medical files on individuals
7. Law-enforcement investigation records whose release would (a) interfere with the investigation, (b) deprive a person of the right to a fair trial, (c) invade a person's privacy, (d) disclose confidential information or confidential sources, (e) disclose investigative techniques, or (f) endanger lives
8. Reports that evaluate financial institutions
9. Reports on geological or geophysical matters

If an agency refuses to release the information it can be taken to court for settlement. Results of the court cases thus far are spotty, but one observer team (Zuckman and Gaynes, 1983) suggests that more than half have succeeded in securing the desired information.

FREE PRESS VS. FAIR TRIAL

The First Amendment of the Constitution guarantees freedom of speech and press. The Sixth Amendment guarantees to anyone accused of a crime a speedy trial by an impartial jury. Sometimes these principles appear to come into sharp conflict, particularly when persons are accused of unusually sensational or repugnant deeds.

Such was the case in the 1954 conviction of Dr. Sam Sheppard, on trial for murder in the bludgeoning death of his wife in a Cleveland suburb. The U.S. Supreme Court, reviewing the case twelve years later, ordered a new trial for Sheppard on the ground that the first was prejudicial because of the massive publicity and general circus atmosphere of media coverage.

In its review, the Court reaffirmed the importance of a free press: "A responsible press has always been regarded as the handmaiden of effective judicial administration, especially in the criminal field." But it castigated the media for "unfair and prejudicial news comment on pending trials." Specifically in the Sheppard case it found these excesses: (1) pretrial clamor for arrest and indictment of Sheppard, (2) publication of damaging information not a part of the court testimony, (3) publication of names and addresses of jurors, causing them to receive numerous communications about the case, (4) general disruption of courtroom decorum by reporters, and (5) publication of the transcript of each day's testimony.

The Court has also overturned other convictions on the ground that excessive publicity had precluded a fair trial. In about half the states, news media and bar representatives have responded by issuing guidelines intended to help both reporters and police officers determine what information about an arrested person can be released without damaging the rights of the accused. These guidelines are essentially a compromise between the two competing principles. They are not legally binding, but they strongly influence police officials who, of course, don't want to risk having their court convictions overturned on the ground of prejudicial pretrial publicity. The guidelines work reasonably well in routine cases, but not especially well in sensational cases, such as the New York "Son of Sam" lover's lane murders.

The bar-press-broadcasters joint statement from Oregon is typical:

> It is generally appropriate to disclose or report the following:
> 1. The arrested person's name, age, residence, employment, marital status, and similar biographical information.
> 2. The charge.
> 3. The amount of bail.
> 4. The identity of and biographical information concerning both complaining party and victim.
> 5. The identity of the investigating and arresting agency and the length of the investigation.
> 6. The circumstances of arrest, including time, place, resistance, pursuit, and weapons used.
>
> It is rarely appropriate to disclose for publication or to report prior to the trial the following:
> 1. The contents of any admission or confession, or in the fact that an admission or confession had been made.
> 2. Opinions about an arrested person's character, guilt, or innocence.
> 3. Opinions concerning evidence or arguments in the case.
> 4. Statements concerning anticipated testimony or the truthfulness of prospective witnesses.
> 5. The *results* of fingerprints, polygraph examinations, ballistic tests, or laboratory tests.
> 6. *Precise* descriptions of items seized or discovered during investigation.
> 7. Prior criminal charges and convictions.
> ("Oregon State Bar-Press-Broadcasters Joint Statement of Principles," 1968.)

These guidelines refer only to *pretrial* publicity, it should be remembered. In 1980 the U.S. Supreme Court ruled that reporters and the public have a constitutional right to attend trials *(Richmond Newspapers* vs. *Virginia)*. And in 1984 the Supreme Court expanded its interpretation to include the presumptive right to attend the attorneys' and judges' questioning and selection of potential jurors *(Press-Enterprise* vs. *Riverside County Superior Court).*

COPYRIGHT

The 1976 Copyright Act grants authors the right to their work for their lifetime plus 50 years. This is a substantial change over the old (1909) law that granted copyright for 28 years, renewable for another 28.

The law is too complex to treat here except to explore briefly the one aspect of copyright that is of concern to most reporters: How much, if any, can a reporter quote from copyrighted material without permission of the copyright holder?

The answer is not simple. A "fair use doctrine" has emerged from court decisions over the years that suggests that a small amount of quotation from copyrighted materials is permissible in the interests of a free flow of ideas within an open society.

The first step in quoting from published materials is to determine if the material is in fact copyrighted. Published material that bears no copyright notice is generally considered in the public domain and may be quoted freely. Material published originally in U.S. Government documents is also in the public domain. So is material on which the copyright has expired.

The 1976 copyright law cites four factors that must be considered when one is quoting copyrighted material without permission.

1. Is the use for commercial or nonprofit purposes?
2. What is the nature of the copyrighted work?
3. How much is being used?
4. Will the use damage the salability of the original?

It is too early at this writing to determine whether and, if so, how the new copyright law might change the fair use doctrine through future court interpretations. The following guidelines, however, might help you in deciding how much to quote without asking permission, assuming you are using copyrighted material in a local newspaper of general circulation.

- In reviews and critical appraisals of an author's work, quote up to 500 words.
- In factual articles, quote up to 200 words of a nonfiction book when using the material to buttress your own points or to give a broader perspective to a situation of public interest.
- In factual articles depicting a situation of public interest, quote not more than 5 percent of an article or essay, or up to 200 words, whichever is less. (For example, use not more than 75 words of a 1,500-word essay.)
- Do not quote from poems or song lyrics without permission.
- Be wary of quoting from purely "literary" works such as novels, short stories, and plays. Have reasonable justification for use of the excerpts.
- Do not reproduce photos, works of art, or statistical tables without permission.

- Have a noble reason for using a quote: public interest, public welfare, public health and safety, the education of the young, and so forth. The more public interest that can be shown, the safer it is to use the material without permission. One notable example is the use by a book publisher of a few frames of the Zapruder movie of the Kennedy assassination. Though the film was copyrighted by Time, Inc., the court held that the great public interest in the event justified the limited use.
- Remember that only the arrangement of words—not the facts them-selves—are copyrightable. Therefore, facts contained in a copyrighted news story can be used, though they should be confirmed by your own independent research (never trust another publication to have the facts straight).
- Always ask permission when quoting from private letters unless they were obviously intended for publication (such as a letter to the editor). Common law protects unpublished materials, and even a snippet of such a letter must not be used without the permission of the author. (Common law is more strict in this matter than statutory copyright.) You must obtain permission from the *sender,* not the receiver. If Smith sends a letter to Jones, then Smith is the one who must grant you permission, even though the letter is in Jones' possession.
- Always credit fully the source of the quotation.
- If in doubt about any of the above considerations, get permission. It's seldom refused when small amounts of quotation are involved, because local newspaper reproduction seldom offers commercial competition to a copyrighted work. Indeed, it may even enhance sales.

POINTS TO REMEMBER

1. Laws of libel and privacy are roughly equivalent to reckless driving laws; they restrict reckless reporting.
2. Libel is false, unprivileged statement of fact that injures the good name of another.
3. Some libelous comments are safe to publish when protected by privilege, such as proceedings of government agencies.
4. FACT reporting—*f*air, *a*ccurate, *c*omplete, *t*emperate—can help prevent legal snarls.
5. Suspect libel when one is accused of doing wrong or when called a nasty name: adulterer, whore, liar, embezzler, etc.
6. The four major defenses against libel are truth, privilege, fair comment, and absence of fault (negligence or actual malice).
7. Privacy laws are sometimes muddled and confusing.
8. The four invasion of privacy areas are appropriation of one's name or likeness for commercial use, intrusion on private life, false light, and publication of embarrassing facts.
9. Most states now have "sunshine laws" prohibiting secret meetings of public agencies.
10. The First and Sixth Amendments may seem to come into conflict, free press versus fair trial, with regard to reporting of criminal arrests, but can work together under bar-media guidelines.
11. The federal government and most states have "freedom of information" laws allowing

public access to government records except those specifically exempted in nine categories.
12. A "fair use" doctrine generally permits small amounts of copyrighted material to be used without written permission.

PROJECT

It is said that newspapers run libelous material every day. From a recent issue of a newspaper, find articles that you think contain potentially libelous statements. ("Potentially libelous" means material that would be defamatory if untrue or unprivileged.) Look for it in accounts of arrests, police activities, court proceedings, and deliberations of major public officials and public bodies. Write a report discussing what legal risk the paper took in publishing the material, what precautions it might have taken, and what defenses it might offer should a legal action be taken against it. Clip the articles and attach them to this report.

19

The Ethics of News Reporting

The ethics of journalism, a newspaper writer once remarked, are neither black nor white. Rather, they're a "rainbow of gray," said Michael Malloy writing in the now-defunct *National Observer*.

Some of the most interesting newsroom discussions on ethics center on the question, "to publish or not to publish." Legal guidelines seldom help here; nobody's denying your *right* to publish. The question is, "Should you?" But they are not the only ethical questions to be resolved in the gray areas of journalistic ethics. You've just received a free invitation to spend a weekend at a posh resort, no strings attached. But will it change your attitude when you write about the resort's request for a change in the county zoning ordinance? Or you've been elected to join the River City Round-table, an association of prominent community leaders. You feel honored. But you will be writing about some of these leaders from time to time. Will your membership intrude on your impartial reporting?

Or let's say you're on the trail of a great story—you heard that an eight-year-old child is shooting heroin. All your contacts talk about him—and perhaps he's not the only one, they say. But you can't quite find him. Why not just make him up—fictionalize—since everybody insists he exists somewhere?

Or suppose a young woman is stabbed to death in Washington, D.C., by an unknown assailant. A brilliant, educated woman, she was the daughter of a prominent and respected family in your hometown. The *Washington Post* publishes a candid story about her life as she dropped out of Radcliffe and became a $50-a-trick prostitute. The story comes to you through your subscription to the

274

The daily meeting of various editors to decide what's going in the first edition of *The Oregonian*. *(Photo by Randy L. Rasmussen.)*

Washington Post Syndicate. Such unsavory material about a local family will no doubt prove upsetting to the hometown populace. But it *is* a true, tragic story, and from tragedy others may learn important lessons of life. Do you publish?

These are all real stories. The problems are real. Reporters and editors face them every day. Young reporters just out of journalism school are often surprised at how much attention must be given to these kinds of decisions. The professor's threat of a failing grade has been replaced by the distraught reader screaming that you haven't been fair and offering to fight you in the alley outside.

ETHICAL DILEMMAS

Ethical problems tend to come in five categories:

1. To publish or not to publish. Does the public's need or right to know—particularly when dealing with unsavory or highly personal material—outweigh the anguish of potentially harmful exposure of private tragedies or family grief?
2. Deceitful newsgathering methods: fraud, intrusion, trickery or other potentially unfair methods.
3. Conflict of interest: A reporter runs for a seat on a public body that might be the subject of future stories by the reporter or his or her colleagues.
4. Personal bias of reporters. Can anyone be truly, cold-bloodedly "objective"?
5. Fictionalization. If you don't have the facts—or, more likely, the juicy quotes and anecdotes—just make them up. Who's to know?

Statements of Journalistic Principles

In addition to legal restrictions, journalists operate within ethical guidelines. The three predominant ones were revised in the mid-1970s. They are the guidelines published by the Society of Professional Journalists in 1973, the Associated Press Managing Editors in 1975, and the American Society of Newspaper Editors (ASNE) in 1975.

"The primary purpose of gathering and distributing news and opinion," says the ASNE statement, "is to serve the general welfare by informing the people and enabling them to make judgments on the issues of the time. Newspapermen and women who abuse the power of their professional role for selfish motives or unworthy purposes are faithless to that public trust."

The three statements express similar points, of which the following comprise the essence:

* A belief in unfettered discussion of public issues and the public's right to know.
* Impartiality, fairness, accuracy, objectivity, care, completeness.
* Separation of news and opinion, with opinion, advocacy, and analysis clearly labeled.
* Avoidance of needless invasion of privacy or pandering to morbid curiosity.
* Public accountability; prompt correction of errors.
* Refusal to accept gifts or to perform journalistic favors for special-interest groups.
* Avoidance of conflicts of interest.

Guidelines can help, but they often fail to cover specific situations. Let's discuss further the five areas of concern with the ethics of reporting.

1: To Publish or Not to Publish

The question ranges over a variety of topics from the trivial to the tragic. Consider these:

* A parent comes in and wants to keep his son's drunk driving arrest out of the paper "because it would just kill his poor old grandmother if she found out about it."
* A friend wants an auto accident kept out of the paper. Seems the two members of a two-car family somehow smashed into one another, and it's a little embarrassing.
* The paper's biggest advertiser threatens to withdraw all advertising if you publish a story about a customer breaking her leg falling down a stairway in the store.

* Police bungled a narcotics arrest, allowing a dozen notorious drug pushers to go free. Publish the story and you risk losing police cooperation in reporting crime incidents. Withhold it and you deny the public an important story that has implications of bureaucratic mismanagement.
* A 15-year-old girl is raped and beaten. Do you publish a story? Do you use the name?
* A teenage girl commits suicide and leaves a dramatic diary of her agonies over drug addiction, loneliness, and general misery. Her parents are willing to have the material excerpted, but the diary is so graphic that you suspect readers will object strenuously. But the story is a touching one, the dramatic kind from which others might learn.

It is here, in a case like the suicide, that the uncertainities evolve. It's not merely a question of publish or not publish. It's also a question of the quality. It depends on how well you do it. You could write a sleazy, sob-sister kind of story "pandering to morbid curiosity." But you could also write with skill, sensitivity, and compassion, producing an article that truly serves a noble purpose as it depicts tragedy.

Tragedy in the classical definition contains a message for the living. Reporters who believe in the noblest aspects of their calling—who believe that writing about the private tragedy of a suicide victim can truly be useful to the living—will find journalism a vastly higher calling than those who are merely out for a sensational story. In that case, and with the parents voicing no objection, the best route might be to publish. We all learn from our mistakes; the publication of a family's mistakes can make it possible for masses of youngsters and parents to learn.

You may disagree. That's the interesting part about ethics: Cases such as this produce lively discussion precisely because of the absence of blacks and whites.

One of the most controversial publishing decisions revolved around the young woman, cited earlier, who became a $50-a-trick prostitute. The *Washington Post* article showed up on an editor's desk one day in January 1979, in Missoula, Montana, the young woman's hometown where her family still lived. The article discussed her musical talent, her academic brilliance, her dissatisfaction with Radcliffe, her entry into prostitution. She'd met a man in a bar in Missoula, a man police later identified as a notorious pimp. She followed him east. It was in Washington that a friend found her sprawled in a parking lot dying of stab wounds.

The editors of the *Missoulian* discussed the story at length and decided to publish. They deleted the $50-a-trick reference and emphasized the meeting with the pimp in the Montana bar, quoting a Washington, D.C., police detective: "There are many of his kind who go out and find girls." The story ran on page 12 under an eight-column headline.

The storm of public outrage was something the paper has not experienced before or since. Editors fielded countless phone calls, and the paper published more than 100 letters assailing the decision to publish.

That decision, one writer insisted, was "a low, dirty, cheap shot at local people that surely don't deserve to be hurt. It must take a special type of bastard that will allow an article like this to be published."

It "served no purpose other than to deepen the pain of an already grief-stricken family," said another.

It "displayed poor taste, bad judgment, and a complete lack of compassion."

It was "the cruelest thing you could have possibly done to those fine people who have contributed so much to our community."

"I can think of no one act in 'news reporting' showing more callous disregard for human feelings than that exhibited by the person or persons who made the decision to print the story."

And so it went. Yet no such storm of protest greeted the *Washington Post's* publication of the original story. That's what's interesting—or frustrating—about the grayish rainbow of journalistic ethics. Clearly, what's okay in one community may not be okay in another.

If they had it to do over, the Montana editors say, they'd do it differently, perhaps write their own story tailored to hometown consumption or leave it out altogether. The trouble is, next week's major ethical decision will probably be on an entirely different matter for which there is little or no precedent. Decisions on ethical matters are seldom easy or simple, and you always have a supreme court of sorts—the court of public opinion—to second guess. This court may be the most unpredictable of all.

In the end the best guide may be your own sense of fair play and objectivity. One test may be to imagine yourself explaining to a jury of residents of your community your decision to publish or not. Remember, your jury has to be a typical collection of residents, not your journalistic colleagues. Can you *sell* your decision? Can you make a convincing case?

2: Reporting by Deceit

Chapter 9, "Reporting from Observation," has already touched on some of the problems, such as masquerades where the reporter poses as someone else. Literary history has more or less accorded John Howard Griffin's *Black Like Me* the status of a classic. His 1961 account of experiences as a white man traveling as a Negro is even credited with helping to usher in the civil rights era. Similarly, Gloria Steinem's Playboy bunny pose may have struck an early blow for her subsequent feminist principles.

On the other hand, the Chicago *Sun-Times'* Mirage Tavern, which helped to catch some shady government officials, was denied a Pulitzer Prize, it is alleged, because the deal smelled of "entrapment." Even so, the journalistic profession, not to mention the supporters of honest government, tended to support the purchase of a tavern for the purpose of documenting dishonesty among city employees. Besides, the tavern turned a profit.

But some poses can put you in jail. Dave Roman, a reporter for the *Potomac News*, serving a suburb of Washington, D.C., interviewed a Death Row inmate and came out with a fine story about prison brutality. The problem was that he'd gone into the state penitentiary posing as a "jail sergeant." The local jail superintendent had promised to take the reporter along on a visit to the penitentiary for the interview, but at the last minute he had to back out. So he handed the reporter a jailer's badge and made him a "sergeant for a day." The badge got him through the gates and to an interview with the prisoner.

The reporter had second thoughts about publishing the story, however, and so did his editors when they discovered how the interview was obtained. The story didn't run. But then the jail superintendent was suspended, partly for having deputized the reporter. Other media began to pick up the story, alluding to a mysterious interview with a Death Row inmate. That's when the *Potomac News* decided to recount the entire episode, including publication of the interview itself.

The result was that reporter Roman spent ten days in jail for impersonating an officer—"a bizarre vacation," he said. The paper also developed a new policy to cover such situations. It concluded that poses may be okay—"at times, for very compelling reasons, when crucial information for a vital story can be gotten no other way"—but only with the concurrence of the editors.

By contrast, some reporter poses are relatively harmless, more in the category of journalistic stunts. Who's harmed when a woman has herself hogtied to a telephone pole or poses as a skid road derelict to obtain glimpses of human nature?

An entire range of minor examples of deceit must be noted here. One is posing as some kind of official, a deputy coroner, for example, for the purpose of getting witnesses to talk. It's not only a shabby tactic, but it's illegal in many jurisdictions.

Other shady tactics include intimidation, threats, harassment, and "ambush" interviewing (the latter largely a television phenomenon in which a crew descends on a hapless victim trapped in a parking lot or outside a residence). "Mutt and Jeff" interviews belong in this category, too. They're the kind in which two reporters gang up on a source; one is nice, the other nasty, and somehow they beat the information out of the source. It's an old police technique that has been largely discarded in the light of court decisions that confessions must be given voluntarily.

Except in rare instances, then, journalists might observe a kind of cards-on-the-table honesty about their identity and purpose. The key word is *sincerity*. You may lose an occasional story by being up front, but you'll gain a lot more in the long run by being known as a sincere reporter whom people can trust. You'll gain respect. Sources may even seek you out with important stories and ideas that they wouldn't give to other reporters.

Sincere motivation may also guide you through the moral thickets of the participant observation questions. Before you assume a pose of someone other than a journalist, consider five questions: Is it relatively innocuous, the kind where you can truthfully say no one will be damaged and that an interesting insight into human nature might result? Conversely, is it an important enough story that it justifies extraordinary means? Are you sure it cannot be obtained by traditional means? Will the ultimate public good outweigh the shady tactics? And, finally, can you temper your zeal for a juicy story with the realization that you might be taking unfair advantage of people? The latter consideration is important, for the practice of quoting people by name and having them say things they might not have said if they'd known your identity is tempting but questionable.

3: Conflict of Interest

The press, says a critic, is all too quick to jump on conflict of interest cases involving government officials and candidates for public office. But what about conflicts of interest among members of the news staff? The media may be privately owned but they come close to being quasi-public, and they wield great power. Political candidates are required by law in many states to disclose their affiliations and financial holdings—what about reporters and editors?

One newspaper actually did report a news staff disclosure. In Idaho the *Lewiston Tribune* in 1978 carried a story listing the civic, political, business, and other connections of its news staff members. Explained the publisher, Albert L. Alford, Jr., "There is no daily newspaper that doesn't have conflicts. You have to eliminate the ones you can't live with and be open to the readers about the rest."

The practice of journalism is one of public trust, yet it is fraught with numerous pitfalls and temptations. Some of them are most seductive. Promoters are all too eager to invest in journalistic good will by providing reporters with free favors ranging from free lunches to expense-paid junkets overseas.

Downright crookedness among journalists is rare, however. Stanford University Professor John Hulteng, in his book, *The Messenger's Motives,* says that "the discovery in recent years that a reporter for a major eastern paper was blackmailing prominent citizens in the community by threatening to publish adverse stories about them was a nine days' wonder in the trade press because it was so unusual and out of character."

The actual conflicts of interest tend to be less dramatic. Let's examine a few instances.

* You cover professional sports for the paper, and at Christmas you get a case of scotch from the manager of the local team as a "token of appreciation."
* You pick up spare cash writing publicity releases for a local business or a sports team—the same organizations you cover for the paper.
* A major hotel chain opens a resort in Hawaii and offers you a free trip to the grand opening.
* You run for the school board or the city council. Could you serve and still keep your reporting impartial?
* The governor holds an annual bash, the social event of the season. The news media people who attend are clearly the governor's favorites—and

how do you suppose they became favorites? Should you cozy up to the governor more in the future, write more favorable stories?

* You cover movie and play reviews for the campus paper and get free tickets. Will your reviews be more favorable because of the free tickets? Will a series of unfavorable reviews dry up your source of tickets?

* As business writer, you have major investments in various corporations, some of them the same ones you're writing about. Will the investments influence your stories?

These are but a few of the areas of potential conflict. In the past decade or so, newspapers have tightened their standards and rewritten their policies so that staff members are clear on how management feels about possible areas of conflict.

Charles W. Bailey, in a conflict of interest study published in 1984, writes about a *Seattle Times* columnist who ran for water commissioner. Informed that if he won the post he'd have to leave his job, the columnist mounted a campaign *against* his election. He "won"—that is, he got defeated at the polls and kept his job.

The lifestyle editor of the Duluth *News-Tribune* wasn't so fortunate. She was told she'd be fired if she ran for city council. She ran anyway. She was fired. And she lost the election.

And the managing editor of the *Seattle Times* was told he'd be transferred to another job if his wife continued to work as press secretary to the mayor of Seattle. She resigned, and the editor kept his job.

Not all newspapers are so strict. The editor-publisher of a small weekly newspaper in Oregon saw nothing wrong in his serving as mayor of the town, except that he was a little shy about quoting himself all the time. But the trend is in the direction of policies that would curtail the possibility of conflict. When a magazine wrote that sports writers in New York City were getting thousands of dollars worth of free tickets to sports events, the *New York Times* promptly decided that all its writers would pay their own way.

Other papers have established similar rules. In just nine years the papers that prohibit news staffs from accepting expense-paid trips grew from 27 percent to 51 percent, according to surveys. The papers that prohibit staff members from holding public office grew from 54 percent to 67 percent. And the papers that prohibit news personnel from accepting all but token gifts grew from 44 percent to 89 percent. (Izard, 1983.)

4: Personal Bias

The term "objectivity" is the center of countless intellectual arguments in newsrooms and journalism schools. The discussion seems to come largely in three veins.

1. That objective reporting means that newsgathering and writing must be done with almost scientific detachment.
2. That objective reporting means gathering the facts and repeating them in order

of descending importance—and that the facts should more or less speak for themselves.
3. That objectivity is really a myth—that human biases simply can't be excluded from the way reporters observe and report events and situations.

Perhaps all three views have merit. The first two arguments, though, fail to acknowledge that it is the human touch that gives newswriting some of its strength and power. It is purely a human and subjective judgment, for example, that a search for a child mysteriously missing from its home has more human power and drama—thus more newsworthiness—than a legislative hearing on corporate tax measures.

Similarly, it is a human judgment to determine what facts to include in a story and which to exclude. It is a human judgment to take facts "raw, and bleeding, and unsorted," to quote Theodore White, and weave them into some kind of coherent whole. It is a human judgment, subject to human biases and even caprices, to rate the facts by descending importance.

Indeed, news values themselves constitute an inherent human bias. News values—which are based largely on perceptions of what interests people—dictate that we report the house that's on fire rather than the ones that aren't. Or we report the airliner that crashed rather than the thousands that landed safely.

Professionalism suggests, in any event, that journalists attempt to be fair-minded: FACT reporting again. Probably objectivity is not attainable given the human condition. FACT reporting—fairness, accuracy, completeness, temperance—is.

5: Fictionalization

Until 1981, newspaper editors gave only passing thought to fabricated stories as an element of journalistic ethics. Outright lies were rare, and reporters caught making up facts were summarily fired. True, some reporters were not above making up occasional anonymous quotes or a fictitious anecdote for a touch of color. But outright fabrications were rare if only because reporters work in the public eye. Their work is subject to easy detection by alert readers when errors are made or if outright falsification occurs.

Indeed, making up a false story requires talent and courage. The more common problem is to be duped by a shady source who makes up a false story, often as a practical joke or for not-so-humorous spite. In one such example, someone called the hometown daily to report an engagement. The daughter of a prominent and wealthy family was reported to be engaged to a man who—the editors discovered to their horror after the story appeared—was well known in the community as a drunken derelict. Editors have learned to double-check engagement reports. Also letters to the editor—lest an unscrupulous writer sign someone else's name.

So until 1981 editors concerned themselves with more important matters than reporters who fabricate stories.

Then along came Jimmy.

Jimmy was an eight-year-old heroin addict who lived for a fix—a "precocious little boy with sandy hair, velvety brown eyes, and needle marks freckling the baby-smooth skin of his thin brown arms." The two-column story about him in the *Washington Post* moved like fiction: "There is an almost cherubic expression on his small, round face as he talks about life—clothes, money, the Baltimore Orioles and heroin. He has been an addict since the age of 5."

The story read like fiction because fiction it was. But that discovery didn't emerge until after its author, Janet Cooke, had won a Pulitzer Prize for feature writing in 1981.

But Jimmy did not exist. The writer quoted anonymous sources. In fact, she said she feared for her life if she revealed her sources, even to her editors.

The discovery that the story was fake brought enormous recrimination and soul-searching among editors. And so a new chapter emerged in the ethics of journalism.

The problem was not new. Claims of doubtful authenticity occasionally focused on books and magazine articles. In one celebrated case, an article on prostitution showed up in *New York* magazine with vivid descriptions of a hooker named Redpants. Redpants never existed; she was a "composite" of several hookers the author had met and interviewed. But Jimmy, unlike Redpants, was the object of great concern among police, social agencies, and the general public. People cared about Jimmy. Authorities tried to locate him with an eye toward rehabilitation. But Jimmy was nowhere to be found. A full-scale investigation by the *Post* ensued, including an all-night questioning session with the author. Janet Cooke finally admitted the story was a hoax, and she resigned. The Pulitzer Prize was rescinded and awarded to another feature writer.

So where do we go from here?

The now defunct National News Council, an agency formed to investigate and comment on complaints about press performance, investigated the Jimmy story at length and surveyed editors on their reactions.

One of Janet Cooke's editors, Bob Woodward, of Watergate fame, remarked that the entire debacle had "driven a spike in my head." But he said it also had inspired many reforms such as:

* Better hiring practices with more diligent checking of resumes. Cooke had falsified hers a little.
* More training for young reporters with heavier emphasis on rules and ethics.
* Better liaison between editors and writers.
* Curbing the use of anonymous sources.
* More double checking.

* Revamping policies on promotion in the newsroom to avoid the presumption that the only way to get ahead at the *Post* is to concentrate on blockbuster stories.
* More diligence in getting responses from affected agencies or persons when running sensitive or controversial stories.
* Use of pairs or teams of reporters to work on sensitive stories, especially the ones involving anonymous sources.
* Enhanced skepticism. Woodward said he'd always taken it for granted that reporters always tell the truth and government officials always lie. "That's not a good mode to be in," he concluded.

The News Council's survey of 30 editors produced similar suggestions for reform, plus some new ones:

* Avoidance of a fortress mentality that obstructs acceptance and action on valid complaints.
* Keeping the pursuit of prizes from becoming an obsession in the newsroom.
* Guarding against a blurring of the line between fact and fancy. Guarding against new journalism and docudrama techniques such as tampering with or inventing quotes, rearranging events, and guessing what goes on in the recesses of people's minds. (From *In the Public Interest III,* National News Council, 1983.)

Perhaps the most devastating indictment of the Jimmy debacle was the cavalier lack of human compassion. Nowhere along the line, critics have pointed out, did the editors show much concern for Jimmy, the youngster they believed real. Ironically, they showed more concern for the safety of the writer who said her life might be endangered if they nosed around too much trying to verify the story. While police and social agencies searched in vain for a child they thought needed help—for a tiny child could easily die of a drug overdose—the editors declined to help.

A final consideration in journalistic ethics, then, could well be human compassion. Concern for one's fellow humans. The Golden Rule. Somehow it has to be balanced against the people's right to know. The decisions are never easy—nor should they be. You'll find few clear-cut answers. You'll be criticized no matter what you do. That is part of the price you pay for daring to venture onto the public forum. It's a price exacted for being part of the human race. It's a price paid for our constitutionally mandated freedom of expression.

In 1982, *Miami News* reporter Christine Wolff, then of the *Bradenton Herald* in Florida, happened upon a suicide attempt on the Sunshine Skyway Bridge over Tampa Bay. She helped to restrain a man bent on self-destruction until assistance arrived. For that she got lots of public commendation. She even got a bonus from one editor. Another said if she weren't the kind of reporter who would assist in such an emergency he wouldn't want her on his staff.

But she also got criticism. A couple of people said she should not have interfered with a person's right to kill himself. Such are the rewards, and the penalties, for doing what you believe in your heart is right.

POINTS TO REMEMBER

1. Journalistic ethics are debatable and often controversial—seldom black and white.
2. Reporters and editors are confronted almost daily by decisions of whether to publish information that might prove uncomfortable to the people involved or to their families.
3. Deceit in newsgathering seldom works for long, may even cause harm in the long run, and journalists should give careful thought to the rare exceptions.
4. Journalistic ethics in newsgathering should be at least equal to those required by law of police: honesty and absence of force, trickery, or deceit. A key word is sincerity.
5. Journalists—if they are true to the concept of seeking truth for the public good—must be careful not only to avoid conflicts of interest but also the appearance of conflict.
6. Pure objectivity is hard to achieve, but fair, accurate, complete, and temperate reporting is a worthy and attainable goal.
7. The Jimmy's world debacle has caused numerous proposals for editorial reform, including avoidance of anonymous sources, better checking for accuracy, team reporting, enhanced editorial skepticism, and careful separation of fact from fiction.

PROJECT

Find in a local paper examples of issues that you think represent some of the ethical considerations mentioned in this chapter. Stories of crime, violence, and tragedy are likely sources. So are letters to the editor that discuss ethical concerns. Write an essay outlining the issues as you see them and expressing your own point of view.

20

Newsroom Practices

Newswriting teachers like to keep track of their former students, somewhat the way General Motors keeps track of its cars and even recalls them if a mass defect appears. No one has yet seriously suggested that journalism alumni be recalled for repair of defects. The suggestion has been made facetiously numerous times, however, often by the young journalism graduates themselves.

A young woman wrote her former teacher, "I couldn't believe the cooperation I was getting from this car salesman for my feature story. He was giving me all kinds of ideas—but the ideas dealt less with auto retailing and more with romantic notions, such as taking the new TransAm to a scenic viewpoint with dinner to come later. I wondered at what point do you blow the whistle? Not much discussion about those kinds of problems in Reporting J-361. How come?"

Male reporters presumably have fewer problems of this sort, though one young man kept getting calls evenings from a woman—much to the dismay of the reporter's girlfriend. The caller was a suspected murderer who subsequently was indicted and convicted for killing one of her children. Should he blow the whistle—tell the woman to quit calling? Or did the inside line to a newsworthy source compensate for the inconvenience? He took the calls, even got a few exclusives through them. The calls stopped when the woman was indicted, tried, and eventually sentenced to life imprisonment. If nothing more, the experience supports Mark Twain's comment that reporters typically form lasting friendships with "some of the worst people in the world."

Twain also wrote spirited accounts of his naive mistakes as a beginning re-

(Photo by Randy L. Rasmussen.)

porter. Similar mistakes can be recounted today. One reporter, new on a daily serving an agricultural area in eastern Washington, had come from an urban background. So when a farmer told him he had 1,000 acres in wheat, 500 in barley, and 500 acres "in summer fallow," the story came out that the farmer grew three crops, "wheat, barley, and summer fallow."

The story showed up in the paper the next day—somehow getting past the copydesk—and the reporter quickly discovered to his embarrassment that "summer fallow" is not a crop—it means the land lies unused through the summer. The paper promptly transferred him to the police beat. His colleagues have been teasing him about it for five years now: "Well, Jim, what's the bushels-per-acre yield of summer fallow this year?"

Jim, fortunately, saw the humor and even tells the story on himself from time to time.

Three lessons emerge from that experience: (1) Learn the jargon of your newsbeat, (2) errors made in real life often extract a higher price than errors made in college classrooms—five years of razzing does seem an excessive price for one small mistake—and (3) reporters should not lose their sense of humor.

Such an experience only serves to confirm what the young journalism graduates say—you can't learn it all from a textbook or even a news reporting class. "My education began," says one, "the first day on the job."

And what is it they learn on the job? Mostly the harsh lessons of professional experience. They learn the unpredictable frustrations of human communication, which can range from stubborn and cantankerous sources to unwanted sexual advances (and occasionally even "wanted" sexual advances, a far-worse problem). The frustrations can even mean suffering the natural consequences of mistakes, such as an angry source claiming misquotation or unfair tactics or unethical practices, maybe even threatening violence or a lawsuit. The new reporters also learn certain tricks of the trade that don't show up in classroom experiences. And they learn that getting jobs requires more than good grades.

Here are some common responses among young journalism graduates who went to work for the news media. Most of them were taken from letters from and conversations with former journalism students.

1. Getting jobs means being competitive. It means having some prior experience, perhaps on the campus paper or a small community paper. One successful job getter not only was a star on the campus daily, but she volunteered to work without pay for a community weekly. The investment paid off. When she applied for work at a nearby daily, the editors recognized her byline from the weekly. It helped her get the job. Internships are also vital.

2. Most students find that conducting interviews for news stories is no longer the ordeal it had been in college. "You don't even think of them as interviews after a while," says a young man. "You just talk to people. It's what you do every day."

3. Techniques that used to get good grades in classes—keeping up with your reading, getting your assignments in on time, having them neatly typed—won't necessarily get you ahead on the job. Editors expect, *in addition* to those qualities, teamwork in the newsroom, initiative (bringing up new ideas), and learning and growing from experience (not making the same mistake twice).

4. Editorial wrath from their bosses continues to fall on the heads of young reporters for poorly developed language skills. You've heard this before, of course, both in this book and from your teachers. But have you heard it from the editors? Or from the beginning journalists themselves? "I should have worked harder on this in college," goes an all-too-frequent lament. The editors complain about the young reporters' spelling, their grammar, and their news story organization. So wary have editors become that they've begun giving language skills exams before choosing new employees. And with so much competition for jobs, they're getting away with it.

5. Their editors also complain that the beginners are weak on civics—such things as government jurisdictions, taxes, local politics, business, local economy—the kinds of things that matter in the local communities where most journalists find their first jobs. This invariably has to be learned on the job, for colleges are notoriously deficient in dealing with local governmental units and local economic matters.

6. A few beginners complain about getting too much editing from their bosses, magnificently crafted stories ripped to shreds, and so on, but

most complain about not getting enough. Rare are the beginners arrogant enough to consider their editors inferior in journalistic skills. The problem is that editing is too light with the result that not much learning occurs.

7. On some papers, beginners are astonished to find that office politics and other nonjournalistic factors enter into questions of who gets ahead. Competition for front-page play of one's stories is intense, and not all decisions derive from news values. It's a fact of life: Reporters with intraoffice political clout get better play for their stories than those lacking the right connections.

8. Some students suffer a loss of idealism because the news media world seldom measures up to their romantic perceptions of it. The romantic analogy is perfect. The honeymoon is shortlived, as a rule, and young reporters soon find themselves up to their elbows in the journalistic equivalent of dirty dishes: council meetings, planning meetings, school board meetings, obituaries, civic announcements, posturing politicians, self-serving bureaucrats, media freaks, and run-of-the-mill bores.

Even so, journalism offers the potential to learn, to gain knowledge and wisdom, to grow intellectually. And as you grow, you'll begin to see the fragments—the planning meetings, the politicians, the bureaucrats—in the shape of a coherent whole rather then seemingly meaningless fragments. Fiction writers call this a writer's "vision," but it's by no means confined to fiction. You have to learn the fragments, piece by piece, before you can assemble the puzzle. And when you begin to piece it all together, seeking a larger truth in the manner of a fine novelist . . . well, that's when journalism can become exciting.

GETTING STREETWISE: TRICKS OF THE TRADE

Working with sources in the real world is seldom as pure as it seemed in the classroom. But as you gain experience, you also gain savvy. You learn, for example, that a certain amount of bargaining goes on between sources and journalists. The sheriff's office will much more willingly provide information under crisis conditions if reminded of the many favors the paper has provided in the past— things like publicity for the policeman's ball or the fund-raising project for the new search-and-rescue equipment.

And in time new reporters learn to recognize some of the typical denizens of the media jungle—such as *media freaks* and *journalistic streetwalkers*. "Media freaks" are persons whose every activity is coldly calculated to attract media attention. They speak in twenty-second staccato bursts for television soundbites (or more slowly for pad-and-pencil reporters). They are keenly aware of what makes news (controversy, negativism, plain talk, hard action, and uniqueness are the essential ingredients).

"Journalistic streetwalker" is a term used by one Honolulu reporter, Jerry Burris, to describe people he often sees walking around provocatively at public occasions such as political conventions or legislative sessions. A reporter who walks up to such a person often encounters this kind of scenario:

> *Reporter:* Hi, how's it going?
> *Streetwalker:* Great, except for that crazy thing on Thursday.

Naturally any gullibly curious reporter will ask, "*What* crazy thing on Thursday?" and out of that will probably come some kind of planned "leak," maybe mere gossip, or maybe important information. It's all part of the journalistic game, a little like Monopoly (some compare it to Trivial Pursuit). Any player who doesn't ask the right question will lose a turn or at least have to go back several spaces. Some sources play the game with great gusto and seem to know the reporter's business better than the reporter does.

They know, for example, that mystery always makes good copy for news-hungry reporters. So if they want lots of publicity for some important situation, they know that the appropriate procedure is to try to cover it up, particularly if it has to do with personal finances of a political candidate. They will tantalizingly attempt to bar reporters from their meetings. That means that reporters will fight to get the story. Editors will put their best investigative reporters on the story. As a result, it will capture headlines and broadcast attention for days maybe weeks. Conversely, if they want very little attention, they will call a press conference and confess everything. Even if the story is negative, it will be a one-day affair and then quickly forgotten.

It's all part of the game. Some bureaucrats and politicians know how to play it; some don't. Had Richard Nixon called a press conference and confessed everything early in the Watergate scandal, he probably would have served out his second term.

Reporters learn to play the game, too.

Jerry Burris, who covers the legislature for the *Honolulu Advertiser,* knows to stay alert for subtle signs. If the Republican leaders are meeting with the Democratic leaders in a conference room with the governor's guard standing outside the door, Burris concludes that something big is in the wind—and the game is afoot, as the fictional detective, Sherlock Holmes, would say. Holmes, who once said his methods of detection are "founded on trifles," would approve of Burris's work: a fragment of information here, another tidbit there, trifles from fifteen or twenty different sources. Eventually a pattern emerges and the story takes shape.

Tricks of the journalistic trade can also include outright deception—though this is rare, fortunately. The media live in the public limelight and thus are in a poor position to blow the whistle on unethical practices of, say, politicians while using shady tactics themselves. Public trust of the media—as shown by poll after poll—descended to new depths in the early 1980s. And on a personal level, the reporter who gains a reputation for using devious methods may win an occasional skirmish but has probably lost the game entirely in the long run.

Even so, it is not uncommon for reporters to use such "gentle deceptions," as one phrased it, as pretending that they have more information than they really have in the hope that their sources will be duped into thinking "they've got the whole story anyway." Or reporters may suggest "facts" they've supposedly gained from other sources—facts fabricated or known to be skewed—in the hope that the correct information will come tumbling out as the source hastens to correct the error.

Some reporters even resort to what one calls "buffalo chipping": publishing highly speculative stories with incomplete information. The reporter hopes that the stink caused by the falling buffalo chip will somehow force out the real story—or at least raise a little hell as it brings forth intemperate denials and cross-charges. An example would be something like this: "Reliable sources in the courthouse today say that Sheriff Ira Carter will soon announce his resignation to run for governor." The reporter hopes that Carter will hotly deny running for governor but will reveal his true intentions.

Reporters have also been known to assume false identities. The folklore of journalism is full of stories about reporters getting a witness to talk by posing as a cop or other official. In Chicago, goes one story, everybody hates reporters and no one will talk to them. So you always pose as some kind of official. One reporter called a rape victim: "This is Detective Macy of the Twenty-third Precinct, and I want to ask you some questions." The woman's husband came on the phone and said gruffly, "This is Sergeant O'Malley of the Twenty-third Precinct, and we don't *have* a Detective Macy—who the hell *are* you?" The reporter quickly hung up.

If reporters are hated in Chicago, it may be because of such tactics, which are both risky and unnecessary. A sincere, honest approach to reporting is always best. Even the occasional participant observation project described in Chapter 9—posing as a Playboy bunny or whatever—must be done in a sincere belief that you can convince the court of public opinion that the end justifies the means.

GETTING SOURCED

Reporters are never better than the quality of their information. Finding the right sources of information is more than a mere "trick of the trade." It's at the heart of the journalistic process. A good reporter goes beyond the official contacts described in Chapter 11 and works to maintain contacts with all kinds of people. Not all of them need be in high positions. One reporter counts among his most productive sources of tips and confidential information the following: (1) a barmaid who serves cocktails where public officials gather after work, (2) a switchboard operator who monitors a lot of comings and goings in a public building, and (3) a night watchman who felt he'd been wronged by certain officials and takes a perverse delight in providing tips whenever certain agencies fall into difficult or awkward situations.

Finding the right sources has special meaning for specialized newspapers such as the *Chronicle of Higher Education* or the *Wall Street Journal*. Frank Allen, a *Wall Street Journal* editor, says one measure of "getting sourced" is a reporter's telephone file containing the names and numbers of important contacts out in the real world. Does the Rolodex bristle with clean white cards that represent new contacts? Are new cards being inserted week by week? Or does it contain the same worn, thumb-smudged cards that have been there forever?

Allen is chief of the newspaper's Philadelphia bureau. His own source file is uniquely diverse. One is a young Philadelphia lawyer with Society Hill connections. Another is a young, impoverished black woman whose connections are world's removed from Society Hill.

Like so many of his contacts, both are symbolic of elements of society that interest the *Journal*. The lawyer stands for the young, ambitious professional with the Right Connections. Frank considers him a source of penetrating insights into the nature of politics and the economy, and his quoted comments have occasionally shown up in *Journal* articles. The other example, a young woman with two children and a "sometime husband," helps Frank monitor the frustrations of some uneducated urban blacks.

In some ways these informal contacts are the heart of journalism, at least the kind practiced by the *Wall Street Journal*. If there were ever a newspaper that had the right to be dull and flat, it would be this one. It contains business, economic, and political news vital to its specialized audience. It could be sober and important and stiffly formal. After all, it doesn't even run comics or photographs. It could be like medicine—good for you but not much fun. It could be but it's not. Like many a good journalistic medium, the *Journal* writes about people. And writing about people is the ultimate payoff in expanding your list of contacts in the real world. Journalists are, after all, story tellers. The most dramatic way to tell a story is through people, specifically, by using people as symbols to show the effect of economic and political decisions often made in plush offices and board rooms. And the *Wall Street Journal's* way of relating the impact of an important economic or political story through the people affected is a model for other journalists to follow.

That's because a lot of news staffs are in a rut. "I never could get my reporters out talking to enough people," lamented one former city editor. "I used to tell them, if you've got an hour to spare, call the city manager or somebody knowledgeable and see if you can come over and talk about, well, anything. His vision of the future, maybe, or his most serious problems. A lot of reporters don't like to do that. They think that unless they have a specific story to work on, specific questions to ask, they shouldn't be out talking."

It doesn't always happen that way. But when it does the result is the worst possible source of ideas: ivory towerish creations that come from editors and reporters who sit around dreaming up what they think is happening rather than keeping in touch with the mainstream thinking in the community. This isolationist concept of reporting is unfortunate because it limits reporters' views of the world to meeting agendas and in-house perceptions of the world around them.

How does one make contacts? Frank Allen often makes them in the most casual of ways—by striking up a conversation with a seatmate on a commuter train, by attending meetings and scanning the list of participants to find whom he'd like to talk with, by asking seemingly innocent questions of bellhops as he checks into hotels. He also likes to wander into a city's ethnic neighborhoods and strike up conversations with sidewalk business people.

Using unofficial and sometimes confidential sources means following certain rules. Here are some important principles:

1. Play fair with people; don't play favorites.
2. Be honest. Trickery and deceit only elicit similar responses among your sources.
3. Be accurate.
4. Do not identify sources to whom you have pledged confidentiality.
5. Believe sincerely that government ought to be clean, honest, fair-minded, and open to public scrutiny. A lot of people agree, and they're willing to provide information to accomplish those goals.
6. Believe sincerely that the news media ought to be clean, honest, fair-minded, and open to public scrutiny.
7. Talk with people. If you are friendly and interested in the people you meet, the tipsters and reliable informants will come to you.

THE POLICE BEAT

Some reporters believe the police beat is the toughest to cover with the possible exception of the military. In Honolulu, a young woman who covered the military beat picked up the phone and called the public information officer of a naval installation and remarked in a friendly voice, "I've been away for a couple of days . . . so how's everything been going out there at CINCPAC?"

The woman at the base replied coolly, "We don't give out that kind of open-ended information. Why don't you think about it and then call us back with a more specific question?"

It's like talking to a computer. The police beat has become almost as bad, some reporters say. Unlike other beats, few self-serving contacts are available to provide tips, and reporters are constantly dealing with traumatic and potentially libelous material. Spencer Heinz of *The Oregonian*, a former police reporter, once wrote his perception of the police beat:

> Things have changed. Former police reporters are astounded that we can no longer stroll into Portland police robbery division and scan clipboards at our leisure, or swing through homicide to exchange a good Truman joke for a banner story.

The changes, he said, are in the direction of tighter control over access to records, which are frequently stored in computer and retrievable only by clerks who push the right buttons. Freedom of information laws aren't always helpful, particularly

30 minutes before a deadline—you might get the report eventually under FOI rules, but probably too late for today's paper.

And the newest problem is women on the police beat, a new trend that takes some getting used to down at police headquarters. Recall, for example, Bonnie Henderson's experiences depicted in Chapter 2. Bonnie was replaced on the police beat by another woman, Gail Bullen, who says her problems are simpler, possibly because of Bonnie's pioneering efforts and also because Gail previously worked as a police dispatcher.

Basically, the cops in many communities simply haven't gotten used to having women around, and they react in one of two ways: They tend to withhold candor from reporters they don't trust or they tend to play flirtatious little games. The former reaction applies to both men and women, but it affects women more because cops simply aren't used to dealing with inquisitive females. The latter is, of course, strictly related to gender.

COPING WITH SEXUAL HARASSMENT

No rules have been written for the problem of sexual harassment, and each woman tends to sort it out for herself. At least that is largely the conclusion drawn from conversations with about a dozen women—all reporters or former reporters—in the preparation of this chapter.* The problem is by no means limited to the police beat. And it's complicated by the fact that women have certain advantages—namely, that men enjoy talking to attractive, intelligent women. They feel less threatened by them. They trust them more, at least with personal kinds of details, and so they often speak with greater candor. Some of the women consulted for this chapter suggest that they would not hesitate to use feminine wiles ("batting my eyelashes," as one explained it) if it would help open up an important but recalcitrant source. Men, after all, do not hesitate to take advantage of a natural, bantering camaraderie among men when interviewing male sources.

But that's a pretty subtle concept compared to the overt sexual harassment some women endure. One statehouse reporter in Ohio was standing in the capitol building when a legislator pinched her posterior. She spun around and slapped him on the face with such force that it echoed in the rotunda. Word quickly got around. In the several years that have elaspsed since then, she's had no further trouble.

The consensus of the women consulted on this question is summarized in the following seven points:

---

*The author is particularly indebted to Professor Sharon Brock of The Ohio State University for enlightenment in this topic. Professor Brock, a former reporter, says that her tall stature—five feet ten inches—gave her the "advantage of not being a cupcake and not having to spend time proving it." Even she, however, confesses that police headquarters could be troublesome.

1. Don't date anyone from whom you must get information.
2. Be patient. Social and business mores don't change overnight. Bantering, horseplay, and practical jokes are a way of life among men in many organizations, especially the police; indeed, being included is a badge of acceptance in some quarters. A good deal of this attitude stems from the teamwork camaraderie experienced by men in sports or the military. Women who have played on scholastic athletic teams recognize this fact of life a good deal sooner than those who haven't. Read Betty Harragan's book, *Games Mother Never Taught You,* which deals with this concept.
3. Do a sincere and conscientious job. Do your homework—prepare for interviews. Ask knowledgeable questions. Sources will come to respect you for the depth of your knowledge and the quality of your writing. (It's a fact of life, however, that sources will more easily forgive a man for a dumb mistake than a woman, according to our female sources.)
4. Dress conservatively.
5. Ignore off-color remarks, sly sexual innuendoes; perhaps pretend you didn't even hear them. Stick to business. (A minority opinion from our source panel—a woman who claims she can tell dirty jokes faster and better than any man—says she's ready if that's the kind of game they want to play.)
6. Don't automatically assume that gender is the reason for practical jokes, ruses, false news leads, and so on. Young male reporters get their share, too, particularly from the cops. Cops can be a playful bunch, but women reporters agreed that the problem is usually confined to a tiny percentage of the total.
7. Take advantage of the natural propensity of men (and probably women, too) to talk more candidly to a woman. Says one reporter, "They bare their souls. Without really digging for them I get the juicier, more intimate details than most of my male counterparts."

IN THE FUTURE

If you have read this far, you deserve a reward. Here it is: a short windup. Relax. Put away the marking pen and lean back. Consider the future.

If you have done some of the things recommended in this book—gone out and reported real events for real newspapers—then you're the kind of person editors are looking for. Experienced. You are also, let us hope, a learning, growing kind of person, flexible and open-minded, one not afraid of the changes that will inevitably take place, both in society and in the newspaper office.

The newspaper of the future will be different, but the change will be evolutionary, not revolutionary. Some newspapers will change faster than others. Among the changes foreseen by the more visionary editors and publishers, as discussed in their speeches and conferences, are these:

* Continued advances in newsroom automation, including greater use of remote and portable word processors.
* Increased use of readership surveys in editing to determine reader needs and interests and how best to respond to them.
* Greater use of data processing in information gathering.
* Expanded use of graphics, often in color: photographs, art, graphs, charts, also increased use of computer graphics.
* More reporting by teamwork, particularly on big, comprehensive news-features.
* More attention to good writing; use of writing coaches.
* More concern for ethics. Questioning and possible curtailing of certain accepted journalistic practices such as use of anonymous sources and fictional composites.
* More emphasis on good information gathering; particularly documentary research, data compilation by computer, and sensitive interviewing. More careful checking of factual detail the way the better magazines do.
* Greater departmentalization of the newspaper.
* Continued emphasis on service journalism.
* Continued specialization among reporters, particularly on scientific and technical subjects.
* Greater use of "literary techniques," such as reporting through people and their activities.

Final words of advice? Certainly. They'll be brief.

1. Be fair—even when people aren't always fair to you. It will cause you to grow in personal stature.
2. Develop a skin thin enough to know what's going on.
3. But develop a skin thick enough not to dwell unnecessarily on other people's tragedies. Otherwise you won't do a good job.
4. Try to curb your need to "express yourself" (a dreadful cliche in journalistic writing).
5. Try, instead, to work for your reader. Try to be of use to people in serving their needs for information about their environment.
6. Never cease to be an eager, curious student of the world around you—it's what makes reporting fun.

POINTS TO REMEMBER

1. It's a different world out there when reporters take their first news jobs.
2. Mistakes are common, and the consequences sometimes harsher than a mere bad grade.
3. Human relationships are unpredictable—a point you learn on the job rather than in classes.
4. Competition for first jobs is best met by people who have a little experience in addition to their college degrees.

5. Among the things that editors expect of new reporters are initiative, teamwork, and continued learning and intellectual growth.

6. Typical weaknesses among beginners, from editors' perspective, are inadequate language skills and naivete about how government works.

7. Office politics and other nonnews factors often govern who gets ahead in newsrooms.

8. Journalism has great potential for intellectual growth once you get past being overwhelmed by public affairs trivia.

9. Tricks of the trade—from bargaining with sources to gentle deceptions—are generally learned on the job rather than from texts or in classrooms.

10. Getting "sourced" means going beyond official sources and making contacts with as wide a variety of people as possible.

11. The police beat is becoming an increasingly difficult one to cover, particularly for women.

12. Women are vulnerable to sexual harassment and off-color banter but can counter it with patience and a few common-sense measures.

Appendix A

Copy Preparation

A newspaper is essentially a manufacturing plant. It gathers, processes, packages, and distributes somewhere between 35,000 and 100,000 words with each issue, the latter figure representing the length of an average novel. To do this daily, newspapers must process a lot of copy in a hurry. Reporters must learn copy-handling procedures so that their copy can be processed quickly and efficiently.

Learning these procedures was simpler in earlier years when newspapers used a standard set of copyediting symbols derived from age-old printing practices. Today, printing practices on many newspapers have undergone such revolutionary changes that paper is no longer used in preparing copy.

It is no longer possible, then, to set forth a standard set of copy procedures and editing symbols that will apply universally throughout the industry. It is not even possible to set forth any standard procedures in electronic editing: They vary from newspaper to newspaper, depending on how the computers are programmed.

Furthermore, some journalism schools and departments are in various stages of conversion. If your school teaches newswriting using VDT copy preparation methods, you will, of course, get instructions there.

TRADITIONAL COPY PREPARATION

The following rules apply to copy prepared on paper to be set in type by a printer.

1. Typewrite all copy, double spaced. Leave at least a one-inch margin all around.
2. In the upper left-hand corner of the first page, put your name and a "slugline" containing a word or two that tells what the story is about. Thus:

   Smith
   Governor's speech

3. Start your copy about a third of the way down the page from the top.
4. On subsequent pages, write your name, slugline, and page number in the upper left-hand corner.

   Smith
   Governor's speech—2

5. At the end of each page except the last, write *(more)* to indicate that the story continues.
6. At the end of your story, put an end symbol such as # or -30- or END.
7. Do not break (hyphenate) words at the end of typewritten lines (it's confusing to the typesetter).
8. Do not break paragraphs from one page to the next (also causes typesetting problems).
9. Do not erase or strike over figures or letters. Mark them out with x's or with soft lead copy pencil. Do not use a pen to edit copy.

COPYEDITING SYMBOLS

The symbols shown on page 300 are standard in the printing industry and remain in day-to-day use despite the changes in technology. Make your changes within the copy, never at the side. (The designations at the side in the following example are merely to explain the nature and use of each symbol.)

VIDEO DISPLAY TERMINAL

The rapid growth of electronic copy processing in newspaper offices is not for the sake of novelty or experimentation. All advances in five centuries of printing technology have been to increase speed, improve efficiency, and/or save money. This instance is no exception. The principle that explains the increasing use of video display terminals is that of "saving keystrokes."

The video display terminal is an electronic typewriter. As you type a story, using

By LARRY BACON

By LARRY BACON

By LARRY BACON

FLORENCE, (Oregon)--Jim Alexander likes to watch a good stand-up fistfight.

So when he saw two men head out the back door of a waterfront tavern after (what appeared to be) a heated argument Thursday evening, he followed to watch the action.

Instead of a fight, alexander was horrified to see one of the men pull a pistol, stick the barrel against the other's neck, and fire a shot. The wounded man, Stanley Eldon Kezar, (twenty-eight), of Portland, began grappling with his somewhat hefty attacker.

Alexander, a 47-year-old builder who lives on Bay (St.) here, acted without hesitation.

"I jumped into the middle of them and took the gun out of his hand," he said.

The gunman fled.

Alexander took the gun into a tavern, gave it to the barkeeper for safekeeping, and asked someone to call an ambulance.

Police credited Alexander with saving Kezar's life.

"It takes a great deal of courage to do what that man did," police officer Bob Peterson said. "Not a hell of a lot of people would do that."

Alexander said, thinking about the whole deal pretty much in retrospect, that maybe he's stupid, but he acted without considering the possibility that he might have been shot. He said he never has been able to tolerate apathy. "I wasn't raised that way," said he. (Story from Eugene (Ore.) Register-Guard.)

⌞	Flush left
⌉ ⌞	Center
⌉	Flush right
◯	Abbreviate the name
│	Separate the words
∾	Transpose letters
⌄	Insert phrase
ℐ	Delete letter and close up
≡	Capital letter
⌃	Insert comma
⌄	Insert apostrophe
◯	Use numerals
⌒	Delete words
│—│	Insert dash
◯	Spell out word
⌄	Insert quote marks
No ¶	No paragraph
⌄	Insert word
⊙	Add period
/	Use small letter
(STET)	Ignore correction; let the original stand
⌒	Run in
│	Separate words
✕	Insert letter
⌞	Paragraph
⊓	Transpose words

a keyboard similar to that of an electric typewriter, your words flash onto a TV screen above the keyboard. The VDT is usually wired ("on-line") to a computer, which drives the typesetting machinery.

"Saving keystrokes" means that the original keystrokes you used to type your story are the ones eventually used to set the type. True, a few of your keystrokes are lost in editing changes along the way, but most remain. A whole battery of typesetters or keypunchers has been eliminated in the process, with tremendous financial savings. Though the equipment is expensive to purchase, the savings soon pay back the cost.

Reporters, even those with years of experience on manual typewriters, seem to adapt quickly to the electronic era. Granted, a few exceptions exist. But most reporters, given time to get accustomed to the system, find the advantages outweigh the disadvantages.

You can revise, add words, strike out characters, move blocks of copy, and rewrite as much as you want. But unlike the case when typing on paper, here you don't end up with messy insertions, scratched-out sections, and hard-to-read marginal notations. When you delete a word or sentence or a faulty paragraph from the VDT, it's gone forever. No more rekeyboarding an otherwise satisfactory story simply because it's so messy that no one but you could read it. In short, no matter how many changes you make on your VDT story, you always end up with clean copy.

You start your day's work on the VDT by "logging on" to the computer. You type in a "password": a word or set of characters that allows you access to your "file" stored in computer memory. (Reporters have had to learn a whole new set of terms to match the new technology; see Glossary.)

The main portion of your keyboard is the same as that of an electric typewriter. As you type, a blip of light, called a "cursor," moves across the screen just ahead of your words (it keeps up with you no matter how fast you type). The cursor is the point at which editing changes can be made. Auxiliary keys, usually to the right of your main keyboard, permit you to move the cursor to any point within your copy and allow you to make editing changes within the copy.

Put the cursor in any point within a certain word, press the DELETE WORD key, and the word disappears from the screen. All the other words to the right and below the deleted word move up to close rank.

Put the cursor at a point where you want to insert a new word, press the INSERT key, and type in your new word or phrase (or even a whole new paragraph). All the other characters to the right and below move back to accommodate the new insertion.

So you fouled up your lead paragraph? Move the cursor to any point within that paragraph, press the DELETE PARA key (you may have to press it twice, a built-in safety factor to avoid eliminating a large block of copy by mistake) and in an instant the offending paragraph is gone.

Although paper is nowhere involved in the VDT operation, you can get "hard copy," as it's called in computer language, by getting a printout on the line printer. This, reporters find, is handy if you want to keep a paper record of your story or a set of notes (many reporters take notes on the VDT when conducting telephone interviews—typing is faster than taking notes by hand).

Some sophisticated systems permit exotic kinds of editing undreamed of in earlier years. Let's say you've typed a 700-word story. A mere fifteen seconds before your deadline, you discover that you have misspelled a name at least a dozen times throughout the story. You spelled it Smith when it should have been Smythe.

No problem. You command the computer to search for every "Smith" in your story and change it to "Smythe." Once you have set up these instructions (it takes only a moment), you press the EXECUTE key. In an instant every misspelled Smith is corrected. And you still have seven or eight seconds to spare in case you discover another mass spelling error.

When you have finished the editing of your story, you press a key that transfers it into computer storage. It can be called back onto your screen for further work or onto an editor's screen for review and editing. If the editor has questions or suggestions, he or she can type them onto the screen as the electronic equivalent of marginal notations (they won't show up in the typesetting). When all editing is completed, the editor executes the typesetting function. The story is thus set in type, usually by phototypesetting at the rate of perhaps 100 to 150 newspaper lines a minute, depending on the equipment.

Disadvantages of the new system, from the reporter's point of view, are occasional malfunctions (more than occasional, it seems, when a new system is first placed into use). These malfunctions include such traumatic experiences as lines voluntarily transposing themselves on the screen or screens suddenly going blank. Static electricity can sometimes play havoc with a VDT. These problems are usually minor, confined to an individual VDT. It's not so minor, of course, to lose your just-completed Pulitzer prize winner moments before deadline. To avoid problems, reporters often file their stories take-by-take (screenful-by-screenful) into computer storage where they are not vulnerable to such eccentricities.

A more serious problem is the "crash," when the entire system is temporarily inoperative (though memory-stored articles are usually not affected). Some newspapers have installed two systems—call them the A and B systems—with one a backup for the other.

OPTICAL CHARACTER RECOGNITION

Optical character recognition (OCR or "scanner") calls for typewritten copy prepared to machine-readable specifications. Some newspapers prepare all or most of their copy that way, using electric typewriters (usually IBM Selectrics) equipped with a machine-readable typeface. Many newspapers use both scanners and VDT's. (Even in a newspaper fully VDT-equipped, scanners are handy for such things as syndicated columns, many of which are sent scanner-ready).

In preparing copy for a scanner, you usually type your story on special copysheets. After being edited at the copydesk, your story is sent to the composing room for typesetting. The copysheets are fed sheet by sheet through the scanner, a machine that looks a little like a small Xerox machine. The scanner either punches a paper tape or moves the copy on-line into computer memory for eventual typesetting. The scanner reads very fast, about 1,200 words a minute.

Appendix B

Style Guide

When you write about a commercial firm, is it Acme Company, Acme company, Acme Co., or what? Do you write 6 cows or six cows? Twenty-three horses or 23? A newspaper style guide is designed to achieve consistency in such matters.

The style guide presented here is an abbreviated one covering the primary areas that require consistency. It is not intended to be complete. For a complete guide, you are urged to secure a copy of *The AP Stylebook and Libel Manual* (order from AP Newsfeatures, 50 Rockefeller Plaza, New York 10020, or the *UPI Stylebook* (Production Director, United Press International, 220 East 42nd Street, New York 10017.)

The style guide below does not fully cover punctuation because the rules of punctuation are standard; consult the back pages of a good dictionary, such as the *Random House College Dictionary* or *Webster's New Collegiate Dictionary*.

CAPITALIZATION

Capitalize titles that precede and are part of names. Lower-case titles that follow names or stand by themselves. *Pres. John C. Brown. President Brown. John C. Brown, president of the River City Bank. Judge Carl E. Wimberly. Judge Wimberly. Carl E. Wimberly, judge of the Circuit Court.*

Capitalize specific regions but not the point of the compass nor directions.

Middle West. Midwest. South. Pacific Northwest. East Coast. Texas Panhandle. He drove south for the winter. She left for the East this morning. He was headed west the last I saw him.

Capitalize names of religious denominations and nouns, pronouns, and adjectives used to designate the Supreme Being in any religion. *Methodist. Catholic Church. Deity. He, His, Him* denoting Deity (but not *who, whose, whom*).

Capitalize ethnic names and nationalities. *Oriental. Caucasian. Anglo. Chinese. Chicano.* But do not capitalize *white* or *black.*

Capitalize abbreviations of college degrees (no space between letters). *B.A. Ph.D. L.L.D.* Do not capitalize when spelled out. *bachelor of arts. doctor of philosophy.*

Capitalize nouns used with names of companies, associations, streets, geographical features, etc. *Yankee Stadium. Hanauma Bay. Plaza Hotel. River City High School. Crampton Hall. Chicago Avenue. Washington and Adams Streets. Waldo Lake. Weyerhaeuser Co. Oregon State University. Acme Manufacturing Co.*

Capitalize congressional committees, governmental agencies, courts, etc. *Senate. House. Legislature. House Ways and Means Committee. Senate Foreign Relations Committee. Board of Selectmen. City Council. Supreme Court. Circuit Court. Juvenile Court. 6th U.S. Court of Appeals.*

Capitalize holidays and special or historic events. *Fourth of July. Battle of the Bulge. Hurricane Anita. Good Friday. Passover. New Year's Eve. Reformation. seventh annual Miss South Dakota Day.*

Capitalize chapter, room, highway, etc., when followed by a number or letter. *Room 2. Highway 101. Appendix B.*

Capitalize names of political parties, but not the same words when used in a general sense. *Democratic Party. John Doe is a Republican. Nationalist China. Communist Party. communism. fascism. republican system. democratic principles.*

Do not capitalize a.m. or p.m. when used with figures. *9:40 a.m. 11 p.m. His workday runs from 8 a.m. to 5 p.m. 12 midnight.*

Do not capitalize seasons of the year. *summer. autumn. winter.*

Do not capitalize former, ex-, or -elect when used with titles. *former Pres. Gerald Ford. ex-President Ford. Pres.-elect John Smith.*

Do not capitalize false titles or occupational titles. *mechanic John Doe. defense attorney Susan Graham. reporter Cindy Johnson. catcher Fred Love. southpaw Lefty Gonzales.*

Do not capitalize the start of fragmentary quotations (but capitalize the first word of a quotation that makes a complete sentence). *Jones said he felt "sick at heart" about the new development. Jones said, "You can imagine how sick at heart I feel."*

ABBREVIATIONS AND TITLES

Abbreviate names of states when used after names of cities; otherwise spell out. *Bloomington, Ind. Red Bank, N.J. Chico, Calif. Jackson, Miss. Amherst, Mass. He's en route to Mississippi. She comes from California.*

Do not abbreviate Alaska, Hawaii, Idaho, Iowa, Maine, Ohio, and Utah.

Omit the name of the state if the city is well known. *Chicago. New York. Boston. Los Angeles. San Francisco.*

Abbreviate the common nouns in the names of business firms. *Acme Manufacturing Co. Warner Bros.*

Abbreviate titles when used with full names but spell out when used with only the surname. *Dist. Atty. Anne Banks. District Attorney Banks. Gen. George C. Marshall. General Marshall.* Abbreviate as follows: *Prof., Gen., Adm., Supt., Dr., Gov., Capt., Lt., 1st Sgt., M. Sgt., Rear Adm., Cmdr., Pfc., Lt. Col., Asst. Gov., Pres., Atty. Gen.*

Abbreviate *saint* in names of saints and cities. *St. Louis. St. Paul. St. Lawrence Seaway.*

Abbreviate *fort* when applied to military bases. *Ft. Lewis, Wash.*

Spell out *mount* when applied to mountains and cities. *Mount Rainier. Mount Vernon, N.Y.*

Spell out port, association, university, college, point, detective, department, secretary, treasurer, manager. *Port Moresby. Detective John Doe. Reed College Alumni Association. Willamette University.*

Abbreviate names of months (except March, April, May, June, July) when used with specific dates; otherwise spell out. *She was born Feb. 2, 1944. She was born in February. She was born in February 1944. Where were you last March 30? The ship leaves Dec. 5.*

Abbreviate names of political parties when used with the name of a Congressman. *Sen. Mark Hatfield, R-Ore., said today. . . .*

Use the abbreviations St., Ave., Blvd., when used with a specific address, but do not abbreviate Lane, Circle, Road, Drive. Spell out when used in a general sense. *876 River Ave. 11 E. Broadway St. 311 Argyle Road. 893 E. 11th Ave. He drove west on University Street. She walked down the avenue.*

Generally use periods in lower case abbreviations, especially if the letters without periods spell words. *c.o.d. f.o.b. s.o.b. m.p.h. a.m. p.m.*

Do not use periods in abbreviations of millimeter or in tape recorder speeds. *35mm film. 105mm howitzer.*

Do not abbreviate names of foreign countries (except U.S.S.R. and U.A.R.), days of the week, people's names (such as *Wm., Jas.,* etc.), percent, United States or United Nations (except as adjective, such as *U.S. attorney general*).

Forms of address such as Mr., Mrs., Miss, and Ms. are ordinarily unnecessary except in a direct quote. Use the full name on first reference and last name only thereafter. *Susan Graham began her public life in 1966. That was the year Graham ran for district attorney.*

When it is necessary to mention husband and wife in the same story, distinguish between the two by using full names throughout.

Rev. should always be preceded by "the" and should be followed by title if appropriate. *the Rev. Thomas L. Brown, pastor of the River City Methodist Church. the Most Rev. James Riley. Father Patrick Casey. Reverend Brown. Father Casey. Archbishop O'Farrell.*

When a person's title is longer than two words, place it after the name. *John Jones, superintendent of public instruction* (not *Supt. of Public Instruction John Jones*). *Paul Kelly, assistant to the chief of protocol.*

Do not use an abbreviation that is not likely to be understood easily. Spell it out the first time, then abbreviate thereafter. *Smith founded the River City Taxpayers Association in 1973. R.C.T.A. membership quickly climbed to 300.*

PUNCTUATION

Period and comma always are placed inside quotation marks. Other punctuation marks go inside when they are part of the quoted material and outside when they are part of the overall sentence. *"We have a small problem here," Captain Smith said. Captain Smith said, "We have a small problem here." "What can we do about it?" she asked. Is it really a "small problem"?*

Use a period after most abbreviations. *B.A. Jr. the Rev.* etc.

Do not use a period after initials of commonly accepted or widely known organizations. *ROTC. FBI. CIA. AFL-CIO.* However, use periods in *U.S., U.N.,* and *U.S.S.R.*

Put periods inside parentheses when a complete sentence is contained therein. But when the parenthetical expression is only a part of the sentence, put the period outside. *(It was too cold for swimming.) It was too cold for swimming (or even for walking).*

Use commas to set off the year in a date and to set off the month and the exact date following the day of the week. *He arrived Feb. 7, 1944, and immediately took control. It was June 30, 1955, when she left for Europe. The ceremony will be held Monday, May 16, in the lobby of Crampton Hall.*

Use commas to set off the name of a state after a city. *She left for Bismarck, N.D., on her 27th birthday.*

Use commas to set off street addresses, but not before an "of" phrase indicating place or position. *John Doe Jr., 23, River City, is missing. John Doe Jr. of River City is missing. John Doe Jr., 2345 First Ave., River City, is missing.*

Do not use a comma before the conjunction (such as "and") when used in a series of three or more words or phrases. *The party included Jim, Fred, Jane and Marsha. He ate his dinner, brushed his teeth and went to his room.*

Do not use a comma between a person's name and Jr. or Sr. *John D. Doe Jr.*

Use quotation marks for titles of books, poems, plays, speeches, songs, works of art, and titles of lectures and magazine articles. *He finished reading "Gone With the Wind" last night. His article, "How to Fly a Kite," appeared in Popular Mechanics last year.*

Do not use quotation marks for names of newspapers or magazines. *She read it in the New York Times. She sold an article to Good Housekeeping.*

Use dashes sparingly to show a significant pause or an abrupt change in thought, or to set off a phrase to be emphasized. *He said—and he pounded the table for emphasis—that he loved his country. She asked for cake and they gave her—a stone.*

NUMERALS

Spell out numerals when they begin a sentence. Spell out numerals one through nine, then use figures. Always use figures for the following: ages, dates, time, addresses, highways, sports scores, voting results. *Jimmy Doe, 9. March 22, 1944. April 3, 1979. 3 p.m. 5 Trenton Road. Highway I–5. Siwash won, 7 to 6. The City Council voted 8–7 in favor of the pension plan.*

Use figures with the dollar sign. *$4. $3.5 million. $2.13.*

Use figures with military units, political divisions, and court districts. *6th Fleet. 2nd Division. 6th U.S. Court of Appeals. 8th Ward. Ward 4.*

Be consistent when using figures in a series. *She ate 2 apples, 11 oranges and 83 raisins. The fleet included five carriers, two cruisers, two minesweepers, two tankers and fourteen destroyers.*

Spell out numbers when used casually or conversationally. *She said, "I told him a hundred times to slow down." She read a novel about the Gay Nineties.*

Do not use roman numerals unless they are part of a name or title. *World War II. King George V. Pope John XXIII. John Doe III (3rd acceptable).*

Use figures for fractions or decimals unless they begin a sentence or are used conversationally. *The study showed only 7.4 percent of the voters preferred Smith for mayor. Add 1¼ cups of sugar. "We're about three-fourths through," she said.*

Appendix C

Keys to Exercises

CHAPTER ONE QUIZ

Spelling

1. accidentally
2. accommodate
3. all right
4. ancient
5. balloon
6. battalion
7. believe
8. ceiling
9. collaborate
10. commitment
11. conceive
12. debatable
13. defendant
14. dependent
15. desirable
16. development
17. diesel
18. embarrassment
19. fiery
20. fluorescent
21. gauge
22. holiday
23. hygiene
24. incidentally
25. interchangeable
26. irrelevant
27. leisure
28. maintenance
29. misspell
30. newsstand
31. occasional
32. opulence
33. parallel
34. pier
35. professor
36. recommend

37. resistant
38. rhythm
39. satellite
40. seize
41. separate
42. sergeant
43. temperament
44. truly
45. vinegar

Grammar and Word Usage

46. bad
47. its
48. who
49. Whom
50. "It's
51. laid
52. me and her
53. is
54. lies
55. I
56. your
57. was
58. were
59. As
60. whoever
61. whom
62. his
63. is
64. are
65. as if
66. whom
67. were
68. farther
69. further
70. lie
71. lay
72. were
73. its
74. badly
75. whom
76. are
77. were
78. me
79. carelessly
80. hanged

Punctuation

81. James and . . . (remove comma)
82. . . . 'Stick 'em up . . . (substitute single quote mark to start the quote within a quote)
83. children's (insert apostrophe)
84. Charles' or Charles's (insert apostrophe, but not Charle's)
85. "It's (insert apostrophe)
86. brigade, (insert comma after brigade)
87. okay (colon should be *outside* quote mark)
88. slim, tanned (remove hyphen, insert comma)
89. celebrity, Mary Tyler Moore, (set off with commas)
90. sharply; (insert semicolon)
91. okay
92. said, (remove semicolon, substitute comma)
93. okay
94. stadium?" (question mark inside quote)
95. center," (comma inside quote)

Sentence Fragments

96. fragment
97. complete
98. complete
99. fragment
100. fragment

Scoring. Allow one point for each correct answer. Total points possible: 100. The ratings below are based on the author's experience in working with students at the University of Oregon.

95 or better. Excellent for a quiz, but please remember that news copy appearing in print should be *perfect.* That, perhaps, is the difference between the student and the professional. If your score is perfect, congratulations. If not, then at least you're on your way toward professionalism. You probably already keep a dictionary handy to help you spell troublesome words.

90–94. Good. But carry a dictionary when writing. Consult a grammar reference book. Keep your tools sharp.

85–89. Passable for a quiz, but you definitely should work on spelling, grammar, and punctuation. Consult a good book on spelling and grammar.

Below 85. If this were a typical classroom situation, you might be satisfied, depending on how close you were to 85. But professional editors won't be impressed, and neither should you. Consult a good book on spelling and grammar, and keep it handy at all times.

CHAPTER FOUR EXERCISES

Auto fatality

A California man died today of injuries received when his car skidded off rain-slickened Highway 123 five miles east of River City.

Sheriff's officers identified him as Harold Alan Kennedy, 33, of San Jose, Calif. He died at Mercy Hospital about 5:30 a.m., an hour and a half after a passing truck driver spotted his wrecked compact car at the edge of the Chickahominy River.

The truck driver, Peter Gooding, 456 Cherry St., River City, told police he saw the vehicle's lights "shining kind of eerie" through the rain that was falling hard at the time. He stopped to investigate and found Kennedy alone and unconscious inside the car, which lay upside down with the back end partly submerged.

Unable to open the door, Gooding summoned help by citizen's band radio.

The body will be sent by River City Mortuary to San Jose for services.

First Citizen Award

Judge Sarah Jane Benchly is River City's "First Citizen of the Year"—the first woman to be so honored in the five-year history of the civic award.

A two-minute standing ovation greeted announcement of her selection last night at the First Citizen banquet held at the Riverview Hotel under sponsorship of the East River Kiwanis Club. Some 300 persons attended.

The award recognizes ten years of work accomplished by Judge Benchly on behalf of underprivileged children. Benchly, of the Holcomb County Court of Domestic Relations, was founder and first president of Bixby House, a shelter home for runaway girls. She has also organized camping, skiing and river excursions for underprivileged children.

River City Mayor Henry W. Wadsworth presented the award. Wadsworth, first winner of the First Citizen Award when it was established five years ago, said 43 men and women had been considered by the selection committee. The committee took three weeks and seven meetings to arrive at its choice of Judge Benchly.

Benchly, who is married to a River City pediatrician, Dr. John E. Benchly, was appointed to the court four years ago to fill the unexpired term of Judge Allen W. Bixby who died in office. She ran unopposed for election a year later.

She is the mother of two teenage boys, Charles and Dana. She taught high school English for four years before attending law school at the University of Southern California.

"I am deeply honored," she said last night, "so much so that for the first time in my life words fail me."

CHAPTER FIVE REFERENCE

Ah, ha! So you *do* have a curious mind! That's good, for this "Oh, Harry" business is a test of curiosity. If your mind is not active and curious enough to pursue these answers, then it is not active and curious enough to be a good journalist. In any event, this scene occurred at the Port Authority Bus Terminal in New York City on New Year's Day, 1964. The college girl was boarding a bus to return to her campus after the holiday. Harry was her old neighborhood boyfriend, and he'd just gotten the word: He was through. The romance was off. After helping her dispose of Harry, Talese and the *Times* describe the hordes of college students who jammed bus, train, and air terminals en route back to their campuses. Talese later went on to better things, such as his book on the Mafia, *Honor Thy Father,* and he became one of a group of activists in a brand of writing popularly called the "new journalism," though today we tend to call it "literary journalism."

CHAPTER FIVE EXERCISES

Situation 1

(Probably too trivial for inclusion.)

Situation 2

Gov. Harry A. Allen escaped injury in a minor traffic accident in River City about midnight last night.

River City police said the governor's compact car was struck broadside by a car that apparently skidded on slippery pavement through a red light. . . .

Situation 3

A minor traffic collision sent a car swerving onto a sidewalk last night, sending a pedestrian to Mercy Hospital with minor injuries.

Police said John H. Roe, 35, 45 Deadwood Lane, River City, was treated for scalp lacerations after being struck by one of two cars that collided at the corner of Main Street and River Avenue. . . .

Situation 4

An Evanston, Ill., man was in satisfactory condition at Mercy Hospital today with injuries suffered in an auto collision at Main Street and River Avenue last night.

Police said Harry A. Allen, 72, was hurt when. . . .

Situation 5

A 72-year-old Evanston, Ill., man died at 9:45 this morning from injuries suffered in an auto collision in River City last night.

Police said the driver of the other car, Charles A. Rush, 33, 3005 Ponderosa Ave., River City, was jailed on a charge of driving while under the influence of intoxicating liquor.

Chief Darrell McManus said police continued to investigate today. . . .

Situation 6

A freak auto accident sent 1,000 pages of a book manuscript flying in a strong wind over an 11-block area of River City last night.

By midmorning today, 814 pages had been recovered by a volunteer search crew that fanned over the area and even climbed trees to retrieve soggy pages.

Police said the pages spilled out of the author's car when it was struck broadside at the intersection of Main Street and River Avenue about midnight.

The pages represent 30 years of work by the author, Harry A. Allen, 72, of Evanston, Ill., to write an autobiographical account of his World War II experiences with the French underground.

Allen, a former U.S. intelligence officer, had parachuted into France during the Nazi occupation and spent two years with the French resistance.

The book, titled "An Underground View," will be published in about a year.

Allen, a retired history professor at Northwestern University, had come to River City to visit the library at Ponderosa College, where. . . .

Variation of 6

A 1,000-page book manuscript of the World War II French underground was about 81 percent intact today after a freak accident and a strong wind scattered them over an 11-block area of River City last night. . . .

CHAPTER SIX EXERCISES

The sample stories here are not intended to represent the *only* way the exercises in Chapter 6 can be handled. Each reporter sees things a little differently. You may have written your story from a different angle, or you may simply have written a better story: smoother, more succinct, more spirited. Good. These sample stories are merely references for students not quite sure of their writing skills and news judgment.

Exercise 2: An Advance Story

Gov. Edward W. McCormack will discuss school finance, law enforcement and several other issues in a River City speech Wednesday.

Arrangements were completed today for the governor to address the weekly luncheon meeting of the River City Downtowners Club on the issues facing the legislature when it convenes in Valley City next month.

The speech begins at 12:45 in the Riverview Hotel. It is open to the public without charge. Chairs will be set up for an expected audience of nonmembers, said John Small, president of the Downtowners. City and county officials were especially invited, Small said.

Ken Farmer, the governor's press secretary, singled out law enforcement and school finances as the primary issues the governor will discuss. He also plans to speak about taxation, land-use planning and mass transportation, Farmer said.

Exercise 3: A Speech

Gov. Edward W. McCormack says he will veto any legislative attempt to restore capital punishment in (this state).

"I don't believe that society has a right to deliberately take a human life," the governor told some 200 persons attending yesterday's luncheon meeting of the Downtowners Club in the Riverview Hotel. The audience was the largest in the 23-year history of the club.

The governor also said he would lead the campaign to defeat capital punishment at the polls should the legislature refer it to a vote of the people.

"We have come too far in this state to fall back to the Dark Ages," McCormack said in announcing his decision to stand "unalterably opposed to capital punishment."

The governor also announced his opposition to construction of a new state prison.

He acknowledged the overcrowded conditions in the state's 45-year-old prison— more than 1,000 prisoners in facilities designed for 675. But he said he opposes building "another concrete fortress" with 20-foot walls at a cost of $50 million.

Governor McCormack said he favored development of regional rehabilitation facilities instead.

"I favor a policy that insures that those who can be helped are helped," he said.

The governor announced plans to take to the legislature several proposals for penal reform, though he did not specify them.

"Rest assured that a new prison and capital punishment will not be among them," he said.

Capital punishment was abolished in (this state) 10 years ago in a statewide vote. McCormack said, however, that he expected at least two bills calling for capital punishment to be introduced into the legislature, which convenes next month in Valley City.

Exercise 4: An Obituary

Walter S. Stewart, retired River City automobile dealer and antique car enthusiast, collapsed and died yesterday of a heart attack. He was (age).

Stewart collapsed yesterday noon while working on one of his four antique cars, a 1934 Dodge. He was taken by ambulance to Mercy Hospital where he died about 4 p.m.

Services will be held tomorrow at 1 p.m. in the Hickman-Edwards Chapel of the Gardens, 747 River Ave., with burial to follow at Valley View Memorial Park.

Stewart operated the Stewart Chevrolet Sales and Service in River City from 1946 until retirement in 1971. In 1956 he founded the River City Antique Cars Club.

"Old cars are an addiction with me," he told a newspaper interviewer a year ago. "Some guys take to alcohol or drugs. Me, I never did drink or smoke. These old cars suit me just fine."

He owned four of them, the Dodge plus a 1924 Model-T, a 1929 Chevrolet and a 1937 Ford V-8. He maintained them in running order and drove the Dodge to church Sundays and the '37 Ford to picnics in the country with his wife.

Stewart, born in Bismarck, N.D., in 1907, also maintained an interest in American Indians. Two years ago he contributed to Ponderosa College some 1,600 books and other documents representing his lifetime collections of material about Indians. Since 1958 he maintained a college scholarship fund for Indians.

He also served on the River City School Board for eight years.

He is survived by his widow, Mary Jane, whom he married in 1934, and three daughters: Elaine Wyman, Prairie View, Tex.; Heather Simmons, Sandy, Ore.; and Cynthia Gonzales, Spearfish, S.D. Five grandchildren also survive.

In lieu of flowers, the family suggests contributions in his memory to the Stewart Scholarship Fund for American Indians, care of Ponderosa College.

Exercise 5: A Follow-Up Story

A dangerous type of flammable paint has been discovered in River City, and Fire Chief Charles Pickering will send inspectors on a tour next week to see if there's any more of it around.

Pickering today blamed the paint—perhaps 30 years old and highly flammable—for the rapid spread of fire in an apartment at 456½ Partridge Ave. Wednesday morning.

The fire, thought to have started from a lighted cigarette, spread so rapidly that a 19-year-old mother was forced to flee with her two infant daughters through a bathroom window. They were taken off a 15-foot-high ledge to safety, but the apartment was destroyed, and the sporting goods store below was damaged by water. Total damage was estimated at $10,000.

Pickering said the fire ignited the old paint in the apartment. The blaze "just flashed through the living room" in seconds. Had his crew arrived 30 seconds later, they might have lost the entire building, the fire chief added.

A crew next week will inspect several old buildings in River City in search of dangerous paint. Pickering said residents who have suspicious paint, old and flammable, may call the fire department for an inspection free of charge.

Exercise 6: A Meeting Story

Mountain climbers in northern California will be asked to carry small citizen's band two-way radios, representatives of five outdoor and rescue agencies decided in River City last night.

The radios are intended to aid in search and rescue operations.

"When a climber gets lost, a lot of people risk their lives searching for him," explained Paul Nelson, River City, who presided over yesterday's meeting. "A couple of pounds of radio gear in a climber's backpack is a small price to pay to make it easier and safer for rescue parties."

Agencies represented at yesterday's meeting include the U.S. Forest Service, Civil Air Patrol, River City Mountaineers, Mountain Rescue and Safety Council and REACT, a citizen's band emergency radio monitoring network.

The 17 persons attending unanimously passed the resolution calling for CB radios. Climbers will be asked to register their radio frequencies along with their planned routes and return times. If the climbing party is 12 hours overdue, an emergency radio monitoring network will be established, Nelson said.

He anticipates that climbers may need a little urging before accepting the proposal. An "educational program" is planned.

"Climbers are an independent bunch," Nelson acknowledged today.

In defense of the proposal, however, he cited a rescue mission two years ago on Mount Multnomah. An observation plane crashed with minor injuries to its two occupants. Because the plane carried an emergency radio "beeper" in the tail, searchers were able to locate it within minutes. One of three lost climbers, meanwhile, died of hypothermia.

"That incident is what started us thinking about CB radios," Nelson said.

CHAPTER SEVEN EXERCISE

A Complex Weather Story

Some 25 minor traffic accidents and a massive traffic jam on Highway 123 resulted from a brief icing condition that glazed River City streets yesterday evening during the homebound rush-hour period.

The ice resulted from rain that started falling around 5:30 p.m. yesterday and froze on contact with the ground. It lasted about 20 minutes.

Continued light rain is expected today and tomorrow, with warmer temperatures also predicted, the National Weather Service said.

Only one injury resulted from the icy streets, according to police agencies. Seven-year-old Cecil Arlington, 2020 River Ave., fell and broke his arm at the River and 18th Street intersection.

Police said a car swerved to avoid hitting the boy and broke a nearby fire hydrant, releasing a large spray of water. Police identified the driver as Louis A. Weltzer, 56, of 85 Salmon St.

A truck-trailer vehicle jacknifed on Highway 123 four miles east of River City, causing a one-hour traffic delay in the eastbound lanes, the State Highway Patrol reported. The tieup involved hundreds of cars stalled all the way back to River City. The truck driver, Charles A. Petrie, 44, of Los Angeles, was not hurt.

Some 50 homes in the Pine Tree Road area east of River City lost electricity for about 90 minutes after a car skidded on icy pavement and sheered off a power pole, Municipal Power Co. reported. The driver, George T. Henry, 1173 Eastway St., River City, was not hurt.

Although the ice momentarily crippled traffic in River City and a wide area to the east, other areas including the airport to the west of town remained unaffected. Meteorologist Fred Denny explained that the warm storm front, approaching from the west, had warmed the terrain west of town to above freezing before the rain started.

CHAPTER EIGHT EXERCISE

Hospital Emergency Story

A fiction writer who works at Mercy Hospital to gather material for a novel called "Emergency!" became an emergency victim herself last night.

Mary Ann McQuillan, 30, of River City—who says a writer "shouldn't be afraid to get blood on her hands or mud on her boots" in search of a story—was found near the hospital about 10 p.m., unconscious and bleeding from a stab wound, police said. Her purse and $20 are missing.

She was rushed to the same Emergency Room where she does volunteer work. She was given a blood transfusion and was reported in good condition in the hospital this morning.

"I didn't really have in mind my own blood, frankly," McQuillan remarked in a bedside interview this morning as she attempted to record the incident in a journal she keeps as a writer.

Getting the experience down on paper proved to be more difficult than she had imagined, however.

"I spent an hour this morning trying to scribble notes about what happened," she said. "It just won't come. I don't feel anything at all. Nothing."

McQuillan is a home extension agent for Holcomb County. She has published some 20 short stories and nonfiction articles in literary magazines. She said her novel will depict a "tense and dramatic" emergency room situation, but she declined to elaborate.

"I don't know myself how the book will turn out," she said. "All of my short stories have been that way. I figure if the endings surprise me, they'll surprise the reader."

She began work as a Red Cross volunteer six months ago, performing nonmedical errands in the Emergency Room, to enhance her understanding of hospital work. Her book is about six months from completion, she said.

"I see this as a kind of semi-documentary about hospital work," she explained. "I detest novels that deal exclusively with intense personal feelings and leave out context. The reader ends up feeling he hasn't learned a thing except 37 ways to make love. I want to get my characters out of the bedroom once in awhile and into the Emergency Room."

She was not sure, however, whether her own experience as an Emergency Room patient will ever find its way into the book. The attack apparently came from behind as she was leaving work for home. She remembered searching through her purse for her car keys when suddenly "the world turned upside down."

"I didn't know I was hurt," she said. "I just felt sort of dizzy. I didn't even feel fear—it all happened so fast. I almost feel cheated, like I ought to ask for my money back."

Police said she had tried to return to the Emergency Room, about 175 yards away, but collapsed just 40 feet from the entrance. There she was found by a passing doctor, Douglas M. Duncan.

Despite the experience, she plans to resume her volunteer work, she said.

Hospital authorities, meanwhile, have scheduled a meeting for this afternoon to discuss security measures, a spokeswoman said. She said two previous cases of purse snatching had occurred at night in the parking lot within the past year.

An Alternate Opening (Narrative Style)

Mary Ann McQuillan, 30, author of some 20 published short stories and articles in literary magazines, believes writers should be where the action is.

"A writer shouldn't be afraid to get blood on her hands or mud on her boots" in search of a story, she says.

So she went to work six months ago as an unpaid volunteer in the Emergency Room of Mercy Hospital to get material for her novel, "Emergency!"

Last night she became an emergency patient herself.

A doctor found her unconscious, bleeding from a stab wound, just 40 feet away from the same Emergency Room where she worked.

Police said her purse and $20 are missing. They said she apparently had been attacked from behind in the parking lot as she was leaving work for home. She tried to return to the Emergency Room, 175 yards away, but collapsed unconscious near the entrance.

She was given a blood transfusion and was in good condition this morning.

"I didn't really have in mind my own blood, frankly," she remarked today in a bedside interview. . . .

CHAPTER 10 QUIZ

1. 6.4%
2. 7.6%
3. 1.45 murders per 100,000 population
4. 53.6 voted yes
5. mean: 30.4, median 21, mode 21
6. .324 batting average
7. fuselage length = 26.6 inches
8. *C* is first at 66.6% "correct," *B* second at 46%, *A* last at 38.8%

CHAPTER SEVENTEEN EXERCISE: THE BIG STORY

Two firefighters died today when a wall collapsed on them as they fought the second most costly fire in the history of River City.

The fire destroyed the Continental Motors Building, 3200 River Ave., and for tense moments around 8:30 a.m. it threatened to spread as a stiff wind dropped burning debris onto three other buildings downwind.

Fire officials estimated the loss to Continental Motors, a Ford dealership and repair facility, at $1.45 million.

The fire also sent three other persons to Mercy Hospital with injuries. It destroyed some 55 cars, caused a three-mile traffic tieup on River Avenue and attracted some 3,000 to 4,000 spectators, 500 of whom witnessed the collapse of the building's north wall on top of four firefighters.

One of the injured was an unidentified woman found unconscious in an alley at the back of the building.

Reports by two witnesses that a woman's screams had been heard inside the burning building shortly after the fire was discovered remained unconfirmed by fire officials.

The dead:

Felix Doerner, a firefighter, 38, 1836 Circle Lane, River City. He was pronounced dead on arrival at Mercy Hospital. Doctors said he probably was killed instantly beneath the rubble of the collapsing wall.

Elbert A. Lindsay, also a firefighter, age 46, 1234 Elkay Drive, River City. He died about five minutes after arrival at the Emergency Room of Mercy Hospital. Hospital officials declined to announce the cause of death pending an autopsy.

The injured:

Charles T. Larson, firefighter, 31, Rural Route 7, River City. He is in satisfactory condition with a broken leg and two cracked ribs.

An unidentified woman, about 40, listed by the hospital in "serious but stable" condition. She remained unconscious at midmorning today, and doctors said her injuries include what appear to be electrical burns.

William A. Kennedy, a firefighter, 35, 12 Dorsey Drive, River City. He was in good condition and due for release from the hospital tomorrow.

Kennedy was one of the crew manning a hose close to the front wall of the building. He had gone back to the street to pull more hose when he saw the wall about to give way above the remaining three men.

"I could see it coming and it was like a nightmare," Kennedy said at the hospital this morning. "I yelled at them to get out, the wall's going. Charlie and Al started running, but Felix just seemed to stand there frozen. He just crumpled up in the middle of a ton of cement and brick."

Fire Chief Charles Pickering said he also saw the wall about to fall.

"I yelled at them but they didn't hear me," Pickering said. "A moment later it all came down."

Another witness said the three men at the hose turned when the fourth yelled a warning.

"Two of them started running back," said James Englemann, 18, who lives near the fire scene. "But the man holding the nozzle couldn't seem to get out in time. He threw up his hands like he was trying to stop the wall. He just crumpled up and went down."

When the wall collapsed the crowd of witnesses surged forward but was restrained by police. Officers did allow about 12 men to go to the scene to help the injured firefighters, joining about a dozen others to remove debris to free the four victims.

City fire officials said the two deaths were the first fatalities among firecrews in the line of duty since 1928.

Fire officials said the building and contents of Continental Motors were a total loss. The loss includes the building valued at $700,000, and cars and equipment valued at another $750,000.

William Harrison, manager of Continental Motors, said the loss is covered by insurance.

Harrison estimated that 55 cars inside the building were destroyed. They include 30 new cars and another 25 customers' cars in the repair shop.

Cause of the fire remains undetermined at press time today.

About 30 new cars standing just outside the burning building were pushed to safety by groups of teenagers.

Witnesses reported hearing numerous explosions inside the building. They were attributed to exploding gas tanks and drums of flammable liquid. Witnesses also reported auto horns occasionally going off inside the building as the fire reached the cars. Some horns blew for as long as three minutes, sounding like "the last cry of some dying monster," as one witness described it.

The first alarm was telephoned to the fire department at 7:46 a.m. by Peter L. Larkin, 37, a lawyer who was driving downtown on River Avenue. Larkin said he caught a glimpse of something "bright orange out of the corner of my eyes."

Stopping to investigate, he heard a muffled explosion inside the building followed by thick gray smoke pouring out of a window.

The first fire truck arrived at 7:50 and immediately called for assistance. At 8:01 the general alarm sounded, alerting the city's entire fire fighting force, including reserve and off-duty crews. By standing arrangement, adjacent communities sent standby trucks to River City to replace those called to the fire.

Two witnesses said they heard a woman's screams inside the back side of the building sometime before the first truck arrived. Firecrews, however, were not able to enter that part of the building to verify the reports.

One witness, Harry A. Lovelace, 69, 443 Abby Lane, said he'd been walking by the building about 7:45 when he heard an explosion followed by a woman's screams.

"I couldn't believe my ears," said Lovelace. "There was kind of a sharp scream, a woman's scream. Then I didn't hear it anymore."

Assistant Fire Chief Red Britton said by the time the first equipment arrived "that part of the building was totally involved. There was no way anyone could get in to check."

Within minutes flames were rising 80 feet in the air and depositing flaming debris on three buildings downwind and across River Avenue from the burning building. The buildings are the River Avenue branch of the city library, the OK Tavern, and the Oakway Building.

The buildings were evacuated shortly after 8 a.m., and crews played water on them to prevent them from catching fire. Damage was minor to the three buildings, though heat from the fire cracked the plate glass windows of the library.

Some 75 firefighters and 12 trucks responded to the fire, bringing it under control by about 9:20, though it continued to burn through the morning.

The fire created a three-mile traffic snarl on River Avenue, and a crowd estimated at 3,000 to 4,000 quickly formed to watch the fire. Some 20 police officers handled crowd and traffic control. Police detoured traffic to side streets to the north of River Avenue. Officers said the crowd was generally well behaved, although two men were arrested in one tussle on charges of disorderly conduct and resisting an officer.

Fire Chief Pickering called the fire "one of the worst in the history of River City."

He said crews were "fighting a hell of a lot more than just a fire. We're fighting wind and we're fighting traffic and we're even fighting bystanders."

Records show that only one fire in River City's history exceeded the estimated $1.45 million loss in today's fire. That was the Acme Manufacturing Co. fire of 1972 ($1.8 million).

Pickering said an official from the State Fire Marshal's office will arrive this afternoon to assist in investigating the fire's cause. Pickering said it would be premature this morning to speculate on the cause—"It could be any one of a hundred different causes."

Plans to rebuild Continental Motors were uncertain this morning, according to Manager William Harrison. The company's controlling stockholder, Alexander Winthrop, of River City, was cutting short a vacation in Hawaii to return and discuss future plans. The firm employs about 120 persons, some of whom may have to be laid off temporarily, Harrison said.

The two-story building, which occupied a quarter of a city block, contained facilities·for both new and used car sales as well as the repair facility.

Glossary

ad   Advertisement.

add   (1) News copy added to material already written. (2) The second or subsequent pages of a news story, usually tagged "add 1," "add 2," and so on.

advance   (1) A story written ahead of a forthcoming event announcing or calling attention to it. (2) A publicity release distributed in advance of a release date. (3) Wire copy moved ahead of a release date.

agate   A 5½-point line of type; standard measure of advertising space.

A.M.   A morning newspaper.

angle   An approach to, concept, or basic thrust of an article.

AP   Associated Press wire service.

art, artwork   Illustrative matter: photos, drawings, charts, graphs, etc.

attribution   Identification of the source of material used in a story.

background   (1) A portion of a story that describes earlier events and circumstances and thus puts new information in historical context. (2) A term ("on background") used by bureaucrats to indicate that their statements are "not for attribution," that is, the informa-tion can be published but the source must not be named.

backgrounder   A feature that focuses on the history of an event or situation to explain how it came to be.

banner   Headline that stretches across a newspaper page.

beat   (1) A set of agencies, offices, and informal contacts called on by a reporter for news and features. (2) A story published exclusively or ahead of competing media.

blow-up   Enlarged photo or art.

body type   Type set for text matter, usually around 7 to 12 point.

boil, boil down   To shorten a story by close editing or rewriting.

bold face   Type that is darker and heavier than normal type, **like this.**

box   Printed rules arranged in rectangular shape, usually to enclose a special feature.

bright, brite   Short, lighthearted featurette.

budget   List of important stories forthcoming that day from the wire service.

bug   Typographical ornament.

bulldog   The first edition of a multi-edition newspaper.

bullet A large dot sometimes used at beginning of paragraphs for special emphasis. Also called a "meatball."

bulletin Brief statement about a major, late-breaking story.

byline Writer's name at the top of an article.

CAM Composition and Makeup: an electronic editing terminal that permits writing, editing, and layout in producing an advertisement or editorial page layout.

canned copy Articles provided by syndicates.

caps Capital letters.

caption Written description that accompanies a photo or artwork. Also called "cutlines."

character generation High speed typesetting by electronic means.

city editor The manager in charge of the newspaper's local reporting staff. A paper may also have a county editor, state editor, regional editor, and foreign editor, each in charge of a reporting staff.

clip News clipping.

coding Designation of symbols for the computer.

cold type Type set by electronic, photographic, or strike-on (typewriter) methods.

color separation Use of color filters to break color art or photos into three primary ink colors (cyan, magenta, and yellow) for color reproduction.

color story A feature article, often a human interest story, usually run in conjunction with a major news story (for example, witness accounts of a flood or major fire).

command An order given to the computer through a terminal.

copy Material (articles, photos, artwork) prepared for publication.

copydesk A desk or set of desks where copy is edited, headlines written, and page layouts prepared.

copyeditor, copyreader A person who edits and prepares written material for publication.

copyfitting Determining the space written copy will occupy when set in type.

correspondent An employee or contributor located away from the main newspaper office, such as a country correspondent or foreign correspondent.

cover To gather information about an event or agency for purposes of writing news, as to cover a meeting or cover the police beat.

CPU Central Processing Unit—the computer that serves to receive, store, and process information such as news articles.

crash Computer malfunction that renders the machine inoperable.

credit line Acknowledgment of source of art or photos.

crop To eliminate unwanted portions of a photo.

cub Beginning reporter.

cursor A block or point of light on the VDT screen indicating where editing changes can be made.

cut (1) A published photo or art. (2) To eliminate portions of a story.

cutlines Caption for photo or art.

data Information, such as news articles, that is stored and processed by a computer.

dateline Designation of place and date of a nonlocal article.

deck A headline, usually consisting of two or three lines of type, located beneath the main headline or banner.

depth reporting Reporting that focuses deeply on a narrow topic. Thoughtful reporting.

dingbat Typographical ornament.

disk A magnetic disk, also called a floppy disk, for storage of computer data.

display type Large type (14 point and up) used for headlines and display matter in advertisements.

double truck Ad or feature layout that occupies two adjacent pages.

duotone Printing a black-and-white photo in two colors (usually black plus one other color) to achieve a third-color effect.

dupe Carbon copy.

ear Boxed material on either side of a nameplate, such as a weather report or promotional copy.

edition One of the two or more versions of a newspaper published in a single day, as a regional edition, suburban edition, city edition.

editorial Nonadvertising material in the paper. (2) An opinion essay.

enterprise copy A story, usually a comprehensive newsfeature, that originates as an idea from the reporter or the paper.

em A printing measurement; an em is the square of the type size.

exclusive A story that competing media missed, also called a "beat" or "scoop."

feature (1) Beyond straight news (see Chapter 13.) (2) To play up or give prominence to a story or a story angle.

file To send a story to the central office from a correspondent or field office. (2) Related data in computer storage.

filler A brief editorial item used to fill out ("justify") a column of type.

flag The nameplate of a newspaper.

flat A composite negative used to make an offset printing plate.

flush Lines of type aligned evenly on either or both sides of a column (flush left, or flush right).

folio A page number.

folo Short for follow or follow up.

font All the characters of a particular typeface in a particular size.

fourth estate The press. Journalism. Historically, a political power that follows the first estate (clergy), second estate (nobility) and third estate (commoners).

freelancer A nonstaffer who provides material for the paper on an assignment or speculative basis.

futures book, future book A reporter's or editor's calendar of forthcoming ideas and events to cover.

FYI "For your information."

glossy A black-and-white photo with a shiny finish.

hack Editorial staffer of limited competence.

hairline Extremely thin printing rule. (2) Thin stroke of a letter.

halftone Photo or art screened into a dot pattern for reproduction via a printing plate.

handout A publicity release.

hard copy In electronic editing, a computer printout.

hard news News of important public events such as government actions, foreign affairs, economic trends, etc.

hardware Physical equipment used in news production, such as computers, VDTs, or phototypesetting equipment.

H&J Hyphenation and Justification: computerized system for inserting hyphens and aligning type flush right.

HFR "Hold for release": material that has a release date.

hot type Type formed by molten metal.

HTK Abbreviation for "head to come" (hed to kum).

input Sending data to a computer.

humanistic reporting Finding the human dimension in journalistic reports.

inverted pyramid A news story structure that places the most important elements at the top of the story with remaining details more or less in order of descending importance.

interpretive reporting Reporting that seeks meaning beyond superficial reports of events.

investigative reporting Comprehensive reporting in depth, usually on wrongdoing.

italic Type with letter slanting toward the right, *like this.* Most typefaces have italic versions for emphasis or for citing names of books, plays, ships, etc.

jump To continue a story from one page to another.

justify To align type on the right so that all lines are even.

keypunch A composing machine that punches a coded paper type for typesetting.

kicker A short, often teasing or provocative line of type located just above a major headline.

kill To discard a story originally intended for publication.

kiss The impression of inked type on paper.

layout A plan or "blueprint" for the location of news stories, headlines, photos, and advertisements.

lead (Pronounced *ledd.*) Metal used for hot type.

lead (Pronounced *leed.*) Opening paragraph(s) of a story.

leading (Pronounced, and often spelled *ledding.*) Space between lines of type.

legman, legwoman A reporter who gathers information at the scene of a story and phones in reports to a rewrite person.

letterpress Printing from raised (usually metal) surfaces, a process now largely supplanted by offset on most papers.

libel False, defamatory written statement about a person or agency.

line engraving, line cut A photoengraving with only solid lines, no intermediate tones.

line printer A device used to print computer output; the printed version is known as "hard copy."

literary journalism Use of fiction devices in writing factual material. Scenes, descriptions, narrative, and so on.

logotype Letters assembled on a printing plate; often refers to a newspaper nameplate or advertising signature.

lower case Small letters of the alphabet, so called because in printing's early years they were assembled by hand from the lower of two type cases.

makeover To redo a newspaper page, as in a second edition.

makeup Assembling type and photos into a page, often called "pasteup" in offset printing.

managing editor The person in charge of a news operation.

masthead Statement of ownership, place of publication, etc.

mechanical Pasteup of an advertisement or newspaper page ready for photographic platemaking.

moire pattern An undesirable pattern formed when one halftone screen is printed over another, as in multicolor printing.

mug shot Photo of a person's face.

nameplate The name of the paper as printed on the front page.

new journalism Use of fiction devices in writing factual material. Scenes, description, narrative, and so on. Also called "literary journalism."

news editor The person in charge of selecting and displaying the day's news.

news hole Nonadvertising space available in a given issue.

news peg A news event or situation that makes it timely to write about a topic; a recent murder would be a news peg for a feature on growing violence.

OCR Optical Character Recognition. A method of setting type by electronic reading of typewritten copy.

offset A photomechanical printing technique that prints images onto a rubber blanket which in turn offsets onto the paper.

off the record Information given to a reporter (as in an interview) that is not intended for publication.

on-line Connected by wire, as a typesetter on-line to a computer.

op ed A section of the newspaper that carries columns, essays, and opinion pieces, so called because it often is located on a page opposite the editorial page.

overset Type set for publication that got left out for lack of space.

pagination Full-page layout on an electronic terminal.

password Word or set of characters that allows access to a computer file.

pasteup A layout with type affixed in place ready for the camera in offset printing method.

pica A printer's measurement, one-sixth of an inch. Used to designate type width, photo dimensions, etc.

pickup Copy that is to be inserted into a story already sent on the wire or set in type.

play Handling of news: "Let's play this on the front page."

play down De-emphasize a point: "Play down the sex angle."

play up To emphasize a point or angle.

P.M. An afternoon paper.

point A printing measurement: $1/72$ of an inch or $1/12$ pica. Used to designate type size: 72-point type is one inch high.

precede A paragraph or bulletin printed at the top of a news story usually to present a last-minute development.

precision journalism Use of scientific methods in reporting.

proof Material in type submitted to editors for correction of typographical errors.

queue A list of stories in computer for editing or typesetting.

rag Slang for newspaper.

replate To redo a page for a new edition or to correct an error.

retraction Correction of an erroneous statement.

rewrite To redo a story such as a press release. (2) Writing stories assembled from information phoned in by reporters.

rewrite desk The site where a reporter takes phoned-in reports and assembles them into a news story.

roman Type with serifs, based on historic letterforms. (2) Upright type, as opposed to *italic*.

rotogravure A printing process in which ink prints onto paper from tiny wells engraved in a copper cylinder. Used to print "roto" sections, such as the Sunday magazine.

rule A printed line, such as a column rule.

runaround Type set around a photo or artwork.

running story An event or situation that prompts frequent stories over a period of days or weeks.

sans serif Type that has no serifs.

saturation reporting Intensive interviewing and observation; often involves hours, days, even weeks of observation.

scanner A computerized device that reads typewritten copy; see Optical Character Recognition.

screamer A large banner headline.

screen Printed matter lightened in tone by rendering it into a dot pattern, such as a "screened" headline. (2) Screen of a computer monitor, such as a VDT.

scroll To move the viewing area in a video display terminal up or down the screen.

serif Small line that extends at right angles from a main stroke of a letter, such as the horizontal lines at the top and bottom of the letter M.

service journalism Writing specifically to serve the reader, usually through how-to-do-it articles on home improvement, financial planning, physical fitness, etc.

sidebar A secondary story that complements a major news story, such as witness interviews accompanying a story about a natural disaster.

situationer A story that ties together loose ends of a complicated event or issue.

slant, slanted story (1) Biased report. (2) Angle or approach to a story (common to magazine journalism).

slot The inside of a U-shaped copy desk. Head copyeditor sits in this position.

slug An identification word to identify a story. (2) A line of metal type.

sob story Human interest story noted for sentimentality or pathos.

soft news News noted more for reader interest than public importance, such as personality features or crime incidents.

software A computer program; a set of stored instructions that enables the computer to process data.

spike To kill (discard) copy.

spot news A timely report of an event, often unexpected.

stereotype A metal printing plate for rotary letterpress.

stet Copyeditor's symbol for "let it stand," used to restore previously changed copy.

stringer A correspondent who is not a regular member of the staff.

stripper A printer who assembles photographic negatives into composite negatives or "flats" for offset platemaking.

stylebook A compendium of capitalization, punctuation, and word usage rules designed to attain consistency in the paper.

subhead Short heads or teasers within a column of type used to break up long blocks of copy.

system A combination of computer hardware and software that performs a specific processing operation.

tabloid A small-sized newspaper, usually about 11 by 17 inches.

take A page of typewritten copy.

tear sheet A sheet torn from the paper, usually to show advertisers their printed advertisements.

terminal A device through which data can enter or leave the computer.

think piece A serious essay on a substantive issue, often containing personal opinion or interpretation.

thirty or **30** End of a story.

time copy News or features not connected to a date.

tint block A block of color ink, either solid or screened, underlying type or art.

type Metal or photo-composed letterforms.

typeface A style of type that has unique identifying characteristics. Type goes by various names (often the name of the type designer) such as Caslon, Goudy, Bodoni, Century.

UPI United Press International wire service.

upper case Capital letters, so called in the early days of printing because type characters were chosen from two cases, an upper and a lower.

VDT Video Display Terminal; an electronic typewriter that displays words on a TV-like screen.

web Continuous roll of paper fed through a rotary press.

widow A line of type containing only a few characters as at the end of a paragraph.

x-height Height in a line of type of lower case primary letters such as a, e, w, m, x—letters without descenders or ascenders.

yellow journalism Cheaply sensational and overplayed reporting.

zinc A relief plate for letterpress etched into zinc metal, usually for a photo or artwork.

Bibliography

After 'Jimmy's World': Tightening up in Editing. New York: National News Council, 1981.

ANDERSON DAVID, and PETER BENJAMINSON. *Investigative Reporting.* Bloomington: Indiana University, 1976.

ATWOOD, L. ERWIN. "How Newsmen and Readers Perceive Each Others' Story Preferences." *Journalism Quarterly* 47 (1970): 296–302.

BABB, LAURA LONGLEY, ed. *Writing in Style.* Washington: The Washington Post, 1975.

BAKER, ROBERT. "Reporter Posed As a Cop." *1983 APME Report.*

BAILEY, CHARLES W. *Conflict of Interest: A Matter of Journalistic Ethics.* New York: National News Council, 1984.

BARZUN, JACQUES. *Simple and Direct: A Rhetoric for Writers.* New York: Harper & Row, 1975.

BERNSTEIN, CARL, and BOB WOODWARD. *All the President's Men.* New York: Simon and Schuster, 1974.

BOGART, LEO. *The Press and Public: Who Reads What, Where, and Why in American Newspapers.* Hillsdale, N.J.: Lawrence Erlbaum Associates, 1982.

BOLCH, JUDITH, and KAY MILLER. *Investigative and In-Depth Reporting.* New York: Hastings House, 1978.

BRADY, JOHN. *The Craft of Interviewing.* Cincinnati: Writer's Digest, 1976.

BREMNER, JOHN B. *Words on Words: A Dictionary for Writers and Others Who Care About Words.* New York: Columbia University Press, 1980.

BRIAN, DENIS. *Murderers and Other Friendly People.* New York: McGraw-Hill, 1973. (Interviews with interviewers.)

CAPPON, RENE J. *The Word: An Associated Press Guide to Good News Writing.* New York: The Associated Press, 1982.

CHANCELLOR, JOHN, and WALTER MEARS. *The News Business.* New York: Harper & Row, 1983.

CLARK, ROY PETER. *Best Newspaper Writing.* St. Petersburg, Fla.: Modern Media Institute, 1979–85. Published annually.

CLARK, RUTH. *Changing Needs of Changing Readers.* Reston, Va.: American Society of Newspaper Editors, 1979.

CLYDE, ROBERT W. "News Readership as a Function of Several Affective Characteristics." *Journalism Quarterly* 45 (1968): 535–37.

CODY, ROBIN. "The Inside Job." *Northwest,* magazine of *The Sunday Oregonian,* March 11, 1984.

COOK, WILLIAM J. *The Joy of Computer Communications.* New York: Dell, 1984.

CROUSE, TIM. *The Boys on the Bus.* New York: Random House, 1973.

DEAKIN, JAMES. *Straight Stuff: The Reporter, the White House and the Truth.* New York: William Morrow, 1984.

DENNISTON, LYLE W. *The Reporter and the Law: Techniques of Covering the Courts.* New York: Hastings House, 1980.

DEVORE, NELSON, *Newsroom Legal Guidebook.* Seattle: Seattle Times Company, 1982.

DORFMAN, RON, and HARRY FULLER JR., eds. *Reporting/Writing/Editing: The Quill Guides to Journalism.* Dubuque, Iowa: Kendall/Hunt, 1982.

DORNFELD, A.A. *Behind the Front Page: The Story of the City News Bureau of Chicago.* Chicago: Academy, 1983.

Editor & Publisher Yearbook. New York: Editor & Publisher, 1984.

FONTAINE, ANDRE. *The Art of Nonfiction Writing.* New York: Thomas Y. Crowell, 1974.

GHIGLIONE, LOREN, ed. *Improving Newswriting: The Best of the Bulletin of the American Society of Newspaper Editors.* Washington: ASNE, 1982.

GILLELAND, LARUE W. "Simple Formula Proves Helpful to Interviewers." *Journalism Educator* 26 (1971): 19–20. See also *Editor & Publisher,* September 18, 1971, p. 54.

GILLMOR DONALD M., and JEROME A. BARRON. *Mass Communications Law.* 4th ed. St. Paul, Minn.: West, 1984.

GIVEN, JOHN L. *Making a Newspaper.* New York: Henry Holt, 1907.

GOODWIN, GENE. "The Ethics of Compassion." *The Quill,* November 1983.

GRIFFIN, JOHN HOWARD. *Black Like Me.* Boston: Houghton Mifflin, 1961.

GROTTA, GERALD L., ERNEST F. LARKIN, and BARBARA DEPLOIS. "How Readers Perceive and Use a Small Daily Newspaper." *Journalism Quarterly,* 52 (1975): 711–15.

HAGE, GEORGE S., EVERETTE E. DENNIS, ARNOLD H. ISMACH, and STEVEN HARTGEN. *New Strategies for Public Affairs Reporting.* 2d ed. Englewood Cliffs, N.J.: Prentice-Hall, 1983.

HALLMAN, TOM JR. "Collision Course." *Northwest,* magazine of *The Sunday Oregonian,* October 9, 1983.

HARRAGAN, BETTY LEHAN. *Games Mother Never Taught You.* New York: Rawson, 1977.

HOLLOWELL, JOHN. *Fact & Fiction: The New Journalism and the Nonfiction Novel.* Chapel Hill: University of North Carolina Press, 1977.

HESS, STEPHEN. *The Washington Reporters.* Washington: The Brookings Institution, 1981.

HUFF DARRELL, and IRVING GEIS. *How to Lie with Statistics* New York: Norton, 1954.

HULTENG, JOHN L. *Playing It Straight.* Reston, Va.: American Society of Newspaper Editors, 1981.

———. *The Messenger's Motives: Ethical Problems of the News Media.* 2d ed. Englewood Cliffs, N.J.; Prentice-Hall, 1985.

HYNDS, ERNEST. *American Newspapers in the Nineteen Eighties.* 2d ed. New York: Hastings House, 1980.

In the Public Interest III. New York: National News Council, 1983.

IZARD, RALPH S. "Gains on the Ethical Front." In *1983 Journalism Ethics Report.* Chicago: Society of Professional Journalists, Sigma Delta Chi, 1983.

JOHNSON, GERALD W. *What Is News?* New York: Knopf, 1926.

KESSLER, LAUREN, and DUNCAN MCDONALD. *When Words Collide: A Journalistic's Guide to Grammar and Style.* Belmont, Calif.: Wadsworth, 1984.

KILPATRICK, JAMES J. *The Writer's Art.* Fairway, Kan.: Andrews, McMeel & Parker, 1984.

KOHLMEIER, LOUIS M., JR., JOHN G. UDELL, and LAIRD B. ANDERSON. *Reporting on Business and the Economy.* Englewood Cliffs, N.J.: Prentice-Hall, 1981.

LIEBLING, A.J. *The Press.* New York: Pantheon, 1981.

LINTHICUM, LESLIE. "High School Revisited," *Albuquerque Tribune,* March 8–12, 1983.

LOVELL, RONALD P. *Reporting Public Affairs: Problems and Solutions.* Belmont, Calif.: Wadsworth, 1982.

MASLOW, ABRAHAM H. *Motivation and Personality.* 2d ed. New York: Harper & Row, 1972.

MERRILL, JOHN C., and HAROLD A. FISHER. *The World's Great Dailies: Profiles of Fifty Newspapers.* New York: Hastings House, 1980.

METZLER, KEN. *Creative Interviewing: The Writer's Guide to Gathering Information by Asking Questions.* Englewood Cliffs, N.J.: Prentice-Hall, 1977.

MEYER, PHILIP. *Precision Journalism.* 2d ed. Bloomington: Indiana University Press, 1979.

MITFORD, JESSICA. *Poison Penmanship.* New York: Knopf, 1979.

MOLLENHOFF, CLARK R. *Investigative Reporting.* New York: Macmillan, 1981.

MULLIGAN, HUGH A. "Getting the Total Picture." In *Reporting: Writing from Front Row Seats,* ed. Charles A. Grumich. New York: Simon & Schuster, 1971.

NEWSON, D.F. *The Newspaper: Everything You Need to Know to Make It in the Newspaper Business.* Englewood Cliffs, N.J.: Prentice-Hall, 1981.

Newspaper Readership Project. "Meeting Readers' Multiple Needs: Content and Readability of News and Features in the Daily News." New York: Newspaper Advertising Bureau, 1984.

NICHOLS, RALPH G., and LEONARD A. STEVENS. *Are You Listening?* New York: McGraw-Hill, 1957.

PEMBER, DON R. *Mass Media Law.* 3d ed. Dubuque, Iowa: Wm. C. Brown, 1984.

PLIMPTON GEORGE. *Paper Lion.* New York: Harper & Row, 1966.

POWELL, JODY. *The Other Side of the Story.* New York: William Morrow, 1984.

PROSSER, WILLIAM LLOYD. *Handbook on the Law of Torts.* 4th ed. St. Paul, Minn.: West, 1971.

RARICK, GALEN. "Differences Between Daily Newspaper Subscribers and Nonsubscribers." *Journalism Quarterly* 50 (1973): 265–70.

ROSENBERG, JERRY M. *Inside the Wall Street Journal.* New York: Macmillan, 1982.

RUEHLMANN, WILLIAM. *Stalking the Feature Story.* Cincinnati: Writer's Digest, 1979.

SACK, ROBERT D. *Libel, Slander, and Related Problems.* New York: Practising Law Institute, 1980.

SCHRAMM, WILBUR. "Measuring Another Dimension of Newspaper Readership." *Journalism Quarterly* 24 (1947): 293–306.

SCHULTE, HENRY H., JR. *Reporting Public Affairs.* New York: Macmillan, 1981.

SEDGWICK, ELLERY. *The Happy Profession.* Boston: Little, Brown, 1946.

SIGAL, LEON V. *Reporters and Officials.* Lexington, Mass.: Heath, 1973.

SMITH, ANTHONY. *Goodbye Gutenberg: The Newspaper Revolution of the 1980s.* New York: Oxford University Press, 1980.

SMITH, ZAY N., and PAMELA ZEKMAN. *The Mirage.* New York: Random House, 1979.

STEWART, KENNETH. *News Is What We Make It.* Boston: Houghton Mifflin, 1943.

TARSHIS, BARRY. *How to Write Like a Pro.* New York: New American Library, 1982.

ULLMANN, JOHN, and STEVE HONEYMAN, eds. *The Reporter's Handbook.* New York: St. Martin's, 1983. (Investigative reporting techniques.)

WEBB, EUGENE J., and JERRY R. SALANCIK. The Interview; or The Only Wheel in Town." *Journalism Monographs,* 2, November 1966.

WEBB, EUGENE J., DONALD T. CAMPBELL, RICHARD D. SCHWARTZ, LEE SECHREST, and JANET BELEW GROVES. *Nonreactive Measures in the Social Sciences.* 2d ed. Boston: Houghton Mifflin, 1981.

WEBER, RONALD. *The Literature of Fact.* Athens: Ohio University Press, 1980.

"What Is News? Who Decides? And How?" Washington: American Society of Newspaper Editors, 1982.

WEIR, DAVID, and DAN NOYES. *Raising Hell.* Reading, Mass.: Addison-Wesley, 1983.

WILHOIT, G. CLEVELAND and DAVID H. WEAVER. *Newsroom Guide to Polls & Surveys.* Washington: American Newspaper Publishers Association, 1980.

WILLIAMS, PAUL N. *Investigative Reporting and Editing.* Englewood Cliffs, N.J.: Prentice-Hall, 1976.

ZAHLER, RICHARD. "A Rage That Filled the Sky." *Seattle Times,* May 25, 1980.

ZINSSER, WILLIAM. *On Writing Well.* 2d ed. New York: Harper & Row, 1982.

———. *Writing with a Word Processor.* New York: Harper & Row, 1983.

ZUCKMAN, HARVEY, L., and MARTIN J. GAYNES. *Mass Communications Law in a Nutshell.* 2d ed. St. Paul, Minn.: West, 1983.

Index

DATE DUE

JAN 1 1 1991			
GAYLORD			PRINTED IN U.S.A.